D0500107

Reader's
Digest

Who? What? When? Where? Why?

A SUBSTANTIAL GATHERING OF
INTRIGUING & DELIGHTFUL
KNOWLEDGE

The Reader's Digest Association, Inc.
Pleasantville, New York / Montreal

Reader's Digest Home & Health Books

PRESIDENT, HOME & GARDEN AND HEALTH & WELLNESS Alyce Alston
EDITOR IN CHIEF Neil Wertheimer
CREATIVE DIRECTOR Michele Laseau
EXECUTIVE MANAGING EDITOR Donna Ruvituso
ASSOCIATE DIRECTOR, NORTH AMERICA PREPRESS Douglas A. Croll
MANUFACTURING MANAGER John L. Cassidy
MARKETING DIRECTOR Dawn Nelson
SENIOR ART DIRECTOR Edwin Kuo

The Reader's Digest Association, Inc.

PRESIDENT AND CHIEF EXECUTIVE OFFICER Mary Berner
PRESIDENT, CONSUMER MARKETING Dawn Zier

This special edition was compiled and published by
The Reader's Digest Association, Inc., by permission of
Sterling Publishing Co., Inc.

The material in this book was originally published as five titles by Sterling
Publishing Co., Inc.: *The 5 W's Who?* ©2005 by Erin McHugh; *The 5 W's
What?* ©2005 by Erin McHugh; *The 5 W's When?* ©2005 by Erin
McHugh; *The 5 W's Where?* ©2005 by Erin McHugh; and *The 5 W's Why?*
©2005 by Erin McHugh.

Library of Congress Data has been applied for.
ISBN 978-0-7621-0557-1

Address any comments about *Who? What? When? Where? Why?* to:
    The Reader's Digest Association, Inc.
    Editor in Chief, Books
    Reader's Digest Road
    Pleasantville, NY 10570-7000

To order copies of *Who? What? When? Where? Why?*, call 1-800-846-2100.
Visit our online store at **rdstore.com** or **rd.ca**

Printed in the United States of America

1 3 5 7 9 10 8 6 4 2

US 6109/L-OP

The Delightful Truth

As you read this, there are roughly one billion children on the planet under the age of eight. And this evening, at least half of them will ask their parents or caregivers a question they will have no idea how to answer.

You did it. All kids do it. And they always will. Why is the sky blue? Do dogs talk to each other? Where do whales sleep? Why does hair grow on Daddy's face, but not Mommy's? Scientists haven't discovered it just yet, but we are certain there is a ask-impossible-questions gene woven into the human DNA.

As we grow older, we tend to suppress our desire to ask bewildering questions. But trust us, they are in most of our grown-up minds nonetheless, sitting there patiently, just waiting for the moment in which we allow them to be voiced.

Welcome to that moment.

Who? What? When? Where? Why? is a potpourri of facts tidbits, lists, charts, and miscellanea that answers questions you've long wondered about—and thousands more.

Whether your mind wanders to off-the-wall corners of the trivial world (What's the recipe for a Big Mac's "special sauce"? Which countries have more TV sets per capita than the United States?), or you tend to brood over more practical matters (Is a Navy Ensign ranked higher than a Lieutenant? Why can the Amish use batteries, but not electricity?), *Who? What? When? Where? Why?* is the most informative, entertaining book you'll read in a very long time. There's no other volume from which you'll learn about Hindu castes, Gershwin music, academic degrees, and Tony Curtis...without turning a page.

And for the child within all of us who never got their questions answered properly, we've taken care of you as well. Once and for all, the truth about Santa's reindeer, the North Pole, Walt Disney films, rabbits' feet, Baskin Robbins' 31 flavors, and other magical topics are revealed in the pages ahead.

So enjoy *Who? What? When? Where? Why?* We suspect that all your secret questions, past and present, will soon be answered.

Table of Contents

Who?

Trees, planets, and hummingbirds are all fascinating topics, but when it comes to what makes life truly strange and unpredictable, the answer inevitably is "people." Without heroes, villains, tinkerers, artists, overachievers and outrageous talkers, life would be sadly dull. This chapter is a vivid collection of folks that we worship, and others we hate; of people who entertain us, and others whose names will go down in infamy. Sit back, settle in, and make their acquaintance.

TRIPLE CROWN WINNERS

ELVIS

FOUNDING FATHERS

PULITZER PRIZE WINNERS

PATRON SAINTS

POPULAR BABY NAMES

MAFIA NICKNAMES

ANGELS

AUTHORS AND PSEUDONYMS

FAMOUS PETS

GREAT PHILOSOPHICAL MINDS

SHAKESPEAREAN CHARACTERS

JAMES BOND'S GIRLS

SATURDAY NIGHT LIVE STARS

FAMOUS ANIMALS IN ADVERTISEMENTS

PERFORMERS AT WOODSTOCK

PHOBIAS OF THE FAMOUS

BEST JOURNALISTS OF THE 20TH CENTURY

DECIPHERING ACADEMIC DEGREES

BRITISH ROYAL LINE OF SUCCESSION

ALLEGEDLY GAY MONARCHS

FAMOUS SCIENTISTS

WORST SERIAL KILLERS IN HISTORY

FAMOUS FOLKS' FINAL WORDS

DISEASES NAMED AFTER PEOPLE

PRESIDENTIAL NICKNAMES

POETS LAUREATE

PRESIDENTS ELECTED WITHOUT A MAJORITY

HURRICAN'TS

Hurricanes So Damaging Their Names Have Been Retired

Name	Last Heard from	Name	Last Heard From
Agnes	1972	Elena	1985
Alicia	1983	Eloise	1975
Allen	1980	Flora	1963
Andrew	1992	Frederic	1979
Anita	1977	Gilbert	1988
Audrey	1957	Gloria	1985
Betsy	1965	Hattie	1961
Beulah	1967	Hazel	1954
Bob	1991	Hilda	1964
Camille	1969	Hugo	1989
Carla	1961	Ione	1955
Carmen	1974	Inez	1966
Carol	1954	Janet	1955
Celia	1970	Joan	1988
Cleo	1964	Klaus	1990
Connie	1955	Luis	1995
David	1979	Marilyn	1995
Diana	1990	Mitch	1998
Diane	1955	Opal	1995
Donna	1960	Roxanne	1995
Dora	1964		

◆

YAWN

Famous Insomniacs

Caligula * Joseph Conrad * Marlene Dietrich * Alexandre
Dumas * W. C. Fields * F. Scott Fitzgerald * Galileo
* Hermann Goering * Rudyard Kipling * Alexander Pope

BLACK PATENT

Curiously, free blacks were allowed to hold U.S. patents, even before the Civil War. Often craftspeople and machinists, African Americans have held some of our most important patents.

Thomas Jennings was the first black man to hold a U.S. patent, which was granted in 1821 for a dry-cleaning process. He spent most of his considerable earnings promoting abolitionist causes.

Henry Blair received a patent in 1834 for his corn-planting machine. Two years later, he invented a corn-harvesting machine as well.

Norbert Rillieux patented an evaporator for refining sugar in 1845 that is still in use.

Elijah McCoy patented a device for lubricating steam engines in 1872, which was the first of fifty-seven patents issued to him in his lifetime.

Lewis Howard Latimer was granted a patent for an electric lamp in 1881 and a carbon light bulb filament in 1882. He was the only black man working in Thomas Edison's lab.

Sarah E. Goode designed a folding cabinet bed, which was patented in 1885, making her the first black woman granted a U.S. patent.

Anna M. Mangin patented a pastry fork in 1892.

Madame C. J. Walker patented a hair-care system for black men and women in the early 1900s, sales of which made her the wealthiest black woman in America. She donated most of her fortune to black charities.

Garrett Augustus Morgan patented a gas mask in 1914, which was widely used in World War I. He went on to design automated traffic lights that were awarded patents in 1923.

George Washington Carver was granted three patents in his lifetime, all issued in 1927 for a processing system he invented for producing paints and stains from the humble soybean. Today, Carver is most widely known for inventing more than three hundred uses for the peanut.

Frederick McKinley Jones patented a refrigeration system in 1938 that revolutionized long-haul trucking. A specialist in refrigeration, Jones gathered more than forty patents in his lifetime.

David Crosthwaite patented a heating system that he went on to install in New York's Radio City Music Hall. Crosthwaite earned more than forty patents in his lifetime for advancements made in heating, ventilating, and air-conditioning systems.

Granville T. Woods held more than sixty patents, his most important for a system that made telegraph communication between two traveling trains possible.

TRIPLE CROWN WINNERS

Horse	Year
Sir Barton	1919
Gallant Fox	1930
Omaha	1935
War Admiral	1937
Whirlaway	1941
Count Fleet	1943
Assault	1946
Citation	1948
Secretariat	1973
Seattle Slew	1977
Affirmed	1978

ALL-TIME GREAT CONEY ISLAND SIDESHOW STARS

Baby Dee the Human Hermaphrodite
Bambi the Mermaid
Christine Hell the Fire Eater
Eak the Geek, the Illustrated Man
Helen Melon ("She needs four men to hug her and
a boxcar to lug her")
Indestructible Indio
Koko the Killer Clown
Ravi the Scorpion Mystic
The Twisted Shockmeister
Ula the Painproof Rubber Girl
Zenobia the Bearded Lady

INVENTORS AND THEIR FAMOUS—
AND LESS FAMOUS—INVENTIONS

Inventor	Famous Invention	Less Famous Invention
Isaac Newton	Laws of gravity (1684)	Reflecting telescope (1668)
Eli Whitney	Cotton gin (1794)	Mass production (1798)
Benjamin Franklin	Lightning conductor (1752)	Bifocal lens (1784)
Robert Fulton	Long-distance steamboat (1807)	Metal-clad submarine (1800)
Samuel F. B. Morse	Morse code (1838)	Underwater telegraph cable (1842)
Alfred Nobel	Dynamite (1867)	Nitroglycerine (1865)
Thomas Alva Edison	Incandescent light bulb (1879)	Mimeograph (1875) and alkaline battery (1900)

◆

ELVIS!

In 1993, the U.S. Postal Service issued a commemorative stamp featuring a portrait of the "King." The most popular stamp ever, more than 124 million have been collected by philatelists since its release. The next bestselling celebrity commemoratives are Marilyn Monroe, which sold 46.3 million stamps (number 6 overall) followed by Bugs Bunny, which sold 45.3 million (number 7 overall).

WHO AM I?
Our Human Ancestors

Who?	How Old?	Profile
Ardipithecus ramidus kadabba	5.8–5.2 million years ago	Walked upright; 4 feet tall
Ardipithecus ramidus ramidus	c. 4.4 million years	Similar to *A. ramidus kadabba*
Australopithecus anamensis	c. 4.2 million years	Walked upright; possible ancestor of Lucy
Australopithecus afarensis	c. 3.2 million years	Lucy; 3.5 feet tall; lived in family groups in Africa
Australopithecus africanus	c. 2.5 million years	Descendant of Lucy
Australopithecus robustus	c. 2 million years	Related to *A. africanus*
Homo habilis	c. 2 million years	Brain enlarged; used simple tools
Homo erectus	c. 1.8 million years	Java Man; used fire; lived in caves; pre–*Homo sapiens*
Homo sapiens idaltu	160,000 years (?)	Anatomically modern human
Homo sapiens sapiens	100,000 years (?)	Anatomically modern human

The World's Most Famous Eight-Man Baseball Club

THE "WHO'S ON FIRST?" TEAM

Abbott and Costello's Shtick from The Naughty Nineties

Who:	First base
What:	Second base
I Don't Know:	Third base
Why:	Left field
Because:	Center field
Tomorrow:	Pitcher
Today:	Catcher
I Don't Give a Darn:	Shortstop

There is no right fielder mentioned in the skit.

WHO WILL HELP?

The 2000 U.S. census points out the heartening statistic that 40 to 50 percent of adults between the ages of thirty-five and forty-four do some volunteer work. Though they are in one of life's busiest times in terms of both family and career, this is also the age group with the highest volunteer percentage. The volunteers in this age group are nearly equally divided between men and women.

◆

THE EDSEL, the longest-running joke in the car indus-try—and one of its biggest flops—was not built by Edsel Ford but named for him after his death in 1943. Edsel him-self was an automobile maker of extraordinary vision and dis-tinction and was the man responsible for the design of the Lincoln Continental Mark I, which debuted in 1939.

QUESTIONABLE KUDOS:
NOT-SO-GREAT FIRSTS FOR WOMEN

Goodwife (Goody) Wright was the first woman wrongly accused of witchcraft in America, in 1622.

Goodwife Norman and **Mary Hammon** were the first women arrested and tried for lesbianism, in the Massachusetts Bay Colony in 1649. In an odd judicial decision, Goody Norman was sentenced to "public acknowledgment," while Ms. Hammon was acquitted.

Alice Thomas, in 1670s Boston, was the country's first female tavern keeper and, haplessly, the first to be arrested—for selling liquor without a license, profaning the Sabbath, receiving stolen goods, and "frequent secret and unseasonable entertainment in her house to Lewd Lascivious and Notorious persons of both sexes, giving them opportunity to commit Carnale Wickedness."

Mary (Molly) Brandt was the first woman found spying against the United States by informing the British of Patriot movements in New York State, in 1777.

Lucy Stone was the first woman arrested on charges of civil disobedience, in 1858, for protesting taxation without representation. Stone was also the first married woman to retain her maiden name.

Lucy Ware Webb Hayes became the first First Lady to ban liquor in the White House, earning her the nickname

"Lemonade Lucy," in 1877. Hayes was also the first woman to enroll at Ohio Wesleyan University.

Sally Tomkins was the first commissioned officer in the Confederate Army, in 1861.

Edith Eleanor McLean was the first premature baby placed in an incubator, then called a "hatching cradle," at Ward's Island in New York City, in 1888. She weighed 2 pounds, 7 ounces.

Evylyn Thomas was the first automobile accident victim, in 1896. She was riding her bicycle in New York City.

Sarah Emma Edmonds was the first woman inducted into the Grand Army of the Republic, an organization of Civil War veterans, in 1897. In 1861, the New Brunswick, Canada, native enlisted in Michigan as Franklin Thompson. Edmonds became a spy ("disguising" herself as a woman), deserted the army, and finally returned as a nurse.

Anna Edson Taylor was the first woman to go over Niagara Falls alone in a barrel (4.5 feet by 3 feet), in 1901. Her feat brought her a cash prize, which she used to save her ranch from foreclosure.

Nan Jane Aspinall was the first woman to ride alone across the United States on horseback, in 1910. She covered 4,500 miles in 301 days, but seriously delayed delivery of the letter she carried from the mayor of San Francisco to the mayor of New York by riding less than half of the time.

Maude B. Campbell was the first paying woman customer on a commercial plane in 1926. Campbell purchased a round trip ticket for $180 and flew from Salt Lake City, Utah, to Los Angeles in an open cockpit biplane. The trip lasted nine hours each way and Ms. Campbell was required to wear a parachute.

Mary Babnick Brown was the first woman whose hair (brunette, 34 inches long) was used as crosshairs for World War II B-17 bombsights.

Roberta A. Kankus was the first woman licensed as a commercial nuclear power plant operator at the pastoral-sounding Peach Bottom Power Plant, in 1976.

Dorothy Dietrich was the first woman ever to catch a bullet in her mouth, at the International Brotherhood of Magicians Convention, in 1980. Many had already found this perilous trick fatal, and even Houdini himself refused to attempt it.

Judith A. Resnick and **Sharon Christa McAuliffe** were the first women to die on a space flight, in 1986, aboard the *Challenger*. Resnick was a career astronaut. McAuliffe was chosen by President Reagan because she was a teacher; she planned to give science lessons to children via the Public Broadcasting System during the flight.

Arlette Rafferty Schweitzer was the first woman to bear her own grandchildren, acting as her daughter's surrogate, in 1991.

◆

BLANCHETTE is Little Red Riding Hood's given name.

FOUNDING FATHERS

Father of the United Nations	Cordell Hull (1871–1955), U.S. secretary of state
Father of the Blues	W. C. Handy (1873–1958), composer
Father of the Irish Republic	Eamon de Valera (1882–1975), president of Sinn Fein
Father of the Four-Letter Word	Henry Miller (1891–1980), author of *Tropic of Cancer*
Father of Country Music	Jimmie Rodgers (1897–1933), singer and guitarist
Father of the Gossip Column	Walter Winchell (1897–1972), U.S. journalist
Father of the Atomic Bomb	Dr. J. Robert Oppenheimer (1904–1967), physicist

◆

THREE STOOGES—SIX NAMES

Moe Howard: Moses Horwitz
Larry Fine: Louis Feinberg
Curly Howard: Jerome Lester Horwitz
Shemp Howard: Samuel Horwitz
Joe Besser: Jerome Besser
Joe DeRita: Joseph Wardell

And yes, all three Horwitzes were brothers.

MULTIPLE PULITZER PRIZE WINNERS

Four

Eugene O'Neill	Drama	*Beyond the Horizon* (1920) *Anna Christie* (1922) *Strange Interlude* (1928) *Long Day's Journey into Night* (1957)
Robert E. Sherwood	Drama	*Idiot's Delight* (1936) *Abe Lincoln in Illinois* (1939) *There Shall Be No Night* (1941)
	Biography	*Roosevelt and Hopkins* (1949)

Three

Edward Albee	Drama	*A Delicate Balance* (1967) *Seascape* (1975) *Three Tall Women* (1994)
Herbert Block (HerBlock)	Editorial cartooning	NEA Service (1942) *Washington Post* and *Times-Herald* (1954) *Washington Post* (1979)
Paul Conrad	Editorial cartooning	Formerly of *Denver Post* (1964), later of *Los Angeles Times* (1971 and 1984)

Edmund Duffy	Editorial cartooning	*Baltimore Sun* (1931, 1934, and 1940)
Rollin Kirby	Editorial cartooning	*New York World* (1922, 1925, and 1929)
Jeffrey K. MacNelly	Editorial cartooning	*Richmond (VA) News-Leader* (1972 and 1978) *Chicago Tribune* (1985)
Thornton Wilder	Drama	*The Bridge of San Luis Rey* (1928), *Our Town* (1938), *The Skin of Our Teeth* (1943)

Two

William Faulkner	Fiction	*A Fable* (1955) *The Reivers* (1963)
Nelson Harding	Editorial cartooning	*Brooklyn Eagle* (1927 and 1928)
George S. Kaufman	Drama	*Of Thee I Sing* (with Morrie Ryskind and Ira Gershwin) (1932) *You Can't Take It with You* (with Moss Hart) (1937)
Bill Mauldin	Editorial cartooning	United Features Syndicate (1945) *St. Louis Post-Dispatch* (1959)
Vaughn Shoemaker	Editorial cartooning	*Chicago Daily News* (1938 and 1947)

Paul Szep	Editorial cartooning	*Boston Globe* (1974 and 1977)
Booth Tarkington	Fiction	*The Magnificent Ambersons* (1919) *Alice Adams* (1922)
Barbara W. Tuchman	Nonfiction	*The Guns of August* (1963) *Stilwell and the American Experience in China, 1911–1945* (1972)
Tennessee Williams	Drama	*A Streetcar Named Desire* (1948) *Cat on a Hot Tin Roof* (1955)
August Wilson	Drama	*Fences* (1987) *The Piano Lesson* (1990)

◆

WHO IS "THE 12TH MAN"?

Originally, "The 12th Man" was a Texas A&M basketball player named E. King Gill, who was asked to hurriedly suit up for an ailing football team member back in 1922. Though Gill never saw any action, he became known as "The 12th Man," and his spirit lives on. Today, the entire Texas A&M student body acts as the 12th Man, and stands at the ready throughout the entire game whenever A&M plays at home. Official preseason tryouts are held for an annual 12th Man position on the bench as well.

50 GREATEST SCREEN LEGENDS

	Actors	*Actresses*
1.	Humphrey Bogart	Katharine Hepburn
2.	Cary Grant	Bette Davis
3.	James Stewart	Audrey Hepburn
4.	Marlon Brando	Ingrid Bergman
5.	Fred Astaire	Greta Garbo
6.	Henry Fonda	Marilyn Monroe
7.	Clark Gable	Elizabeth Taylor
8.	James Cagney	Judy Garland
9.	Spencer Tracy	Marlene Dietrich
10.	Charlie Chaplin	Joan Crawford
11.	Gary Cooper	Barbara Stanwyk
12.	Gregory Peck	Claudette Colbert
13.	John Wayne	Grace Kelly
14.	Lawrence Olivier	Ginger Rogers
15.	Gene Kelley	Mae West
16.	Orson Welles	Vivien Leigh
17.	Kirk Douglas	Lillian Gish
18.	James Dean	Shirley Temple
19.	Burt Lancaster	Rita Hayworth
20.	The Marx Brothers	Lauren Bacall
21.	Buster Keaton	Sophia Loren
22.	Sidney Poitier	Jean Harlow
23.	Robert Mitchum	Carole Lombard
24.	Edward G. Robinson	Mary Pickford
25.	William Holden	Ava Gardner

Source: American Film Institute, 2004.

THE WOMEN OF PLAYBOY
Famous Girls, Infamous Covers of the Twentieth Century

The Fifties
Marilyn Monroe (December 1953 and September 1955)
Jayne Mansfield (February 1956)
Zsa Zsa Gabor (March 1957)
Julie Newmar (May 1957)
Sophia Loren (September 1957)
Kim Novak (October 1959)

The Sixties
Elizabeth Taylor (January 1963)
Elke Somers (September 1964)
Ursula Andress (July 1965)
Jane Fonda (August 1966)
Ann-Margret (October 1966)
Joan Collins (March 1969)
Vanessa Redgrave (April 1969)

The Seventies
Melanie Griffith (October 1976)
Raquel Welch (February 1977)
Margaux Hemingway (June 1978)
Farrah Fawcett (December 1978)
Nastassia Kinski (August 1979)

The Eighties
Suzanne Somers (February 1980)
Crystal Gayle (November 1981)
Rae Dawn Chong (May 1982)
Mariel Hemingway (April 1982)
Kim Bassinger (February 1983)
Bridget Bardot (March 1985)
Madonna (September 1985)

Mamie Van Doren (February 1986)
Vanna White (July 1986)
Morgan Fairchild (August 1986)
Jessica Hahn (November 1987)
LaToya Jackson (March 1989)

The Nineties
Sharon Stone (July 1990)
Sherilyn Fenn (December 1990)*
Stephanie Seymour (March 1991)
Mimi Rogers (March 1993)
Elle Macpherson (May 1994)
Patti Davis (July 1994)
Robin Givens (September 1994)
Drew Barrymore (January 1995)
Nancy Sinatra (March 1995)
Cindy Crawford (July 1988 and October 1998)
Katarina Witt (December 1998)

*Sherilyn Fenn also enjoyed a career as a *Playboy* Bunny, along with other superchicks Lauren Hutton (1960), Gloria Steinem (1963), and Deborah Harry (1968).

◆

WHO SHOT J. R.?

Kristin Shepard, J. R. Ewing's sister-in-law
on March 21, 1980 in *Dallas*, Texas

◆

Since the game's invention in 1935, THE MONOPOLY GUY was known as Rich Uncle Moneybags. It was only with the millennium that he was renamed Mr. Monopoly.

HEAVENS ABOVE!
Patron Saints, the People They Protect,
and Their Strange Symbols in Art

Patron Saint	Who Is Protected	Symbols
Agatha	Bellmakers, nurses	Tongs
Agnes of Rome	Girls	Lamb
Ambrose of Milan	Beekeepers	Bees
Anne	Canada, mothers	Door
Antony	Domestic animals	Hog
Augustine of Hippo	Printers	Pen
Barbara	Artillerymen	Cannon
Bartholomew the Apostle	Leathermakers	Tanner's knife
Benedict	Poison sufferers	Broken cup
Blais	Throat ailments	Wax candle
Catherine of Siena, Italy	Fire prevention	Stigmata
Cecelia	Musicians	Organ
Christopher	Bookbinders, travelers	Forest, giant
Cosmos and Damian	Druggists	Box of ointment
Dominic	Choirboys	Rosary
Elizabeth of Hungary	Bakers	Bread

Patron Saint	Who Is Protected	Symbols
Francis of Assisi	Animals	Birds, deer, fish
Francis Xavier	Emigrants and immigrants	Ship
Genevieve	Disasters, Paris	Keys
George	Soldiers	Dragon
Gregory the Great	Singers	Tiara
Hilary of Poitiers	Snake bite victims	Stick
Jerome	Librarian	Lion
John the Baptist	Lambs	Head on a platter
Lawrence	Cooks, France	Gridiron
Lucy of Syracuse	The blind	Eyes
Luke the Apostle	Artists	Palette
Margaret	Pregnant women	Dragon
Martha	Housewives, servants	Holy water sprinkler
Mary Magdalen	Penitent sinners	Alabaster box of ointment
Maurus	Gout sufferers	Crutch
Monica	Married women	Girdle and tears
Nicholas of Myra	Pawnbrokers	Three purses

Patron Saint	Who Is Protected	Symbols
Patrick	Engineers, Ireland	Harp and shamrock
Peter the Apostle	Fishermen	Rooster
Philip Neri	Rome	Altar
Roch	Dogs and dog lovers	Dog
Rose of Lima	Florists, the Americas	City
Sebastian	Archers, athletes	Arrows
Vincent de Paul	Charities, volunteers	Children
Vincent Ferrer	Builders	Captives

◆

WHO GOES THERE?

Dr. Byron McKeeby and Nan Wood were the real folks who modeled in 1930 for Grant Woods's famous *American Gothic*. They were neither married nor farmers, being the dentist and sister of the artist. In fact, they never even sat together for the portrait.

KEEPING UP WITH THE JONESES
The Ten Most Common Surnames in the United States

Smith * Johnson * Williams * Jones * Brown * Davis *
Miller * Wilson * Moore * Taylor

PEOPLE MAGAZINE'S SEXIEST MEN

Year	Hunk	Age
1985	Mel Gibson	29
1986	Mark Harmon	34
1987	Harry Hamlin	35
1988	John F. Kennedy Jr.	27
1989	Sean Connery	58
1990	Tom Cruise	27
1991	Patrick Swayze	38
1992	Nick Nolte	51
1995	Brad Pitt	31
1996	Denzel Washington	41
1997	George Clooney	35
1998	Harrison Ford	55
1999	Richard Gere	50
2000	Brad Pitt	36
2001	Pierce Brosnan	47
2002	Ben Affleck	29
2003	Johnny Depp	39
2004	Jude Law	32
2005	Brad Pitt	41

◆

In 1848 in Seneca Falls, New York, the FIRST WOMEN'S RIGHTS CONVENTION met and drew up a Declaration of Sentiments, which was signed by sixty-eight women and thirty-two men.

WOODROW WILSON is the only president to ever hold a Ph.D. (Johns Hopkins, Political Science, 1886).

SATANIC MONIKERS
Better the Devil You Know . . .

Name	Biblical Reference
Abaddon	Revelation 9:11
The accuser of our brethren	Revelation 12:10
The adversary	1 Peter 5:8
Apollyon	Revelation 9:11
Beelzebub	Matthew 12:24; Mark 3:22; Luke 11:15
Belial	2 Corinthians 6:15
The Devil	Matthew 4:1
Dragon	Revelation 12:9 and 20:2
The enemy	Matthew 13:39
Father of all lies	John 8:44
God of this world	2 Corinthians 4:4
King of Babylon	Isaiah 14:4
King of Tyrus	Ezekiel 28:12
Little horn	Daniel 7:8
Lucifer	Isaiah 14:12
Man of sin	2 Thessalonians 2:3
That old serpent	Revelation 12:9 and 20:2

Name	Biblical Reference
Power of darkness	Colossians 1:13
Prince of the power of the air	Ephesians 2:2
Prince that shall come	Daniel 9:26
Prince of Tyrus	Ezekiel 28:2
Prince of this world	John 12:31
Ruler of the darkness of this world	Ephesians 6:12
Satan	Job 1:6
Serpent	Genesis 3:1
Son of perdition	John 17:12
The tempter	Matthew 4:3
The wicked one	Matthew 13:19

WORLD'S GREATEST CALLING CARD

Miss Holly Golightly Travelling	Hats off to *Breakfast at Tiffany's* . . .

◆

PINOCCHIO means "pine-eye" in Italian.

NEWFANGLED PROBLEMS,
NEW PATRON SAINTS
Some Actual Modern-Day Assignments of the Catholic Church

Patron of	*Saint*
Advertisers and advertising	St. Bernardine of Siena, known for the power of his sermons
Aircraft pilots and crew	The Virgin Mary; her Assumption into heaven shows her ascending through the clouds
Flight attendants	St. Bona of Pisa, famous pilgrim
Astronauts	St. Joseph of Cupertino, chosen for his ability to levitate
Motorists	St. Frances of Rome, as her continuous vision of her guardian angel enabled her to see at night
Telecommunications	St. Gabriel the Archangel (the word archangel means "chief messenger")
Highways	John the Baptist, who wrote "Make straight the way of the Lord" (John 1:23)
Scientists	St. Albertus Magnus, a Dominican priest and scientist considered to be the equal of Aristotle in his time

NUMBER, PLEASE
What Your Social Security Number Means . . .

AREA NUMBERS
The first three numbers originally represented the state in which a person first applied for a social security number. Since 1973, the Social Security Administration has assigned numbers and issued cards based on the zip code.

GROUP NUMBERS
The two middle digits, which range from 01 to 99, are simply used to break all the social security numbers with the same area number into smaller blocks.

SERIAL NUMBERS
The last four serial numbers are randomly generated and run consecutively from 0001 through 9999, subdividing each middle group of numbers.

◆

GOT A CLUE?

Anyone who played the board game Clue as a kid remembers the names of the playing pieces and their attendant colors:

Mr. Green	green
Colonel Mustard	yellow
Mrs. Peacock	blue
Professor Plum	purple
Miss Scarlet	red
Mrs. White	white

. . . but less well known is the name of the victim: Mr. Boddy.

WITCHCRAFT, WICKED WITCHCRAFT

Lady Alice Kyteler (1280–?) was a wealthy Irish woman accused of witchcraft by her fourth husband and his family, who all believed she had lured him into marrying her for his money. Soon, the children of her former husbands accused her of hastening their fathers' deaths, leaving them impoverished. Her alleged transgressions ranged from heresy to nocturnal meetings with the devil himself (in the form of a large black dog). A servant claimed Lady Alice had taught her to become a witch, and that they flew through the air on a broomstick. Kyteler eventually escaped to England, banished, and disappeared from sight.

Joan of Navarre (1370–1437), the wife of King Henry IV of England, was accused in 1419 of being a witch and of conspiracy to depose the king. She was later pardoned and reinstated as queen in 1422.

Anne Boleyn (1507–1536), second wife of King Henry VIII, was claimed to be a witch when she was unable to bear him a son. That she had a sixth finger (or more likely a vestigial sixth nail, the mark of a witch) on one hand didn't help. Boleyn was executed on patently false charges of witchcraft, incest, and adultery.

Elisabeth Sawyer (?–1621), upon being condemned to death, confessed her "long and close-carried witchery." The devil, she said, came to her and assisted her in the injuries she inflicted. Mother Sawyer confessed that she had plagued her neighbors' cattle and caused the death of two infants. She was hanged, and shortly thereafter a famous play, *The Witch of Edmonton*, was written.

Margaret Jones (?–1648), a Massachusetts Bay Colony physician, became the first woman accused of being a witch to be executed, when patients under her care got sicker instead of well. (It turned out that many of her patients simply weren't taking their medicine.) She was hanged in 1648.

Mother Shipton (most likely Ursula Sonthiel, 1488–1561) was a fifteenth-century Yorkshire woman and England's most famous witch. She was said to have powers of healing and spell-casting; she set forth many prophecies about modern times, scientific inventions, new technology, wars, and politics, which were later interpreted as having come true, from the Great Fire of London in 1666 to the advent of modern technology, and even her own death in 1561.

The Mother Shipton Prophecies

The fiery year as soon as O'er,
Peace shall then be as before;
Plenty everywhere be found,
And men with swords shall plough the ground.
The time shall come when seas of blood
Shall mingle with a greater flood.
Carriages without horses shall go.
And accidents fill the world with woe.

Around the world thoughts shall fly
In the twinkling of an eye.

Waters shall yet more wonders do,
How strange yet shall be true.
The world upside down shall be,

And gold found at the root of a tree.
Through hills men shall ride
And no horse or ass be by their side;
Under water men shall walk,
Shall ride, shall sleep, shall talk;
In the air men shall be seen,
In white, in black, and in green.

Iron in the water shall float
As easy as a wooden boat;
Gold shall be found, and found
In a land that's not now known.
Fire and water shall more wonders do
England shall at last admit a Jew;
The Jew that was held in scorn
Shall of a Christian be then born.

A house of glass shall come to pass
In England, but alas!
War will follow with the work
In the land of the Pagan and Turk
And state and state in fierce strife
Will seek each other's life
But when the North shall divide the South
An eagle shall build in the lion's mouth.

An Ape shall appear in a Leap year
That shall put all womankind in fear
And Adam's make shall be disputed
And Roman faith shall like rooted,
And England will turn around.
Thunder shall shake the earth;
Lightning shall rend asunder;

Water shall fill the earth;
Fire shall do its work.

Three times shall lovely France
Be led to dance a bloody dance;
Before her people shall be free.
Three tyrant rulers shall she see;
Three times the People rule alone;
Three times the People's hope is gone;
Three rulers in succession see,
Each spring from different dynasty.
Then shall the worser fight be done,
England and France shall be as one.

Waters shall flow where corn shall grow
Corn shall grow where waters doth flow
Houses shall appear in the vales below
And covered by hail and snow;
White shall be black then turn grey
And a fair Lady be married thrice.

All England's sons that plough the land
Shall be seen, book in hand;
Learning shall so ebb and flow,
The poor shall most wisdom know.

◆

NO LOVE

Frederick Louis, eldest son of George II, quarrelled bitterly
with his father and led the political opposition to the king.
The feud ended when Frederick died in 1751 as a result of
being struck by a tennis ball.

OOH, BABY, BABY
*The Most Popular Names for Children
in the Year 1900 . . .*

1.	John	Mary
2.	William	Helen
3.	James	Anna
4.	George	Margaret
5.	Charles	Ruth
6.	Joseph	Elizabeth
7.	Frank	Marie
8.	Henry	Rose
9.	Robert	Florence
10.	Harry	Bertha

And Today* . . .

1.	Jacob	Emily
2.	Michael	Emma
3.	Joshua	Madison
4.	Matthew	Olivia
5.	Ethan	Hannah
6.	Andrew	Abigail
7.	Daniel	Isabella
8.	William	Ashley
9.	Joseph	Samantha
10.	Christopher	Elizabeth

*2004, according to the Social Security Administration

◆

WILLIAM KEMMLER was the first American criminal to be executed, in Auburn, New York, on August 6, 1890.

WHO

DOG TAGS DECODED
November 1941 to July 1943

First line	First name of soldier, second initial, surname	CLARENCE R JONES
Second line	Army serial number Tetanus immunization Tetanus	37337566 T42 43 O
Third line	Name of next of kin	FRED JONES
Fourth line	Street address of next of kin	2843 FEDERAL PL
Fifth line	city and state; religion	DENVER COLO P

Current Version

First line	Last name
Second line	First name, middle initial
Third line	Social Security number
Fourth line	Blood Type
Fifth line	Religion

◆

Though U.S. presidents have never been known to be a musical bunch, "COOL CAL" COOLIDGE apparently played a pretty mean harmonica.

"THE HOLLYWOOD TEN"

This famous—or infamous—group was blacklisted from the movie industry for refusing to testify about communism in Hollywood in 1947 before the House Un-American Activities Committee. They were convicted of contempt of Congress and served prison sentences. Their futures were checkered.

Alvah Bessie (1904–1985) worked as a stage manager in San Francisco, then turned to novel writing.

Herbert Biberman (1900–1971) financed his own work, including the 1954 movie *Salt of the Earth* with Adrian Scott, which was not allowed to be shown in the United States until 1965.

Lester Cole (1904–1985), fired from writing *Viva Zapata!* in 1952, penned his work under an assumed name for the rest of his life, including the screenplay for the extremely popular *Born Free* in 1965.

Edward Dmytryk (1908–1999), after reconsidering, reappeared before HUAC in 1951 and named names. This change of heart resulted in a future in directing; one of his films was *The Caine Mutiny*.

Ring Lardner Jr. (1915–2000), sacked by Fox, worked under a pseudonym until the blacklist lifted, and won an Oscar in 1970 for Best Original Screenplay for *M*A*S*H*.

John Howard Lawson (1894–1977), blacklisted by all the studios, moved to Mexico and wrote Marxist interpretations of drama and filmmaking until his death.

Albert Maltz (1908–1985) wrote without credit for *The Robe* in 1953, and, in the 1970s, worked on other less successful movies under his own name.

Samuel Ornitz (1890–1957) spent the rest of his life as a novelist; one of his titles was the bestselling *Bride of the Sabbath*, in 1951.

Adrian Scott (1912–1973), blacklisted for twenty-one years, wrote under a pseudonym for television. He sued RKO Studios for wrongful dismissal; his case was finally thrown out by the Supreme Court in 1957.

Dalton Trumbo (1905–1976) was the first blacklisted writer to resume using his own name in 1960, with *Spartacus*. He wrote screenplays for several popular movies until his death.

◆

WE KNEW THEM WHEN
What They Were Called Before They Became Big

Radiohead	On a Friday
The Beach Boys	Carl and the Passions
Procul Harem	The Paramounts
Talking Heads	The Artistics
The Byrds	The Beefeaters
The Who	The High Numbers
Depeche Mode	Composition of Sound
Blondie	The Stilettos
Black Sabbath	Earth

ANIMAL HOUSES

Animal	Male	Female	Young
Ass	Jack	Jenny	Foal
Bear	Boar	Sow	Cub
Cat	Tom	Queen	Kitten
Cattle	Bull	Cow	Calf
Chicken	Rooster	Hen	Chick
Deer	Buck	Doe	Fawn
Dog	Dog	Bitch	Pup
Duck	Drake	Duck	Duckling
Elephant	Bull	Cow	Calf
Fox	Dog	Vixen	Cub
Goose	Gander	Goose	Gosling
Horse	Stallion	Mare	Foal
Lion	Lion	Lioness	Cub
Sheep	Ram	Ewe	Lamb
Swan	Cob	Pen	Cygnet
Swine	Boar	Sow	Piglet
Tiger	Tiger	Tigress	Cub
Whale	Bull	Cow	Calf
Wolf	Dog	Bitch	Pup

◆

BILLBOARD'S #1 RECORD RECORDS

Artist: The Beatles—20
Writer: Paul McCartney—32
Producer: George Martin—23
Label: Columbia—92

THE POCAHONTAS EXCEPTION

Pocahontas (1595–1617) is an early American heroine born Matoaka, daughter of Powhatan, an Indian chief, but from childhood she was known as Pocahontas. She made her first mark on history when she helped save the fledgling colony of Jamestown, Virginia, from extinction by supplying its new residents with food, at which time she befriended founding colonist John Smith.

Pocahontas married Englishman John Rolfe, who took her to England, where she became the toast of high society, including English royalty. She contracted smallpox while in England, however, and died there. Many years later, her only son, Thomas, sailed back to Virginia, claimed his grandfather's land, and killed or enslaved many of his mother's Indian relatives.

Regardless of Thomas's feelings, his parents had wed with the approval of Virginia's governor, and because Pocahontas was of royal (albeit aborigine) blood, the statutes in Virginia made an exception in their case at a time when interracial marriages were prohibited. The Virginia Colony's racist laws stated that virtually any black or Native American blood made a "white" person black or Native American; however, there was a colonial statutory Pocahontas Exception for the English descendants of Rolfe and Pocahontas, which in 1924 was reenacted by the U.S. Virginia State legislature. The Pocahontas Exception remained on the books in Virginia until overturned in the Supreme Court decision *Loving v. Virginia* in 1967. Today, white descendants of the Native American heroine often list her with pride atop their family tree.

POPEYE 'N' PALS

Popeye	Salty sailorman and love of Olive Oyl
Poopdeck Pappy	Popeye's dad, imprisoned on Goon Island
Peepeye, Pipeye, Poopeye, and Pupeye	Popeye's rambunctious quadruplet nephews
Olive Oyl	Anorexic, high-strung, girlfriend of Popeye
Swee' Pea	Snugglie-clad baby left on the doorstep and adopted by Popeye, who called him his "adoptid orphink"
Castor Oyl	Olive's brother
Cole and Nana Oyl	Olive and Castor's dad and mom
Ham Gravy	Pre-Popeye boyfriend of Olive Oyl
Bluto	Muscle-bound and determined bully who's out to deck Popeye and steal Olive Oyl
Brutus	Later Bluto lookalike
Alice the Goon	Flowerpot-hatted, near-mute giantess whose perpetual mission was to kidnap Popeye and spirit him away to Goon Island
Eugene the Jeep	mischievous pup given as a birthday gift to Popeye from Olive Oyl

J. Wellington Wimpy	Popeye's penny-pinching, hamburger-craving mooch of a best friend, known to his friends simply as Wimpy
Sea Hag	longtime stalker and archenemy
Toar	Sea Hag's flunkie, now Popeye ally
George G. Geezil	Shoe cobbler and Wimpy's nemesis
Rough House	Chef/owner of Rough House's Café

◆

TENNIS RULES FOR BLACK BOYS

Arthur Ashe said that as a youth, a black player followed unwritten rules playing tennis against white kids:
- Engage—never enrage—white opponents
- When in doubt, call your opponent's ball in
- Before changing court sides, pick up your opponent's balls and hand them to him
- Always make sure your behavior is beyond reproach

◆

CINDY LOU WHO: Literature's most famous Who, and one of the Who-ville Whos; melted the heart of the Grinch in Dr. Seuss's holiday tale *How the Grinch Stole Christmas*.

The NEW YORK YANKEES have been honored seven times in a New York City tickertape parade, the most ever.

WHO YOU CALLIN' MOB?
The Very Best Mafia Nicknames

Louis "Pretty" Amberg (1897–1935)	Independent racketeer and killer
Otto "Abbadabba" Berman (1880–1935)	Policy game fixer
Ruggerio "Richie the Boot" Boiardo (1891–1984)	New Jersey Mafia patriarch
Joseph "Joe Bananas" Bonanno (1905–2002)	New York "Big 5" family boss
Ralph "Bottles" Capone (1893–1974)	Al's brother and Chicago overlord
Vincent "Mad Dog" Coll (1909–1932)	Quintessential Irish 1930s gangster
William "Willie Potatoes" Daddano (1925–1975)	Chicago outfit torturer
Jack "Legs" Diamond (1896–1931)	Lone-wolf racketeer
Sam "Momo" Giancana (1908–1975)	Most powerful boss west of New York
Sam "Golf Bag" Hunt (?–1956)	Capone hit man
Ellsworth "Bumpy" Johnson (1906–1968)	Black mafioso from Harlem
Alvin "Creepy" Karpis (1907–1979)	Public Enemy wooed by Mafia

Joseph "Socks" Lanza (1904–1968)	Genovese captain and fish industry boss
Thomas "Three-Finger Brown" Lucchese (1900–1967)	"Five Families" Don
Peter "The Clutching Hand" Morello (1870–1930)	Took over Black Hand with brothers
Samuel J. "Nails" Morton (?–1924)	Jewish Chicago mobster
Abe "Kid Twist" Reles (1907–1941)	Murder, Inc. hit man
Paul "The Waiter" Ricca (1897–1972)	Top Chicago outfit man
Jacob "Gurrah" Shapiro (1900–1947)	Murder, Inc. right-hand man

. . . And If You Wonder Why They Call Them Animals:

Anthony "Tony Ducks" Corallo (1913–2000)	Lucchese boss
Sammy "The Bull" Gravano (1945–)	John Gotti's underboss
Murray Llewellyn "The Camel" Humphries (1899–1972)	Chicago chieftain
Matthew "Matty the Horse" Ianniello (1920–?)	Genovese capo and porn czar
George "Bugs" Moran (1893–1957)	Chicago Prohibition gangster

Ignazio "Lupo the Wolf" Mafia Saietta (1877–1947)	Organized New York City activity
Benjamin "Bugsy" Siegal (1906–1947)	Gangster and Las Vegas developer
Tony "The Ant" Spilotro (1938–1986)	Vegas mobster; model for Joe Pesci character in *Casino*
Angelo "Quack-Quack" Ruggiero (?–1986)	Talkative Gotti capo
Jimmy "The Weasel" Fratianno (1913–1993)	Mobster-turned-informant
Philip "Chicken Man" Testa (1924–1981)	Philadelphia underboss

"THEY'RE GIVIN' YOU A NUMBER, AND TAKIN' AWAY YOUR NAME"
Types of Secret Agent Men

Agent: A person, usually foreign, who obtains information for an intelligence organization.

Notional agent: A nonexistent agent created by an intelligence agency to deceive the enemy.

Secret agent: An undercover agent or anyone acting as a clandestine spy or saboteur for an intelligence operation.

Agent of influence: A person whose job is to wield opinion in important places. Agents of influence are usually politicians, academics, journalists, scientists, and the like.

Agent provocateur: An agent who provokes illegal rioting, rebellion, mutiny, treason, or sabotage by those under suspicion, making them liable to punishment.

Bagman: An agent who handles the money, either by acting as paymaster to spies, or by handing out bribes to those in authority.

Counterspy: An agent who works with a counterintelligence agency to expose or squelch a spy's ability to obtain information, usually by leaking disinformation.

Courier: An agent who retrieves and/or delivers messages, documents, and so on, usually with no idea of informational content.

Defector-in-place: An agent who has defected, but remains in his previous position in order to act as a double agent.

Defector: A spy who voluntarily changes sides.

Double agent: A spy who works for both sides, but who is loyal to only one; in other words, a spy who is employed by the enemy and performs a real service for them, while reporting valuable information back to his original agency.

ANGEL HIERARCHY

Seraphim
Cherubim
Thrones
Dominions
Virtues
Powers
Principalities
Archangels
Angels

WHO'S ON THE MONEY
The Faces of U.S. Currency

Since the U.S. government started issuing currency in 1861, bills and gold certificates have been printed in denominations from $1 to $100,000. Today, only the $1, $2, $5, $10, $20, $50, and $100 Federal Reserve Notes are printed. Bills in the denominations of $500 and $1,000 may still be found in circulation, and there are approximately two hundred $5,000 and three hundred $10,000 bills out there, though most of them are with collectors. The $100,000 bill was primarily used in intragovernment transactions between banks, but the advent of electronic transfers has made its use all but obsolete.

Only three of the denominations have not pictured U.S. presidents: these three show the first secretary of the treasury (Alexander Hamilton), a statesman and inventor (Benjamin Franklin), and the creator of the national banking system (Salmon P. Chase).

$1	George Washington	$100	Benjamin Franklin
$2	Thomas Jefferson	$500	William McKinley
$5	Abraham Lincoln	$1,000	Grover Cleveland
$10	Alexander Hamilton	$5,000	James Madison
$20	Andrew Jackson	$10,000	Salmon P. Chase
$50	Ulysses S. Grant	$100,000	Woodrow Wilson

By 1792, Congress was intent on establishing a coin system for the new country. The Coinage Act authorized the Mint and prescribed the standards, with the smallest denomination the half cent—soon known as the "little sister"—which was first struck in July 1793, just four months after the one-cent coin. Since then, several denominations have been minted:

1792	Half disme (½ dime), and cent	1796	Quarter dollar
		1850	$20 double eagle
1794	Half dollar	1851	3 Cent
1794	Silver dollar	1854	$3
1795	$5 Half eagle	1864	2 Cent
1795	$10 Eagle	1866	Nickel
1796	Dime	1875	20 Cent

CURRENT U.S. COINAGE

One cent	Abraham Lincoln	Half dollar	John F. Kennedy
Nickel	Thomas Jefferson	Silver dollar	Susan B. Anthony
Dime	Franklin D. Roosevelt	Golden dollar	Sacagawea
Quarter dollar	George Washington		

◆

SHORT-LIVED

Arguably the two biggest jobs on earth have each had one incredibly short-term occupant. Pope John Paul I served for a mere 33 days in 1978, and President William Henry Harrison held the chief executive post for just 32 days before his death.

◆

ADOLF AND RUDOLF DASSLER were very sneaky brothers, the creators of Adidas (1920) and Puma (1948) shoes, respectively.

AUTHOR! PSEUDONYM!

Name	*Pseudonym*
Kingsley Amis	Robert Markham
Hans Christian Andersen	Villiam Christian Walter
François-Marie Arouet	Voltaire
Isaac Asimov	Dr. A. Paul French
Louis Auchincloss	Andrew Lee
Robert Benchley	Guy Fawkes
Mildred Wirt Benson	Carolyn Keene
Marie Henri Beyle	Stendahl
Ambrose Bierce	Don Grile
Eric Arthur Blair	George Orwell
Charlotte Brontë	Lord Charles Wellesley
Charlotte Brontë	Marquis of Duoro
Emily Jane Brontë	Ellis Bell
Pearl Buck	John Sedges
William Burroughs	William Lee
Agatha Christie	Mary Westmacott
Samuel Langhorne Clemens	Mark Twain
Manfred B. Lee and Frederic Dannay	Ellery Queen
Charles Dickens	Boz
Charles L. Dodgson	Lewis Carroll
Cecily Isabel Fairfield	Rebecca West
Howard Fast	E. V. Cunningham
Edward Gorey	Hyacinthe Phypps
Dashiell Hammett	Peter Collinson
Carolyn Heilbrun	Amanda Cross
Josef Teodor Konrad Korzeniowski	Joseph Conrad

Name	Pseudonym
Evan Hunter	Ed McBain
Edna St. Vincent Millay	Nancy Boyd
Dorothy Parker	Constant Reader
Jean-Baptiste Poquelin	Molière
William Sydney Porter	O. Henry
Anne Rice	A. N. Roquelaure
William Saroyan	Sirak Goryan
Irving Tennenbaum	Irving Stone
Gore Vidal	Edgar Box

◆

IT'S THE SAME OLD STORY . . .
Boys versus Girls in the Old Testament

Books Named After Boys

Joshua
Samuel (First Book)
Samuel (Second Book)
Ezra
Nehemiah
Tobit
Job
Sirach
Isaiah
Jeremiah
Baruch
Ezekiel
Daniel
Hosea
Joel
Amos
Obadiah
Jonah
Micah
Nahum
Habakkuk
Zephaniah
Haggai
Zechariah
Malachi

Books Named After Girls

Ruth
Judith
Esther

TOTALS: BOYS: 25, GIRLS: 3

PET NAMES
Animals We Know and Love

Name	Animal	Owner
Dinah	Cat	Alice in Wonderland
Garfield	Cat	Jim
Heathcliff	Cat	The Nutmeg Family
Mr. Bigglesworth	Cat	Dr. Evil of *Austin Powers*
Fred	Cockatoo	Baretta
Asta	Terrier	Nick and Nora Charles of *The Thin Man*
Astro	Mutt	The Jetsons
Brain the Wonder Dog	Mutt	Inspector Gadget
Brian	Mutt	The Griffins of *Family Guy*
Brandon	Golden Labrador	Punky Brewster
Daisy	Mutt	Dagwood Bumstead of *Blondie*
Dino	Dinosaur Dog	The Flintstones
Eddie	Jack Russell Terrier	Martin Crane of *Frasier*
Krypto	Super-Dog	Superboy

Lassie	Collie	Timmy Martin
Meathead	Bulldog	"Dirty Harry" Callahan
Mignon	Yorkshire Terrier	Lisa Douglas of *Green Acres*
Neil	St. Bernard	The Kerbys of *Topper*
Rin Tin Tin	German Shepherd	Corporal Rusty
Ruff	Airedale mix	Dennis the Menace
Snoopy	Beagle	Charlie Brown of *Peanuts*
Tiger	Sheepdog	The Brady Bunch
Tiger	Sheepdog	Patty Duke
Togo	Terrier	Nancy Drew
Triumph	Yugoslavian mountain dog	Conan O'Brien
Wishbone	Jack Russell	Joe Talbot
Woofer	Mutt	Winky Dink
Flipper	Dolphin	Sandy and Porter Ricks
Bimbo	Elephant	Corky of *Circus Boy*
Flicka	Horse	Ken McLaughlin
Silver	Horse	The Lone Ranger
Tornado	Horse	Zorro
Oscar	Lizard	Opie of *The Andy Griffith Show*

GREAT MINDS, RARELY THINKING ALIKE

Name	Philosophy
Anthisthenes (445–365 BCE)	Founder of Cynicism
Aristotle (384–322 BCE)	Offered roots of modern science and Western civilization nature
Saint Thomas Aquinas (1225–1274)	Provided Catholic Church much of its official dogma
Saint Augustine (354–430)	Founder of theology and cornerstone of the Christian Church
Martin Buber (1878–1965)	Dialogue between man and God is possible
August Comte (1798–1857)	Father of sociology; replaced the idea of God with the idea of mankind as a whole
René Descartes (1596–1650)	Father of the scientific method
John Dewey (1859–1952)	Pragmatist and educational theorist

Some Philosophies of Life . . . and Their Proponents

Best-known Work	Quote
No primary works survive	"I would rather go mad than feel pleasure!"
Organon	"Man is a political animal."
Summa Theologica	"Reason in man is rather like God in the world."
Confessions	"Will is to grace as the horse is to the rider."
I and Thou	"All journeys have secret destinations of which the traveler is unaware."
Introduction to Positive Philosophy	"Nothing at bottom is real except humanity."
Discourse on Method	"I think, therefore I am."
Democracy and Education	"Education is a social process. Education is growth. Education is, not a preparation for life; education is life itself."

Name	*Philosophy*
Friedrich Engels (1820–1895)	Cofounder of Marxism; originated philosophy of dialectical materialism
Epicurus (341–270 BCE)	Founder of Epicureanism
Georg Friedrich Wilhelm Hegel (1770–1831)	Thesis versus antithesis leads to synthesis
David Hume (1711–1776)	Argued against proofs of the existence of God
William James (1842–1910)	One of the founders of pragmatism; reality is what we make it
Immanuel Kant (1724–1804)	Founder of modern philosophy; the "thing-in-itself" cannot be known
Søren Kierkegaard (1813–1855)	Founder of existentialism; "truth is subjectivity"
Gottfried Wilhelm Von Leibniz (1646–1716)	Inventor of calculus; forefather of modern mathematical logic

Best-known Work	Quote
Dialectics of Nature	"The ruling ideas of each age have ever been the ideas of its ruling class."
Letter to Herodotus, Letter to Pythocles, Letter to Menoeceus	"The magnitude of pleasure reaches its limit in the removal of all pain."
Phenomenology of Spirit	"What is reasonable is real; that which is real is reasonable."
Enquiry Concerning Human Understanding	"Custom, then, is the great guide of human life."
The Will to Believe	"A thing is important if anyone think it important."
Critique of Pure Reason	"Though our knowledge begins with experience, it does not follow that it arises out of experience."
Either/Or	"Life can only be understood backwards; but it must be lived forwards."
Monadology	"I often say a great doctor kills more people than a great general."

Name	Philosophy
John Locke (1632–1704)	Ideas come from experience; none are innate
Niccolò Machiavelli (1469–1527)	Any act by a ruler to gain and hold power is permissible
Karl Marx (1818–1883)	It is human nature to transform nature
Friedrich Nietzsche (1844–1900)	God is dead
Blaise Pascal (1623–1662)	God cannot be known through reason, only through mystical understanding
Plato (c. 427–347 BCE)	Father of Western philosophy; recorded dialogues of Socrates
Jean-Paul Sartre (1905–1980)	One of the founders of existentialism; man is condemned to be free
Pyrrho of Elis (365–275 BCE)	Founder of Skepticism

Best-known Work	Quote
An Essay Concerning Human Understanding	"No man's knowledge here can go beyond his experience."
The Prince	"Among other evils which being unarmed brings you, it causes you to be despised."
Manifesto of the Communist Party	"Religion . . . is the opium of the people."
Thus Spake Zarathustra	"That which does not kill you makes you stronger."
Pensées	"Men blaspheme what they do not know."
Republic	"Democracy passes into despotism."
Existentialism and Human Emotions	"Hell is—other people."
No primary works survive	"Since nothing can be known, the only proper attitude is 'freedom from worry.'"

Name	Philosophy
Arthur Schopenhauer (1788–1860)	Believed the will is entirely real, but not free, nor does it have any ultimate purpose
Adam Smith (1723–1790)	Laissez-faire economic policy
Socrates (464–399 BCE)	Invented the practice of philosophical dialogue
Baruch Spinoza (1632–1677)	Mind and body are aspects of a single substance expressing God's plan
Alfred North Whitehead (1861–1947)	Integrated twentieth-century physics into a metaphysics of nature; "theology of organism"
Ludwig Wittgenstein (1889–1951)	Philosophical problems are often caused by linguistic confusions
Zeno of Citium (336–264 BCE)	Founder of Stoicism

Best-known Work	Quote
The World as Will and Idea	"Every man takes the limit of his own field of vision for the limits of the world."
Wealth of Nations	"A monopoly granted either to an individual or to a trading company has the same effect as a secret in trades or manufactures."
No writings—Plato recorded his thoughts	"The unexamined life is not worth living."
Ethics	"Will and Intellect are one and the same thing."
Principia Mathematica (with Bertrand Russell)	"A culture is in its finest flower before it begins to to analyze itself."
Tractatus	"Whereof one cannot speak, thereof one must be silent."
No primary works survive	"Follow where reason leads."

WHO ROCKS
Rock & Roll Hall of Fame Members

CHARTER 1986 PERFORMER INDUCTEES
Chuck Berry * James Brown * Ray Charles * Sam Cooke
* Fats Domino * Everly Brothers * Buddy Holly * Jerry Lee
Lewis * Elvis Presley * Little Richard

1987
The Coasters * Eddie Cochran * Bo Diddley
* Aretha Franklin * Marvin Gaye * Bill Haley * B. B. King
* Clyde McPhatter * Ricky Nelson * Roy Orbison
* Carl Perkins * Smokey Robinson * Big Joe Turner
* Muddy Waters * Jackie Wilson

1988
The Beach Boys * The Beatles * The Drifters
* Bob Dylan * The Supremes

1989
Dion * Otis Redding * The Rolling Stones
* The Temptations * Stevie Wonder

1990
Hank Ballard * Bobby Darin * The Four Seasons
* The Four Tops * The Kinks * The Platters
* Simon and Garfunkel * The Who

1991
LaVern Baker * The Byrds * John Lee Hooker
* The Impressions * Wilson Pickett * Jimmy Reed
* Ike and Tina Turner

1992
Bobby "Blue" Bland * Booker T. and the MG's * Johnny Cash * The Isley Brothers * The Jimi Hendrix Experience * Sam and Dave * The Yardbirds

1993
Ruth Brown * Cream * Creedence Clearwater Revival * The Doors * Frankie Lymon and the Teenagers * Etta James * Van Morrison * Sly and the Family Stone

1994
The Animals * The Band * Duane Eddy * The Grateful Dead * Elton John * John Lennon * Bob Marley * Rod Stewart

1995
The Allman Brothers Band * Al Green * Janis Joplin * Led Zeppelin * Martha and the Vandellas * Neil Young * Frank Zappa

1996
David Bowie * Gladys Knight and the Pips * Jefferson Airplane * Little Willie John * Pink Floyd * The Shirelles * The Velvet Underground

1997
The (Young) Rascals * The Bee Gees * Buffalo Springfield * Crosby, Stills and Nash * The Jackson Five * Joni Mitchell * Parliament-Funkadelic

1998
The Eagles * Fleetwood Mac * The Mamas and the Papas * Lloyd Price * Santana * Gene Vincent

1999
Billy Joel * Curtis Mayfield * Paul McCartney * Del
Shannon * Dusty Springfield * Bruce Springsteen *
The Staple Singers

2000
Eric Clapton * Earth, Wind & Fire * Lovin' Spoonful
* The Moonglows * Bonnie Raitt * James Taylor

2001
Aerosmith * Solomon Burke * The Flamingos * Michael
Jackson * Queen * Paul Simon * Steely Dan * Ritchie
Valens

2002
Isaac Hayes * Brenda Lee * Tom Petty and the
Heartbreakers * Gene Pitney * Ramones * Talking Heads
* Chet Atkins

2003
AC/DC * The Clash * Elvis Costello and the Attractions
* The Police * The Righteous Brothers

2004
Jackson Browne * The Dells * George Harrison
* Prince * Bob Seger * Traffic * ZZ Top

2005
Buddy Guy * The O'Jays * The Pretenders
* Percy Sledge * U2

◆

JAMES K. POLK was the first U.S. president to have a
presidential photograph taken.

GROUP MYTHOLOGY

Fates (3)

The three daughters of Necessity: Life is woven by Clotho and measured by Lachesis, and the thread of life is cut by Atropos.

Winds (4)

Aeolus is the keeper of the winds; Boreas, the north wind; Eurus, the east wind; Notus, the south wind; Zephyrus, the west wind.

Muses (9)

The daughters of Zeus and Mnemosyne preside over arts and sciences: Calliope, epic poetry; Clio, history; Erato, lyric and love poetry; Euterpe, music; Melpomene, tragedy; Polyhymnia, sacred poetry; Terpsichore, choral dance and song; Thalia, comedy and bucolic poetry; and Urania, astronomy.

Furies (3)

The avenging spirits, daughters of Mother Earth: Alecto, unceasing in pursuit; Megaera, jealous; and Tisiphone, blood avenger.

LICENSE AND REGISTRATION, PLEASE . . .

We all know where the Three Wise Men were headed . . . but where were they from?

> Balthazar was from Ethiopia and carried myrrh
> Caspar came from Tarsus with frankincense
> Melchior hailed from Arabia and brought gold

F. O. S.

Friends of Shakespeare . . . or, at Least,
Who and What He Wrote About

Antony and Cleopatra: One of history's greatest couples, the
Roman general Antony and the Egyptian queen Cleopatra.
All Rome called her a sorceress as Antony gave away parts of
the empire to Cleopatra and her children.

Coriolanus: Victorious yet prideful Roman general exiled
from his native city; widely acknowledged to be the least
sympathetic protagonist among Shakespeare's tragic figures.

Cymbeline: Wise and gracious king of Britain nearly
destroyed by his wicked and conniving queen.

Hamlet: Shakespeare's most famous hero; a tragic prince who
must choose between moral integrity and the need to avenge
his father's murder.

Henry IV: The aging king of England joins with his wild
adolescent son, Harry, to regain control of the country crum-
bling around him.

Henry V: England's rabble-rousing young prince becomes a
brilliant young king and the revered ruler who conquers
France.

Henry VI: A weak king who was never able to live up to the
glories of his father, and who desired only to be an ordinary
citizen.

Henry VIII: The larger-than-life king who changed England forever, bringing many wives and a new church to the palace.

Julius Caesar: Idolized Roman general and senator who falls prey to his public's idolization and belief in his own invincibility.

King John: Son of Henry II, though technically not next in line for the monarchy. Eventually he lost support and was killed by monks for stealing from their monasteries.

King Lear: The mad king whose demands on his daughters drove his family to rage and murder.

Macbeth: A murderous man determined to be king, whose power both rises and falls with the strength and fate of his wife.

Othello: Eloquent, respected, and powerful, this Moorish general is undone by jealousy and dies at his own hand.

Pericles: Like Job, a good man who conquers both men and fear, suffers many hardships, and is rewarded at last by reuniting with his own family.

Richard II: A regal, poetic young king attached much more to money and possessions than his people; eventually he is overthrown for his sins and assassinated.

Richard III: Deformed in body, twisted in mind, politically brilliant—and will stop at nothing, including murder, to be king.

Romeo and Juliet: Perhaps the most famous young couple in history, destined to die rather than live without each other.

Timon of Athens: Generous, wealthy man who later goes bankrupt, only to find he has no friends. He becomes a hermit, fortuitously finds a pot of gold, and uses it to have Athens destroyed.

Titus Andronicus: Heroic soldier and Shakespeare's bloodiest hero, he pursues revenge to the end (including cooking and serving his enemies), dying in the process.

Troilus and Cressida: Love goes bad between the prince of Troy, a valiant warrior, and a less-than-monogamous young woman, Cressida.

◆

LADIES AND GENTLEMEN, THE BACH FAMILY!

Johann Sebastian Bach was the most famous musician of several generations of Bach musicians, starting with his great-grandfather, Veit Bach (1555–1619). Of J. S. Bach's twenty children, only three made anything of their musical training, none of them nearing the success of their prolific father.

When the family musicians became numerous and widely dispersed, they agreed to meet annually to discuss, compose, and play music together. This continued until the middle of the eighteenth century, with as many as 120 persons assembling, the fruits of which eventually formed a collection known as the Bach Archives. Here, a family tree on the most musical of the Bachs . . .

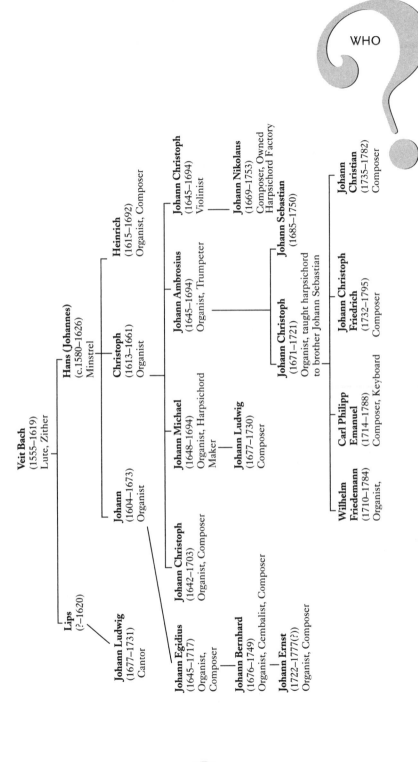

WHO ?

Veit Bach
(1555–1619)
Lute, Zither

Lips
(?–1620)

Hans (Johannes)
(c.1580–1626)
Minstrel

Johann Ludwig
(1677–1731)
Cantor

Johann
(1604–1673)
Organist

Christoph
(1613–1661)
Organist

Heinrich
(1615–1692)
Organist, Composer

Johann Christoph
(1642–1703)
Organist, Composer

Johann Michael
(1648–1694)
Organist, Harpsichord Maker

Johann Ambrosius
(1645–1694)
Organist, Trumpeter

Johann Christoph
(1645–1694)
Violinist

Johann Egidius
(1645–1717)
Organist, Composer

Johann Bernhard
(1676–1749)
Organist, Cembalist, Composer

Johann Ernst
(1722–1777(?))
Organist, Composer

Johann Ludwig
(1677–1730)
Composer

Johann Christoph
(1671–1721)
Organist, taught harpsichord to brother Johann Sebastian

Johann Nikolaus
(1669–1753)
Composer, Owned Harpsichord Factory

Johann Sebastian
(1685–1750)

Wilhelm Friedemann
(1710–1784)
Organist,

Carl Philipp Emanuel
(1714–1788)
Composer, Keyboard

Johann Christoph Friedrich
(1732–1795)
Composer

Johann Christian
(1735–1782)
Composer

BOND, JAMES BOND'S GIRLS
The Many Women in 007's Life

Lois Maxwell: Miss Moneypenny (1962–1985)
Caroline Bliss: Miss Moneypenny (1987–1989)
Samantha Bond: Miss Moneypenny (1995–present)
Ursula Andress: Honey Ryder: *Dr. No* (1962)
Daniela Bianchi: Tatiana Romanova:
From Russia with Love (1963)
Honor Blackman: Pussy Galore: *Goldfinger* (1964)
Shirley Eaton: Jill Masterson: *Goldfinger* (1964)
Claudine Auger: Domino Derval: *Thunderball* (1965)
Molly Peters: Patricia Fearing: *Thunderball* (1965)
Akiko Wakabayashi: Aki: *You Only Live Twice* (1967)
Diana Rigg: Tracy Di Vicenzo:
On Her Majesty's Secret Service (1969)
Jill St. John: Tiffany Case: *Diamonds Are Forever* (1971)
Jane Seymour: Solitaire: *Live and Let Die* (1973)
Britt Ekland: Mary Goodnight:
The Man with the Golden Gun (1974)
Barbara Bach: Anya Amasova: *The Spy Who Loved Me* (1977)
Lois Chiles: Dr. Holly Goodhead: *Moonraker* (1979)
Carole Bouquet: Melina Havelock: *For Your Eyes Only* (1981)
Maud Adams: Octopussy: *Octopussy* (1983)
Tanya Roberts: Stacey Sutton: *A View to a Kill* (1985)
Fiona Fullerton: Pola Ivanova: *A View to a Kill* (1985)
Maryam D'Abo: Kara Milvoy: *The Living Daylights* (1987)
Carey Lowell: Pam Bouvier: *Licence to Kill* (1989)
Talisa Suto: Lupe Lamora: *Licence to Kill* (1989)
Famke Janssen: Xenia Onatopp: *GoldenEye* (1995)
Teri Hatcher: Paris Carver: *Tomorrow Never Dies* (1997)
Michelle Yeoh: Wai Lin: *Tomorrow Never Dies* (1997)

Denise Richards: Dr. Christmas Jones:
The World Is Not Enough (1999)
Halle Berry: Jinx: *Die Another Day* (2002)
Dame Judi Dench: M (1995–present)

◆

HOLLYWOOD'S MOST CELEBRATED
The Envelope, Please. . .
Oscar Winners with Four Wins

FOUR-TIME BEST ACTRESS WINNER
Katharine Hepburn
Morning Glory (1933)
Guess Who's Coming to Dinner (1967)
The Lion in Winter (1968)
On Golden Pond (1981)

FOUR-TIME BEST DIRECTOR WINNER
John Ford
The Informer (1935)
The Grapes of Wrath (1940)
How Green Was My Valley (1941)
The Quiet Man (1952)

SNOOPY'S SIBS

Before Charlie Brown, everyone's favorite beagle had
another family at the Daisy Hill Puppy Farm . . .

Andy * Marbles * Rover * Olaf * Spike * Belle * Molly

Live from New York, It's
THE ALBERT BROOKS SHOW
Or, As We All Know and Love It . . . Saturday Night Live

ORIGINAL NOT READY
FOR PRIME TIME PLAYERS
Dan Aykroyd (1975–1979)
John Belushi (1975–1979)
Chevy Chase (1975–1977)
Jane Curtin (1975–1980)
Garrett Morris (1975–1980)
Laraine Newman
 (1975–1980)
Gilda Radner (1975–1980)

NOT FEATURED
George Coe (1975)
Michael O'Donoghue
 (1975–1979)

CAST MEMBERS
Fred Armisen
 (2002–present)
Peter Aykroyd (1979–1980)
Morwenna Banks
 (1994–1995)
Jim Belushi (1983–1985)
Jim Breuer (1995–1998)
A. Whitney Brown
 (1985–1991)
Beth Cahill (1991–1992)
Dana Carvey (1986–1993)

Ellen Cleghorne
 (1991–1995)
Billy Crystal (1984–1985)
Joan Cusack (1985–1986)
Tom Davis (1977–1980)
Denny Dillon (1980–1981)
Jim Downey (1979–1980)
Robert Downey Jr.
 (1985–1986)
Brian Doyle-Murray
 (1979–1982)
Rachel Dratch
 (1999–present)
Robin Duke (1980–1984)
Nora Dunn (1985–1990)
Christine Ebersole
 (1981–1982)
Dean Edwards (2001–2003)
Chris Elliott (1994–1995)
Jimmy Fallon (1998–2004)
Siobhan Fallon (1991–1992)
Chris Farley (1990–1995)
Will Ferrell (1995–2002)
Tina Fey (2000–present)
Will Forte (2002–present)
Al Franken (1977–1980 and
 1985–1995)

Janeane Garofalo
(1994–1995)
Ana Gasteyer (1996–2002)
Gilbert Gottfried
(1980–1981)
Mary Gross (1981–1985)
Christopher Guest
(1984–1985)
Anthony Michael Hall
(1985–1986)
Brad Hall (1982–1984)
Rich Hall (1984–1985)
Darrell Hammond
(1995–present)
Phil Hartman (1986–1994)
Jan Hooks (1986–1991)
Yvonne Hudson (1980–1981)
Melanie Hutsell (1991–1994)
Victoria Jackson (1986–1992)
Chris Kattan (1995–2003)
Tim Kazurinsky (1980–1984)
Laura Kightlinger
(1994–1995)
David Koechner
(1995–1996)
Gary Kroeger (1982–1985)
Matthew Laurance
(1980–1981)
Julia Louis-Dreyfus
(1982–1985)
Jon Lovitz (1985–1990)
Norm MacDonald

(1993–1998)
Gail Matthius (1980–1981)
Michael McKean
(1993–1995)
Mark McKinney
(1994–1997)
Tim Meadows (1990–2000)
Laurie Metcalf (1980–1981)
Seth Meyers (2001–present)
Dennis Miller (1985–1991)
Jerry Minor (2000–2001)
Finesse Mitchell
(2003–present)
Jay Mohr (1993–1995)
Tracy Morgan (1996–2003)
Eddie Murphy (1980–1984)
Bill Murray (1976–1980)
Mike Myers (1988–1995)
Kevin Nealon (1986–1995)
Don Novello (1978–1980
and 1985–1986)
Cheri Oteri (1995–2000)
Chris Parnell (1998–present)
Joe Piscopo (1980–1984)
Amy Poehler (2001–present)
Randy Quaid (1985–1986)
Colin Quinn (1995–2000)
Jeff Richards (2001–2004)
Rob Riggle (2004–present)
Ann Risley (1980–1981)
Chris Rock (1990–1993)
Charles Rocket (1980–1981)

Tony Rosato (1980–1982)
Maya Rudolph
  (1999–present)
Adam Sandler (1990–1995)
Horatio Sanz (1998–present)
Tom Schiller (1979–1980)
Rob Schneider (1990–1994)
Molly Shannon (1994–2001)
Harry Shearer (1979–1980
  and 1984–1985)
Martin Short (1984–1985)
Sarah Silverman (1993–1994)
Robert Smigel (1991–1993)
David Spade (1990–1996)
Pamela Stephenson
  (1984–1985)

Ben Stiller (1988–1989)
Julia Sweeney (1990–1994)
Terry Sweeney (1985–1986)
Kenan Thompson
  (2003–present)
Danitra Vance (1985–1986)
Dan Vitale (1985–1986)
Nancy Walls (1995–1996)
Damon Wayans (1985–1986)
Patrick Weathers
  (1980–1981)
Fred Wolf (1995–1997)
Alan Zweibel (1979–1980)

Over the years; Saturday night's favorite TV show has also been known as:

The Albert Brooks Show (working title)
NBC's Saturday Night (1975 original title)
SNL 25 (2000 new title)
SNL (1975)
Saturday Night Live '80 (1980 new title)

◆

WALT DISNEY often washed his hands up to thirty times an hour—while Louis XIV hated washing so much it is believed that he bathed only three times in his entire life.

THE VALKYRIES

These beautiful young women scout battlefields to choose the bravest of the slain and bring them to Valhalla. The flickering light off their armor is the aurora borealis.

As they appear in traditional Norse mythology:

Brynhildr * Geriskögul * Göll * Göndul * Gudr
* Gunn * Herfjoturr * Hildr * Hladgunnr * Hlokk * Hrist
* Mist * Rathgrith * Rota * Sigrdrifa * Sigrún * Skagull
* Skeggjald * Skuld * Svafa * Thrud

As they appear in Richard Wagner's *Der Ring des Nibelungen:*

Brunnhilde * Gerhilde * Grimgerde * Helmwige * Ortlinde
* Rossweisse * Schwertleite * Siegrune * Waltraute

◆

WHO'S ON TOP
Notable Women Given Honorary Degrees at
Harvard Since Its Founding in 1636

Martha Graham (1966)
Georgia O'Keeffe (1973)
Beverly Sills (1974)
Barbara Jordan (1977)
Eudora Welty (1977)
Mother Teresa (1982)
Louise Nevelson (1985)
Toni Morrison (1989)

Ella Fitzgerald (1990)
Madeleine Albright (1997)
Gertrude B. Elion (1998)
Julia Kristeva (1999)
Ruth J. Simmons (2002)
Kathering Dunham (2002)
Margaret Atwood (2004)
Shirley M. Tilghman (2004)

MUSICAL GROUPS AND THEIR ORIGINAL MEMBERS

THE ANDREWS SISTERS
LaVerne Sofia, Maxene Angelyn, and Patty Marie Andrews

THE BAND
Robbie Robertson, Rick Danko, Richard Bell, Levon Helm,
Garth Hudson, and Richard Manuel

THE BEATLES
George Harrison, John Lennon, Paul McCartney,
and Stuart Sutcliffe

BUFFALO SPRINGFIELD
Richie Furay, Dewey Martin, Bruce Palmer, Stephen Stills,
and Neil Young

THE DAVE CLARK FIVE
Dave Clark, Lenny Davidson, Rick Huxley, Denis Payton,
and Mike Smith

DESTINY'S CHILD
Beyoncé Knowles, LaTavia Roberson,
Kelendria (Kelly) Rowland, and LeToya Luckett

THE DIXIE CHICKS
Emily Erwin, Martie Erwin, Laura Lynch,
and Robin Lynn Macy

THE DOORS
John Densmore, Robby Kreiger, Ray Manzarek,
and Jim Morrison

THE FOUR TOPS
Levi Stubbs, Renaldo "Obie" Benson, Abdul "Duke" Fakir, and Lawrence Payton

THE GRATEFUL DEAD
Jerry Garcia, Bob Weir, Ron "Pigpen" McKernan, Phil Lesh, and Bill Kreutzmann

GUNS N' ROSES
Steve Adler, Mike "Duff" McKagan, Axl Rose, Slash, and Izzy Stradlin

THE INK SPOTS
Ivory "Deek" Watson, Jerry Daniels, Charles Fuqua, and Orville "Hoppy" Jones

THE JACKSON 5
Jackie, Marlon, Jermaine, Tito, and Michael Jackson

THE McGUIRE SISTERS
Christine, Dorothy, and Phyllis McGuire

THE MONKEES
Micky Dolenz, Davy Jones, Mike Nesmith, and Peter Tork

THE OSMONDS
Alan, Wayne, Merrill, Jay, Donny, and Jimmy Osmond

THE ROLLING STONES
Mick Jagger, Brian Jones, Keith Richards, Charlie Watts, and Bill Wyman

THE SUPREMES
Florence Ballard, Diana Ross, and Mary Wilson

THE TEMPTATIONS
Eldridge Bryant, Melvin Franklin, Eddie Kendricks,
Otis Williams, and Paul Williams

TRAFFIC
Dave Mason, Steve Winwood, Chris Wood, and Jim Capaldi

THE WHO
Roger Daltrey, John Entwhistle, Keith Moon, and
Pete Townshend

FIFTH BEATLEMANIA!

Three people have been tagged the Fifth Beatle over the years: The first was original bass guitarist, Stu Sutcliffe, who played with the group until 1961; the second, manager Brian Epstein, so knighted by New York DJ Murray the K, and later, Beatles recording manager George Martin. Nowadays the term "fifth Beatle" is used to describe anyone who's missed out on success.

YANKEE INGENUITY?

In the nearly century-long history of the World Series, the New York Yankees have taken home baseball's greatest title twenty-six times. Second-place winners could hardly even be called runners-up: The St. Louis Cardinals have won nine times (the last time back in 1982).

REIGNS SUPREME

Supreme Court Justice William O. Douglas sat on the Big Bench for the longest time: thirty-six years, from 1939 to 1975.

Though Thomas Johnson served the shortest amount of time—he was sworn in August 6, 1792, and resigned on January 16, 1793—he is credited with writing the Supreme Court's very first decision.

Several religious denominations have been represented only once in the Supreme Court history:

John Rutlege (1790–1791 and 1795)	Church of England
Gabriel Duval (1811–1835)	French Protestant
Henry Baldwin (1830–1844)	Trinity Church
Noah H. Swayne (1862–1881)	Quaker
Joseph R. Lamar (1910–1916)	Church of Disciples
James C. McReynolds (1914–1941)	Disciples of Christ
William H. Rehnquist Jr. (1972–present)	Lutheran

And though several of the earlier justices came to America from Europe, two in the twentieth century were foreign-born: Justice David J. Brewer (1889–1910) was born in Asia Minor (in what is now Turkey) in 1837 to missionary parents who returned to the United States shortly after his birth; and Justice Felix Frankfurter (1939–1962) hailed from Vienna, Austria, and came to the United States in 1894 at the age of twelve.

◆

EZRA J. WARNER invented the first can opener in 1858. Unfortunately, this was forty-five years *after* the invention of the tin can.

ADVERTISING ANIMALS

Axelrod	Flying "A" Service Stations dog
Bingo	Cracker Jack dog
Bucky Beaver	Ipana toothpaste
Charlie the Tuna	Starkist Tuna
The Counting Sheep	Serta Mattress
Dinky	Taco Bell chihuahua
Elsie the Cow	Borden's Milk
Farfel	Nestlé Quik dog
Frank and Louie	Budweiser frogs
The Gecko	Geico Insurance
Geoffrey	Toys "R" Us giraffe
Joe Camel	Camel cigarettes
Leo	MGM lion
Morris the Cat	Nine Lives Cat Food
Nipper and Lil' Nipper	RCA dogs
Polly	NBC peacock
Sharpie the Parrot	Gillette
Smokey the Bear	USDA Forest Service
Snoopy	Metropolitan Life (and *Peanuts*) beagle
Snuggle	Snuggle fabric softener bear
Sonny	Cocoa Puffs cuckoo bird
Spuds McKenzie	Bud Lite dog
Sugar Bear	Sugar Pops
Tige	Buster Brown Shoes dog
Tony the Tiger	Kellogg's Frosted Flakes
Toucan Sam	Froot Loops cereal bird
UBU Roi	UBU Productions (*Spin City*) dog
Willie	Kool penguin
Woodsy Owl	U.S. Forest Service

PRESIDENT RONALD REAGAN was older than JFK, Nixon, Ford, and Carter—four presidents who occupied the Oval Office before him.

◆

FREE CONCERT!
Performers at Woodstock, August 15–17, 1969

AUGUST 15

Richie Havens
Country Joe McDonald
John Sebastian
Incredible String Band
Bert Sommer
Sweetwater

Tim Hardin
Ravi Shanker
Melanie
Arlo Guthrie
Joan Baez

AUGUST 16

Quill
Keef Hartley
Santana
Mountain
Canned Heat
Grateful Dead

Creedence Clearwater
Revival
Janis Joplin
Sly and the Family Stone
The Who
Jefferson Airplane

AUGUST 17

Joe Cocker
Country Joe and the Fish
Ten Years After
The Band
Blood, Sweat and Tears
Johnny Winter

Crosby, Stills, Nash
and Young
Paul Butterfield Blues Band
Sha Na Na
Jimi Hendrix

THE DISRUPTERS
CEOs Who've Changed the Face of Business

Janus Friis and Niklas Zennstrom, KaZaA: Inventors of the world's leading file-sharing software, which allows worldwide distribution of licensed works using peer-to-peer technology. They have also launched Skype, software that lets users place telephone calls over the Internet virtually free of charge and threatens to upend the telecommunications industry.

Bill Gates: Founder of the Microsoft Corporation, the largest software company in the world. Gates is also the richest man in the world.

Ray Kroc: Founder of McDonald's, the world's largest fast-food chain. Recognized that Americans don't dine—they eat and run.

Eli Pariser, MoveOn.org: This political activist changed the nature of the beast by creating this citizen mobilization Web site composed of three entities: helping members elect candidates; education and avocation on national issues; and education of voters on positions, records, views, and qualifications of political candidates.

Jim Press, Toyota: The only American on the Japanese company's board of directors is bringing the United States into the future with the much-vaunted hybrid automobile, the Prius, the gas-electric vehicle voted 2004 Car of the Year by *Motor Trend* magazine.

Mike Ramsay and Jim Barton, TiVo: In conceiving TiVo, these two men transformed the way people watch television. This popular DVR (digital video recorder) has enjoyed one of the most rapid adoption rates ever in consumer electronics.

James Sinegal, CostCo: The founder of the members-only warehouse—who got his chops at Price Club—is selling to both consumers and small and medium retailers. Revenues and popularity are making even Wal-Mart take notice.

Martha Stewart: America's most trusted style guru, famous for her Emmy Award–winning *Martha Stewart Living* television show, many books, and magazines.

Sam Walton: Founder of Wal-Mart, the largest U.S. retailer, featuring low prices and one-stop shopping. Walton changed the face of retailing today, contributing to the downsizing of family-run Mom and Pop stores throughout the country.

◆

After selling his steel business, ANDREW CARNEGIE pursued his lifelong dream: trying to give away all his money. Interest on his money grew so fast, however, that he never managed to fulfill his dream, though when he died in 1919, Carnegie had donated 90 percent of his $125 million, primarily through the Carnegie Endowment for International Peace and the Carnegie Corporation, the latter a philanthropic trust to fund libraries; aid colleges, universities, and technical schools; and promote scientific research.

GREAT SONGS ABOUT EPHEMERAL SOMEONES

Who put the bomp in the bomp ba bomp ba bomp,
Who put the ram in the rama lama ding-dong?
Who Put the Bomp in the Bomp Ba Bomp Ba Bomp?

Who threw the overalls in Mrs. Murphy's chowder?
Nobody spoke, so she shouted all the louder
It's an Irish trick that's true,
I can lick the mick who threw
The overalls in Mrs. Murphy's chowder.
Who Threw the Overalls in Mrs. Murphy's Chowder?

Who's that knocking at my door?
Barnacle Bill the Sailor

Who's sorry now?
Who's sorry now?
Who's heart is aching for breaking each vow?
Who's Sorry Now?

Who's afraid of the big bad wolf?
Who's Afraid of the Big Bad Wolf? (based on Johann Sebastian Strauss's
"Champagne Song" from *Die Fledermaus*)

◆

HERMANN RORSCHACH'S SECRET

Actually, there are ten secrets. The inkblots the general
public typically sees as examples of Rorschach inkblots are
just that: examples. The real inkblots used in Rorschach's
psychological testing are copyrighted and kept under tight
wraps, so that testees have no prior knowledge.

MUTUALLY INCLUSIVE

The only person to be featured in both the "Got milk?"
mustache ads and "What becomes a legend most?"
Blackglama mink ads:

Lauren Bacall

The only character to be part of both the *Sesame Street* and
The Muppet Show casts:

Kermit

The only men to sign both the Declaration of Independence
and the Constitution:

Roger Sherman of Connecticut
Benjamin Franklin of Pennsylvania
Robert Morris of Pennsylvania
George Clymer of Pennsylvania
James Wilson of Pennsylvania
George Read of Delaware

MAN, OH, MAN
*The Seven Ages of Man, According to the Bard, William
Shakespeare*

The infant
The whining schoolboy
The lover
The soldier
The justice
The lean and slipper'd pantaloon
Second childishness and mere oblivion

WHO'S YOUR GOD?
Top 10 Organized World Religions by Population Ranking

Religion	Members
Christianity	2.1 billion
Islam	1.3 billion
Hinduism	900 million
Buddhism	376 million
Sikhism	23 million
Judaism	14 million
Baha'i Faith	7 million
Confucianism	5.3 million
Jainism	4.2 million
Shinto	4 million

SCAREDY CATS
A Few Phobias of the Famous

Katharine Hepburn	Trichopathophobia (fear of dirty hair)
Madonna	Brontophobia (fear of thunder)
Queen Christina of Sweden	Acarophobia (fear of fleas)
Elizabeth I	Anthophobia (fear of roses)
Sid Caesar	Tonsurphobia (fear of haircuts)
Sigmund Freud	Siderodromophobia (fear of train travel)
Augustus Caesar	Ailurophobia (fear of cats)

◆

CHRISTOPHER PLUMMER on Julie Andrews:
"Working with her is like being hit over the head with a Valentine's card."

BASIC ORGANIZATION OF THE ROMAN LEGION

Contubernium	Tent party	8
Ten contubernium	One century (basic unit of imperial legion)	80
Two centuries	One maniple (administrative/training)	160
Six centuries	One cohort (main battlefield/tactical unit)	480*
Ten cohorts	One legion	5,120*

*The first cohort, made up of the elite troups, consisted of five double centuries, 800 men, rather than the 480 in each of the remaining cohorts.

Ranking of Soldiers

Legatus	Commander of a legion who had six tribunes as subordinates; these officers were generally drawn from the senatorial class
Tribune	Generally a young aristocrat
Centurion	Lowest commissioned rank
Cornicularius	Top sergeant
Optio	Sergeant
Signifer	Standard-bearer
Librarius legionus	Divisional clerk, a sort of cushy clerical job
Legionary	Backbone of the Roman army
Auxiliary	Drawn from Roman colonies or provinces

WHO'S UP THERE?

In his 1972 book *The UFO Experience: A Scientific Study*, Dr. J. Allen Hynek, an astronomy professor at Ohio State University, devised one of the most famous contributions to UFOlogy, the Hynek Classification System—a way to categorize or group UFO sightings as either "distant sightings" or "close encounters."

Close Encounter of the First Kind (CEI)	A UFO is within 500 feet of the experiencer
Close Encounter of the Second Kind (CEII)	A UFO leaves marks on the ground, may cause burns or paralysis to humans, scares animals, interferes with car engines or TV and radio reception
Close Encounter of the Third Kind (CEIII)	A CEI or CEII that has visible occupants
Close Encounter of the Fourth Kind (CEIV)	Abduction
Close Encounter of the Fifth Kind (CEV)	Communication between human and alien

◆

PRESIDENT JOHN TYLER (1841–1845) has earned the title Father of Our Country in more ways than one. He had more offspring than any other Oval Office resident—fifteen children—though it took him two wives and several years after The Job to do it.

POP TOPS

*Top Pop Music Artists of Each Decade of the Twentieth Century
and Their Most Popular Song*

1900–1909	Billy Murray	"Take Me Out to the Ball Game"
1910–1919	Henry Burr	"In the Shade of the Old Apple Tree"
1920–1929	Paul Whiteman	"It's Only a Paper Moon"
1930–1939	Bing Crosby	"Out of Nowhere"
1940–1949	Bing Crosby	"White Christmas"
1950–1959	Elvis Presley	"Hound Dog"
1960–1969	The Beatles	"She Loves You"
1970–1979	The Bee Gees	"Stayin' Alive"
1980–1989	Michael Jackson	"Thriller"
1990–1999	Mariah Carey	"Sweetheart"

Bing Crosby had the most Top 40 tunes in the twentieth century with ninety-three songs. They ranged from "Out of Nowhere" in 1931 (number 1 for three weeks, number 7 for the year) to "True Love" in 1956 (number 27 for the year). His biggest hit was "White Christmas," which spent eleven weeks at number 1 in 1945—though the film by the same name was not released until 1954.

HERE COMES THE GROOM

At an estimated 1,400 pounds, Jon Brower Minnoch outweighed his 110-pound wife, Jeanette, by at least 1,290 pounds, the world's greatest recorded marital weight difference. They had two children before Mr. Minnoch died at age forty-two in 1983.

FOLKS WHO ARE SO BIG THEY HAVE THEIR OWN FESTIVAL

Festival	Honoring
Abraham Lincoln National Rail-Splitting Festival	Celebrates young lawyer's efforts to bring railroad through town
Annie Oakley Days	Famous Wild West sharpshooter
Bill Williams Rendezvous	Rough-and-ready frontier scout
Chester Greenwood Day	Inventor of the earmuffs
Daniel Boone Festival	Archetypal American
Defeat of Jesse James	Notorious Wild West outlaw
Hemingway Days	Writer, drinker, reveler

From the "Isn't America Great?" Files—

Locale	Events
Lincoln, Illinois	Junior and senior rail-splitting competitions, flea market, frontier display
Greenville, Ohio	Shooting contests, balloon rallies, old-time melodramas, parade
Williams, Arizona	Roping, parade, black powder shoot, cowboy barbecue, arts and crafts, music and dancing
Farmington, Maine	Old-time vaudeville shows, invention displays, parade
Barbourville, Kentucky	Pioneer village, pioneer long-rifle shootout, square dancing, pioneer crafts, quilt show, parade
Northfield, Minnesota	Reenactment of raid, rodeo, parade, outdoor art and food fair
Key West, Florida	Storytelling competitions, armwrestling contests, "Papa" Hemingway lookalike show, Caribbean street festival

Festival	Honoring
The Jeanie Auditions	Mrs. Stephen Foster "with the light brown hair"
Jim Butler Days	Lost a burro, found a silver mine
Lum 'n' Abner Days	Slice-of-Arkansas- life radio stars
Stonewall Jackson Heritage Jubilee	Revered Confederate General
Tom Sawyer Days	Fictional all-American boy

. . . And a Couple of Very Special Groups

Cowboy Poetry Reading	Sensitive, sentimental cowpokes
National Hobo Convention	Newspaper gag turned nostalgic fete

Locale	Events
White Springs, Florida	Contest for composer Stephen Foster's wife ("I Dream of Jeanie with the Light Brown Hair"), vocal competition, folk art exhibit and ball
Tonopah, Nevada	Miner competitions, chili cook-offs, barbecue, catfish fry, stock-car races, Old West entertainment, parade
Mena, Arkansas	Children's beauty pageant, quilt show, basketball camp, arts fair
Weston, West Virginia	Mountain crafts and music, traditional dancing, Civil War reenactment, food booths, arts fair
Hannibal, Missouri	Whitewashing competition, jumping frog contest, tomboy games, fireworks, tours of Hannibal, Missouri, mud volleyball tournament
Elko, Nevada	Poetry readings, seminars in songwriting, rawhide braiding, silversmithing, and western cooking
Britt, Iowa	Carnivals, talent show, hobo parade, serving of mulligan stew

WHO'S WHO

Since the first *Who's Who* (8,602 people were listed) in 1899, Marquis, the publishing house, has built a biographical fiefdom that includes:

Who's Who in America
Who Was Who in America
Who's Who in 20th Century America
Who's Who in the World
Who's Who on the Web

Who's Who in the East
Who's Who in the Midwest
Who's Who in the South and Southwest
Who's Who in the West

Who's Who in American Art
Who's Who in American Education
Who's Who in American Law
Who's Who in American Politics
Who's Who of American Women
Who's Who in Finance and Business
Who's Who in Medicine and Healthcare
Who's Who in Science and Engineering

◆

Moby-Dick author HERMAN MELVILLE died as a patent clerk, so out of fashion and forgotten that his *New York Times* obituary repeatedly referred to him as Henry Melville.

WHO

NOTES FROM THE SYMPHONY
Who's in Charge at America's Biggest, or, Different Notes for Different Folks

TWO SYMPHONIES, ONE MUSICAL DIRECTOR
Michael Tilson Thomas serves as musical director of the New World Symphony and San Francisco Symphony

JoAnn Falletta is at both the Buffalo Philharmonic and the Virginia Symphony

WOMEN IN CHARGE
(IN ADDITION TO MS. FALLETTA, ABOVE)
Anne Manson at the Kansas City Symphony
Kate Tamarkin at the Monterey Symphony
Gisèle Ben-Dor at the Santa Barbara Symphony Orchestra

MUSICAL DIRECTORS WHOSE NAMES HAVE AN UMLAUT
Paavo Järvi of the Cincinnati Symphony Orchestra
Franz Welser-Möst at the Cleveland Orchestra
Neeme Järvi at the Detroit Symphony Orchestra
Gürer Aykal at the El Paso Symphony Orchestra
Osmo Vänskä at the Minnesota Orchestra

THE KFC 3

Colonel Harlan Sanders shared his secret recipe with only two others—his wife, Claudia, and Jack C. Massey, head of the syndicate that bought the corporation in 1964. Others learn only how to cook the chicken, not what's in the secret recipe.

BEST JOURNALISTS OF THE 20TH CENTURY*
So Good They Were Voted the Top 100—More Than Once

Edward R. Murrow	Battle of Britain, CBS radio (1940) Report of the Liberation of Buchenwald, CBS radio (1945)
Edward R. Murrow and Fred Friendly	Investigation of Senator Joseph McCarthy, CBS (1954)
Edward R. Murrow, David Lowe, and Fred Friendly	*Harvest of Shame*, documentary, CBS television (1960)
Tom Wolfe	*The Electric Kool-Aid Acid Test*, book (1968) *The Kandy-Kolored Tangerine-Flake Streamline Baby*, collected articles (1965) *The Right Stuff*, book (1979)
James Baldwin	*The Fire Next Time*, book (1963) "Letter from the South: Nobody Knows My Name," *The Partisan Review* (1959)
W. E. B. Du Bois	*The Souls of Black Folk*, collected articles (1903) Columns on race while editor of *The Crisis* (1910–1934)
John Hersey	"Hiroshima," *The New Yorker* (1946) *Here to Stay*, collected articles (1963)

98

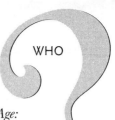

Murray Kempton	*America Comes of Middle Age: Columns 1950–1962*, collected articles (1963) *Part of Our Time: Some Ruins and Monuments of the Thirties*, book (1955)
Norman Mailer	*The Armies of the Night*, book (1968) *The Executioner's Song*, book (1979)
Bob Woodward and Carl Bernstein	Investigation of the Watergate break-in, *The Washington Post* (1972) *All the President's Men*, book (1979)

*According to a New York University Journalism Department panel vote.

HISPANIC AMERICAN NOBEL PRIZE WINNERS

Severo Ochoa, biochemist, for work on the synthesis of RNA (1959)

Luis Walter Alvarez, physicist, inventor of radio distance and direction indicator (1968)

Mario Molina, chemist, for work in atmospheric chemistry, particularly his study of the ozone layer (1995)

◆

GORE VIDAL on RONALD REAGAN: "A triumph of the embalmer's art."

HINDU CLASSES

Hindi are separated into castes, a hereditary social class system stratified according to ritual purity.

Brahmins: the highest, or priestly, class
Kshatriyas: royal and warrior class
Vaisyas: mercantile and professional class
Sudras: working class

General Hierarchal Hindu Caste System

1. Persons of holy descent
2. Landowners and administrators
3. Priests
4. Craftsmen
5. Agricultural tenants and laborers
6. Herders
7. Despised persons, or untouchables

The Hindu caste system is thought to have begun around 1500 BCE with the invasion of India by the Aryans, and though "untouchability" has been officially abolished, it is still somewhat in practice.

◆

"Who could ask for anything more?" Not the GERSHWIN BROTHERS, apparently. They used the phrase in three of their songs:

"I Got Rhythm," from 1930's *Girl Crazy*
"I'm About to Be a Mother," from *Of Thee I Sing* in 1931
"Nice Work If You Can Get It," from the 1937 movie
A Damsel in Distress

TITLE-ISTS: HOW TO READ THE SHEEPSKIN

AB	artium baccalaureus (bachelor of arts)
AM	artium magister (master of arts)
BA	bachelor of arts
BD	bachelor of divinity
BS	bachelor of science
DB	divinitatis baccalaureus (bachelor of divinity)
DD	dovonitatis doctor (doctor of divinity)
DDS	doctor of dental surgery
DO	doctor of osteopathy
DVM	doctor of veterinary medicine
JD	juris doctor (doctor of law)
LHD	litterarum humaniorum doctor (doctor of humanities)
LittD	litterarum doctor (doctor of letters)
LLB	legum baccalaureus (bachelor of laws)
MA	master of arts
MD	medicinae doctor (doctor of medicine)
MLitt	master of literature
MS	master of science
PhB	philosophiae baccalaureus (bachelor of philosophy)
PhD	philosophiae doctor (doctor of philosophy)
PhG	graduate in pharmacy
PsyD	doctor of psychology
RN	registered nurse
SB	scientus baccalaureus (bachelor of science)
SM	scientus magister (master of science)
STB	sacrae theologiae baccalaureus (bachelor of sacred theology)

◆

TONY CURTIS on Marilyn Monroe: "It's like kissing Hitler."

FANNY BRICE on Esther Williams: "Wet she's a star. Dry she ain't."

◆

BRITISH ROYAL LINE OF SUCCESSION*

1. HRH Prince Charles, the Prince of Wales (1948)
2. HRH Prince William of Wales, eldest son of Prince Charles (1982)
3. HRH Prince Henry of Wales, younger son of Prince Charles (1984)
4. HRH Prince Andrew, the Duke of York, second son of Queen Elizabeth II (1960)
5. HRH Princess Beatrice of York, elder daughter of Prince Andrew (1988)
6. HRH Princess Eugenie of York, younger daughter of Prince Andrew (1990)
7. HRH Prince Edward, the Earl of Wessex, youngest son of Queen Elizabeth II (1964)
8. Lady Louise Alice Elizabeth Mary Mountbatten Windsor, daughter of Prince Edward, the Earl of Wessex (2003)
9. HRH Princess Anne, the Princess Royal, only daughter of Queen Elizabeth II (1950)
10. Peter Phillips, son of Princess Anne (1977)
11. Zara Phillips, daughter of Princess Anne (1981)
12. David Armstrong-Jones, Viscount Linley, son of Princess Margaret (1961)
13. The Honorable Charles Patrick Inigo Armstrong-Jones, son of David, Viscount Linley (1999)
14. Margarita Elizabeth Rose Alleyne Armstrong-Jones, daughter of David, Viscount Linley (2002)
15. Lady Sarah Chatto, daughter of Princess Margaret (1964)

*As of 2004.

AKA

Prince Charles of Great Britain holds all of these titles (and more):

Prince of Wales
Duke of Cornwall
Duke of Rothesay
Earl of Carrick
Baron of Renfrew
Lord of the Isles
Prince and Great Steward of Scotland
Earl of Chester

ORDER OF BRITISH PEERAGE

1. Duke and duchess
2. Marquess and marchioness
3. Earl and countess
4. Viscount and viscountess
5. Baron and baroness

◆

VICTORIA CLAFLIN WOODHULL (1838–1927)

was the first woman nominated for the U.S. presidency. In 1872, the Equal Rights Party picked Woodhull to represent them for her early advocacy of an eight-hour workday, graduated income tax, social welfare programs, and profit sharing. Her candidacy was supported by laborers, female suffragists, spiritualists, and communists. The Equal Rights Party also nominated Frederick Douglass, the first African American to run for vice president in U.S. history.

FORTUNE 500 TOP MINORITY EMPLOYERS

Company	Percentage of Minority Employees
Union Bank of California	55.6
McDonald's	53.1
PNM Resources	48.5
Sempra Energy	48.0
Denny's	47.4
Southern California Edison	44.9
Fannie Mae	44.7
U.S. Postal Service	36.4
Freddie Mac	33.5
PepsiCo	27.3

◆

PROFILES IN COURAGE, written by then-Senator John F. Kennedy, is the only Pulitzer Prize–winning biography by a U.S. president. It is the story of eight other U.S. senators and how they manifested what JFK considered the most admirable of human virtues, and what Ernest Hemingway called "grace under pressure"—courage.

John Quincy Adams (1767–1848)
Daniel Webster (1782–1852)
Thomas Hart Benton (1782–1858)
Sam Houston (1793–1863)
Lucius Quintas Cincinnatus Lamar (1825–1893)
Edmund G. Ross (1826–1907)
George Norris (1861–1944)
Robert A. Taft (1889–1953)

VERY, VERY MARRIED

"She cried, and the judge wiped her tears with my checkbook."
—TOMMY MANVILLE

King Mongut of Siam (1804–1868), depicted in *The King and I*	9,000 wives and concubines
King Solomon of the Old Testament (970–928 BCE)	700 wives
Brigham Young, Mormon of Salt Lake City (1801–1877)	27 wives
Calamity Jane (*née* Martha Cannary) of the United States (1852–1903)	12 husbands
Tommy Manville of the United States (1894–1967)	11 wives
Pancho Villa of Mexico (1878–1923)	9 wives
Artie Shaw of the United States (1910–2005)	8 wives
Mickey Rooney of the United States (1920–)	8 wives
Elizabeth Taylor of Hollywood (1932–)	7 husbands

◆

IT'S THEIR PARTY

Presidents Elected Without Any Party Affiliation

George Washington (1789)
John Quincy Adams (1824)

Author WINSTON CHURCHILL (1871–1947) wrote several bestsellers—mostly historical fiction of the American south—at the turn of the century. His most outstanding success, *Richard Carvel,* sold 2 million copies upon publication in 1899 . . . in a country of only 72 million people. This particular Winston Churchill did not go on to become the prime minister of England, though he met and occasionally communicated with that British statesman. In fact, because the 10 Downing Street resident's works reached the bookshelves later, his book jackets always read Winston S. Churchill.

◆

MERRY CHRISTMAS!
Born on December 25

Sir Isaac Newton, scientist (1642)
Conrad Hilton, hotelier (1887)
Dame Rebecca West, novelist (1892)
Cab Calloway, jazz singer (1907)
Anwar Sadat, statesman (1918)
Little Richard, singer (1932)
Annie Lennox, singer (1954)

LOGGING ON @ THE START

Some surprising folks were the Internet's earliest computer geeks . . .

• The first world leader to send an e-mail was Queen Elizabeth in 1976.
• Jimmy Carter and Walter Mondale used e-mail to plan their campaign events, also in 1976.
• Novelist William Gibson coined the word *cyberspace* in 1984.

WHO DIED AND MADE YOU QUEEN?

The Reigns of Ten Allegedly Gay Monarchs

William II of England 1087–1100
Richard I of England 1189–1199
Edward II of England 1307–1327
John II of France 1350–1364
James III of Scotland 1469–1488
Henri III of France 1574–1589
James I of England (James VI of Scotland) 1603–1625
Louis XIII of France 1610–1643
Mary II of England, Scotland, and Ireland 1689–1694
Anne of Great Britain and Ireland 1702–1714

CURIOUS, THE AMISH . . .

They May Not	*But They May*
Have a phone at home, as it might promote gossip	Use a phone outside the home
Own a car	Hitch a ride from an "English" friend
Have electricity in their home	Use 12-volt batteries to run appliances
Swear an oath in court	Make an "affirmation of truth" in court

◆

WARD MCALLISTER was the coiner of several high-society words and *bon mots*, including *snob* and *bon vivant*; he also named Mrs. Astor's closest pals The Four Hundred.

BETTER LIVING THROUGH SCIENCE
Some Scientists and Their Steps Through Time

Hippocrates (c. 460–377 BCE)
Father of medicine

Euclid (c. 300 BCE)
Geometry

Nicholas Copernicus (1473–1543)
Sun is center of the solar system

Galileo Galilei (1564–1642)
Father of astronomy and physics

Robert Hooke (1635–1703)
Invented the quadrant,
Gregorian telescope,
and microscope

Sir Isaac Newton (1642–1727)
Law of Gravity

Charles Darwin (1809–1882)
Theory of evolution

Jean Foucault (1819–1868)
Foucault's pendulum

Gregor Johann Mendel (1822–1884)
Modern genetics

Louis Pasteur (1822–1895)
Immunization and
pasteurization

Wilhelm Conrad Roentgen (1845–1923)
X-ray machine

Sigmund Freud (1856–1939)
Father of psychoanalysis

Leo Baekeland (1863–1944)
Bakelite, the first popular plastic

Marie Curie (1867–1934) and Pierre Curie (1859–1906)
Radiology

Wilbur Wright (1867–1912) and Orville Wright (1871–1948)
Heavier-than-air flight

Ernst Rutherford (1871–1937)
Father of nuclear physics

Albert Einstein (1879–1955)
Theory of relativity

Edwin Hubble (1889–1953)
Universe is expanding

Robert J. Oppenheimer (1904–1967)
Father of the Atomic Bomb

Philo T. Farnsworth (1906–1971)
Vacuum tube television

Rachel Carson (1907–1964)
Environmental movement

Jonas Salk (1914–1995)
Polio vaccine

James Dewey Watson (1928–) and Francis Crick
(1916–2004)
DNA double helix

◆

WOMEN OF MANNERS
Modern-Day Grandes Dames of Etiquette

EMILY POST
"Manners are a sensitive awareness of the feelings of others. If you have that awareness, you have good manners, no matter what fork you use."

AMY VANDERBILT
"Good manners have much to do with the emotions. To make them ring true, one must feel them, not merely exhibit them."

LETITIA BALDRIDGE
"When you put your foot in your mouth, eject it—quickly!"

MISS MANNERS (NÉE JUDITH MARTIN)
"We are all born charming, fresh and spontaneous, and must be civilized before we are fit to participate in society."

◆

W. E. B. DU BOIS was the first African American to receive a Ph.D. from Harvard, in 1895.

BIG DAY

On these dates, someone famous died . . . and someone famous was born.

Date	Died	Born
May 19, 1795	Biographer James Boswell	Philanthropist Johns Hopkins
July 4, 1826	Presidents John Adams and Thomas Jefferson	Songwriter Stephen Foster
October 15, 1917	Spy Mata Hari	Historian Arthur Schlesinger Jr.
May 23, 1934	Bank robbers Clyde Barrow and Bonnie Parker	Inventor Robert Moog
January 5, 1945	Seer Edgar Cayce	Musician Stephen Stills
November 21, 1945	Humorist Robert Benchley	Actress Goldie Hawn

. . . and these folks were born on the very same day.

James Cagney and Erle Stanley Gardner, born July 17, 1899
Marlon Brando and Doris Day, born April 3, 1924
Eartha Kitt and Roger Vadim, born January 26, 1928
Luciano Pavarotti and Joan Rivers, born October 12, 1935
Princess Margaret and Janis Joplin, born January 19, 1943
George Foreman and Linda Lovelace, born January 10, 1949

KILLING MACHINES

Name/Handle	When and Where	Number of Victims
David Berkowitz/ "Son of Sam"	1970s New York	Killed 6; wounded 7
Kenneth Bianchi and Angelo Buono/ "The Hillside Stranglers"	1977–1978 United States	9 convictions
Ted Bundy	1970s United States	28 confessions
Jeffrey Dahmer	1980s Milwaukee	16
Albert DeSalvo	1962–1964	13 women
Albert Fish	1919–1928 United States	8–15
John Wayne Gacy/ "The Killer Clown"	1978–1981 Chicago	30+
Pedro Lopez/ "Monster of the Andes"	1970s Peru, Ecuador, and Colombia	300+
Robert Pickton	1990s Vancouver	30+
Aileen Wournos	1989–1990	6 convictions

Some of History's Most Gruesome Serial Killers

M.O.	Weird Fact
44-caliber killer; stalked lovers' lanes	Took his orders from a dog
Sodomize, strangle, leave on a hillside	Posed as policemen
Charming psychopath raped college girls	Urban legend has Deborah Harry as an escaped victim
Cannibalism and necrophilia of young boys	Impaled animal heads on sticks as a child
Sex and murder	"Measuring Man" told women he was from a modeling agency
Rape, torture, cannibalize, and try new children recipes; Hannibal Lector model	Liked to be beaten with a nail-studded paddle
Torture, rape, and murder young men; hid remains under the floorboards	Had his photo taken with First Lady Rosalyn Carter
Rape and murder of young girls, often three a week	Had "tea parties" with little girls after he killed them
Killed prostitutes and kept body parts in freezers	Chopped body parts into pig feed
Lesbian who worked as prostitute and killed men	Played in the movie *Monster* by one of Hollywood's most beautiful actresses, Charlize Theron

DAY JOBS
Famous People, Ordinary Work

Jeffrey Archer (author): Deckchair attendant
Hannah Arendt (political philosopher): First Princeton
woman professor
Jon Bon Jovi (rock star): Christmas ornament maker
Dominick Dunne (writer, investigative journalist): Producer
T. S. Eliot (poet): Bank clerk
Benjamin Franklin (scientist and statesman): Promoter
Washington Irving (author): Diplomat
James Fenimore Cooper (author): Gentleman farmer
Ralph Waldo Emerson (poet): Unitarian minister
Friedrich Engels (coauthor of *The Communist Manifesto*):
Textile manufacturer
Che Guevara (Cuban revolutionary): Doctor
Nathaniel Hawthorne (author): Surveyor
Adolf Hitler (Leader of the Third Reich): House painter
Mick Jagger (rock star): Mental hospital porter
Cyndi Lauper (pop star): Dog kennel cleaner
Malcolm X (Nation of Islam leader): Burglar
Herman Melville (author): Customs inspector
Gertrude Stein (author): Medical student
Wallace Stevens (poet): Insurance executive
Rod Stewart (rock star): Gravedigger
Harriet Beecher Stowe (abolitionist): Housewife
Hunter S. Thompson (author): Sportswriter
Henry David Thoreau (naturalist): Pencil maker
Lionel Trilling (literary critic): College professor
Mark Twain (author): Riverboat pilot
William Carlos Williams (poet): Pediatrician

SEBASTIAN CLOVER became the youngest person ever to sail the Atlantic single-handedly in 2003. He was just fifteen years old and was racing against his father.

SOME YOUNG MEN RAISED AS YOUNG LADIES

Boy	Girlish Past	Macho Future
Robert Peary (1856–1920)	"Bertie" wore frills and sun-bonnets	North Pole explorer
Douglas MacArthur (1880–1964)	Skirts and curls	General
Ernest Hemingway (1899–1961)	Frilly dresses	Great American novelist
Peter Paul Rubens (1577–1640)	Lacy underwear, gowns, and wigs	Flemish artist
Rainier Maria Rilke (1875–1926)	"Sophie," ages one to six	Austrian poet
Oscar Wilde (1854–1900)	Dresses of blue velvet	Irish playwright
Thomas Wolfe (1900–1938)	Long, hand-curled hair	U.S. novelist
Alexander Woollcott (1887–1943)	Dressed as "Alexandra"	U.S. essayist

HONORARY CITIZENS OF
THE UNITED STATES

In the history of the United States, there have been only six:

Sir Winston Churchill (1874–1965)	British Prime Minister during World War II; citizenship conferred 1963
Raoul Wallenberg (1912–?)	Swedish diplomat and Holocaust hero; citizenship conferred 1981
William Penn (1644–1718) and Hannah Penn (1671–1727)	Founder of Pennsylvania and his second wife, who administered the Province of Pennsylvania after his death; citizenship conferred 1984
Mother Teresa, *née* Agnes Gonxha Bojaxhim (1910–1997)	Macedonian nun and civil rights advocate; citizenship conferred 1996
The Marquis de Lafayette (1757–1834)	The French supporter of the American Revolution was made an honorary citizen many times, but not of the United States as a whole until 2002

◆

GEORGE W. BUSH was the president elected with the most popular votes: 62,028,772 (yet with only 50.8 % of the popular vote) in 2004.

LESSER-KNOWN GOLDWYNISMS

"Every director bites the hand that lays the golden egg."
"I had a monumental idea last night but I didn't like it."
"Tell me, how did you love my picture?"
"I never liked you, and I always will."
"It's more than magnificent—it's mediocre."
"It's spreading like wildflowers."
"This makes me so sore it gets my dandruff up."
"Color television! Bah, I won't believe it until I see
it in black and white."
"If I could drop dead right now, I'd be the happiest
man alive."
"A bachelor's life is no life for a single man."

◆

THE WORLD'S MOST PROLIFIC PAINTER

Created an estimated
13,500 paintings and designs,
100,000 prints and engravings,
34,000 book illustrations and
300 sculptures and ceramics

and quite possibly possessed the longest artist's name:

Pablo Diego José Francisco de Paula Juan Nepomuceno
Crispin Crispiniano los Remedios Cipriano de la Santisima
Trinidad Ruiz Blasco y Picasso Lopez
AKA
Pablo Picasso

AT LAST . . .
Famous Folks' Final Words

"Why not, why not, why not. Yeah." —Timothy Leary

"Stand away, fellow, from —Archimedes
　my diagram."

"Damn it....Don't you dare ask God —Joan Crawford
to help me out."

"It is very beautiful over there." —Thomas Edison

"I'm losin'." —Frank Sinatra

"All my possessions for a —Elizabeth I
moment of time."

"This is the last of earth! —John Quincy Adams
　I am content."

"Get my swan costume ready." —Anna Pavlova

"Moose. Indian." —Henry David Thoreau

"I'll finally get to see Marilyn." —Joe DiMaggio

"Crito, I owe a cock to Asclepius; —Socrates
　will you remember to pay the debt?"

"I've never felt better." —Douglas Fairbanks Jr.

"Go on, get out. Last words are —Karl Marx
　for fools who haven't said enough."

"Please put out the lights." —Theodore Roosevelt

"I have a terrific headache." —Franklin Delano
　　Roosevelt

"Curtain! Fast music! Lights! —Florenz Ziegfeld
　Ready for the last finale! Great!
　The show looks good.
　The show looks good."

"I am not the least afraid to die." —Charles Darwin

"We've caught them napping!" —General Custer,
　　at Little Big Horn

"I go to seek the great Perhaps." —Francois Rabelais
"Well, I must arrange my pillows for —Washington Irving
another weary night! When will
this end?"
"Thou, too, Brutus, my son!" —Julius Caesar
"Let us go in; the fog is rising." —Emily Dickinson

◆

WOMEN'S WORK
Leading Occupations Held Predominantly by Females

Job	Median Weekly Earnings ($)
1. Secretary	591
2. Registered nurse	887
3. Nursing, home health care	372
4. Cashier	315
5. Customer service representative	503
6. Office supervisor	609
7. Retail supervisor	496
8. Bookkeeping, auditing clerk	512
9. Receptionist	446
10. Accountant	756
11. Retail sales	382
12. Maid	317
13. High school teacher	824
14. Waitress	318
15. Teaching assistant	344
16. Office clerk	502
17. Financial representative	823
18. Preschool teacher	493
19. Cook	317

DISEASES NAMED AFTER PEOPLE

Creutzfeld-Jakob Disease: Encephalopathic disease commonly known as "Mad Cow" (1920)

Legionnaire's Disease: Infection that leads to pneumonia, named for the initial two hundred Philadelphia conventioneers who contracted it (1976)

Down Syndrome: Condition in which a person has three of chromosome 21 instead of two (1866)

Cushing's Disease: Hormonal condition brought on by high levels of cortisol (1932)

Hodgkin's disease: Cancer of the lymphatic system whose cause remains unknown, but may be related to Epstein-Barr virus, which causes mononucleosis (1832)

Marfan Syndrome: Connective tissue problems found in very tall people (1896)

Munchausen Syndrome: Hypochondriac's obsessive need to procure attention (1951)

Munchausen-by-Proxy: Condition in which, to garner attention, a parent causes a child to become sick (1977)

Parkinson's Disease: Neurological condition affecting the central nervous system (1817)

Raynaud's Disease: Vessel contraction in the fingers and toes, causing numbness and tingling (1862)

Reyes Syndrome: Children's organ disorder resulting from chicken pox or flu (1963)

Tay-Sachs Disease: Rare inherited disease causing slow destruction of the central nervous system (1969)

Tourette's Syndrome: Neurological disorder manifesting itself in tics (1885)

FAMOUSLY ILLEGITIMATE

Sarah Bernhardt, actress
Pope Clement VII
Leonardo da Vinci, artist
Frederick Douglass, abolitionist
Josephine de Beauharnais, Napoleon's wife
Alexander Hamilton, U.S. secretary of the treasury
Jenny Lind, singer
Marilyn Monroe, actress
Richard Wagner, composer
William the Conquerer, first Norman ruler

◆

DID YOU WHISTLE FOR ME?

A majority of the thirty most popular pet names are also people names, according to the ASPCA. Some of the top monikers are:

Max * Sam * Kitty * Molly * Buddy * Brandy * Ginger
* Misty * Missy * Jake * Samantha * Muffin * Maggie
* Charlie * Rocky * Rusty * Buster

Some are named for other types of animals:

Bear * Tiger

And some are actually named for what most pets think they
in fact are—royalty:

Lady * Princess

121

AMERICA'S BEST PRESIDENTIAL NICKNAMES

George Washington: Sword of the Revolution
John Adams: Old Sink or Swim
Thomas Jefferson: Pen of the Revolution
James Monroe: Last of the Cocked Hats
John Quincy Adams: Accidental President
Andrew Jackson: King Andrew the First
Martin Van Buren: Petticoat Pet
W. H. Harrison: Old Granny
Millard Fillmore: American Louis Philippe
Franklin Pierce: Purse
James Buchanan: Ten-Cent Jimmy
Abraham Lincoln: Illinois Baboon
Andrew Johnson: Sir Veto
Ulysses S. Grant: Useless Grant
Rutherford B. Hayes: His Fraudulency
Chester A. Arthur: Dude President
Grover Cleveland: Buffalo Hangman
Benjamin Harrison: Grandfather's Hat
William McKinley: Wobbly Willie
Theodore Roosevelt: Great White Chief
Woodrow Wilson: Coiner of Weasel Words
Herbert Hoover: Hermit Author of Palo Alto
Franklin D. Roosevelt: Sphinx
Harry S. Truman: Haberdasher Harry

◆

MARY FAIRFAX SOMERVILLE was the first woman to have a scientific paper presented before the British Royal Society, in 1826.

OVAL OFFICE ODDITIES

Clothes Hog
Chester Allan Arthur owned more than 80 pairs of trousers.

The "Hanging Sheriff"
Grover Cleveland was the only president to personally hang anyone. "Buffalo's Hangman" threw the noose and sprung the trap on two convicted criminals while sheriff of Erie County, New York.

In the Raw
John Quincy Adams insisted on swimming in the nude.

STD
JFK had a nearly perpetual case of chlamydia.

Backroom Politics
Warren G. Harding gambled White House china in a poker game—and lost the china. The lucky winner took it home.

. . . And the Most Expensive Non–White House Race
Michael R. Bloomberg ran the most costly nonpresidential campaign in U.S. history. In his 1998 New York City mayoral campaign, he spent $73 million.

WHO APPEARS MOST OFTEN IN CROSSWORD PUZZLES?

Prophets
In order of popularity:

Major
Isaiah * Jeremiah * Ezekiel * Daniel

Minor
Hosea * Obadiah * Nahum * Haggai * Joel * Jonah
* Habakkuk * Zechariah * Amos * Micah * Zephaniah
* Malachi

Canadian Jurists
In word-length order, alphabetically:
Caron * Jette * Armour * Davies * Mulock * Stuart
* Doherty * Lacoste * Fournier * Haultain * Newcombe
* Richards * Robinson * Haliburton * Fitzpatrick

Hunting Dogs
In word-length order, alphabetically:
Alan * Brach * Rache * Ratch * Alaund * Basset * Hunter
* Kennet * Lucern * Racche * Saluki * Seizer * Setter
* Slough * Courser * Dropper * Harrier * Pointer * Striker

Playwrights from Around the World
Chambers (Australia) * Maeterlinck (Belgium)
* Rose (Canada) * Tammsaare (Estonia) * Ilg (Switzerland)
* Evans (Wales) * Chikamatsu (Japan) * Gamboa (Mexico)
* Silva (Portugal) * Blaga (Romania)

U.S. POETS LAUREATE

Joseph Auslander (1937–1941)

Allen Tate (1943–1944)

Robert Penn Warren (1944–1945)

Louise Bogan (1945–1946)

Karl Shapiro (1946–1947)

Robert Lowell (1947–1948)

Leonie Adams (1948–1949)

Elizabeth Bishop (1949–1950)

Conrad Aiken (1950–1952)

William Carlos Williams (1952)

Randall Jarrell (1956–1958)

Robert Frost (1958–1959)

Richard Eberhart (1959–1961)

Louis Untermeyer (1961–1963)

Howard Nemerov (1963–1964)

Reed Whittemore (1964–1965)

Stephen Spender (1965–1966)

James Dickey (1966–1968)

William Jay Smith (1968–1970)

William Stafford (1970–1971)

Josephine Jacobsen (1971–1973)

Daniel Hoffman (1973–1974)

Stanley Kunitz (1974–1976)

Robert Hayden (1976–1978)

William Meredith (1978–1980)

Maxine Kumin (1981–1982)

Anthony Hecht (1982–1984)

Robert Fitzgerald and Reed Whittemore (1984–1985)

Gwendolyn Brooks (1985–1986)

Robert Penn Warren (1986–1987)

Richard Wilbur (1987–1988)

Howard Nemerov (1988–1990)

Mark Strand (1990–1991)

Joseph Brodsky (1991–1992)

Mona Van Duyn (1992–1993)

Rita Dove (1993–1995)

Robert Hass (1995–1997)

Robert Pinsky (1997–2000)

Stanley Kunitz (2000–2001)

Billy Collins (2001–2003)

Louise Gluck (2003–2004)

Ted Kooser (2004–   )

U.S. poets laureate are appointed for one year, but eligible for reappointment.

PRESIDENTS ELECTED WITHOUT A MAJORITY

Year	Winner
1824	John Quincy Adams (D-R)
1844	James K. Polk (D)
1848	Zachary Taylor (W)
1856	James Buchanan (D)
1860	Abraham Lincoln (R)
1876	Rutherford B. Hayes (R)
1880	James A. Garfield (R)
1884	Grover Cleveland (D)
1888	Benjamin Harrison (R)
1892	Grover Cleveland (D)
1912	Woodrow Wilson (D)
1916	Woodrow Wilson (D)
1948	Harry S. Truman (D)
1960	John F. Kennedy (D)
1968	Richard M. Nixon (D)
1992	William J. Clinton (D)
1996	William J. Clinton (D)
2000	George W. Bush (R)

D-R: Democratic-Republican; D: Democrat; W: Whig; R: Republican

Though Americans are now quite used to close presidential elections and a long wait for results, the 1876 vote between Rutherford B. Hayes and Samuel B. Tilden still holds first

Fifteen of Our Commanders in Chief—
And Three of Them Twice

Opponent	Percentage of Electoral Votes	Percentage of Popular Votes
Andrew Jackson	32.2	30.9
Henry Clay	61.8	49.5
Lewis Cass	56.2	47.3
John C. Fremont	58.8	45.3
John C. Breckinridge	59.4	39.8
Samuel J. Tilden	50.1	47.9
Winfield S. Hancock	58.0	48.3
James G. Blaine	54.6	48.5
Grover Cleveland	58.1	47.8
Benjamin Harrison	62.4	46.0
Theodore Roosevelt	81.9	41.8
Charles E. Hughes	52.2	49.2
Thomas E. Dewey	57.1	49.6
Richard M. Nixon	56.4	49.7
Hubert H. Humphrey	56.0	43.4
George H. Bush	68.8	43.0
Robert J. Dole	70.5	49.2
Albert A. Gore	50.4	47.9

place in America's collective political breath-holding record books. Hayes was announced the winner of the November 7 race on March 2, 1877—three days before his inauguration.

ROBERT URICH starred in fifteen television series, more than any other actor to date:

Bob & Carol & Ted & Alice (1973)
S.W.A.T. (1975–76)
Soap (1977–81)
Tabitha (1977–78)
Vega$ (1978–81)
Gavilan (1982)
Spenser: For Hire (1985–88)
American Dreamer (1990–91)
National Geographic Explorer (1991–94)
Crossroads (1992)
It Had to Be You (1993)
The Lazarus Man (1996)
Vital Signs (1997)
Boatworks (1997)
Love Boat: The Next Wave (1998–99)

◆

A POPULAR, TRENDY COCKTAIL
The Dr. Kevorkian

1 oz Amaretto
1 oz Southern Comfort whiskey
1 oz Jack Daniels whiskey
1 oz gin
1 oz vodka
8 oz orange juice
Serve over ice.

WHO BOLTED?
The Confederate States of America

State	Date Seceded from Union	Date Readmitted to Union
1. South Carolina	Dec. 20, 1860	July 9, 1868
2. Mississippi	Jan. 9, 1861	Feb. 23, 1870
3. Florida	Jan. 10, 1861	June 25, 1868
4. Alabama	Jan. 11, 1861	July 13, 1868
5. Georgia	Jan. 19, 1861	July 15, 1870
6. Louisiana	Jan. 26, 1861	July 9, 1868
7. Texas	March 2, 1861	March 30, 1870
8. Virginia	April 17, 1861	Jan. 26, 1870
9. Arkansas	May 6, 1861	June 22, 1868
10. North Carolina	May 20, 1861	July 4, 1868
11. Tennessee	June 8, 1861	July 24, 1866

◆

SNL HOSTS WITH THE MOST
Celebs Who Keep Coming Back for More

Steve Martin (13 appearances)
* John Goodman (12 appearances) * Alec Baldwin
(11 appearances) * Buck Henry (10 appearances)
* Chevy Chase (8 appearances)

SNL'S LONGEST-LASTING CAST MEMBERS

Al Franken (11 years) * Tim Meadows (10 years)
* Darrell Hammond (10 years) * Kevin Nealon (9 years)
* Phil Hartman (8 years)

THE SIX WIVES OF HENRY VIII

Queen	Birth–Death	Wifely Years	Fate
Catherine of Aragon	1485–1536	1509–1533	Divorced
Anne Boleyn	1507?–1536	1533–1536	Executed
Jane Seymour	1509?–1537	1536–1537	Died
Anne of Cleves	1515–1557	January–July 1540	Divorced
Katherine Howard	?–1542	1540–1542	Executed
Katherine Parr	1512–1548	1543–1547	Widowed

◆

ALGONQUIN ROUND TABLE
1919–1943

Dorothy Parker * Alexander Woollcott * Heyward Broun
* Robert Benchley * Robert Sherwood * George S. Kaufman
* Franklin P. Adams * Marc Connelly * Harold Ross
* Harpo Marx * Russel Crouse

MUSICIANS WHO DIED IN PLANE CRASHES

Glenn Miller (1944) * Big Bopper (1959) * Buddy Holly
(1959) * Richie Valens (1959) * Patsy Cline (1963) * Otis
Redding (1967) * Jim Croce (1973) * Ricky Nelson (1985)
* Stevie Ray Vaughn (1990) * John Denver (1997)

What

What should I say? What does it mean? What were they thinking? The following pages offer meanings and definitions, codes and rules, and other clever ways that we people organize our world and communicate about it. What does "86" stand for at the diner, or "187" on a police scanner? What is the proper gift to give, and what about those weird town names? Turn the page and break the code.

POLICE SCANNER CODES

PROPER TABLE SETTINGS

SLEEPWALKING

WINNING SPELLING BEE WORDS

ODD LAWS

YIDDISH PUTDOWNS

METAL ALLOYS

THE DOW JONES INDUSTRIAL AVERAGE

SIZES OF EVERYDAY THINGS

PHOBIAS

DIAMONDS AND DIAMOND SYNTHETICS

MORSE CODE

DEATH ROW MEALS

GRATUITIES

POPULAR TOWN NAMES

SUPERSTITIONS

LUCKY NUMBER SEVEN

ANNIVERSARY GIFTS

ZODIAC SIGNS

SPORTS MASCOTS

OLD WIVES' TALES ABOUT PREGNANCY

SLOT MACHINE LINGO

ASTRONAUT TERMINOLOGY

MINOR POLITICAL PARTIES

TOP MOVIES AT THE BOX OFFICE

MILITARY RANKS

OSCAR AND THE OSCARINIS

In 1938, Walt Disney won an Academy Award for his animated feature *Snow White and the Seven Dwarfs*—or, more precisely, he received one for himself, and seven miniatures for his little friends.

MANILA FOLDERS are made from and named after Manila hemp, or abaca, a sturdy fiber derived from a relative of the banana plant. Indigenous to the Philippines, its light weight, durability, and strength make it a natural choice for paper products.

POLITICAL PARTY

The signers of the United States Constitution apparently had a "work hard, play hard" mentality. Just two days before signing, they ordered a few drinks. When the bill came, it included:

> 54 bottles of Madeira
> 60 bottles of claret
> 30 to 50 bottles of whiskey, beer, hard cider, and port
> 7 bowls of spiked punch

Many experts believe that the back brace PRESIDENT KENNEDY wore on November 22, 1963, was part of the reason he didn't survive the assassination in Dallas. The first bullet passed through his neck, but did not kill him. However, Kennedy's back brace prevented his body from slumping over, leaving a clear target for the second bullet, a fatal shot to his head.

COP TALK

"10-4, over and out!" is just one code in the lexicon of police jargon, some of which we've learned from watching television cop shows. Although the codes vary between police departments, here are some examples:

10-1	You are being received poorly
10-10	Fight in progress
10-15	Civil disturbance
10-16	Pick up prisoners
10-24	Trouble at station
10-31	Crime in progress
10-32	Person with gun
10-34	Riot
10-39	Urgent—use light and siren
10-45	Animal carcass
10-79	Notify coroner
10-80	Vacation check
10-85	Will be late
10-90	Bank alarm
10-94	Drag race
10-98	Jailbreak
11-12	Dead animal/loose livestock
11-14	Animal bite
11-15	Ball game in street
code 7	Out for lunch
187	Homicide
288	Lewd conduct
311	Indecent exposure
390D	Drunk unconscious
415G	Gang disturbance
470	Forgery

595	Runaway car
903L	Low-flying aircraft
905V	Vicious animal
908	Begging
914H	Heart attack
915	Dumping rubbish
921P	Peeping Tom
927	Suspicious person
927A	Person pulled from telephone
949	Gasoline spill
962	Suspect is armed and dangerous
975	Can your suspect hear your radio?
967	Outlaw motorcyclists
966	Sniper
995	Labor trouble
996	Explosive
5150	Mental case
21958	Drunk pedestrian in roadway

◆

STERLING SERVICE
The Proper Setting for the Elegant Table

Left of the Plate

Napkin
Fish fork
Dinner fork
Salad fork

Right of Plate

Service knife
Fish knife
Soup spoon

Above the Plate

Butter knife (on butter plate)
Dessert spoon (bowl left)
Cake fork (tines right)

Crystal or glassware
(from left to right)

Water glass
Red wineglass
White wineglass

MAD FADS
Nutty Obsessions of the Twentieth Century

1920s

Flagpole sitting
Flappers
Freudianism
Mah Jongg
Dance marathons

1930s

Stamp collecting
Board games
Drive-in movies
Miniature golf
Zoot suits

1940s

Swallowing goldfish
Silly putty
Pea shooters
"Kilroy was here"
Slinky

1950s

Phone booth stuffing
Hula hoop
3-D movies
Coonskin caps
Panty raids

1960s

The Twist
Fallout shelters
Troll dolls
Ouija boards
Bouffants

1970s

String art
Streaking
Puka shells
Mexican jumping beans
Pet rocks

1980s

Rubik's Cube
Boom boxes
Cabbage Patch dolls
Break dancing
Smurfs

1990s

Beanie Babies
Grunge
Furby
Tattoos
Piercing

WHO—AND WHAT—AM I?

Autosomal DNA determines much of who we are, and consists of all of a cell's DNA, except the X and Y chromosomes and the mitochondrial DNA. Fifty percent of your autosomal DNA comes from your father, and 50 percent comes from your mother, and it contains a broad picture of your genetic ancestry. It is currently used to legally verify Native American blood when questions of land inheritance arise.

THE FEATHER LAW

Federal laws that prohibit the killing, possession, or use of several types of birds, such as the bald eagle, were enacted to protect various bird species from hunters, but Native Americans enrolled in federally recognized tribes may legally possess eagle feathers for use in religious ceremonies. A provision mandates that these feathers be obtained, via permit, from a central distribution office and they cannot be sold, bartered, or given away to anyone other than another enrolled member of a federally recognized tribe.

◆

SOCIAL SECURITY currently offers U.S. citizens four types of protection:

1. Retirement benefits
2. Survivors' benefits
3. Disability benefits
4. Medicare medical insurance benefits

◆

Ancient Romans considered FLAMINGO TONGUES a delicacy.

THE PULITZER PRIZE

All winners, except for Public Service, are awarded a $10,000 cash prize and a certificate of recognition. The Public Service Award winner receives a gold medal.

Current Pulitzer Prize Categories

Beat Reporting
Biography or Autobiography
Breaking News Photography
Breaking News Reporting
Commentary
Criticism
Drama
Editorial Cartooning
Editorial Writing
Explanatory Reporting
Feature Photography
Feature Writing
Fiction
General Non-Fiction
History
International Reporting
Investigative Reporting
Music
National Reporting
Public Service
Biography or Autobiography (by an American author)
Fiction (by an American author)
General Non-Fiction (by an American author)
U.S. History
Poetry

Discontinued Pulitzer Prize Categories

Correspondence
Explanatory Journalism (replaced by Explanatory Reporting)
General News Reporting
Local General or Spot News Reporting
Local Investigative Specialized Reporting
Local Reporting
Local Reporting, Edition Time
Local Reporting, No Edition Time
The Novel (now the Pulitzer Prize for Fiction)
Photography (replaced by Feature Photography
    and Breaking News Photography)
Specialized Reporting
Spot News Photography
Spot News Reporting
Telegraphic Reporting—National and Internationa

THE EMANCIPATION PROCLAMATION

When it was enacted on New Year's Day 1863, Abraham
Lincoln called the Emancipation Proclamation "a fit and
necessary war measure for suppressing rebellion." Lincoln's
proclamation applied only to freed slaves in Southern states
that had already seceded from the Union, making it virtually
unenforceable. It did not apply to slaves in the North, nor in
the border states of Delaware, Maryland, Kentucky, and
Missouri. It was not until 1865, when Congress passed the
Thirteenth Amendment, that slavery was abolished in the
United States.

PEARLS will dissolve in vinegar.

THE NOBEL PRIZE

Since their first presentation in 1901, Nobel laureates have received a cash prize, a gold medal, and a diploma. Winners can be either individuals or institutions and currently share approximately US$1.3 million per category. There can be up to three winners per category, with all winners for each category dividing the prize money. A prize may not be awarded if no candidate is chosen, but each prize must be awarded at least once every five years. Any money declined by laureates remains the property of the Nobel Prize Foundation and remains in its trust.

Nobel Prize categories

Nobel Prize in Chemistry
Nobel Prize in Economic Sciences*
Nobel Prize in Literature
Nobel Prize in Physics
Nobel Prize in Physiology or Medicine
Nobel Peace Prize

*Instituted in 1968 by the Bank of Sweden in Memory of Alfred Nobel, founder of the Nobel Prize.

◆

The JOLLY ROGER is an English euphemism for a pirate flag and is thought by some to come from the French "joli rouge" or "pretty red," a wry description of the red banner flown by pirates that declared they would show no mercy to victims. Seventeenth-century privateers designed their own personal banners, often flown along with the national flag, and what we think of today as the Jolly Roger—the skull and crossbones on a black background—first appeared on the high seas in the eighteenth century. It may have come from the captain's log, in which the skull and crossbones indicated the death of a crew member.

"I SAY, OLD CHAP"

For the feel of Hollywood in its heyday or an afternoon at the races, when it comes to men's neckwear, only an ascot will do. Here is how it's properly tied:

1. Pull the ascot around the back of your neck as you would a tie. Let the left end hang slightly more than two inches longer than the right.
2. Wrap the left end one and a half times over the right. Continue around as if you were going to complete a second turn, and push the left end up through the neck loop so that it emerges over the top.
3. Center the top flap so that it is the only visible portion of the ascot. Spread the sides slightly, creating a "waterfall" of fabric from the base of your neck.
4. Undo only one button of your shirt. Tuck the ends of the ascot into your shirt.
5. Secure the ends of the ascot with a stick pin if desired.

◆

AMERICA'S CUP?

The America's Cup, often called the oldest trophy in sports, did not travel from its home in the New York Yacht Club from 1851 until 1983, when it was won by an Australian team. The cup has since resided in San Diego; Sydney, Australia; and Auckland, New Zealand; and has taken a trip back to its original home, the Royal Yacht Squadron in Cowes, England. The cup always flies accompanied by two security guards in its own seat in business class. It also has its own specially crafted Louis Vuitton travel case, so that it may travel in comfort and style.

SPEED RACKING

In bars, the good liquor, referred to as "top shelf," is kept behind the bartender, and the least expensive liquor, called "well drinks," is kept in what is called the "speed rack," below the lip of the bar. They usually line up, left to right, in the following order: vodka, bourbon, gin, scotch, rum, brandy, tequila, triple sec, rye, and kahlua.

◆

WHAT DID YOU SAY?

The longest word (containing forty-five letters) currently listed in any dictionary is pneumonoultramicroscopicsilicovol-canoconiosis and is defined in *Webster's Third New International Dictionary, Unabridged* as "a pneumoconiosis caused by the inhalation of very fine silicate or quartz dust and occurring especially in miners." This easily beats the more familiar antidisestablishmentarianism (the only one of the über-long words that is not science-based), which has a mere twenty-eight letters. Other contenders are:

Otorhinolaryngological	22 letters
Immunoelectrophoretically	25 letters
Psychophysicotherapeutics	25 letters
Thyroparathyroidectomized	25 letters
Pneumoencephalographically	26 letters
Radioimmunoelectrophoresis	26 letters
Psychoneuroendocrinological	27 letters
Hepaticocholangiogastrostomy	28 letters
Spectrophotofluorometrically	28 letters
Pseudopseudohypoparathyroidism	30 letter

MUSICAL JEWELS

In 1958 the Recording Industry Association of America began issuing award records—a facsimile disc mounted on a plaque—as industry recognition of top-selling recordings based on their audits. Originally a gold record was presented in recognition of 500,000 copies sold. Along with the explosive growth and rapid technological changes of recent decades came recording industry changes. RIAA announced different award levels, adding the Platinum record in 1976 and Multi-Platinum in 1984, and introduced a diamond record award in 1999. Currently the awards are based on U.S. unit sales (including military post exchanges abroad) and are:

Record	Number Sold
Gold	500,000
Platinum	1,000,000
Multi-Platinum	2,000,000
Diamond	10,000,000

The number sold to receive one of these awards is the same, whether the record is a single or an album.

DR. BUNTING TO THE RESCUE

Noxzema is a trademark name with a personal history. Soon after its invention, it was marketed as an efficient cold cream as well as a remedy for relieving sunburn under the name "Dr. Bunting's Sunburn Remedy." Shortly after its introduction, a surprised and happy customer wrote to the company, reporting, "Your cream knocked my eczema!" and a new name and use were announced for the remedy.

WHAT ARE THE 6,469,952 BLACK SPOTS ON THAT SCREEN?

They are the total number of spots that appear on the dogs in the animated film *101 Dalmatians*.

◆

SOMNAMBULISM

If you're worried that you walk in your sleep and have a vague memory of doing so, you may be right: About 18 percent of the population does so at least once during their lifetime. The majority of somnambulists are prepubescent, and their somnambulism is unlikely to last through their teens. However, if childhood sleepwalking begins after the age of nine, it will often last well into adulthood.

Autonomic (independently functioning) behavior during somnambulism can involve dressing, eating, and, rarely, criminal or harmful activity. Here are a few helpful hints should you suddenly discover you're strolling during the night:

- Being overtired can trigger a sleepwalking episode; be sure to get enough rest.
- Practice meditation or perform relaxation exercises to calm yourself before going to sleep.
- Remove anything from the bedroom that could be dangerous to you when sleepwalking.
- Sleep on the ground floor if possible.
- Carefully review with your physician any current medications you're taking.
- Try a hypnotherapy treatment.

SOME KIND OF HOT

The substance in chili peppers that makes them hot is called capsaicin. In 1912, pharmacist Wilbur Scoville created a scale to measure pepper hotness using a solution of pepper extract that was diluted in increasing amounts of sugar water until the "heat" of the pepper was no longer detectable to a panel of (usually five) tasters. Scoville developed Scoville Units as a measure, with 0 being no heat and with heat increasing along with the Scoville Unit number. Pure capsaicin would measure 16 million Scoville Units.

Type of Pepper	Number of Scoville Units
Habanero	100,000–350,000
Tien tsin	40,000–60,000
Dundicut	40,000–60,000
Cayenne	30,000–50,000
de Arbol	15,000–30,000
Ground hot red	20,000
Serrano	5,000–15,000
Chipotle pepper	5,000–10,000
Jalapeño	2,500–8,000
Ancho pepper	1,000–3,000

451° FAHRENHEIT is the temperature at which paper will ignite and books will burn, according to Ray Bradbury's horrific tale of the future, *Fahrenheit 451*. The novel, and the movie adapted from it, takes place in what is known as a dystopia, a fictional society that is the opposite of utopia, usually existing in the future, when conditions of life are extremely bad, often due to deprivation, oppression, or terror.

PORTMANTEAUS
A Short List of "Blended" Words—New Words
Formed by Joining Two Words

Anacronym	From anachronism and acronym
Backronym	From back and acronym
Blaxploitation	From black and exploitation
Bootylicious	From booty and delicious (as sung by Destiny's Child)
Chortle	From chuckle and snort (coined by Lewis Carroll)
Cocacolonization	From Coca-Cola and colonization
Corpsicle	From corpse and Popsicle
Cyborg	From cybernetic and organism
Digipeater	From digital and repeater
Dramedy	From drama and comedy
Ebonics	From ebony and phonics
Ecoteur	From ecological and saboteur
Ginormous	From gigantic and enormous
Guesstimate	From guess and estimate
Hasbian	From has been and lesbian
Jazzercise	From jazz and exercise
Mantastic	From man and fantastic
Mockumentary	From mock and documentary
Moped	From motor and pedal
Motel	From motor and hotel
Oxbridge	From Oxford and Cambridge
Posistor	From positive and thermistor
Procrasturbate	From procrastinate and masturbate
Sexcellent	From sex and excellent
Sexercise	From sex and exercise
Skort	From skirt and short (as in short pants)
Smog	From smoke and fog

Soundscape	From sound and landscape
Spork	From spoon and fork
Squiggle	From squirm and wiggle
Stagflation	From stagnation and inflation
Swaption	From swap and option
Tangelo	From tangerine and pomelo
Televangelist	From television and evangelist
Woon	From wooden and spoon (flat wooden utensils for eating dished ice cream)

OH, REINDEER!

They may be caribou to you:

1. They are approximately three and a half feet in height.
2. They run about fifty miles per hour at top speed.
3. They weigh more than three hundred pounds, and can carry up to their own weight.
4. Both males and females have antlers.
5. Their milk is used for drinking and making cheese in Lapland.
6. They live in Europe, Asia, Alaska, and Canada.
7. Their skins are used to make clothing and tents.
8. They *are* used to pull sleighs.

◆

NINE-BANDED ARMADILLOS (the variety found in the U.S.) are always born as same-sex identical quadruplets. They will often eat forty thousand ants in a single sitting and are excellent in water, able to hold their breath for up to ten minutes by inhaling air into their lungs, stomach, and intestines (which can also make them buoyant). Letting their breath out enables armadillos to feed by walking along the bottom of a body of water.

SWORN STATEMENT

The presidential oath of office is taken by every president of the United States on first entering office, as specified in Article II, Section 1 of the Constitution:

I do solemnly swear (or affirm) that I will faithfully execute the office of President of the United States, and will to the best of my ability, preserve, protect, and defend the Constitution of the United States.

The "affirm" option is given the president-elect because members of the Quaker religion do not swear on a Bible (this is also true for any Quaker serving as a witness in court).

◆

A FEW FACTS ABOUT THE FAIR FOWL
All Things Chicken

Bantam or banty: A small version of a large fowl
Pullet: Young female chicken who has not yet begun to lay eggs
Capon: A castrated rooster
Chanticleer: A loud crower
Cock or rooster: Adult male of the domestic fowl
Cockerel: A young, male, domesticated fowl
Hen: A mature female of the common domestic fowl
Bantamweight: 118 pounds and under (usually refers to a human)

A cock has no penis. He and the hen both have a single orifice called a *cloaca* (from the Latin word for sewer), which serves a multitude of functions, including reproduction.

NO-WAY BAY

Items that can't be sold on eBay include:

alcohol * animals and wildlife products * cable TV
descramblers * counterfeit items * current catalogs *
drugs and drug paraphernalia * embargoed goods * firearms *
fireworks * government IDs and licenses * human body parts *
lock-picking devices * lottery tickets * postage meters *
prescription drugs and materials * recalled items * stocks
and other securities * stolen property * surveillance
equipment * tobacco

WHAT IS BEYOND BEYOND?

There is a number so incomprehensible it is rarely used, even
in physics and astronomy. In 1938, mathematician Edward
Kasner asked his nine-year-old nephew, Milton Sirotta, to
come up with a name for the number that Kasner had
invented, a one followed by 100 zeroes. "Googol" was little
Milton's big idea, and if that's not big enough, there's
googolplex, which is defined as one to the power of googol.
A googolplex is written like this:

$$10^{10^{100}}$$

The largest number ever in a real mathematical problem is
called Graham's Number, for Ronald L. Graham, a juggler,
acrobat, and mathematician. It is incomprehensibly large, and
occurs in combinatorics, the branch of mathematics that
studies the enumeration, combination, and permutation of
sets of elements and the mathematical relations that char-
acterize their properties. It is often used in probability and
statistics.

SOME JACKPOT!

The largest individual lottery win came to an incredible $314.9 million and was won by Andrew "Jack" Whittaker Jr. of Scott Depot, West Virginia, in 2002. He took half the prize in a lump sum of $111.7 million after taxes rather than the full prize in thirty annual installments. Whittaker tithed a tenth of his winnings to his church and created a foundation for the less-fortunate citizens of West Virginia, which he has subsequently closed. Alas, he lost some of his winnings while at a West Virginia nightclub, where he was robbed of a suitcase containing $545,000 in cash and cashiers' checks. He has also been arrested for drunk driving twice, has been in rehab, and has been involved in a number of lawsuits. You win some, you lose some.

◆

No WORD in the English language rhymes with:

month * nothing * orange * pint * purple * silver

◆

SNAKE-EATING SNAKES

What kind of snake would pick on another snake? The larger of the two, naturally, normally preys on the smaller snake; it's nature's way.

Asian coral snake	Krait
Black-headed python	North American king snake
Burrowing asp	Ring-necked snake
King snake	Texas coral snake
King cobra	

ADDING COMPLICATIONS

The annual Rube Goldberg Machine Contest celebrates the Pulitzer Prize winner's "Invention" cartoons. Entrants eschew conventional problem solving, relying instead on imagination and intuition to create the most convoluted solutions possible. Goldberg (1883–1970) said his inventions—or, more precisely, noninventions—were symbolic of man's capacity for exerting maximum effort to accomplish minimal results. He believed there were two ways to do things: the simple way and the hard way, and many people prefer the hard way. The 2005 challenge asked entrants to remove the old batteries from a two-battery flashlight, install new batteries, and turn the flashlight on—in twenty or more steps. Other recent twenty steps–plus challenges have been:

1988	Adhere a stamp to a letter
1989	Sharpen a pencil
1990	Put the lid on a ball jar
1991	Toast a slice of bread
1992	Unlock a combination padlock
1993	Screw a lightbulb into a socket
1994	Make a cup of coffee
1995	Turn on a radio
1996	Put coins in a bank
1997	Insert and then play a CD
1998	Shut off an alarm clock
1999	Set a golf tee and tee up a golf ball
2000	Fill, seal a time capsule with 20th-century inventions
2001	Select, clean, and peel an apple
2002	Select, raise, and wave a national flag
2003	Select, crush, and recycle an empty soft-drink can
2004	Select, mark, and cast an election ballot

HALLS OF FAME

They're not just for ballplayers anymore. Here are some lesser-known halls of fame that honor the best of their best:

Accounting	Great Americans
Advertising	Hamburgers
Afro-Americans	Hollywood Stuntmen
Agriculture	Hot Dogs
Astronauts	Inventors
Automotive	Jewish-Americans
Aviation	Nashville Songwriters
Business	National Teachers
Burlesque	National Women
Car Collectors	Nurses
Checkers	Photography
Chess	Police
Circus	Quilters
Classical Music	Rivers
Clowns	Rock and Roll
Comedy	RVs/Motor Homes
Country Music	Songwriters
Cowgirls	Space
Ecology	

IT'S FLOTSAM OR JETSAM

Both words originally pertained to the sea: *Flotsam* in maritime law applies to wreckage or cargo left floating on the sea after a shipwreck. *Jetsam* applies to cargo or equipment thrown overboard (jettisoned) from a ship in distress and either sunk or washed ashore. The common phrase *flotsam and jetsam* is now used loosely to describe any objects found floating or washed ashore.

DID I DREAM THAT?

Sea monkeys are indeed real; here are a few facts:

- Sea monkeys are actually a type of brine shrimp, *Artemia salina.*
- Sea monkeys breathe through their feet.
- Sea monkey eggs can survive for years without water by hibernating.
- Sea monkeys are born with one eye but develop two more.
- Sea monkeys are attracted to light and can be taught tricks with a flashlight.
- Sea monkeys require water and feeding only every five days.
- If sea monkeys are not bred on their own in captivity, they will be eaten by other inhabitants of the deep (or not-so-deep: never put them in a tank with other fish).

WORDS OF WISDOM

According to the 1893 *Farmer's Almanac* (the first edition of that now-ubiquitous book) the four things that should never flatter us are:

1. Familiarity with the great
2. The caresses of women
3. The smiles of our enemies
4. A warm day in winter

The word UMLAUT doesn't have one. (It's the double dot over the "u.")

STEP RIGHT UP, LADIES AND FLEAS!

Although already centuries old, the flea circus became the talk of London during the 1830s, due to L. Bertolotto, the P. T. Barnum of his time. Bertolotto had flea orchestras playing audible flea music, flea foursomes in games of flea whist, and flea waltzing, complete with dresses and frock coats. Fleas drew miniature coaches, carried guns, and fired cannons "not larger than a common pin," and fleas dressed as Napoleon and the Duke of Wellington. Bertolotto's flea circus became so popular that other impresarios developed their own flea extravaganzas, with flea circuses becoming popular fixtures in carnivals and circus sideshows throughout Europe and the United States. As late as the 1950s there was a popular flea circus near New York's Times Square. A lot has been written about the "condition" of the fleas—dead or alive—and many flea circus acts relied on dead fleas glued to their seats, to tightropes, or to other circus equipment, or on fleas manipulated by magnets hidden below a tiny flea stage. Bertolotto's playbill announced that his superior flea equipment "precludes all charges of cruelty to the fleas." Other acts, also refuting such tricks, had fleas rigged in wire harnesses so the fleas could move in only a particular manner.

Today flea circus ringmasters control their "trained" performers using several odd and sometimes difficult methods. A trainer can limit the height of a flea's jump, for example, with a glass ceiling, or by having the flea in a test tube lying on its side. (Fleas don't like to bump their heads.) And certain chemicals will bother a flea: Put some on a small ball and fleas will push it away with their legs, giving the illusion that they are playing football. Their sensitivity to heat and light can also be used to manipulate appearances—or perform tricks, if you will—by forcing them to move in a specific direction. Following, some little-known flea facts:

- There is said to be a flea in a Kiev museum that wears horseshoes made of real gold.
- A flea may be able to pull up to 160,000 times its own weight.
- A flea can jump over 200 times its own height.
- When jumping, the flea accelerates faster than the space shuttle.
- Fleas can jump 30,000 times without a break.
- It was popular in the 1920s to collect dead fleas dressed as wedding couples.
- Fleas are attracted to carbon dioxide.

◆

WINNING WORDS AT THE NATIONAL SPELLING BEE

Spelling bees are almost always won or lost because of one word. Here are some winners:

Easy	*More Difficult*
Fracas	Schappe
Deteriorating	Syllepsis
Knack	Troche
Therapy	Cacolet
Interning	Hydrophyte
Sanatarium	Elucubrate
Initials	Odontalgia
Luge	Elegiacal
Deification	Spoliator
Incisor	Fibranne
Abalone	Antipyretic
Chihuahua	Xanthosis
Croissant	Euonym
Sycophant	Succedaneum

IT OUGHTA BE ILLEGAL

And apparently—at least in some places—it is. A few oddities that are against the law:

Have sexual relations with a porcupine in Florida

Pay a debt higher than 25 cents with pennies in Canada

Fall asleep under a hair dryer in Florida, even if you're the salon owner

Kill or even threaten a butterfly in Pacific Grove, California

Duel in Paraguay if both parties are not registered blood donors

Have sex in a butcher shop's meat freezer in Newcastle, Wyoming

Hunt camels in the state of Arizona

Have sex on a parked motorcycle in London, England

Wear a fake mustache that causes laughter in church in Alabama

Bar owners in Nebraska may not sell beer unless they have a kettle of soup on the stove

Beer and pretzels cannot be served at the same time in any bar or restaurant in North Dakota

Throw a ball at someone's head for fun in New York

Lie down and fall asleep with your shoes on in North Dakota

Get a fish drunk in Ohio

Tie a giraffe to a telephone pole or street lamp in Atlanta, Georgia

"POWDER OF SYMPATHY"

One longitudinal theory proposed in 1688 employed a substance made primarily of sulfuric acid and was called the "Powder of Sympathy."

It was believed that a person who had been stabbed, no matter how long ago, would feel the same intensity of pain when Powder of Sympathy was sprinkled onto the same knife that caused the original wound. It became a popular medical treatment in the seventeenth century, and patients often jumped or swooned when practitioners powdered swords that had cut them or cloths that had dressed their wounds.

During that century it was believed that if dogs, all wounded by the same knife, were placed on each of His Majesty's ships and every day at Greenwich time noon that same knife was plunged into a bowl full of the Powder of Sympathy, all the dogs on every ship would yelp, no matter where they were. Ship captains would then know that it was exactly noon in Greenwich, England, and could calculate their longitude from this.

◆

The SWEDES invented a kind of ladies' glove that was made of leather and worked to have a slight nap on one side by brushing the smooth surface with an emery board. The French gave it a name—suede—which is French for "Swedish." Today suede is buffed and brushed in essentially the same manner.

◆

The PETER PRINCIPLE decrees: "In a hierarchy, every employee tends to rise to his level of incompetence."

157

THE LAST WORD ON DADAISM

Dada, or *Dadaism* (French, from *dada*, a child's word for horse) was a Nihilistic art movement that flourished chiefly in France, Switzerland, and Germany from about 1916 to 1920, and was based on the principles of deliberate irrationality, anarchy, and cynicism, and which rejected laws of beauty and social organization.

Views on Dada from the Artists Themselves

Dada is beautiful like the night, who cradles the
young day in her arms.
—HANS ARP

Dada speaks with you, it is everything,
it envelops everything, it belongs to every religion, can be
neither victory nor defeat, it lives in space and not in time.
—FRANCIS PICABIA

Dada is the sun, Dada is the egg. Dada is the
Police of the Police.
—RICARD HUELSENBECK

Dada doubts everything. Dada is an armadillo.
Everything is Dada, too. Beware of Dada. Anti-dadaism is
a disease: self-kleptomania, man's normal condition, is Dada.
But the real Dadas are against Dada.
—TRISTAN TZARA

◆

MEET THE PRESS debuted on NBC in 1947 and continues to hold the record as television's longest-running program. It was also TV's first news show.

USEFUL YIDDISH PUTDOWNS

shikker	drunkard
shkapeh	hag
shlak	a nuisance
shlatten shammes	busybody
shlecht veib	shrew
shlemiel	dope, fool
shlimazel	unlucky person
shlooche	slut
shlub	stupid person
shlump	sloppy person
shmendrick	nincompoop
shmoe	dunce
shmuck	self-made fool
shnook	patsy
shnorrer	beggar
shtunk	lousy human being

◆

TEN STEPS TO A DECATHLON MEDAL
The Events That Comprise the Two-Day Olympic Decathlon

Day 1	*Day 2*
100-meter run	110-meter hurdles
Long jump	Discus throw
Shot put	Pole vault
High jump	Javelin throw
400-meter run	1,500-meter run

159

WHAT WAS SERVED AT THE LAST SUPPER?

Many believe the Last Supper was actually a seder. Jesus and the apostles were served:

- Passover lamb to remind them of the lambs' blood sprinkled on their doors so that the Angel of Death would spare the firstborn of the Jews
- Unleavened bread to remind them of the haste with which their ancestors left Egypt
- Salt water to remind them of the many tears shed during the years of slavery in Egypt
- Bitter herbs to remind them of the bitterness of slavery
- A sweet mixture of apples, dates, pomegranate, nuts, and cinnamon sticks, to symbolize the clay and straw their ancestors used to make bricks while in slavery
- Four cups of wine during the course of the meal to remind them of the four promises of God's deliverance in Exodus 6:6–7

◆

CATS ENTERTAINMENT!

The top ten longest-running Broadway plays of all time:

1. Cats
2. The Phantom of the Opera
3. Les Misérables
4. A Chorus Line
5. Oh! Calcutta!
6. Beauty and the Beast
7. Miss Saigon
8. Rent
9. 42nd Street
10. Grease

CONTINENTAL DIVIDES

The basic definition of a continent requires that it be a large, nonsubmerged land mass, and that it have geologically significant borders. As the definition is so vague, some sources list as few as four or five continents, although it is commonly acknowledged that there are six—the generally accepted geologists' count—or seven:

Seven continents: Africa, Antarctica, Asia, Europe, North America, Oceania, South America

Six continents: Africa, Antarctica, Oceania, Eurasia, North America, and South America

Six continents: Africa, America, Antarctica, Asia, Oceania, and Europe

Five continents: Africa, America, Oceania, Antarctica, Eurasia

Five continents: Africa, America, Oceania, Europe, Asia

Four continents: America, Oceania, Antarctica, Eurafrasia

Various Continental Definitions

Eurasia: Europe and Asia

Eurafrasia: Europe, Africa, and Asia

Oceania: A name used for varying groups of islands of the Pacific Ocean. In its narrow usage it refers to Polynesia (including New Zealand), Melanesia (including New Guinea), and Micronesia. In its wider usage it includes Australia.

RELATIVE RELATIONSHIPS

Relationships are hard enough—understanding the complex terms of genealogy is even more confusing:

Cousin is the term used to signify the relationship between the offspring of two siblings.

The number in front of the word *cousin* corresponds to going another generation down both sides of the family tree; for example, the grandparents of second cousins would be siblings. These are considered whole cousins.

If two people are not descended by the same number of generations from siblings, count the number of steps "removed" between them, and you will have the exact kinship. For example, the relationship between two persons, one descended two generations from a sibling and the other three generations from the other sibling, would be second cousins, once removed (one person would be the grandchild of one of the siblings, and the other a great-grandchild of the other sibling).

More confusion . . .

Great signifies being one generation removed from the relative specified; it is often used in combination, for example, great-granddaughter.

Collateral lineage is when two people have a common ancestor, but neither one is an ancestor of the other.

Fictive kinship is a relationship, such as with a godparent, modeled on relations of kinship but created by customary convention rather than the circumstances of birth.

Consanguinity is relationship by blood (i.e., presumed biological) ties. A consanguine is a relative by birth, as distinguished from an in-law ("affine") or step-relative.

Affinity is relationship by marriage ties. Whenever the connection between two relatives includes one or more marital links, the two have no necessary biological relationship and are classed as an affinal relative, or affine.

◆

ORDER UP!

According to most accounts, the Fourth Earl of Sandwich, John Montagu, invented the tasty concoction the world now so enjoys—the sandwich. But what drove him to such a brilliant brainstorm? The most popular story, most likely false, places him at a marathon poker game in 1762. Unwilling to miss a single hand, he sent his valet off to concoct the original sandwich with what was available in the larder: a piece of salt beef between two slices of toasted bread. But the more likely story, according to the earl's biographer, N.A.M. Rodger, places Montagu at sea. Needing a portable meal, he put a piece of meat between two slices of bread: hence, the sandwich!

◆

LETTERS FROM THE PAST

Words like *encyclopedia* are occasionally spelled *encyclopaedia*, a throwback to old English, when the letter called *ash* (a and e together) was still part of the alphabet. Another vestige of old English is found in signs saying "Ye Olde..."—the letter called *thorn*, which made a th sound, looked similar to the modern y in handwriting.

METALLIC COMBINATIONS

An alloy is a combination of two or more elements, at least one of which is a metal (usually both are), and where the resultant material has metallic properties.

Alloys of Aluminum

Al-Li = aluminum + lithium
Alumel = aluminum + nickel
Duralumin = aluminum + copper + manganese + magnesium
Magnox = aluminum + magnesium oxide

Alloys of Potassium

NaK = potassium + sodium

Alloys of Iron

Steel = iron + carbon
Stainless steel = iron + chromium + nickel
Surgical stainless steel = iron + chromium + molybdenum
 + nickel
Silicon steel = iron + silicon
Tool steel = iron + tungsten *or* iron + manganese
Cast iron = iron + carbon (smaller amount of carbon than
 in steel)
Spiegeleisen = iron + manganese + carbon

Alloys of Cobalt

Stellite = cobalt + chromium + tungsten + carbon
Talonite = cobalt + chromium

Alloys of Silver

Sterling silver = silver + copper

Alloys of Nickel

German silver = nickel + copper + zinc
Chromel = nickel + chromium
Mu-metal = nickel + iron
Monel metal = nickel + copper + iron + manganese
Nichrome = nickel + chromium + iron
Nicrosil = nickel + chromium + silicon + magnesium
Nisil = nickel + silicon + magnesium

Alloys of Copper

Brass = copper + zinc
Constantan = copper + nickel
Prince's metal = copper + zinc
Gilding metal = copper + zinc
Bronze = copper + tin, aluminum, or any other element
Phosphor bronze = copper + tin + phosphorus
Bell metal = copper + tin
Beryllium copper = copper + beryllium
Cupronickel = copper + nickel
Nickel silver = copper + nickel
Billon = copper + silver
Nordic gold = copper + aluminum + zinc + tin

Alloys of Tin

Pewter = tin + lead + copper
Solder = tin + lead

Rare Earth Alloys

Misch metal = cerium + lanthanum + various traces

Alloys of Gold

Electrum = gold + silver

18K gold = 18 parts gold + 6 parts another metal
   (75 percent gold)

14K gold = 14 parts gold + 10 parts another metal
   (58.3 percent gold)

12K gold = 12 parts gold + 12 parts another metal
   (50 percent gold)

10K gold = 10 parts gold + 14 parts another metal
   (41.7 percent gold)

(Other metals present in gold alloys allow jewelers to vary the color; nickel, palladium, copper, and silver are some of those used.)

Alloys of Mercury

Amalgam = mercury + silver *or* mercury + tin

Alloys of Lead

Solder = lead + tin
Terne = lead + tin (ratio differs from that in solder)
Type metal = lead + tin + antimony

◆

DID HE GO TO BURGER KING?

"Elvis has left the building" was the message actually used over PA systems after the King's concerts, in the hope that it would persuade people to go home.

THE RICHTER EARTHQUAKE SCALE

In 1935, American seismologist Charles F. Richter created a scale to measure how much the ground shakes during an earthquake. On the Richter Scale, magnitudes increase logarithmically: energy increases tenfold with each magnitude number.

Descriptor	Magnitude	Effects	Estimated Frequency
Micro	<2.0	Microearthquakes, recorded, but not felt	8,000 per day
Very minor	2.0–2.9	Generally not felt, but recorded	1,000 per day
Minor	3.0–3.9	Often felt; rarely cause damage	49,000 per year
Light	4.0–4.9	Rattling indoor items; noises	6,200 per year
Moderate	5.0–5.9	Slight damage to buildings	800 per year
Strong	6.0–6.9	Destruction in 100-mile radius	120 per year
Major	7.0–7.9	Serious damage over larger areas	18 per year
Great	8.0–8.9	Serious damage over a diameter of more than 500 miles	1 per year
Rare great	>9.0	Major damage over 1,000 miles	1 per 20 years

FROM BAD TO WORSE

The Saffir/Simpson Hurricane Scale is based on a hurricane's intensity.

Category	Wind Speed (mph)	Storm Surge (wave footage)	Damage
1	74–95	4–5	Minor
2	96–110	6–8	Moderate
3	111–130	9–12	Major
4	131–155	13–18	Severe
5	> 155	> 18	Catastrophic

COURTSIDE MAGIC

One of the least understood occupations in plain view of the public is the court reporter. What are they doing with that weird typewriter? How could anyone type anything with so few keys?

The shorthand machine has come a long way since the first modern version was developed in Ireland by Miles Bartholemew in 1879. Later improvements made by Americans led to the modern stenographic machine which became common after World War II. The key to the amazing speed at which a machine stenographer could record speech was the limited number of keys on the shorthand machine's keyboard. Some less common letters are recorded by pressing more than one key at a time, thus cutting down on hand movement. Also, machine stenography, like shorthand, frequently breaks words down into syllables, rather than letters.

Today, computer aided transcription (CAT) devices have replaced the old shorthand machines and have taken court reporting to a new level of speed and simplicity.

MOODY BLUES . . . AND GREENS

While mood rings don't really reflect your mood with scientific accuracy, some say they are reliable indicators of your body's involuntary physical reactions. The stone in a mood ring has thermotropic liquid crystals that change according to changes in the temperature in your hand, and thus change the color of the crystals:

> **Dark blue:** Happy, romantic, or passionate
> **Blue:** Calm or relaxed
> **Blue-green:** Somewhat relaxed
> **Green:** Normal
> **Amber:** A little nervous or anxious
> **Gray:** Very nervous or anxious
> **Black:** Stressed

◆

DISORIENTATION

The Möbius strip is what's known as a nonorientable surface—it has only one side and one edge. This circular conundrum is named after August Ferdinand Möbius, a nineteenth-century German mathematician and astronomer. You can build one with a strip of paper, making a half twist and taping the ends together. (If you're the suspicious sort, paint each side of the paper a different color before taping it.) Its usefulness? Well, picture this: Möbius strips were commonly used as car fan belts, as both sides are utilized equally, therefore halving the wear and tear. Today, the majority of cars have a regular loop fan belt; some say this is planned obsolescence.

THE DOW-RE-MI

In 1896, Charles Dow created the Dow Jones Industrial Average (DJIA) with just twelve stocks:

1. American Cotton Oil
2. American Sugar Refining Co.
3. American Tobacco
4. Chicago Gas
5. Distilling & Cattle Feeding Co.
6. General Electric Co.
7. Laclede Gas Light Co.
8. National Lead
9. North American Co.
10. Tennessee Coal, Iron & Railroad Co.
11. U.S. Leather
12. U.S. Rubber Co.

The number of stocks in the DJIA climbed to twenty in 1916, and then to thirty in 1928, where it remains today (though the stocks chosen for the DJIA change). General Electric is the only one of the original twelve stocks to remain. The present stocks are:

1. 3M Corporation
2. Alcoa
3. American International Group
4. Altria (was Philip Morris)
5. American Express
6. Boeing
7. Caterpillar
8. CitiGroup
9. Coca-Cola

10. E.I. DuPont de Nemours
11. Exxon Mobil
12. General Electric
13. General Motors
14. Hewlett-Packard
15. Home Depot
16. Honeywell
17. Intel
18. International Business Machines
19. J.P. Morgan Chase
20. Johnson & Johnson
21. McDonald's
22. Merck
23. Microsoft
24. Pfizer
25. Procter and Gamble
26. SBC Communications
27. United Technologies
28. Verizon Communications
29. Wal-Mart Stores
30. Walt Disney

THE MONASTIC HOURS

Hour of the Day	Latin Name
Midnight	Matins
3 A.M.	Lauds
6 A.M.	Prime
9 A.M.	Terce
Noon	Sext
3 P.M.	None
Sunset	Vespers
Nightfall	Compline

MR. SHERIDAN'S WRITE STUFF

Mrs. Malaprop, introduced in Richard Sheridan's 1775 play *The Rivals*, lived in an etymological world filled with colorful turns of phrase that were always just a bit off. Her mistakes arose from substituting a similar-sounding word for the word that she intended, called a malapropism, from the French phrase *mal à propos*, inappropriate. These slips are divided into two types: classical malapropisms, mistakes due to ignorance (as in the case of Mrs. Malaprop), and temporary slips of the tongue, in which the intended word is known by the speaker but has been inadvertently replaced. A related word gaffe is the *mondegreen*, which is a misheard saying or phrase. It is a sort of aural malapropism, usually used in regard to song lyrics.

A few of Mrs. Malaprop's original -isms from *The Rivals*:

"Promise to forget this fellow—to illiterate him, I say, quite from your memory." (obliterate)

"If ever you betray what you are entrusted with . . . you forfeit my malevolence for ever." (benevolence)

"She's as headstrong as an allegory on the banks of Nile." (alligator)

"I am sorry to say, Sir Anthony, that my affluence over my niece is very small." (influence)

"He is the very pine-apple of politeness!" (pinnacle)

"Why, murder's the matter! slaughter's the matter! killing's the matter!—but he can tell you the perpendiculars." (particulars)

"I have since laid Sir Anthony's preposition before her." (proposition)

SECRET STASH

The main reason for opening a Swiss bank account is nothing clandestine, merely the legendary privacy it affords. Long a haven for ordinary people around the world as well as James Bond's nemeses, Swiss banks require a minimum amount for deposit of a mere $15,000. The Swiss currently charge a hefty 35 percent tax on interest earned in their banks' accounts, but Americans, for example, can receive 30 percent of that back by showing they're not Swiss residents. Of course, then it's not a secret anymore, is it?

◆

AAAACH-HOW?

Some illnesses are viral and others bacterial. Here's a short list of what's what:

Viruses	*Bacteria*
AIDS	Botulism
Chicken pox	Diphtheria
Common cold	Gonorrhea
Encephalitis	Lyme disease
Hepatitis	Whooping cough
Herpes simplex	Scarlet fever
Mononucleosis	Syphilis
Influenza	
Measles	
Mumps	
Poliomyelitis	
German measles	
Yellow fever	

ENDANGERED

According to the United States Fish and Wildlife Service, as of 2004, the number of endangered or threatened species breaks down as follows:

Mammals	346	Flowering Plants	716
Birds	272	Conifers and Cycads	5
Fishes	126	Ferns and Allies	26
Reptiles	115	Lichens	2
Clams	72		
Insects	48	PLANT TOTAL	749
Snails	33		
Amphibians	30		
Crustaceans	21		
Arachnids	12		
ANIMAL TOTAL	1075	GRAND TOTAL	1824

THE TEN PLAGUES

The Old Testament speaks of ten plagues that would befall Egypt if the Pharaoh did not release the Jewish people from slavery. They are:

1. Blood
2. Frogs
3. Lice or gnats
4. Flies
5. Cattle disease

6. Boils
7. Hail
8. Locusts
9. Darkness
10. Death of the firstborn

◆

A typical LIGHTNING BOLT is two to four inches wide and two miles long.

TAKING MEASURE
Universal Sizes of Everyday Things

Chopsticks: Chinese are blunt-ended and 10 inches long; Japanese are pointed and are 8 inches for men and 7 inches for women

Scallops: 36.3 scallop meats per pound (weighed out of shell, as per a 1982 U.S. federal regulation)

U.S. dollar bills: 6⅛ inches by 2⅝ inches (any denomination) . . . and speaking of money, a quarter is about 1 inch, and a penny ¾ inch

Standard linoleum tiles: 12 inches square

Credit card: 3⅜ inches by 2⅛ inches

Residential plumbing pipe: ⅛ inch smaller than outside diameter

Most business cards: 3½ inches by 2 inches

Marbles: Shooter is between ½ inch and ¾ inch; target is ⅝ inch

Pizza: The European Union Traditional Pizza Association insists that crust diameter not exceed 30 centimeters

Badminton shuttlecock: 14 to 16 feathers, 4.74 to 5.5 grams

Osprey nesting site: 4-foot by 4-foot platform, 15 to 20 feet high, ½ mile apart from one another

Napkins: Cloth, dinner, 16 to 18 inches unfolded; cloth, cocktail, 10 to 12 inches unfolded; cocktail, paper, 9½ inches

Threaded handles: Brooms, paint rollers, extension poles for window-washing brushes, and squeegees have universal threading—¾ inch in diameter, 5 threads per inch

Sari: 4 feet wide, 12 to 27 feet long

FEELING FRIGHTENED?
Seems Like Everybody's Afraid of Something

Aerophobia: Fear of swallowing air
Anemophobia: Fear of wind
Anthrophobia: Fear of flowers
Arachibutyrophobia: Fear of peanut butter sticking to the roof of the mouth
Aulophobia: Fear of flutes
Barophobia: Fear of gravity
Bibliophobia: Fear of books
Blennophobia: Fear of slime
Chaetophobia: Fear of hair
Chronophobia: Fear of time
Clinicophobia: Fear of going to bed
Deciophobia: Fear of making decisions
Dendrophobia: Fear of trees
Eleutherophobia: Fear of freedom
Eosophobia: Fear of daylight
Epistemophobia: Fear of knowledge
Ergophobia: Fear of work
Geliophobia: Fear of laughter
Geniophobia: Fear of chins
Genuphobia: Fear of knees
Geumaphobia: Fear of taste
Helmintophobia: Fear of being infested with worms
Hippopotomonstrosesquippedaliophobia: Fear of long words
Linonophobia: Fear of string
Melophobia: Fear of music
Metrophobia: Fear of poetry
Nebulaphobia: Fear of fog
Ophthalmophobia: Fear of opening one's eyes

Ostraconophobia: Fear of shellfish
Papyrophobia: Fear of paper
Pentheraphobia: Fear of mothers-in-law
Phobophobia: Fear of fear
Phronemophobia: Fear of thinking
Sophophobia: Fear of learning
Stasibasiphobia: Fear of walking
Thaasophobia: Fear of sitting
Triskadekaphobia: Fear of the number 13
Xanthophobia: Fear of the color yellow

◆

THE TARTAN

The use of tartans by Scottish clans is quite new, historically speaking. Few precede the Jacobite uprising of 1745, and most belong to regions rather than specific families. Dress at that time often also signified rank and status; for example, servants wore clothes of only one color, rent-paying farmers used two colors, and so on, all the way up to seven colors for a king's wardrobe.

In Scotland, the word *tartan* is used to describe cross-checked fabric. Plaid describes a primitive garment, originally made by sewing together two twenty-seven-inch widths of hand-woven tartan cloth, each twelve feet long, for a five-foot by seven-foot garment or blanket. The design of a tartan is formed by an arrangement of colored stripes in the warp (length) and weft (threads across the width of cloth). It becomes a tartan when two sets of threads are interwoven at right angles. Most tartans are a mirror repeat—one half of the design is the exact reverse of the other.

ART FROM THE SEA

Scrimshaw is an indigenous American craft adopted by American whalers in the early 1800s who were frequently at sea for up to four or five years. In their monotony, whalers turned to etching and carving parts of their catch, such as the teeth, jawbones, or baleen of the whale; these valuable whale parts were often part of their pay, and later they would use them as barter with shopkeepers in port.

Scrimshanders etched their designs into the piece with sailing needles or knives—whaling scenes, ships, and women were popular subjects—which were then covered with India ink brought on board by the whalers. The surface was then rubbed with a cloth, which left ink in the etched areas. The origin of the word is obscure; one interesting etymology is a Dutch phrase meaning "to waste one's time." Today, artisans use plastics; any ivory used in the United States has been reduced to "pre-embargo ivory," which was brought into the states before sanctions were set in place.

◆

THAT IS SO HARD
The Mohs Scale for Mineral Hardness

Devised by Frederich Mohs (1773–1839), a German mineralogist, the Mohs scale is a relatively arbitrary ranking of hardness for a selection of widely available substances.

1. Talc	6. Orthoclase
2. Gypsum	7. Quartz
3. Calcite	8. Topaz
4. Fluorite	9. Corundum
5. Apatite	10. Diamond

WHAT

BUT, OFFICER . . .

The following are actual statements to insurance companies offered by drivers involved in auto accidents:

The guy was all over the road. I had to swerve a number of times before I hit him.

An invisible car came out of nowhere, struck my car, and vanished.

I pulled away from the side of the road, glanced at my mother-in-law, and headed over the embankment.

In an attempt to kill a fly, I drove into a telephone pole.

I collided with a stationary truck coming the other way.

My car was legally parked as it backed into the other vehicle.

I told the police I was not injured, but on removing my hat, found that I had a fractured skull.

The guy had no idea which way to run, so I ran over him.

I was sure the old fellow would never make it to the other side of the road when I struck him.

The telephone pole was approaching. I was attempting to swerve out of its way when it struck the front end.

A pedestrian hit me and went under my car.

I saw a slow-moving, sad-faced old gentlemen as he bounced off the hood of my car.

I had been driving for forty years when I fell asleep at the wheel and had an accident.

HERE COMES THAT SOUND AGAIN

What is a musical instrument that has no strings, pipes, frets, or keys, and that you don't touch to play? It's the Theremin, invented in 1919 by Russian scientist Léon Theremin. The instrument consists of a box with two projecting radio antennas around which the user moves his or her hands to play. The Theremin is considered to be an early precursor to the electronic synthesizer. It produces an unforgettably eerie sound that became extremely popular in experimental music and film circles in the 1950s and 1960s—the Beach Boys' "Good Vibrations" and science fiction films, most notably *The Day the Earth Stood Still*, are probably the best-remembered examples. Though many consider it nothing more than a novelty, there are kits for sale and even an occasional Theremin festival for aficionados.

HOW HOT IS HOT?

What it feels like inside your washing machine . . .

Hot: 140–160°F   Medium: 100–140°F
Warm: 80–120°F   Cool: 60–80°F

◆

CHEFS' TOQUES date back as far as the sixteenth century, but it wasn't until the mid-1800s that Marie-Antoine Carême redesigned chefs' uniforms and decided that the hats should be different sizes to distinguish the mighty from the sous: tall hats for the chefs, caps for the cooks. The folded pleats of a toque—usually more than a hundred—are said to indicate the number of ways in which a chef can cook an egg.

DISASTROUS
Fatalities of the United States' Biggest Epidemics

SPANISH INFLUENZA
Killed 500,000 in 8 months during 1918.

YELLOW FEVER
Killed more than 13,000 in 1878 in the Mississippi Valley.

AIDS
Reported toll is more than 500,000 people since 1981.

CHOPSTICKS, MUSICAL AND OTHERWISE

The use of chopsticks to eat food began more than five thousand years ago, when the Chinese would take their food from the fire using sticks or branches broken from trees. Later, people began to cut food into smaller pieces so they could eat individually and because the smaller portions cooked faster. Chopsticks became the utensil of choice. Today, Japan is the only country that uses chopsticks as its only utensil.

"Chopsticks"—the piano piece—was written by a sixteen-year-old girl named Euphonia Allen, who published it under the name of Arthur de Lulli. The song's title comes not from the Asian eating utensils but from the young composer's sheet music instructions: "Play with both hands turned sideways, the little fingers lowest, so that the movements of the hands imitates the chopping from which this waltz gets its name." Sadly, Euphonia—or rather, Arthur—never wrote another song.

WORTH WAITING FOR
Interesting Exports and Where They Come From

Afghanistan: Opium, precious gems
Antigua and Barbuda: Live animals
Armenia: Brandy
Australia: Coal
Bahamas: Crawfish
Bangladesh: Jute, frozen fish
Bhutan: Electricity (to India), cardamom, cement
British Virgin Islands: Sand
Cape Verde: Shoes
Cayman Islands: Turtle products
Chad: Gum arabic, cattle
China: Sporting goods
Comoros: Ylang-ylang, vanilla, cloves
Democratic Republic of the Congo: Cobalt
Costa Rica: Electronic components
Côte d'Ivoire: Tropical woods
Cyprus: Potatoes, grapes, wine
Denmark: Ships, windmills
Dominican Republic: Ferronickel
East Timor: Sandalwood
Ecuador: Shrimp, cut flowers
El Salvador: Electricity
Eritea: Livestock, sorghum
Ethiopia: Qat
Fiji: Molasses
France: Pharmaceutical products
Gabon: Uranium
Georgia: Grapes, tea
Grenada: Nutmeg, mace
Iceland: Diatomite, ferrosilicon

Indonesia: Plywood
Ireland: Computers
Israel: Software
Jordan: Potash
Kiribati: Seaweed
Kyrgyzstan: Hydropower
Laos: Tin
Lesotho: Wool and mohair
Liechtenstein: Dental products, stamps
Luxembourg: Glass
Marshall Islands: Copra cake
Micronesia: Black pepper
Mongolia: Cashmere, fluorspar
Mozambique: Prawns, cashews
Namibia: Karakul skins
Niger: Cowpeas, onions
Papua New Guinea: Logs
Portugal: Cork
Qatar: Steel
St. Vincent and the Grenadines: Eddoes and dasheen,
             tennis racquets
Samoa: Beer
Seychelles: Cinnamon bark
Sierra Leone: Rutile
Somalia: Charcoal, scrap metal
South Africa: Platinum
South Korea: Ships
Swaziland: Soft-drink concentrates, refrigerators
Tonga: Squash
Tunisia: Hydrocarbons
Turks and Caicos Islands: Conch shells
United Arab Emirates: Dried fish, dates
Vanuatu: Kava

Leonardo da Vinci's MONA LISA is a mere 2'6½" by 1'8⅞". Modern technology has revealed there are three different versions of the painting under the visible one.

◆

BURNING CALORIES

According to the National Heart, Lung, and Blood Institute (U.S.A.), even everyday activities burn a surprising number of calories per hour (estimated for a 150-lb. person):

Dancing	370
Gardening	324
Office Work	240
Light Cleaning	240
Playing with Kids	216
Strolling	206
Vacuuming	150
Sitting	81
Watching TV	72
Sleeping	45

◆

THE BEATLES hold the record for the greatest number of recordings sold in the United States at 166.5 million. Elvis Presley holds the number two position with 117.5 million recordings sold.

HONEY is the only natural food that doesn't spoil. The nectar brought to the hive by the bees is about 60 percent water, and they "cure" it to less than 20 percent water. With a pH of 3–4, it can last for centuries.

MASTERS OF THE HOUSE

The Bauhaus (1919–1933) motto was "Art and technology—a new unity." Founded by Walter Gropius, the school included these other original Bauhaus masters:

Josef Albers * Herbert Bayer * Marcel Breuer * Lyonel Feininger * Johannes Itten * Wassily Kandinsky * Paul Klee * Hannes Meyer * Mies van der Rohe * Laszlo Moholy-Nagy * Georg Muche * Oskar Schlemmer

---

LAST WORDS TO LIVE BY

Popular advice on "How to Stay Young" from Baseball Hall-of-Famer Satchel Paige, later inscribed on his tombstone:

1. Avoid fried meats which angry up the blood.
2. If your stomach disputes you, lie down and pacify it with cool thoughts.
3. Keep the juices flowing by jangling around gently as you move.
4. Go very light in the vices, such as carrying on in society. The social ramble ain't restful.
5. Avoid running at all times.
6. Don't look back. Something might be gaining on you.

A GOLDFISH is the only animal that is known to be able to see in both the ultraviolet and infrared light frequencies.

COMPARISON OF DIAMOND AND DIAMOND SYNTHETICS

Stone	Hardness (Mohs scale)	Degree of Dispersion (color refraction through facets)
Diamond	10 (hardest known natural substance)	High; lots of fire and liveliness
Strontium titanate (Fabulite or "Wellington")	5–6 (soft)	Too high; lots of blue flashes
Cubic zirconia (CZ)	8.5 (hard)	Very high; lots of life
Gadolinium gallium garnet (GGG, synthetic)	6.5 (somewhat soft)	High; almost identical to diamond
Yttrium aluminum garnet (YAG, synthetic)	8.5 (hard)	Very low; almost no fire
Synthetic rutile (shows yellowish color)	6.5 (soft)	Extremely high; strong yellow flashes
Zircon	7.5 (moderately hard)	Good; lively
Synthetic sapphire	9 (very hard)	Very low; little life

1 = soft; 10 = hard.

Stone	Hardness (Mohs scale)	Degree of Dispersion (color refraction through facets)
Synthetic spinel	8 (hard)	Low; little life
Glass	5–6.5 (soft)	Variable—low to good depending on cut quality

◆

ANIMAL ONOMATOPOEIA

The sound of the word imitates the animal it's describing:

Bee: "Buzz"

Cat: "Meow"

Chickadee: "Chickadee"

Chicken: "Cluck"

Rooster: "Cockadoodledoo"

Cow: "Moo"

Crow or raven: "Caw"

Dog: "Woof" or "Grr"

Duck: "Quack"

Frog: "Ribbit"

Lion: "Roar"

Humans: "Prattle," "blab," and "brouhaha"

Mouse: "Squeak"

Owl: "Hoo"

Road runner: "Beep beep"

Pig: "Oink"

Sheep: "Baa"

◆

ANTARCTICA is the only continent that doesn't have ants. That's ANTarctica.

The relationship between Matt Groening's mysteriously identical fez-wearing comic strip characters AKBAR AND JEFF was finally revealed to be "lovers or brothers or both."

MORSE CODE
Complete with the Radio Alphabet

A	Alpha	. -
B	Bravo	- . . .
C	Charlie	- . - .
D	Delta	- . .
E	Echo	.
F	Foxtrot	. . . - .
G	Golf	- - .
H	Hotel	. . . .
I	India	. .
J	Juliet	. - - -
K	Kilo	- . -
L	Lima	. - . .
M	Mike	- -
N	November	- .
O	Oscar	- - -
P	Papa	. - - .
Q	Quebec	- - . -
R	Romeo	. - .
S	Sierra	. . .
T	Tango	-
U	Uniform	. . -
V	Victor	. . . -
W	Whiskey	. - -
X	X-ray	- . . -
Y	Yankee	- . - -
Z	Zulu	- - . .
0		- - - - -
1		. - - - -
2		. . - - -
3		. . . - -

4	. . . . -
5	. . . . .
6	- . . . .
7	- - . . .
8	- - - . .
9	- - - - .
Period	. - . - . -
Comma	- - . . - -
Question mark	. . - - . .
Semicolon	- . - . - .
Colon	- - - . . .
Hyphen	- . . . . -
Apostrophe	. - - - - .

◆

NEON NOTATIONS

Neon signage is most often neon or argon gas in a vacuum tube.

The neon sign is attributed to Georges Claude, who popularized it in Paris in 1910.

Neon signage came to America when Earle C. Anthony bought two signs for $2,400 in Paris and installed them in his Los Angeles Packard dealership.

Neon gas is fiery orange-red; argon is soft lavender; argon gas enhanced with mercury is brilliant blue.

The smaller the diameter of the tube, the more intense the light produced and the higher the voltage required.

More than 150 colors can be achieved by combining different gases (including krypton, xenon, and helium) and phosphors that coat the inside of the glass tube.

DEATH ROW MENU

ANTHONY FUENTES (NOVEMBER 2004):
Fried chicken with biscuits and jalapeño peppers, steak and
French fries, fajita tacos, pizza, a hamburger, water, and Coca-Cola

FRANK RAY CHANDLER (NOVEMBER 2004):
A Pizza Hut thin-crust medium pizza topped with
extra cheese, pepperoni, ham, Canadian taco, mushrooms,
and black olives served with iced milk

FREDERICK PATRICK MCWILLIAMS (SEPTEMBER 2004):
Six fried chicken breasts with ketchup, French fries, six-layer
lasagna (ground chicken, beef, cheese, minced tomatoes,
noodles, and sauteed onions), six egg rolls, shrimp fried rice
and soy sauce, six chimichangas with melted cheese and salsa,
six slices of turkey with liver and gizzard dressing, dirty rice,
cranberry sauce, and six lemonades with extra sugar

DEMARCO MARKEITH MCCULLUM (NOVEMBER 2004):
A big cheeseburger, lots of French fries, three Cokes,
apple pie, and five mint sticks

ROBERT WALKER (NOVEMBER 2004):
Ten pieces of fried chicken (leg quarters), two double-meat,
double cheeseburgers with sliced onions, pickles, tomatoes,
mayonnaise, ketchup, salt, pepper, and lettuce, one small chef
salad with chopped ham and thousand island dressing, one

large order of French fries cooked with onions, five big buttermilk biscuits with butter, four jalapeño peppers, two Sprites, two Cokes, one pint of rocky road ice cream, and one bowl of peach cobbler or apple pie

LORENZO MORRIS (NOVEMBER 2004):
Fried chicken and fried fish, French bread, hot peppers, apple pie, butter pecan ice cream, two soft drinks, either Sprites or Big Reds, and a pack of Camel cigarettes and matches. The request for the Camels was denied.

DOMINIQUE GREEN (OCTOBER 2004):
No final meal request

CHARLES WESLEY ROACHE (OCTOBER 2004):
Sirloin steak, popcorn shrimp, salad with blue cheese dressing, a honey bun, and vanilla Coke

RICKY MORROW (OCTOBER 2004):
A cheeseburger, French fries, onion rings, and iced tea

ADREMY DENNIS (OCTOBER 2004):
Chef salad with French/ranch dressing, fried chicken breasts and legs, French fries, a cheeseburger, chocolate cake, deviled eggs, and biscuits and gravy

TONY WALKER (SEPTEMBER 2002):
French fries, five pieces of fried chicken, three Dr Peppers

RAN SHAMBURGER (SEPTEMBER 2002):
Nachos with chili and cheese, one bowl of sliced jalapeños,
one bowl of picante sauce, two large onions (sliced and
grilled), tacos (with fresh tomatoes, lettuce, and cheese), and
toasted corn tortilla shells

T. J. JONES (AUGUST 2002):
Triple-meat cheeseburger with fried bun and everything,
French fries, ketchup, four pieces of chicken (two legs, two
thighs), and one fried pork-chop sandwich

STANLEY BAKER JR. (MAY 2002):
Two sixteen-ounce rib eyes, one pound turkey breast
(sliced thin), twelve strips of bacon, two large hamburgers
with mayonnaise, onion, and lettuce, two large baked potatoes
with butter, sour cream, cheese, and chives, four slices of
cheese or one-half pound of grated cheddar cheese, chef salad
with blue cheese dressing, two ears of corn on the cob,
one pint of mint chocolate ice cream, and four vanilla Cokes

WALTER MICKENS (JUNE 2002):
Baked chicken, rice, and carrots

DANIEL RENEAU (JUNE 2002):
French fries with salt and ketchup, one tray of nachos with
cheese and jalapeños, one cheeseburger with mustard and
everything, and one pitcher of sweet tea

RONFORD STYRON (MAY 2002):
Mexican platter with all the works, two Classic Cokes, pickles, olives, and cookies and cream ice cream

LESLIE DALE MARTIN (MAY 2002):
Boiled crawfish, crawfish stew, garden salad, cookies, and chocolate milk

◆

DOWNRIGHT BALMY

The highest temperatures ever recorded on each continent:

Continent	Temperature (°F)	Location
Africa	136	Libya
N. America	134	California
Asia	129	Israel
Australia	128	Queensland
Europe	122	Spain
S. America	120	Argentina
Antarctica	59	Scott Coast

MOTHER GOOSE'S DAYS OF BIRTH:

Monday: Fair of face
Tuesday: Full of grace
Wednesday: Full of woe
Thursday: Has far to go
Friday: Loving and giving

Saturday: Works hard for
a living
Sunday: Bonny and blithe,
good and gay

POETIC FEET

There are five different rhythmic groups of syllables that can make up a unit of verse:

Anapestic:	Two unaccented + one accented
Dactylic:	One accented + two unaccented
Iambic:	One unaccented + one accented
Spondaic:	Two accented
Trochaic:	One accented + one unaccented
Pyrrhic:	Two unaccented

Each of these units is called a "foot," and any poet who doesn't know it won't have a leg to stand on.

◆

POETIC LINE LENGTH

The names for the number of feet within a line of poetry:

Monometer:	One foot
Dimeter:	Two feet
Trimeter:	Three feet
Tetrameter:	Four feet
Pentameter:	Five feet
Hexameter:	Six feet
Heptameter:	Seven feet
Octameter:	Eight feet

For example, Shakespeare's most popularly used poetic verse is iambic pentameter—five feet, each with one unaccented and one accented syllable.

INTERNATIONAL DAY OF PANCAKES

In England, Shrove Tuesday (the last Tuesday before the start of Lent, when Mardi Gras is also celebrated, especially in parts of the United States and Canada that have a strong French influence) is best known for the Pancake Day Race at Olney in Buckinghamshire. It has been held continuously since 1445 and remains much unchanged. The race came about after a woman cooking pancakes heard the shriving bell summoning her to confession. She ran to church wearing her apron and still holding her frying pan, and thus inspired a tradition that has lasted for more than five centuries. Under the current rules, only women wearing a dress (no slacks, no jeans), an apron, and a hat or scarf may take part in the race. Each contestant has a frying pan containing a hot, cooking pancake. She must toss it three times—causing it to land back in the pan each time—during the race. The first woman to complete the winding 375-meter course and arrive at the church, serve her pancake to the bellringer, and receive a kiss from him is the winner. She also receives a prayer book from the vicar. The record, by the way, is 63 seconds, set in 1967.

WORLD MOTOR VEHICLE PRODUCTION

In 2003, the top ten countries in the world for manufacturing automobiles were:

1. United States	6. South Korea
2. Japan	7. Spain
3. Germany	8. Canada
4. China	9. Brazil
5. France	10. United Kingdom

A GOOD TIP

Some advice on what's expected in various situations:

Airports
Skycaps: $1 per bag
Wheelchair attendant: $3–5
Electric cart driver: $2

Casinos
Blackjack dealer: $5 per session
Waitress: $1 per drink
Slot machine manager: $1 per session

Tow truck
Jump: $3–5
Tow: $5
Locked out: $5–10

Others who generally receive a tip:
DJ: $1 per song; $5 if it has to be the next song
Buffet-style restaurant waiter: 5–10%
Exotic dancer: $3 per song per person
Dog groomer: $2 per dog, or 15%
Limo driver: $20
Massage therapist: 10–20%
Cruise cabin steward: $3 per day

Holiday Tipping

Babysitter: Two nights' pay
Day care: $15–25 plus a gift
Garbage collector: $15–20
Trainer: $50
Cleaning person: One week's pay

International Eating and Drinking Tips

Canada: The tip range is 10–20 percent and is expected for restaurants, bars, food delivery, and taxis. If service is bad, it's fine not to tip at all.

China: No tipping.

France: In restaurants, a service charge is included in the price by law. It is usually about 15 percent or so. Tip about the same in bars.

Italy: Not expected in restaurants; leave some change on the table if you like.

Japan: No tipping.

Mexico: Tipping is expected for almost every service; pay is so scant that what people make in tips is truly part of their salary.

United Kingdom: No tipping in a bar or pub; buy a drink for the barkeep's service, if you like.

And one last international tipping tip: tip no one in New Zealand and Australia; tip everyone in South Africa.

◆

In 1969, MIDNIGHT COWBOY became the first and only X-rated production to win the Academy Award for Best Picture. Its rating has since been changed to R.

◆

Ten inches of SNOW equals one inch of rain in water content.

IT'S DIFFERENT FOR GIRLS

Rules have never been the same for girls and boys . . .

The Girl Scout Law

I will do my best to be
honest and fair,
friendly and helpful,
considerate and caring,
courageous and strong, and
responsible for what I say and do,
                           and to
respect myself and others,
respect authority,
use resources wisely,
make the world a better place, and
be a sister to every Girl Scout.

The Boy Scout Law

The Boy Scout Law varies from country to country. Here
are a few different versions:

United States: A Scout is: Trustworthy, Loyal, Helpful,
Friendly, Courteous, Kind, Obedient, Cheerful, Thrifty, Brave,
Clean, Reverent.

South Africa: A Scout's honor is to be trusted. A Scout is loyal.
A Scout's duty is to be useful and to help others. A Scout is a
friend to all and a brother to every other Scout. A Scout is
courteous. A Scout is a friend to animals. A Scout obeys orders.
A Scout smiles and whistles under all difficulties. A Scout is
thrifty. A Scout is clean in thought, word and deed.

Thailand: A Scout's honor is to be trusted. A Scout is loyal to his Nation, his Religion, his King and is faithful to his benefactors. A Scout's duty is to be useful and to help others. A Scout is a friend to all, and a brother to every other Scout in the world. A Scout is courteous. A Scout is kind to animals. A Scout respectfully obeys the orders of his parents and his superiors. A Scout is very cheerful and is not afraid of troubles. A Scout is thrifty. A Scout is clean in thought, word and deed.

France: A Scout's honor is to be trusted. A Scout is loyal for life. A Scout's duty is to be useful and to help others. A Scout shares with everyone. A Scout is courteous and fights against injustice. A Scout protects life because it was created by God. A Scout obeys and finishes what he starts. A Scout smiles under all difficulties. A Scout is careful of possessions and property. A Scout is pure and shines pureness.

China: Honesty, Loyalty and Filial Devotion, Helpfulness, Loving Kindness, Courtesy, Justice, Responsibility, Cheerfulness, Industriousness and Thrift, Courage, Cleanness, Public Spirit

◆

ON FIRE

Though species of trees vary in their density, for use as firewood the energy content of the wood does not vary substantially enough to make a difference in efficacy. Availability, dryness, and a proper cut are equally important. But all things being equal, here are the top ten hardest species for your burning pleasure:

Rock elm * Shagbark hickory * White oak * Bitternut hickory
* Sugar maple * Beech * Red oak * Yellow birch
* Red elm * White ash

WHAT'S IN A NAME
The Most Popular Names for Towns in the United States

Town	How Many	Source/Derivation
Franklin	28	Statesman Benjamin Franklin
Madison	27	President James Madison
Clinton	26	Mainly local founders or politicians
Washington	26	President George Washington
Chester	25	English town
Greenville	24	Description
Marion	24	Revolutionary War general
Salem	24	Biblical place
Springfield	24	Description
Manchester	23	English city
Monroe	22	President James Monroe
Troy	22	Greek city
Ashland	21	Tree; home of Henry Clay
Milford	21	English town
Clayton	20	Mainly local founders or politicians
Fairfield	20	Description
Jackson	20	President Andrew Jackson
Jamestown	20	English king; personal name
Jefferson	20	President Thomas Jefferson
Newport	20	Description
Oxford	20	English city
Cleveland	19	President Grover Cleveland
Lebanon	19	Biblical place
Plymouth	19	English city

TOP TEN BRIGHTEST STARS

These are the ten brightest stars in the night sky as visible from Earth:

Name	Distance from Earth (in light years)	Constellation
Sirius	9	Canis Major
Canopus	313	Carina
Alpha Centauri	4	Centaurus
Arcturus	37	Bootes
Vega	25	Lyra
Capella	42	Auriga
Rigel	773	Orion
Procyon	11	Canis Minor
Achernar	144	Eridanus
Betelgeuse	427	Orion

THE INTERNATIONAL SPACE STATION

The following sixteen nations cooperated in the design, construction, and operation of the International Space Station:

Canada, Belgium, Brazil, Denmark, France, Italy, Japan, Netherlands, Norway, Russia, Spain, Sweden, Switzerland, United Kingdom, and the United States

◆

Air holes must be cut in the roof of an IGLOO to prevent suffocation.

MAGIC 8 BALL MESSAGES

In the late 1940s, Alabe Crafts Co. of Cincinnati, Ohio, invented a quirky item that would be the biggest prognosticator on the toy market since the Ouija board took hold in the 1880s. Herewith the prophetic answers offered up by the icosahedron (20-sided polyhedron) inside the mysterious sphere . . .

As I see it, yes.
Ask again later.
Better not tell you now.
Cannot predict now.
Concentrate and ask again.
Don't count on it.
It is certain.
It is decidedly so.
Most likely.
My reply is no.

My sources say no.
Outlook not so good.
Outlook good.
Reply hazy, try again.
Signs point to yes.
Very doubtful.
Without a doubt.
Yes.
Yes—definitely.
You may rely on it.

◆

MAGNETIC PERSONALITY

Magnetic resonance imaging (MRI) is used increasingly to diagnose various conditions, particularly those in the brain. MRI uses radio waves (safer than X-rays) to bring molecules into phase—in other words, aligns the molecules in the area being examined—and then observes the differences as the molecules "relax" or return to their various characteristic phases. The resulting changes are then captured with a computer. To see the body in three dimensions, the MRI device moves along the body and administers pulses of radio waves to each "slice" of tissue, and all these are reassembled into a three-dimensional image.

HOW HIGH?
The Ten Tallest Buildings in the World (as of 2005)

Building	Location	Stories	Height (ft)
1. Taipei 101	Taipei, Taiwan	101	1,670
2. Petronas Tower One	Kuala Lumpur, Malaysia	88	1,483
2. Petronas Tower Two	Kuala Lumpur, Malaysia	88	1,483
4. Sears Tower	Chicago, United States	110	1,450
5. Jin Mao Tower	Shanghai, China	88	1,380
6. Two International Finance Center	Hong Kong	88	1,362
7. CITIC Plaza	Guangzhou, China	80	1,283
8. Shun Hing Square	Shenzhen, China	69	1,260
9. Empire State Building	New York, United States	102	1,250
10. Central Plaza	Hong Kong	78	1,227

◆

The first flight of the WRIGHT BROTHERS was a distance less than the wingspan of a jumbo jet.

EXECUTED
U.S. Executions by State (1976–2004)

State		State	
Texas	336	Utah	6
Virginia	94	Mississippi	6
Oklahoma	75	Washington	4
Missouri	61	Maryland	4
Florida	59	Pennsylvania	3
Georgia	36	Nebraska	3
North Carolina	34	Federal	3
South Carolina	32	Oregon	2
Alabama	30	Montana	2
Louisiana	27	Kentucky	2
Arkansas	26	Wyoming	1
Arizona	22	Tennessee	1
Ohio	15	New Mexico	1
Delaware	13	Idaho	1
Illinois	12	Colorado	1
Indiana	11		
Nevada	11	TOTAL EXECUTIONS:	944
California	10		

The forms of capital punishment used in the U.S. today are
lethal injection, gas chamber, electrocution, firing squad, and
hanging.

LETHAL INJECTION

Alabama	Florida
Arizona	Georgia
Arkansas	Idaho
California	Illinois
Colorado	Indiana
Connecticut	Kansas
Delaware	Kentucky

Louisiana
Maryland Mississippi
Missouri
Montana
Nevada
New Hampshire
New Jersey
New Mexico
New York
North Carolina
Ohio
Oklahoma
Oregon
Pennsylvania
South Carolina
South Dakota
Tennessee
Texas
Utah
U.S. military
U.S. government
Virginia
Washington
Wyoming

ELECTROCUTION
Alabama

Arkansas
Florida
llinois
Kentucky
Nebraska
Oklahoma
South Carolina
Tennessee
Virginia

LETHAL GAS
Arizona
California
Maryland
Missouri
Wyoming

HANGING
New Hampshire
Washington

FIRING SQUAD
Idaho
Oklahoma
Utah

U.S. Executions by Method (through July 2005)

Lethal injection	799	Hanging*	3
Electrocution	151	Firing squad*	2
Lethal gas	11		

* All states that used this method had lethal injection as an alternative choice.

AIN'T SUPERSTITIOUS?
What to Do to Keep Luck on Your Side

If you say good-bye to a friend on a bridge, you'll never see each other again.

Sweep trash out the door after dark and a stranger will visit.

Dropping the comb while you're combing your hair is a sign of a coming disappointment.

It's bad luck to cut your fingernails on a Friday or a Sunday.

Always eat a fish from the head toward the tail.

Never say the word *pig* while fishing at sea.

Drop a fork and a man will visit.

Ivy growing on a house protects the inhabitants from witchcraft and evil.

If you catch a falling leaf on the first day of autumn, you won't catch a cold all winter.

A dream about a lizard means you've got a secret enemy.

A wish will come true if you make it while burning onions.

It's bad luck to see an owl in the sunlight.

Use the same pencil to take a test that you used for studying for the test, and the pencil will remember the answers.

Salty soup is a sign that the cook is in love.

Sing before seven, cry before eleven.

A swan feather sewn into a husband's pillow ensures fidelity.

A yawn is a sign that danger is near.

Seeing an ambulance is very unlucky unless you pinch your nose or hold your breath until you see a black or a brown dog.

Wear a blue bead to protect yourself from witches.

◆

STARS AND STRIPES WHENEVER

In the early years of nationhood, the U.S. flag went through several permutations; in fact, many states designed their own versions of the stars and stripes. But in 1818, Congress voted to keep the number of stripes on the flag at thirteen, to honor the original colonies, and to add one star to the field for every new state. Each new star is officially added on the July 4 following a state's admission to the Union. A fairly recent American flag is rarely seen: the forty-nine-star version, flown for just one year between the time Alaska and Hawaii became states. Technically, the United States was a forty-nine-state country for just over seven months: Alaska was admitted on January 3, 1959, and Hawaii the following August 21, thus missing that year's July 4 "new flag" cutoff. Dwight D. Eisenhower was the only president to serve under the forty-nine-star American flag.

THINGS GOD MADE DURING EARTH'S SEVEN DAYS OF CREATION

1. Light, resulting in day and night
2. Sky
3. Earth and ocean, grass, herbs, and fruit trees
4. Sun, moon, and stars
5. Birds, fish, and whales
6. Cows, creeping things, wild animals, man, and woman
7. The Sabbath—God rested

GRAY SKIES

Sometimes science shows its whimsical side—witness these cloud names, which owe their beginnings to sailors, farmers, and old wives . . .

Cloud	Descriptive Name	Height	Description
Cirrus	Mares' tails	4 or more miles	Thin, feathery
Cirrocumulus	Mackerel sky	4 or more miles	Small patches of white
Cirrostratus	Bedsheet clouds	4 or more miles	Thin, white sheets
Stratus*	High fogs	0–1 mile	Low, gray blanket
Cumulus	Cauliflowers	¼–4 miles	Flat bottomed, white puffy
Cumulonimbus*	Thunderheads	¼–4 miles	Mountains of heavy, dark clouds

*Rain or snow clouds

◆

In many parts of the South, the American CIVIL WAR is still referred to as "The War of Northern Aggression."

-OF-THE-MONTH CLUBS

Just a Few Things You Can Get by Mail, Twelve Times a Year

Wine * Bacon * Books * Cookies * Meals * Fruit * Coffee *
Chocolate * Pizza * Flowers * Plants * Fruits * Jelly *
Salsa * Tea * Cheesecake * Beer * Candles * Popcorn * Pie *
Software * Cigars* Champagne.

THE VERMILLION GATE BRIDGE

Though the U.S. Navy would have preferred black with bright
yellow stripes for visibility in a city often swathed in fog, the
Golden Gate Bridge has been painted orange vermillion—or
"international orange"—ever since its completion. Architect
Irving Morrow selected the color to blend with the bridge's
stunning natural setting. Contrary to legend, the bridge is not
constantly painted end-to-end, nonstop; it has been painted
only twice. Presently, to avoid corrosion and meet air-quality
requirements, it sports an inorganic zinc silicate primer and an
acrylic emulsion topcoat.

THE 1909-11 T206

For some, this code signifies the holy grail of baseball-card
collecting. Rarest of the T206 series is "The Flying
Dutchman," Honus Wagner, and estimates are that only 50
to 100 copies of this card exist. The last time one of these
Honus Wagner cards was sold, in 2000, it went for over $1.1
million.

Want to see one? A Honus Wagner T206 card is in the
collection of New York's Metropolitan Museum of Art.

THE BEST-SELLING
BOOKS OF ALL TIME

Title	First Published	Approximate Sales
The Bible	ca. 1450	More than 6 billion
Quotations from the Works of Chairman Mao Tse-Tung	1966	1 billion
American Spelling Book, by Noah Webster	1783	100 million
The Guinness Book of World Records	1955	90 million
The World Almanac	1868	75 million

◆

PATENTLY ABSURD?

According to the United States Patent and Trademark Office
Web site, only the inventor may apply for a patent, with certain exceptions. If a person who is not the inventor applies
for a patent, the patent, if it is obtained, becomes invalid.
The person applying in such a case who falsely states that he
or she is the inventor is also subject to criminal penalties. If
the inventor is dead, the application may be made by legal
representatives, that is, the administrator or executor of the
estate. If the inventor is insane, the application for patent
may be made by a guardian. If an inventor refuses to apply
for a patent or cannot be found, a joint inventor or a person
having a proprietary interest in the invention may apply on
behalf of the nonsigning inventor.

MAC WORLD

Since 1968, the Big Mac, McDonald's flagship sandwich, has been sung about and scarfed down by the billions. It's universally known that its main ingredients are:

Two all-beef patties   Pickles
Special sauce   Onions
Lettuce   Sesame seed bun
Cheese

Many have tried to replicate the "special sauce." Herewith a popular copycat recipe:

½ cup mayonnaise
2 tablespoons French dressing
4 teaspoons sweet pickle relish
1 tablespoon finely minced white onions
1 teaspoon white vinegar
1 teaspoon sugar
⅛ teaspoon salt

McDonald's officially lists its secret sauce ingredients as:

Soybean oil, pickles, distilled vinegar, water, egg yolks, high fructose corn syrup, sugar, onion powder, corn syrup, spice and spice extracts, salt, xanthan gum, mustard flour, propylene glycol alginate, sodium benzoate and potassium sorbate as preservatives, mustard bran, garlic powder, hydrolyzed (corn gluten, wheat, and soy) proteins, caramel color, extractives of paprika, turmeric, calcium disodium EDTA to protect flavor.

WHO? WHAT? WHEN? WHERE? WHY?

THE DEWEY DECIMAL SYSTEM

Devised by library pioneer Melvil Dewey in the 1870s, this organizational system provides a logical structure for the organization of a library's unique collection. This classification is still used today in more than two hundred thousand libraries worldwide.

000	*Generalities*
100	*Philosophy and psychology*
200	*Religion*
300	*Social sciences*
400	*Language*
500	*Natural sciences and mathematics*
600	*Technology (Applied sciences)*
700	*The arts*
800	*Literature and rhetoric*
900	*Geography and history*

SAYS WHO?

Ventriloquism is much more than dummies and voice throwing. Its magical illusion relies on the fact that the ear is quite unreliable when it comes to pinpointing the direction of sound. Without visual cues, the accuracy is even poorer. To work, a ventriloquist must keep his mouth open only about a quarter of an inch at all times, muffling and faking word sounds that require the lips to be joined. Additional stagecraft includes gestures, eye movements, and patter to distract the audience. The dummy's "voice" must also have a different personality as well—pitch, cadence, and the voice's assumed sex and age can all be altered to confuse the viewer/listener.

ECHOES OF THE ALPS

Yodeling is a vocal art form begun in the Swiss and Austrian Alps, originally serving as a form of communication between houses and towns, and used for spreading simple messages and warnings. Though yodeling consists mostly of nonsense words that are sung primarily for the way they sound, it does have a specific form, switching rapidly from the lower alto, tenor, or bass "chest voices" to a falsetto or "high voice." The yodeler sounds syllables continuously upward until the voice breaks into an upper octave, then down again and up until the voice breaks again. This is done repeatedly and loudly, though some purists complain that acrobatics and speed play too much a part in modern yodeling. A piece will still occasionally end with a few real words, for example, *drobn auf da Alm*, which is Austrian dialect for "up there on the mountain."

GLOBAL EXHALE

In 2002, the top ten producers of carbon dioxide emissions into the atmosphere, the main cause of global warming, were:

1. United States	1568	6. Germany	229
2. China	906	7. Canada	161
3. Russia	415	8. United Kingdom	151
4. Japan	322	9. South Korea	123
5. India	280	10. Italy	122

(million metric tons carbon equivalent)

◆

HOMICIDE is the premiere cause of death of pregnant women.

LUCKY (AND SACRED) SEVEN

History and religion seem to have a predilection for the number seven . . .

Seven Days of Creation: The amount of time cited in the Bible in which God made the world

Seven Churches of Asia: Referred to by St. John in the Book of Revelation, they were located in Ephesus, Smyrna, Pergamum, Thyatira, Sardia, Philadelphia, and Laodicea

Seven Churches of Rome: The basilicas of St. John Lateran, St. Peter, St. Mary Major, St. Paul-Outside-the-Walls, St. Lawrence-Outside-the-Walls, St. Sebastian-Outside-the-Walls, and Holy Cross-in-Jerusalem

Seven Deadly Sins: Pride, covetousness, lust, anger, gluttony, envy, and sloth

Seven Names for Constantinople: By-sance, Antonia, New Rome, the town of Constantine, the Separator of the World's Parts, the Treasure of Islam, Stamboul

Seven Gifts: Wisdom, understanding, counsel, fortitude, knowledge, piety, and fear of the Lord

Seven Angels: In Arabian legend, they cool the sun with ice and snow, so the Earth will not burn up

Seven Holy Days of Obligation: Solemnity of Mary, Easter, Solemnity of the Ascension, Solemnity of the Assumption, Solemnity of All Saints, Solemnity of the Immaculate Conception, and Christmas

Seventh Son: Mythical personages often father seven sons. It is especially fortunate to be the seventh son of the seventh son.

Seven as the Age of Reason: In Christianity, seven is considered the age of reason, and the age when a child is held accountable for sins and begins confession.

Seven Sacraments: Baptism, Confirmation, the Eucharist, Penance, Holy Orders, Matrimony, and Anointing of the Sick

Seven Wedding Blessings: A special set for the bride and groom at Jewish weddings

Seven States of Purification: Egyptian dogma for the stages of the transmigration of the soul

Seven Deities: Egyptians had seven original and higher gods; the Phœnicians seven kabiris; the Persians, seven sacred horses of Mithra; the Parsees, seven angels opposed by seven demons, and seven celestial abodes paralleled by seven lower regions.

◆

WHO IS THIS EMILY, AND WHAT IS HER LIST?

She's not a woman, she's an acronym. EMILY's List stands for "Early Money Is Like Yeast" ("It makes the dough rise"), a financial network to promote pro-choice Democratic women political candidates. It was started in 1985, not by an Emily, but by Ellen R. Malcolm, a Washington, D.C., activist.

SWIM WITH CARE!

These sea creatures can be dangerous, even fatal:

Cone-Shell: A beautiful, small mollusk that lives in the South Pacific and Indian Oceans. It shoots poison barbs into its victims. For humans, they cause mild paralysis and, infrequently, death.

Octopus: All varieties of this common animal produce a paralysis-causing venom, but none is known to be fatal to humans.

Portuguese Man-of-War: This warm-water jellyfish, with tentacles up to 70 feet long, defends itself with painful stings which can cause shock, and thus be indirectly fatal to humans.

Sea Wasp: A warm-water jellyfish with 30-foot-long tentacles, whose deadly stings cause an immediate collapse of the human circulatory system.

Stingray: Although their sting is seldom fatal, an encounter with a stingray can cause vomiting, breathing difficulties, and/or gangrene.

Stonefish: Dangerous because it lies motionless in shallow South Pacific and Indian Ocean waters, a stonefish bite causes severe pain, rapid paralysis, but is only infrequently fatal.

———————————————————◆———————————————————

SALT is the only rock that can be eaten by humans, making it, one might say . . . worth its salt.

It is believed by some scholars that Joseph's COAT OF MANY COLORS was an early tie-dyed garment.

◆

WHAT ARE THE ODDS?

If you toss the dice, these are the chances you take . . .

Total on Dice	Odds
2	35 to 1
3	17 to 1
4	11 to 1
5	8 to 1
6	31 to 5
7	5 to 1
8	31 to 5
9	8 to 1
10	11 to 1
11	17 to 1
12	35 to 1

. . . or deal the cards and take your chances:

Poker Hand	Odds
Royal flush	649,739 to 1
Straight flush	72,192 to 1
Four of a kind	4,164 to 1
Full house	693 to 1
Flush	508 to 1
Straight	254 to 1
Three of a kind	46 to 1
Two pairs	20 to 1
One pair	2.37 to 1

REMEMBER YOUR ANNIVERSARY?

What you give and what you get has changed some over the last several decades. Parts of the traditional list of anniversary gifts, however, have existed since medieval times. The silver and golden landmarks reach back to medieval Germany, where garlands of these materials were presented as gifts for the twenty-fifth and fiftieth celebrations, respectively. Perhaps surprisingly, the "traditional" list did not exist until 1937, when the American National Retail Jeweler Association published options that included suggestions for the first fifteen years and then every five years thereafter, up to sixty. The origin of the modern list is unclear, but like the original, each year seems to be more precious and extravagant than the one before.

Anniversary	Traditional Gift	Modern Gift
First	Paper	Clocks
Second	Cotton	China
Third	Leather	Crystal/Glass
Fourth	Fruit/Flowers	Appliances
Fifth	Wood	Silverware
Sixth	Candy/Iron	Wood
Seventh	Wool/Copper	Desk Sets
Eighth	Bronze/Pottery	Linens/Lace
Ninth	Pottery/Willow	Leather
Tenth	Tin/Aluminum	Diamond Jewelry
Eleventh	Steel	Fashion Jewelry
Twelfth	Silk/Linen	Pearls
Thirteenth	Lace	Textiles/Furs
Fourteenth	Ivory	Gold Jewelry
Fifteenth	Crystal	Watches
Twentieth	China	Platinum

Anniversary	Traditional Gift	Modern Gift
Twenty-fifth	Silver	Silver
Thirtieth	Pearl	Diamond
Thirty-fifth	Coral	Jade
Fortieth	Ruby	Ruby
Forty-fifth	Sapphire	Sapphire
Fiftieth	Gold	Gold
Fifty-fifth	Emerald	Emerald
Sixtieth	Diamond	Diamond

◆

NOTHING IS AS IT SEEMS

Lettuce is from the sunflower family.

The cashew nut and poison ivy are relations.

Both apples and pears are from the rose family.

Those cute baby carrots? No such thing. They're the usual carrot, shaved down to pint-sized pieces.

◆

Q is the only letter in the alphabet that does not appear in the name of any state of the United States.

◆

TOP 10 U.S. States ranked by American Indian and Alaska Native population:

1. California
2. Oklahoma
3. Arizona
4. New Mexico
5. Texas
6. North Carolina
7. Alaska
8. Washington
9. New York
10. South Dakota

THE (EXTRA)ORDINARY OLIVE

The goddess Athena planted the first olive tree near the Acropolis, or so legend has it, and a tree that grows there today is said to have come from the seeds of the original. The olive tree is one of the most prestigious trees in history. As far back as Noah and the ark, a dove returned from the deluge with an olive branch, a sign of life; since then, the branch has also become a symbol of peace. Though it is believed that trees have been cultivated separately in both Syria and Crete as far back as 3000 B.C.E., recent carbon-dating in Spain has found an olive seed, *O. europaea,* thought to be eight thousand years old.

These days, olive oil enjoys a wide variety of uses:

- To unstick a zipper
- To silence squeaky doors
- To shine stainless steel
- As an alternate to shaving cream
- To feed to your cat as hairball prevention
- A sip before sleep to coat the throat and stop snoring
- A swallow to stop a tickle in the throat

And then there's the fruit: salty, deep, rich, and almost as varied in size as in taste. Below, a list of olive count ranges per kilogram:

Bullet (351–380)	Extra Jumbo (161–180)
Fine (321–350)	Giant (141–160)
Brilliant (291–320)	Colossal (121–140)
Superior (261–290)	Super Colossal (111–120)
Large (231–260)	Mammoth (101–110)
Extra Large (201–230)	Super Mammoth (91–100)
Jumbo (181–200)	

PETS IN THE WHITE MOUSE . . . ER, HOUSE

Just a Few of the Crawlers—Creepy and Otherwise—
Who've Lived at 1600 Pennsylvania Avenue

John Quincy Adams raised silkworms.

Aside from the expected bear, of course, Teddy Roosevelt and his clan had dogs, cats, squirrels, raccoons, rabbits, guinea pigs, a badger, a pony, a parrot, and a green garter snake.

William Howard Taft enjoyed peeking out the Oval Office window to watch Pauline Wayne, his cow, who grazed on the front lawn. Pauline was often accompanied by Enoch, her gander friend.

William McKinley often chatted with his Mexican yellow parrot.

And Andrew Johnson did, in fact, keep white mice as pets.

Other White House occupants have included zebras, coyotes, badgers, guinea pigs, hyenas, alligators, lizards, snakes, turtles, and ponies.

◆

TRULY PUZZLING

Word squares—the progenitor of the crossword puzzle—go back to ancient times; in fact, one was found in the Roman ruins of Pompeii. In nineteenth-century England, word squares had become the basis for primitive crossword puzzles for children, but adults didn't do them until *The World* newspaper's word-cross in 1913. Oddly, one of the last newspapers to hold out on what had become a worldwide craze was *The New York Times*, which did not publish a Sunday puzzle until 1942, and a daily puzzle until 1950.

TEA TOTALING

Though the British have made tea an integral part of their lives for more than 350 years, the legend of the first cup of tea dates back to 2737 B.C.E. China and the emperor Shen Nung. A scientist and herbalist, he was sitting beneath a tree while his servant boiled drinking water. Dried leaves dropped into the water and the emperor decided to try the brew. The tree was a wild tea tree.

The Duchess of Bedford is reputed to have originated the idea of afternoon tea in the early 1800s to ward off hunger between lunch and dinner. Two tea services evolved: "high" and "low." "Low" tea was for the wealthy and featured delicate gourmet tidbits and sandwiches, served between 3 and 5 P.M. "High" tea, eaten between 5 and 7 P.M., was the major meal for the middle and lower classes, consisting of dinner items.

More tea is drunk worldwide that any other beverage except water. India, China, Sri Lanka, Kenya, and Indonesia account for nearly 80 percent of the world's tea production.

Top Ten Countries in World Tea Consumption (as of 1997):

Country	Percentage of World Tea Consumption
India	23
China	16
Russia/CIS	6
United Kingdom	6
Japan	5
Turkey	5
Pakistan	4
United States	4
Iran	3
Egypt	3

THE PERFECT FOOD—IN EVERY SIZE

Several things influence the size of an egg: the major factor is the age of the hen, as her eggs increase in size with her age. The breed and weight of the bird also make a difference. Lastly, heat, stress, and overcrowding will affect the size of the eggs. Consumers generally will see only medium-size eggs and larger; below are egg monikers and minimum weight per dozen (in ounces) in the United States and United Kingdom.

Peewee (15)   Large (24)
Small (18)   Extra Large (27)
Medium (21)   Jumbo (30)

◆

HOW MUCH?

What part of *one* don't you understand?

Prefix	Equivalent	Prefix	Equivalent
Atto	Quintillionth part	Deci	Tenth part
Femto	Quadrillionth part	Deka	Tenfold
Pico	Trillionth part	Hecto	Hundredfold
Nano	Billionth part	Kilo	Thousandfold
Micro	Millionth part	Mega	Millionfold
Milli	Thousandth part	Giga	Billionfold
Centi	Hundredth part	Tera	Trillionfold

WHAT'S YOUR SIGN?

The word *zodiac* comes for the Greek *zodiakos*, meaning "circle of animal"; evidence points to the Greek scheme of twelve zodiacal constellations appearing about 300 B.C.E. The zodiac is an imaginary belt extending approximately 8 degrees on either side of the Sun's apparent path, called the ecliptic. It includes the apparent paths of the Moon and all the planets except Pluto, whose path is eccentric. Each sign of the zodiac is approximately 30 degrees and is an artificial division of the Sun's path through the twelve constellations. (Libra, the scales, by the way, is the only inanimate symbol in the zodiac.)

Sign	Symbol	Birthdates
Aries	Ram	March 21–April 19
Taurus	Bull	April 20–May 20
Gemini	Twins	May 21–June 21
Cancer	Crab	June 22–July 22
Leo	Lion	July 23–August 22
Virgo	Virgin	August 23–September 22
Libra	Scales	September 23–October 23
Scorpio	Scorpion	October 24–November 21
Sagittarius	Archer	November 22–December 21
Capricorn	Goat	December 22–January 19
Aquarius	Water	January 20–February 18
Pisces	Fish	February 19–March 20

◆

The TREATY OF FORT JACKSON (1814) compelled the Creek Indians to cede 23 million acres of land to the United States, comprising about half of Alabama and part of Georgia.

STRIPES AND SOLIDS

Everyone knows that when you're "behind the eight ball" things are looking pretty black, but here's a bit more about the color of the cue and the fifteen "object balls" around the rest of the pool table. The number, type, diameter, color, and patterns of billiard balls differ, depending on the game at hand:

1. Yellow	9. White with yellow stripe
2. Blue	10. White with blue stripe
3. Red	11. White with red stripe
4. Purple	12. White with purple stripe
5. Orange	13. White with orange stripe
6. Green	14. White with green stripe
7. Plum	15. White with plum stripe
8. Black	Cue ball: White

Eight ball, **straight pool**, and related games used all 16 balls

Nine ball uses only object balls 1 to 9
Regulation balls for these games have a 2¼" diameter and weigh 5½ to 6 ounces

Snooker uses 15 red balls, 6 colored balls (yellow, green, brown, blue, pink, and black) and one cue ball; all are unnumbered and are 2¹⁄₁₆" in diameter

Carom billiards uses 2 object balls and 1 cue ball on a pocketless table

◆

The photographs ANDY WARHOL used to silkscreen his 1964 *Marilyn* series are stills from her film *Niagara*.

MOST POPULAR BABY NAMES
ACROSS THE U.S. IN 2003

Boys

Alabama	William
Alaska	Jacob
Arizona	Jacob
Arkansas	Jacob
California	Daniel
Colorado	Jacob
Connecticut	Matthew
Delaware	Michael
District of Columbia	Michael
Florida	Michael
Georgia	William
Hawaii	Joshua
Idaho	Ethan
Illinois	Michael
Indiana	Jacob
Iowa	Jacob
Kansas	Ethan
Kentucky	Jacob
Louisiana	Jacob
Maine	Jacob
Maryland	Joshua
Massachusetts	Matthew
Michigan	Jacob
Minnesota	Jacob
Mississippi	William
Missouri	Jacob
Montana	Jacob
Nebraska	Jacob

Nevada	Anthony
New Hampshire	Jacob
New Jersey	Michael
New Mexico	Joshua
New York	Michael
North Carolina	Jacob
North Dakota	Ethan
Ohio	Jacob
Oklahoma	Jacob
Oregon	Jacob
Pennsylvania	Michael
Puerto Rico	Luis
Rhode Island	Michael
South Carolina	William
South Dakota	Jacob
Tennessee	William
Texas	José
Utah	Ethan
Vermont	Ethan
Virginia	Jacob
Washington	Jacob
West Virginia	Jacob
Wisconsin	Jacob
Wyoming	Jacob

TOTALS: JACOB: 25, MICHAEL: 8, ETHAN: 5, WILLIAM: 5, JOSHUA: 3, MATTHEW: 2, ANTHONY: 1, DANIEL: 1, JOSÉ: 1, LUIS: 1

Girls

Alabama	Madison
Alaska	Hannah
Arizona	Emily
Arkansas	Madison
California	Emily
Colorado	Emily
Connecticut	Emma
Delaware	Emily
District of Columbia	Kayla
Florida	Emily
Georgia	Emily
Hawaii	Emma
Idaho	Emma
Illinois	Emily
Indiana	Emma
Iowa	Emma
Kansas	Emma
Kentucky	Emily
Louisiana	Madison
Maine	Emma
Maryland	Emily
Massachusetts	Emily
Michigan	Emma
Minnesota	Emma
Mississippi	Madison
Missouri	Emma
Montana	Emma
Nebraska	Emma
Nevada	Emily
New Hampshire	Emma

New Jersey	Emily
New Mexico	Alexis
New York	Emily
North Carolina	Emma
North Dakota	Emma
Ohio	Emma
Oklahoma	Emily
Oregon	Emma
Pennsylvania	Emily
Puerto Rico	Alondra
Rhode Island	Emily
South Carolina	Madison
South Dakota	Emma
Tennessee	Madison
Texas	Emily
Utah	Emma
Vermont	Emma
Virginia	Emily
Washington	Emma
West Virginia	Madison
Wisconsin	Emma
Wyoming	Emma

TOTALS: EMMA: 23, EMILY: 18, MADISON: 7, ALEXIS: 1, ALONDRA: 1 HANNAH: 1, KAYLA: 1

Source: Social Security Administration, 2003.

◆

CONFETTI, the Italian word for "sweets," has its origins in Italian villages, where treats were thrown over the newlyweds as they left the church as a sort of fertility ritual. In poorer towns, rice, raisins, flower petals, and Jordan almonds were tossed.

WHAT WERE THEIR RANKS?
Of Forty-three American Presidents, Only Twenty-eight
Have Served in the Military

General of the Army	Dwight D. Eisenhower
	Ulysses S. Grant
Lieutenant General	George Washington
Major General	James Garfield
	William Henry Harrison
	Rutherford B. Hayes
	Andrew Jackson
	Zachary Taylor
Brigadier General	Benjamin Harrison
	Andrew Johnson
	Franklin Pierce
Quartermaster General	Chester A. Arthur
Colonel	James Madison
	Theodore Roosevelt
Lieutenant Colonel	James Monroe
Lieutenant Commander (Navy)	Gerald Ford
	Lyndon Baines Johnson
	Richard M. Nixon
Lieutenant	George H. W. Bush
	Jimmy Carter
	John F. Kennedy (Navy)
Lieutenant (National Guard)	George W. Bush
Major	William McKinley
	Harry S. Truman

Captain	Ronald Reagan
Captain (Militia)	Abraham Lincoln
	John Tyler
Private	James Buchanan

◆

COLD VERSUS FLU

According to the National Institute of Allergy and Infectious Diseases, there are several symptomatic differences between the cold and flu, or for the layman, lots of different ways of feeling crummy . . .

Symptom	Cold	Flu
Fever	Rare	High (102–104°F), for 3–4 days
Headache	Rare	Prominent
Aches and pains	Slight	Usual, often severe
Fatigue, weakness	Mild	May last 2–3 weeks
Extreme exhaustion	Never	Early and prominent
Stuffy nose, sore throat	Common	Sometimes

◆

SUBARU is the Japanese name for the constellation we know as the Pleiades, or Seven Sisters. The car's logo only shows six stars, because the Japanese constellation only contains the six brightest stars in the cluster.

MASCOTS

National Basketball Association

Atlanta Hawks	Harry the Hawk
Charlotte Bobcats	Rufus Lynx
Chicago Bulls	Da Bull
Cleveland Cavaliers	Moondog
Dallas Mavericks	Mavs Man
Denver Nuggets	Rocky the Mountain Lion
Golden State Warriors	Thunder
Houston Rockets	Clutch
Indiana Pacers	Boomer
Miami Heat	Burnie
Milwaukee Bucks	Bango
Minnesota Timberwolves	Crunch
New Jersey Nets	Sly
New Orleans Hornets	Hugo
Orlando Magic	Stuff the Magic Dragon
Philadelphia 76ers	Hip-Hop
Phoenix Suns	Gorilla
Sacramento Kings	Slamson
San Antonio Spurs	A coyote
Seattle Supersonics	Squatch
Toronto Raptors	The Raptor
Utah Jazz	A bear
Vancouver Grizzlies	Grizz
Washington Wizards	G-Wiz

The New York Knicks have no mascot.

Major League Baseball

Atlanta Braves	Rally
Anaheim Angels	Rally Monkey
Arizona Diamondbacks	Baxter D. Bobcat
Baltimore Orioles	Oriole Bird
Boston Red Sox	Wally the Green Monster
Chicago White Sox	Southpaw
Cincinnati Reds	Mr. Red and Gapper
Cleveland Indians	Slider
Colorado Rockies	Dinger
Detroit Tigers	Paws
Florida Marlins	Billy the Marlin
Houston Astros	Junction Jack
Kansas City Royals	Sluggerrr
Milwaukee Brewers	Bernie Brewer
Minnesota Twins	TC
New York Mets	Mr. Met
Oakland A's	Stomper
Philadelphia Phillies	Phillie Phanatic
Pittsburgh Pirates	Pirate Parrot
St. Louis Cardinals	Fredbird
San Diego Padres	The Swinging Friar
San Francisco Giants	Lou Seal
Seattle Mariners	Mariner Moose
Tampa Bay Devil Rays	Raymond
Texas Rangers	Rangers Captain
Toronto Blue Jays	Ace and Diamond
Washington Nationals	Screech

The L.A. Dodgers and the New York Yankees don't have mascots. The Chicago Cubs have no official mascot, but a fan called "Ronnie Woo-woo" is the team's unofficial mascot.

National Hockey League

Mighty Ducks of Anaheim	Wild Wing
Atlanta Thrashers	Thrash
Boston Bruins	Blades the Bruin
Buffalo Sabres	Sabretooth
Calgary Flames	Harvey the Hound
Carolina Hurricanes	Stormy
Chicago Blackhawks	Tommy Hawk
Colorado Avalanche	Howler
Columbus Blue Jackets	Stinger
Florida Panthers	Stanley C. Panther
Nashville Predators	Gnash
New Jersey Devils	N. J. Devil
New York Islanders	Sparky
Ottawa Senators	Spartacat
Pittsburgh Penguins	Iceburgh
San Jose Sharks	S. J. Sharkie
Tampa Bay Lightning	ThunderBug
Toronto Maple Leafs	Carlton the Bear
Vancouver Canucks	Fin
Washington Capitals	Slapshot

The remaining ten NHL teams do not have mascots.

National Football League

Arizona Cardinals	Big Red
Atlanta Falcons	Freddie the Falcon
Baltimore Ravens	Edgar, Allan, and Poe
Buffalo Bills	Buffalo Billy
Carolina Panthers	Sir Purr
Chicago Bears	Staley Da Bear

Dallas Cowboys	Rowdy
Denver Broncos	Thunder
Detroit Lions	Roary the Lion
Jacksonville Jaguars	Jaxson de Ville
Kansas City Chiefs	K. C. Wolf
Miami Dolphins	T. D.
Minnesota Vikings	Ragnar the Viking
New England Patriots	Pat Patriot
New Orleans Saints	Gumbo
Philadelphia Eagles	Swoop
San Francisco 49ers	Sourdough Sam
Tampa Bay Buccaneers	Captain Fear

GREAT (NICK)NAMES IN SPORTS

Tara "Terrorizer" Dakides (snowboarder)
George "The Iceman" Gervin (San Antonio Spurs)
Wayne "The Great One" Gretzky (New York Rangers)
Earvin "Magic" Johnson (Los Angeles Lakers)
Randy "The Big Unit" Johnson (New York Yankees)
Walter "The Big Train" Johnson (Washington Senators)
Michael "Air" Jordan (Chicago Bulls)
Karl "The Mailman" Malone (Los Angeles Lakers)
Shaquille "Shaq Attack" O'Neal (Los Angeles Lakers)
Gary "The Glove" Payton (Los Angeles Lakers)
William "The Refrigerator" Perry (Chicago Bears)
Walter "Sweetness" Payton (Chicago Bears)
Ted "Double Duty" Radcliffe (Homestead Grays)
Frank "The Big Hurt" Thomas (Chicago White Sox)
Dominique "Human Highlight Film" Wilkins
  (Atlanta Hawks)

SEXUAL HEALING?

Aphrodisiacs are substances that are thought to cause sexual excitement—but that's just the modern spin. Originally they were thought to be remedies for sexual anxiety, such as inadequate performance or infertility. Before science took over in the sexual potency department, substances that by their very nature represented birth or seeds, such as eggs or bulbs, were considered potency helpers; also considered sexual aids were foods that bore any resemblance to genitalia.

Today, science is at best skeptical about the effects of foods and other substances on the libido. Nevertheless, hope springs eternal. Believe this list of aphrodisiacs at your peril—or delight!

almond	mustard
aniseed	nutmeg
arugula	orchid bulbs
asparagus	oysters
avocado	pine nuts
bananas	pineapple
basil (sweet)	pistachio nuts
carrots	raspberries
celery	river snails
chocolate	sage
coffee	sea fennel
coriander (cilantro seed)	skink flesh
figs	Spanish fly
garlic	strawberries
ginger	truffles
gladius root	turnips
honey	vanilla
licorice	wine
musk	

Oh, and by the way, the ancients warned against "anaphrodisiacs"—items that they believed decreased potency:

dill * lentil * lettuce * rue * watercress * water lily

◆

THE FIRST BOOK

Although it is known that books were being printed at least one hundred years before, the earliest printed and dated book is a copy of the *Diamond Sutra*. It was printed in China and is dated May 11, 868, in a colophon at the end of the book. Now safely ensconced in the British Library, it had been hidden in a sealed cave in China with forty thousand other books and manuscripts—a secret library discovered by a monk in 1900, which had been sealed for nearly nine hundred years.

The *Diamond Sutra* is simply seven pages, and was printed from carved wooden blocks. Though written in Chinese, it is a sacred Buddhist work, whose original Sanskrit title is *Vajracchedika-prajnaparamita-sutra*. The Buddha himself gave the *Diamond Sutra* its name, saying it should be called "The Diamond of Transcendent Wisdom" because "its teaching will cut like a diamond blade through worldly illusion to illuminate what is real and everlasting."

The note at the end of this tiny treasure reads, "Reverently made for universal distribution by Wang Jie on behalf of his two parents"; this does not mean that Wang Jie produced the volume, but rather that he had it made as a pious act.

It would be several hundred more years before Johannes Gutenberg invented the printing press; not until about 1454 did 180 Bibles come off his rudimentary invention.

237

WHAT'S IT GOING TO BE?

Old wives, opinionated people, and just plain nosy folks have had their say on pregancy since time immemorial. Herewith some of the best of the old saws:

"Radiant" is how a pregnant woman is so often described. But if she's unusually moody as well, she's having a girl.

If a woman carries her weight in front, she's having a boy. If others can easily see the pregnancy from behind, a girl will be born.

If the mom-to-be was the more aggressive partner when the baby was conceived, the baby will be a boy. If the father took the lead, the baby's a girl.

If the numerals in the mother-to-be's age when she conceived are either both even or both odd, the baby will be a girl. If one is even and one odd, she's having a boy.

A pregnant woman dreams of a child of the opposite sex from the one she will have.

When asked to show her hands, a pregnant woman will show them with palms up for a girl and with palms down for a boy.

If the mother-to-be has a young boy already, he will show interest in the pregnancy only if the baby is a girl.

If a woman lies on her left when taking a rest, she's having a boy; if she lies on her right, she's having a girl.

Acne during pregnancy means a girl will be born.

Women often sleep with their pillow in a different place while pregnant: north for a boy, south for a girl.

Headaches during pregnancy mean a boy will be born.

Craving fruit during pregnancy means a girl is on the way.

If a woman suddenly feels her feet are colder, she will have a boy.

If a woman chooses the heel of a loaf of bread, the baby is a boy.

If the father-to-be stays slim during the pregnancy, the baby will be a girl.

A gray-haired maternal grandmother will have a grandson; a maternal grandmother with dyed hair or hair that is still its original color will have a granddaughter.

A woman with morning sickness early in pregnancy is expecting a girl.

When a needle on a thread held over a pregnant belly moves in circles, a boy is on the way.

Dull urine color indicates a girl; if it's neon yellow, the baby will be a boy.

If the mom-to-be craves sweets, a girl is on the way; salty cravings mean she's having a boy.

A pregnant woman whose nose spreads will have a boy.

A pregnant woman will pick up a key from the round end only if she's having a boy. If she picks it up at the long end, she's having a girl. If she grips it at the middle, twins are on the way.

◆

To improve her memory, ELEANOR ROOSEVELT ate three chocolate-covered garlic balls every day.

OXYDENTALLY ON PURPOSE

Some favorite oxymorons—the combination of two normally contradictory terms—old and new:

accurate estimate	easy labor
accurate rumors	elevated subway
act naturally	false hope
actual reenactment	fire water
alone together	firm estimate
altogether separate	freezer burn
amateur expert	good grief
among the first	ill health
authentic reproduction	jumbo shrimp
assistant supervisor	junk food
athletic scholarship	living dead
baby grand piano	midnight sun
bad health	minor disaster
bad sport	mud bath
balding hair	natural artifact
black light	new classic
books on tape	nothing much
brief survey	only choice
calm winds	open secret
certain risk	organized confusion
clearly confused	paid volunteer
clogged drain	peace force
cold sweat	plastic glasses
constant change	pretty ugly
constant variable	pure evil
deliberate mistake	quiet storm
detailed summary	recent history
devout atheist	recycling dump
double solitaire	rock opera

round corners
science fiction
silent scream
steel wool
student teacher
sun shade
taped live

tentative conclusion
thinking aloud
tight slacks
turned up missing
virtual reality
working vacation

MIRANDA RIGHTS
Miranda v. Arizona, 384 U.S. 436 (1966)

Let's just say it's always good to know . . .

Before a law enforcement officer may question you regarding the possible commission of a crime, he or she must read you your Miranda rights. He or she must also make sure that you understand them.

WARNING OF RIGHTS

1. You have the right to remain silent and refuse to answer questions. Do you understand?
2. Anything you say can and will be used against you in a court of law. Do you understand?
3. You have the right to consult an attorney before speaking to the police and to have an attorney present during questioning now or in the future. Do you understand?
4. If you cannot afford an attorney, one will be appointed for you before any questioning if you wish. Do you understand?
5. If you decide to answer questions now without an attorney present you will still have the right to stop answering at any time until you talk to an attorney. Do you understand?
6. Knowing and understanding your rights as I have explained them to you, are you willing to answer my questions without an attorney present?

SLOT TALK
Slot Machine Terminology

Bonus feature: Some slot machines offer you a chance to win additional coins. This may be a second screen, free spin, and so on.

Coin size: The size of each bet

Coins per spin: The maximum number of coins that can be played for each spin

Payline: The combination of symbols that will result in the player getting paid off. In the old days, it was three cherries; many new machines offer several lines per play.

Payout percentages: What a slot machine pays out. For example, if a slot machine pays out 99 percent, that means that for every $100 that is taken in by the machine, $99 gets paid back out, meaning that the machine will "hold" $1 for $100. Payouts are listed, and a player should look for numbers in the high nineties.

Pay table: Winning combinations. You will find these listed on the slot machine or close by; the pay table explains how much each symbol on the machine pays out.

Progressive jackpot: A jackpot that continuously grows; that is, every time any player bets, a portion of that bet increments the jackpot; the higher the bet, the higher the increment.

Reels: This is the part of the machine where the symbols are displayed.

Wild symbol: Like a wild card, it's a symbol that counts as any other symbol, thus allowing a jackpot.

EXACTLY HOW SPECTACULAR?

New York City's famous Radio City Music Hall features its *Christmas Spectacular* for several weeks every holiday season. The renowned Radio City Rockettes are the primary stars of the show, but there are many other reasons this musical extravaganza is billed as "spectacular":

- There are more than thirteen hundred colorful costumes.
- The Rockettes change their costumes eight times during each show, often in as little as 78 seconds.
- The "Music Hall Menagerie" is a small herd of two donkeys, three camels, five sheep, and one horse.
- Radio City's Great Stage measures 144 feet by 66 feet. It is made up of three elevators, which may be set at any level from the sub-basement to 13 feet above the stage—a vertical drop of 40 feet. The orchestra uses a fourth elevator. Together, all four weigh 380,000 pounds.
- The "Mighty Wurlitzer Organ" is played during all performances: eleven rooms honeycomb around the theater housing the one-of-a-kind organ's 4,328 pipes and 1 million moving parts.
- Twenty-five hundred pounds of "snow" fall upon the Great Stage during the Christmas Spectacular's annual run.
- The complex sound system enables audiences to hear the orchestra from any seat in the theater—the traveling band car allows the orchestra to continue playing while moving back and forth on the stage and being raised and lowered on the elevators.

---◆---

The CRANBERRY, the blueberry, and the Concord blue grape are the only native fruits of North America.

WHAT FOOD GOES WITH TANG?

Astronautical meals do not require cooking as we know it here on Earth. The natural-state foods are in the same form as here on the ground; other foods are freeze-dried and vacuum-packed before takeoff and must be rehydrated with hot or cold water through the nozzle in the package.

ABBREVIATIONS:

RSB   Rehydratable spoon bowl (package shape)
RD   Rehydratable drink
IM   Intermediate moisture
D   Dehydrated
T   Thermostabilized
NS   Natural state

MENU ITEMS:
Bacon Squares (8) (IM)
Beef Jerky (IM)
Beef Stew (RSB)
Canadian Bacon and Applesauce (RSB)
Chicken Salad (8 ounces) (T)
Cinnamon Toasted Bread Cubes (4) (D)
Cocoa (RD)
Coffee (RD)
Cranberry-Orange Sauce (RSB)
Creamed Chicken Bites (6) (D)
Fruit Cocktail (RSB)
Grape Punch (RD)
Jellied Fruit Candy (IM)
Lobster Bisque (RSB)
Peach Ambrosia (RSB)
Peanut Cubes (4) (NS)

Pea Soup (RSB)
Pineapple Fruitcake (IM)
Pineapple-Grapefruit Drink (RD)
Pork and Scalloped Potatoes (RSB)
Scrambled Eggs (RSB)
Spiced Fruit Cereal (RSB)
Turkey Bites(4) (D)

◆

ARRGGGH! POISON!

Though sometimes useful in drug or food compositions, in their natural form these are absolute poison:

Aconite
Apple, Balsam
Apple, Bitter
Baneberry
Bloodroot
Bryony, Black
Bryony, European White
Bryony, White
Cabbage Tree
Calabar Bean
Calotropis
Cherry Laurel
Clematis
Coca, Bolivian
Cocculus, Indicus
Dropwort, Hemlock Water
Foxglove
Gelsemium

Hemlock
Hemlock, Water
Hemp, Indian
Ignatius Beans
Ivy, Poison
Laburnum
Laurel, Mountain
Lovage, Water
Mescal Buttons
Nightshade, Black
Nightshade, Deadly
Nux Vomica
Paris, Herb
Poppy, White
Saffron, Meadow
Spurges
Stavesacre
Strophanthus

PARTY PLANNING

Should you want to run for president—or perhaps just dog catcher—you can choose your affiliation from among these current United States minor political parties.

- Alaskan Independence Party
- Aloha Aina Party
- America First Party
- American Heritage Party
- American Independent Party
- American Nazi Party
- American Party
- American Reform Party
- Balanced Party
- Charter Party of Cincinnati, Ohio
- Christian Falangist Party of America
- Communist Party USA
- Conservative Party of New Jersey
- Conservative Party of New York State
- Constitutional Action Party
- Covenant Party (Northern Mariana Islands)
- Family Values Party
- Freedom Socialist Party
- Grassroots Party
- Independence Party of Minnesota
- Independent American Party
- Independent Citizens' Movement (US Virgin Islands)
- Labor Party
- Liberal Party (New York State)
- Liberty Union Party (Vermont)
- Light Party
- Marijuana Party

- Mountain Party (West Virginia)
- Natural Law Party
- New Party
- New Progressive Party of Puerto Rico
- New Union Party
- New York State Right to Life Party
- Peace and Freedom Party
- Personal Choice Party
- Popular Democratic Party of Puerto Rico
- Populist Party (unrelated to earlier so-named parties)
- Progressive Party (Vermont)
- Prohibition Party
- Puerto Rican Independence Party
- Reform Party
- Republican Moderate Party (Alaska)
- Revolutionary Communist Party
- Socialist Action
- Socialist Alternative
- Socialist Equality Party
- Socialist Labor Party
- Socialist Party USA
- Socialist Workers Party
- Southern Party
- Southern Independence Party
- Spartacist League
- The Greens/Green Party USA
- United Citizens Party
- U.S. Pacifist Party
- Vegetarian Party
- We the People Party
- Workers World Party
- Working Families Party
- Workers Party, USA

WATCH AND EARN

The top 100 movies in all-time worldwide box office, according to the International Movie Database (2005):

1.*Titanic* (1997)	$1,835,300,000
2.*The Lord of the Rings: The Return of the King* (2003)	1,129,219,252
3.*Harry Potter and the Sorcerer's Stone* (2001)	968,600,000
4.*Star Wars: Episode I, The Phantom Menace* (1999)	922,379,000
5.*The Lord of the Rings: The Two Towers* (2002)	921,600,000
6.*Jurassic Park* (1993)	919,700,000
7.*Shrek 2* (2004)	880,871,036
8.*Harry Potter and the Chamber of Secrets* (2002)	866,300,000
9.*Finding Nemo* (2003)	865,000,000
10.*The Lord of the Rings: The Fellowship of the Ring* (2001)	860,700,000
11.*Independence Day* (1996)	811,200,000
12.*Spider-Man* (2002)	806,700,000
13.*Star Wars* (1977)	797,900,000
14.*Star Wars: Episode III, Revenge of the Sith* (2005)	790,200,000
15.*Harry Potter and the Prisoner of Azkaban* (2004)	789,458,727
16.*Spider-Man 2* (2004)	783,577,893
17.*The Lion King* (1994)	783,400,000
18.*E.T. the Extra-Terrestrial* (1982)	756,700,000
19.*The Matrix Reloaded* (2003)	735,600,000

20. *Forrest Gump* (1994) — 679,400,000
21. *The Sixth Sense* (1999) — 661,500,000
22. *Pirates of the Caribbean:* — 653,200,000
    The Curse of the Black Pearl (2003)
23. *Star Wars: Episode II,* — 648,200,000
    Attack of the Clones (2002)
24. *The Incredibles* (2004) — 624,037,578
25. *The Lost World: Jurassic Park* (1997) — 614,300,000
26. *The Passion of the Christ* (2004) — 604,370,943
27. *Men in Black* (1997) — 587,200,000
28. *Star Wars: Episode VI,* — 572,700,000
    Return of the Jedi (1983)
29. *Armageddon* (1998) — 554,600,000
30. *Mission: Impossible II* (2000) — 545,300,000
31. *Home Alone* (1990) — 533,800,000
32. *Star Wars: Episode V,* — 533,800,000
    The Empire Strikes Back (1980)
33. *Monsters, Inc.* (2001) — 528,900,000
34. *The Day After Tomorrow* (2004) — 527,939,919
35. *Ghost* (1990) — 517,600,000
36. *Terminator 2: Judgment Day* (1991) — 516,800,000
37. *Aladdin* (1992) — 501,900,000
38. *War of the Worlds* (2005) — 498,300,000
39. *Indiana Jones and the Last Crusade* (1989) — 494,800,000
40. *Twister* (1996) — 494,700,000
41. *Toy Story 2* (1999) — 485,700,000
42. *Troy* (2004) — 481,228,348
43. *Saving Private Ryan* (1998) — 479,300,000
44. *Jaws* (1975) — 470,600,000
45. *Pretty Woman* (1990) — 463,400,000
46. *Bruce Almighty* (2003) — 458,900,000
47. *The Matrix* (1999) — 456,300,000

48. *Gladiator* (2000)	456,200,000
49. *Shrek* (2001)	455,100,000
50. *Mission: Impossible* (1996)	452,500,000
51. *Pearl Harbor* (2001)	450,400,000
52. *Ocean's Eleven* (2001)	444,200,000
53. *The Last Samurai* (2003)	435,400,000
54. *Tarzan* (1999)	435,200,000
55. *Meet the Fockers* (2004)	432,667,575
56. *Men in Black II* (2002)	425,600,000
57. *Die Another Day* (2002)	424,700,000
58. *Dances with Wolves* (1990)	424,200,000
59. *Cast Away* (2000)	424,000,000
60. *The Matrix Revolutions* (2003)	424,000,000
61. *Mrs. Doubtfire* (1993)	423,200,000
62. *The Mummy Returns* (2001)	418,700,000
63. *Terminator 3: Rise of the Machines* (2003)	418,200,000
64. *The Mummy* (1999)	413,300,000
65. *Batman* (1989)	413,200,000
66. *Rain Man* (1988)	412,800,000
67. *The Bodyguard* (1992)	410,900,000
68. *Signs* (2002)	407,900,000
69. *X2* (2003)	406,400,000
70. *Robin Hood: Prince of Thieves* (1991)	390,500,000
71. *Gone with the Wind* (1939)	390,500,000
72. *Raiders of the Lost Ark* (1981)	383,900,000
73. *Grease* (1978)	379,800,000
74. *Beauty and the Beast* (1991)	378,300,000
75. *Ice Age* (2002)	378,300,000
76. *Godzilla* (1998)	375,800,000
77. *What Women Want* (2000)	370,800,000
78. *The Fugitive* (1993)	368,700,000
79. *Hitch* (2005)	367,600,000
80. *True Lies* (1994)	365,200,000

81. *Die Hard: With a Vengeance* (1995)	365,000,000
82. *Notting Hill* (1999)	363,000,000
83. *Jurassic Park III* (2001)	362,900,000
84. *There's Something About Mary* (1998)	360,000,000
85. *Planet of the Apes* (2001)	358,900,000
86. *The Flintstones* (1994)	358,500,000
87. *Toy Story* (1995)	358,100,000
88. *Minority Report* (2002)	358,000,000
89. *A Bug's Life* (1998)	357,900,000
90. *The Exorcist* (1973)	357,500,000
91. *My Big Fat Greek Wedding* (2002)	356,500,000
92. *Basic Instinct* (1992)	352,700,000
93. *The World Is Not Enough* (1999)	352,000,000
94. *Madagascar* (2005)	351,800,000
95. *Golden Eye* (1995)	351,500,000
96. *Ocean's Twelve* (2004)	351,331,634
97. *Back to the Future* (1985)	350,600,000
98. *Se7en* (1995)	350,100,000
99. *Who Framed Roger Rabbit* (1988)	349,200,000
100. *Hannibal* (2001)	349,200,000

◆

RELIGION AND SPORTS—TOGETHER AT LAST!

The House of David was a barnstorming baseball team from Benton Harbor, Michigan. The House of David Players were all white, but they frequently traveled with and played exhibition games against the top teams in the Negro Leagues.

The House of David was a religious community whose founder was a sports enthusiast. The community also had a girls' baseball team.

TEN-HUT!
Military Ranks

NAVY	ARMY
Fleet admiral (wartime use only)	General of the army
Admiral	General
Vice admiral	Lieutenant general
Rear admiral (upper half)	Major general
Rear admiral (lower half)	Brigadier general
Captain	Colonel
Commander	Lieutenant colonel
Lieutenant commander	Major
Lieutenant	Captain
Lieutenant junior grade	First lieutenant
Ensign	Second lieutenant
Master chief petty officer of the navy	Sergeant major of the army
Master chief petty officer	Command sergeant major
Senior chief petty officer	Sergeant major
Chief petty officer	First sergeant
Petty officer first class	Master sergeant
Petty officer second class	Sergeant first class
Petty officer third class	Staff sergeant
Seaman	Sergeant
Seaman apprentice	Corporal
Seaman recruit	Specialist
	Private first class
	Private

MARINE CORPS	AIR FORCE
General	General
Lieutenant general	Lieutenant general
Major general	Major general
Brigadier general	Brigadier general
Colonel	Colonel
Lieutenant colonel	Lieutenant colonel
Major	Major
Captain	Captain
First lieutenant	First Lieutenant
Second lieutenant	Second lieutenant
Sergeant Major or Master gunnery sergeant	Command chief master sergeant
Master Sergeant or First Sergeant	Senior master sergeant
Gunnery sergeant	Master sergeant
Staff sergeant	Technical sergeant
Sergeant	Staff sergeant
Corporal	Senior airman
Lance corporal	Airman first class
Private first class	Airman
Private	Airman basic
Cadet	Cadet
Recruit	Recruit

SO BAD THEY'RE GOOD

There are many common drugs made from poisonous plants. Here are some of the most familiar:

Plant	Drug	Use
Amazonian liana	Curare	Muscle relaxant
Annual mugwort	Artemisinin	Antimalarial
Autumn crocus	Colchichine	Antihumor agent
Coca	Cocaine	Local anaesthetic
Common thyme	Thymol	Antifungal
Deadly nightshade (belladonna)	Atropine	Anticholinergic
Dog button (nux-vomica)	Strychnine	Central nervous stimulant
Ergot fungus	Ergotamine	Analgesic
Foxglove	Digitoxin, digitalis	Cardiotonic
Indian snakeroot	Resperine	Antihypertensive
Meadowsweet	Salicylate	Analgesic
Mexican yam	Diosgenin	Birth control pill
Opium poppy	Codeine, morphine	Analgesic
Pacific yew	Toxol	Antihumor agent
Rosy periwinkle	Vincristine, vinblastine	Antileukemia
Thornapple	Scopolamine	Sedative
Velvet bean	L-dopa	Antiparkinsonian
White willow	Salicylic acid	Topical analgesic
Yellow cinchona	Quinine	Antimalaria, antipyretic

When?

History, at its essence, is the study of important moments in time. But for both fun and insight, it's often better to focus on all the odd and unusual stuff that happens *between* the "important" moments. The following pages chronicle minor flickers in time that impact our daily lives, as well as long-standing traditions or movements that shaped modern history. When did that happen? When will this end? The chronologies and events in the pages ahead show yet again that timing, as they say, is everything.

MOST EXTREME WEATHER IN HISTORY

CHINESE CALENDAR

DAYLIGHT SAVINGS TIME

ANIMAL LIFE EXPECTANCIES

COPYRIGHT AND PUBLIC DOMAIN

FULL MOONS

ELLIS ISLAND'S CHRONOLOGY

FOOD EXPIRATION DATES

BUBONIC PLAGUE

HITCHCOCK'S FILM CAMEOS

CONCENTRATION CAMPS

INAUGURAL LUNCHEONS

A PUBLISHING TIMELINE

A HISTORY OF WORLD'S FAIRS

A YEAR'S WORTH OF WEIRD HOLIDAYS

THE SUMMER OF LOVE

PASSING OF CONSTITUTIONAL AMENDMENTS

GREAT MOMENTS IN PIZZA

SEVEN WONDERS OF THE WORLD

BIORHYTHMS

GREAT INVENTIONS

BABIES' MILESTONES

GAY RIGHTS MILESTONES

PROPER NAMES OF DURATIONS

A HISTORY OF FOOD

COME AND GET IT!
American Cuisine Changes Forever

What do you do with ten railroad cars of turkey? That's exactly what the management of the C. F. Swanson Company wondered back in 1953. They were stuck with too much meat (520,000 pounds of it) after Thanksgiving, and it was riding back and forth across the country in boxcars that would refrigerate only when riding the rails. The mandate to their employees: Find a home for the poultry. Salesman Gerry Thomas did just that, combining the concept of airline table trays and the shape of America's newest fad, the television. In went the frozen traveling turkey, accompanied by cornbread dressing with gravy, sweet potatoes, and buttered peas. The TV dinner was born.

The genius part of the frozen dinner, of course, was that each item in the tray was blanched at a different rate, so that when the dinner was cooked at home, the entire meal was ready at the same time. What Swanson didn't expect was that by calling the product a TV dinner, they would actually begin to change how—and where—American families gathered for their nightly meal. The first TV dinners cost ninety-eight cents, and a year later, Americans bought more than 10 million of them.

◆

HELLO?

The SS *Great Eastern* laid the first successful transatlantic telegraph cable, 1,852 miles in length, between Valentia Island, Ireland, and Newfoundland, between July 13 and September 18, 1866.

WEATHER WATCH

August 1860–July 1861	Greatest twelve-month rainfall, in Cherrapunji, India: 1,042 inches
September 13, 1992	Highest temperature, in El Azizia, Libya: 136°F
July 21, 1983	Lowest temperature, in Vostok, Antarctica: −129°F

A **monsoon** occurs when there is a greater annual temperature variation over a large area of land than over its neighboring ocean surfaces. Its seasonal shift of winds usually blows out of the southwest from April to October, and out of the northeast from October to April.

A **snowstorm** is considered a blizzard when, for a duration of three hours or more, there is extreme cold, winds are over thirty-five miles per hour, and enough snow either falls or blows to reduce visibility to a quarter mile or less.

A **flood** is temporary submersion, partial or complete, of ordinarily dry land by water or mud, typically caused by an overflow of waters, whether inland, tidal, or from any accumulated runoff from any source.

NO GRAY AREA

The Pentagon was built in the early 1940s with twice as many bathrooms as were necessary. At that time, the state of Virginia still had segregation laws requiring separate toilet facilities for blacks and whites.

WHY YOU FORGET WHEN YOU FORGET

Amnesia is a disturbance of the memory of information in long-term memory. Types of amnesia are:

Anterograde amnesia: Inability to remember ongoing events after the incidence of trauma or the onset of the disease that might have caused said amnesia.

Emotional/hysterical amnesia: Memory loss caused when psychologically traumatized; usually a temporary condition.

Lacunar amnesia: Memory loss in which one is unable to remember a specific event.

Korsakoff syndrome: Memory loss caused by chronic alcoholism.

Posthypnotic amnesia: Memory loss sustained when one has been in a hypnotic state; can include inability to recall events that occurred during hypnosis or information stored in long-term memory.

Retrograde amnesia: Inability to remember events that occurred before the incidence of trauma or the onset of the disease that caused the amnesia.

Transient global amnesia: Spontaneous memory loss that can last from minutes to several hours; usually seen when one is middle-aged or elderly.

◆

The worst FLOOD in history occurred in 1931 along the Yangtze River in China; drowning, starvation, and disease caused the deaths of 3.7 million people.

THE YEAR OF YOU

The Chinese lunar calendar is the oldest chronological record in history, dating from 2600 BCE. Each year in the calendar is associated with an animal, in a cycle of twelve. The Chinese believe that of the twelve calendrical animals, the animal that rules the year in which a person is born has a profound influence on that person's personality: "This is the animal that hides in your heart." Beware, though, the beginning of the Chinese year is variable, from mid-January to mid-February.

Animal	Characteristics	Years
Rat	Humorous, charming, honest, yet greedy	1924, 1936, 1948, 1960, 1972, 1984, 1996, 2008
Ox	Tenacious, a leader, yet obstinate	1925, 1937, 1949, 1961, 1973, 1985, 1997, 2009
Tiger	Independent, courageous, warmhearted, yet resistant to authority	1926, 1938, 1950, 1962, 1974, 1986, 1998, 2010
Rabbit	Happy, refined, virtuous, yet superficial	1927, 1939, 1951, 1963, 1975, 1987, 1999, 2011
Dragon	Magical, lucky, artistic, sometimes ferocious	1928, 1940, 1952, 1964, 1976, 1988, 2000, 2012
Snake	Wise, philosophical, calm, can be calculating	1929, 1941, 1953, 1965, 1977, 1989, 2001, 2013

Animal	Characteristics	Years
Horse	Popular, quick-witted, hardworking, can be obstinate	1930, 1942, 1954, 1966, 1978, 1990, 2002, 2014
Sheep	Unassuming, innately intelligent, altruistic, yet misanthropic	1931, 1943, 1955, 1967, 1979, 1991, 2003, 2015
Monkey	Talkative, inquisitive, tricky, and egotistical	1932, 1944, 1956, 1968, 1980, 1992, 2004, 2016
Rooster	Courageous, frank, born organizers, yet blunt	1933, 1945, 1957, 1969, 1981, 1993, 2005, 2017
Dog	Humanitarian, just, empathic, yet defensive	1934, 1946, 1958, 1970, 1982, 1994, 2006, 2018
Boar	Pure, honest, fun, and extravagant	1935, 1947, 1959, 1971, 1983, 1995, 2007, 2019

◆

GOING, GOING, GONE

There are two ways that a person may be declared legally and medically dead: when the heart stops beating, or when the brain stops functioning. The latter is commonly called brain death and is caused by interruption in the flow of blood or oxygen to the brain. At this point, the patient cannot think, feel anything, or breathe on his or her own.

THE BEGINNING OF TIME

The Greenwich meridian, or prime meridian, is also longitude zero and marks the starting point of every time zone in the world. Greenwich mean time is the mean—or average—time it takes the earth to rotate from noon to noon.

Since 1884, Greenwich mean time has also been known as world time, and sets official time around the globe. It is measured from the Greenwich meridian line (yes, there is an actual line on the ground) at the Royal Observatory at Greenwich, England. Hourly time signals from Greenwich Observatory were first broadcast on February 5, 1924.

Although Great Britain was the first nation to adopt a daylight saving plan, in 1908, Greenwich mean time forever remains the same all year round.

Countries and Territories Operating on Daylight Saving Time

NORTHERN HEMISPHERE

Albania	Cuba
Andorra	Cyprus
Armenia	Czech Republic
Austria	Denmark
Azerbaijan	Denmark—Faroe Islands
Bahamas	Denmark—Greenland
Belarus	Egypt
Belgium	Estonia
Bosnia and Herzegovina	Finland
Bulgaria	France
Canada	Gaza Strip
(except Saskatchewan)	Georgia
Croatia	Germany

Greece
Haiti
Hungary
Iran
Iraq
Ireland
Israel
Italy
Jordan
Kyrgyzstan
Latvia
Lebanon
Liechtenstein
Lithuania
Luxembourg
Macedonia
Malta
Mexico
Moldova
Monaco
Mongolia
Montenegro
Netherlands
Nicaragua
Norway
Poland
Portugal—Azores

Portugal—Madeira
Romania
Saint Pierre and Miquelon
San Marino
Serbia
Slovak Republic
Slovenia
Spain
Spain—Canary Islands
Sweden
Switzerland
Syria
Tunisia
Turkey
Turks and Caicos Islands
Ukraine
United Kingdom—Bermuda
United Kingdom—England
United Kingdom—Gibraltar
United Kingdom—Northern
   Ireland
United Kingdom—Scotland
United Kingdom—Wales
United States (except
   Hawaii, Arizona, part of
   Indiana)
Vatican City

SOUTHERN HEMISPHERE

Antarctica—Amundsen-Scott
   (South Pole)

Antarctica—McMurdo
   Station (United States)

Antarctica—Palmer Station
  (United States)
Antarctica—Scott Station
  (New Zealand)
Australia—Lord Howe Island
Australia—New South Wales
Australia—South Australia
Australia—Tasmania
Australia—Victoria
Brazil (part)

Chile
Chile—Easter Island
Namibia
New Zealand
New Zealand—Chatham
  Island
Paraguay
United Kingdom—Falkland
  Islands (Malvinas)
Uruguay

STICKY SOLUTION

It's a story of a dog and his burr. George de Mestral, tired of picking the prickly plant seed sacs from both his pooch and his pants after walking in the Alps, and curious as to their annoying sticking power, took off his trousers and put them under a microscope. Close examination showed that the small hooks on the burrs clung to the tiny loops of fabric. De Mestral found a way to manufacture this "locking tape" (he found that sewing nylon under infrared light formed indestructible hooks), and in 1948 decided to name it Velcro, a combination of the words "velvet" and "crochet."

The MELTING POINT of a solid is the same temperature as the freezing point of a liquid. This changes slightly with the addition of salt; it disrupts the molecular equilibrium, so that melting actually occurs faster than freezing.

MIGHTY WINDS
When It's This Windy, Watch Out!

Small craft advisory: A warning for sustained winds of 20–33 knots

Gale warning: A warning for sustained surface winds, or frequent gusts, in the range of 34–47 knots

Storm warning: A warning for sustained surface winds, or frequent gusts, in the range of 48–63 knots

Tropical storm warning: A warning for sustained surface winds, associated with a tropical cyclone, within the range of 34–63 knots

Hurricane-force wind warning: A warning for sustained winds, or frequent gusts, of 64 knots or greater

Hurricane warning: A warning for sustained surface winds of 64 knots or higher associated with a hurricane and expected in a specified coastal area within 24 hours or less; a hurricane or typhoon warning can remain in effect when dangerously high water or a combination of dangerously high water and exceptionally high waves continues, even though winds may be less than hurricane force.

◆

ON THE BLINK
*Just When Do You Close Your Eyes for a Second
and Miss Something?*

A person generally blinks about nineteen times a minute. This is an average, and may differ if one is working in front of a computer, crying, or winking in a lascivious manner.

LEAVING IT ALL BEHIND?

In case you were thinking of leaving everything to your beloved Fifi, you'd better figure out who's liable to outlive whom. Here are estimated average life expectancies of some of our favorite pets. (And in case you were wondering about human life expectancy, it's presently near 75 years for men, and almost 80 for women.)

DOGS

Airedale terrier	10 to 12 years
Beagle	12 to 15 years
Bloodhound	9 to 11 years
Border terrier	13 to 16 years
Boxer	9 to 11 years
Bull terrier	10 to 16 years
Cairn terrier	12 to 15 years
Chihuahua	15 to 18 years
Chow-chow	9 to 11 years
Cocker spaniel	14 to 16 years
Collie	12 to 15 years
Dachshund	15 to 18 years
Dalmatian	10 to 13 years
Doberman	12 to 15 years
German shepherd	10 to 13 years
Golden retriever	10 to 13 years
Great dane	7 to 10 years
Irish setter	14 to 16 years
Irish terrier	12 to 15 years
Newfoundland	7 to 10 years
Papillion	12 to 15 years
Pomeranian	12 to 15 years
Poodle	15 to 18 years

Schnauzer	14 to 16 years
Scottish terrier	12 to 15 years
St. Bernard	9 to 11 years
Wire fox terrier	12 to 14 years
Yorkshire terrier	12 to 15 years

CATS

Indoor	12 to 18 years
Outdoor	4 to 5 years

BIRDS

African gray parrot	50 to 60 years
Amazon	50 to 60 years
Budgie	10 to 15 years
Canary	7 to 9 years
Cockatiel	15 to 20 years
Cockatoo	up to 70 years
Lovebird	15 to 30 years
Macaw	up to 80 years
Parakeet	8 to 10 years

REPTILES AND AMPHIBIANS

Anole	4 years
Ball python	40 years
Bearded dragon	4 to 10 years
Boa constrictor	20 to 40 years
Chameleon	1 to 3 years
Corn snake	10 years
Frog	4 to 15 years
Iguana	15 years
King snake	20 years
Leopard Gecko	up to 20 years
Toad	20 years

RODENTS

Chinchilla	15 years
Gerbil or hamster	3 years
Guinea pig	5 to 7 years
Mouse	3 to 4 years
Rabbit	5 to 15 years

OTHER

Pot-Bellied Pig	12 to 18 years
Sugar Glider	12 to 14 years
Tarantula	20 to 30 years

◆

THE MAKINGS OF A SAINT

The process of becoming a Catholic saint is very lengthy, often taking decades—or even centuries—to complete. The steps to sainthood:

1. A local bishop investigates the candidate's life and writings for evidence of heroic virtue. The findings are sent on to the Vatican.
2. A panel of theologians and the cardinals of the Congregation for the Causes of Saints evaluate the candidate's life.
3. If the candidate is approved, the pope proclaims the person venerable, which means that he or she is a role model of Catholic virtues.
4. Beatification is the next step and is contingent on proof of a posthumous miracle by the candidate; the candidate is now also allowed to be honored by a particular group or region.
5. The final step for canonization is a second posthumous miracle. With this proof, the candidate in canonized in the Vatican as a saint.

"SIX BELLS AND ALL IS WELL!"

On board a ship, time is counted by the ringing of the ship's bell. The ship's crew takes turns being "on watch" in four-hour shifts* and rings the ship's bell every half hour (starting with one chime at 0030 hours military time, up to eight bells at 0400, then beginning with one bell again at 0430) to alert all keeping watch on different parts of the ship.

Watch	Twenty-four-Hour Clock	Twelve-Hour Clock
Middle	0000–0400	Midnight to 4 A.M.
Morning	0400–0800	4 A.M. to 8 A.M.
Forenoon	0800–1200	8 A.M. to noon
Afternoon	1200–1600	Noon to 4 P.M.
First Dog*	1600–1800	4 P.M. to 6 P.M.
Last Dog*	1800–2000	6 P.M. to 8 P.M.
First	2000–2400	8 P.M. to midnight

*Dog watches are only two hours long, to allow crew members to eat dinner.

Bell Time Sequence	Number of Rings
First half hour	One bell
First hour	Two bells
First hour and a half	Three bells
Second hour	Four bells
Second half-hour and a half	Five bells
Third hour	Six bells
Third hour and a half	Seven bells
Fourth hour	Eight bells

WHEN U.S. WORKS PASS INTO THE PUBLIC DOMAIN

Copyright

The U.S. Patent and Trademark Office defines a copyright as a form of protection provided to the authors of "original works of authorship," including literary, dramatic, musical, artistic, and certain other intellectual works, both published and unpublished.

Public Domain

A public domain work is a creative work that is not protected by copyright and which may be freely used by everyone. The reasons that the work is not protected include:

- The term of copyright for the work has expired.
- The author failed to satisfy statutory formalities to protect the copyright.
- The work is a work of the U.S. government.

Date of Work	Conditions	Term
Created January 1, 1978, or later	When work is fixed in tangible medium of expression	Life plus 70 years[1] (or if work of corporate authorship, the shorter of 95 years from publication, or 120 years from creation[2])
Published before 1923	In public domain	None

Published from 1923 to 1963	When published with notice	28 years plus could be renewed for 47 years, now extended by 20 years for a total renewal of 67 years. If not so renewed, is now in public domain
Published from 1964 to 1977	When published with notice[3]	28 years for first term; now automatic extension of 67 years for second term
Created before January 1, 1978, but not published	January 1, 1978, the effective date of the 1976 act, which eliminated common-law copyright	Life plus 70 years or December 31, 2002, whichever is greater
Created before January 1, 1978, but published between that date and December 31, 2002	January 1, 1978, the effective date of 1976 act, which eliminated common-law copyright	Life plus 70 years, or December 31, 2047, whichever is is greater

1. Term of joint works is measured by life of the longest-lived author.
2. Works for hire and anonymous and pseudonymous works also have this term (17 U.S.C. § 302[c]).
3. Under the 1909 act, works published without notice went into the public domain upon publication. Works published without notice between January 1, 1978, and March 1, 1989, the effective date of the Berne Convention Implementation Act, retained copyright only if efforts to correct the accidental omission of notice were made within five years, such as by placing notice on unsold copies (17 U.S.C. § 405).

"I DO," FOR NOW . . .
A Prenuptial Agreement Is Often Made When:

- You have assets such as a home, stock, or retirement funds
- You own all or part of a business
- You may receive an inheritance
- You have children or grandchildren, or both, from a previous marriage
- You are more financially stable than your betrothed
- You have family who need to be taken care of
- You are pursuing a degree in a potentially profitable profession, such as law or medicine
- You see a huge future for yourself

◆

KIDS TODAY!

Boys and girls truly *are* growing up earlier than ever before. Females enter puberty between ages eight and thirteen, though they may not menstruate for several years after this; boys enter puberty between ages nine and fourteen. This change is attributed to better health and nutrition; for example, in North America the age of menstruation has decreased by three to four months each decade after 1850. Present U.S. statistics for growth increases are:

	Female Growth Ages 10 to 14	*Male Growth Ages 12 to 16*
Weight	15 to 55 pounds	15 to 65 pounds
Height	2 to 10 inches	4 to 12 inches
Age of puberty	8 to 13 years of age	9.5 to 14 years of age

WHEN are the call letters for SportsRadio 620 AM in Syracuse, New York.

WHO SCREAMED FOR ICE CREAM?

Before there was ice cream (as unimaginable as that is), it seems that people were hard at work trying to invent it. History tells us that Alexander the Great (356–323 BCE) delighted in snow and ice covered with honey and nectar. Quite soon thereafter, in about 200 BCE, the Chinese were adding milk and a rice mixture to snow. Next came Emperor Nero Claudius Caesar (37–68 CE), who sent runners into the mountains to bring back snow, then flavored it with fruit and juices. And by the time of King Tang of Shang, China (618–697 CE), the recipe was improving: a little buffalo milk, flour, and camphor was added to the ice. By the mid-seventeenth century, Europeans were enjoying something they called creme ice, and the first ice cream parlor in the United States appeared in New York City in 1776.

Just over one hundred years ago, the population of LAS VEGAS, NEVADA, was thirty people.

SKY LIGHT

Edmond Halley (1656–1742) predicted that the comet the world saw in 1531, 1607, and 1682 would return in 1758. He was right, and the comet was named for him posthumously. His calculations proved that the comet's average orbit is seventy-six years; its last sighting was in 1986, so we can expect the next sky show in 2061.

SHINE ON

Every September, skywatchers observe a special phenomenon in the sky: the harvest moon. It's no ordinary full moon: throughout the year the moon rises on a completely different schedule than the sun, on average about 50 minutes later each night. But near the autumnal equinox, the retardation of the moon's rising has sunset and moonrise nearly coinciding for a few special evenings. Because it comes in handy for farmers working long days to harvest their crops before a frost, the extra dose of lighting afforded by the full moon gave the harvest moon its name. If the sky is unclouded, there is full moonlight from sunset to sunrise.

The Farmers Almanac gave every month's full moon a very colorful, yet descriptive name:

January	Wolf Moon
February	Snow Moon
March	Worm Moon
April	Pink Moon
May	Flower Moon
June	Strawberry Moon
July	Buck Moon
August	Sturgeon Moon
September	Harvest Moon
October	Hunter's Moon
November	Beaver Moon
December	Cold Moon

◆

In the course of one year, the average person has more than 1,460 DREAMS.

274

AFTER SINGING AULD LANG SYNE

...How to say "Happy New Year!" in far-flung places:

Language	Happy New Year!
Afrikaans	Voorspoedige nuwe jaar
Arabic	Kul 'am wa antum bikhair
Basque	Urte Berri on
Bengali	Shuvo noboborsho
Chinese (Mandarin)	Xin nian yu kuai
Czech	Stastny Novy Rok
Dutch	Gelukkig nieuwjaar
Esperanto	Bonan Novjaron
Finnish	Onnellista uutta vuotta
Greek	Eutychismenos o kainourgios chronos
Hawaiian	Hauoli Makahiki hou
Hebrew	Shana Tova
Hungarian	Boldog uj evet
Indonesian (Bahasa)	Selamat Tahun Baru
Italian	Felice Anno Nuovo or Buon anno
Japanese	Akemashite Omedetou Gozaimasu
Korean	Sehe Bokmanee Bateuseyo
Laotian (Hmong)	Nyob Zoo Xyoo Tshiab
Latin	Felix sit annus novus
Nigerian (Hausa)	Barka da sabuwar shekara
Norwegian	Godt Nytt År
Philippines (Tagalog)	Manigong Bagong Taon
Polish	Szczesliwego Nowego Roku
Romanian	La Multi Ani si Un An Nou Fericit
Samoan	Ia manuia le Tausaga Fou
Swahili	Heri za Mwaka Mpya
Swedish	Gott Nytt År
Vietnamese	Chuc mung nam moi
Welsh	Blwyddyn Newydd Dda

PUTTING ON THE FEEDBAG
A Food Timeline: The Discovery of Culinary Delights
We Couldn't Live Without

Date	*Food*	*Where Discovered*
6000 BCE	Wine	Iran
6000 BCE	Cheese	Iraq
4000 BCE	Watermelon	Egypt
3600 BCE	Popcorn	Mexico
2000 BCE	Marshmallows*	Egypt
1500 BCE	Chocolate	Mexico
490 BCE	Pasta	Italy
1300 CE	Guacamole	Mexico
1475 CE	Pork and Beans	Italy
1475 CE	Coffee	Turkey
1592 CE	Pot luck	England
1650 CE	Rum	Caribbean Islands
1754 CE	Swedish meatballs	Sweden
1784 CE	Lollipops	England
1826 CE	Fondue	Switzerland
1927 CE	Pez	Austria
1953 CE	Peeps*	United States

*It took nearly four thousand years for the civilized world to progress from plain marshmallows to Peeps, though to be fair, the Peep is not actually made from marshmallow. Until the mid-nineteenth century, marshmallow candies were indeed made with the sap of the root of the marsh-mallow plant (*althea officinalis*). Since then, gelatin has taken its place.

◆

MAMIE SMITH recorded the first vocal blues song, "Crazy Blues," in 1920.

PLAY BALL!

Talk about opening day! April 20, 1912, was the first day at two of America's longest-lasting ballparks: Fenway Park in Boston, home of the Red Sox, and now-defunct Detroit's Tiger Stadium.

◆

SCRAPING THE SKY

Though only ten stories tall, Chicago's Home Insurance Building, built in 1885 and designed by William LeBaron Jenney (1832–1907), is considered the first true skyscraper. While the marriage of a steel framework combined with masonry gave way to tall buildings like the Home Insurance Building, the load-bearing capacity problem that stood in the way of truly enormous height was only solved when a system was invented in which the metal framework supported both the floors and the walls. Because of his work in this field, it is George A. Fuller (1851–1900), and not Jenney, who is credited as the "inventor" of the skyscraper; in fact, the Flatiron Building in New York City was formerly named the Fuller Building.

◆

HANDS ON

Watches and clocks are often displayed with the hands at either 10:10 or 7:22. Theorists say the former is found mostly in the display of clocks and watches because the symmetry is pleasing to the eye. As to the latter time, which is often seen on displayed antique timepieces, legend has it that it's a tribute to Abraham Lincoln. The time of his death was 7:22 A.M., April 15, 1865.

"GIVE ME YOUR POOR . . ."

An inconsequential dot of land in New York Harbor known as Gull Island was first purchased by the colonist governors of Nieuw Amsterdam (later New York) from Native Americans on July 12, 1630, for "certain cargoes, or parcels of goods." And from 1894 to 1954 it took in over 16 million pieces of precious cargo indeed: the immigrants who came through what is now known as Ellis Island. Today, more than 100 million people count themselves descendants of someone who came through Ellis Island's Registry Room.

1620s	Dutch settlers name the island Oyster Island after finding beds nearby.
1785	The current owner, Samuel Ellis, tries unsuccessfully to sell the property; it is sold to New York after his death in 1807.
1808	The U.S. government buys Ellis Island from New York for $10,000.
1813	Ellis Island becomes known as Fort Gibson and houses huge amounts of ammunition.
1847	The first proposal to make Fort Gibson a stopping place for incoming immigrants is made; the U.S. government opts for Castle Garden instead.
1861	Fort Gibson is dismantled; the land is renamed Ellis Island.
1890	The federal government establishes the Bureau of Immigration; Ellis Island is chosen as the site for a new federal immigration station for the port of New York.

1892	The immigration station on Ellis Island is opened on January 1.
1907	11,747 immigrants pass through Ellis Island in one day—1,025,000 will be the record-breaking number of immigrants who pass through the doors in this year.
1924	The number of immigrants passing through Ellis Island begins to decrease.
1943	Ellis Island is used as a detention center for enemy aliens.
1954	Ellis Island officially closes and is offered for bid.
1965	Ellis Island is classified as a National Monument in conjunction with the Statue of Liberty National Monument.
1990	The Ellis Island Immigration Museum opens on September 10.

◆

THE BIRDS

Though legend has it that the swallows return to San Juan Capistrano every year on March 19, scientists insist that what some perceive as a miracle is less mysterious than meets the eye. The birds do return to build their nests in the old mission every year some time near the vernal equinox, and depart around October 23 for their six-thousand-mile journey south to Goya, Corrientes, Argentina. But, as with aviary migration in general, scientists know little more than the fact that weather and the lack of food are the main factors governing when birds take flight.

GIVE ME YOUR CASH

A Chemical Bank in Rockville Centre, New York, was the first bank to feature an automated teller machine in 1969. It was not exactly a "teller": it dispensed only cash. Today, the average American visits an ATM on an average of five times per month.

◆

How often does LIGHTNING strike? About six thousand times per minute worldwide.

◆

HOORAY FOR HOLLYWOODLAND

In 1923, the Hollywoodland Real Estate Group erected a temporary sign up in the terrain of the Hollywood Hills to advertise a housing development of the same name. It cost $21,000 and was meant to last less than two years. Each letter of the "HOLLYWOODLAND" sign initially stood four stories high, at fifty feet, and was thirty feet along the base; the sign was lit by four thousand lightbulbs, and a nearby cabin housed a maintenance man whose sole job was to change them.

The years went by, and the company has long since gone under, but the locals loved the sign and the movie industry—the whole idea of "Hollywood"—had captured America's imagination. There's still no easy way to reach the sign. It's not on a road, it's fenced in to keep out the curious, and it's fitted with a new high-tech alarm system. It's maintained by the Hollywood Sign Trust, whose trustees are named by the Hollywood Chamber of Commerce and the City of Los Angeles. Today it reads just "HOLLYWOOD," but it means a whole lot more.

WHEN IT'S GOOD, IT'S VERY, VERY GOOD . . .

But when it's bad, it's horrid! Here are guidelines used by many manufacturers for food consumption.

- Dating is not federally required, except for infant formula and baby food.
- States have varying laws. Most states require that milk and other perishables be sold before the expiration date.
- Stores are not legally required to remove other food from their shelves once the expiration date has passed. The dates are only advisory in nature.

A Guide to the System

Sell By:	Don't buy the product after this date. This is what we think of as the expiration date.
Best If Used By:	Flavor or quality is best by this date, but the product is still edible thereafter.
Use By:	The last day that the manufacturer vouches for the product's quality.

NOTHING TO CELEBRATE

U.S. Holidays with the Most Alcohol-Related Traffic Fatalities

1. New Year's Eve
2. New Year's Day
3. Super Bowl Sunday
4. St. Patrick's Day
5. Memorial Day
6. Fourth of July
7. Labor Day Weekend
8. Halloween
9. Thanksgiving
10. Christmas

BUBONIC PLAGUE

The history of the plague is terrifying and its sword was swift. It was said that people "ate lunch with their friends and dinner with their ancestors in paradise."

1330s: Bubonic plague begins in the Gobi Desert of China, killing 35 million Asians. Fleas that make their homes on infected rats are the culprits.

1347: Italian merchants return from trips to the Black Sea, infected with the plague.

1352: By now, 25 percent of Europe's population is wiped out—approximately 25 million people.

1400–1542: The plague makes sporadic appearances in Italy, France, and Turkey.

1665: The plague reappears in London; within a year, 15 percent of the city's population is dead.

1892: The plague spreads from China to India, killing more than 6 million people in India alone.

1900–1909: A small outbreak of plague hits San Francisco. It is finally wiped out with the help of the 1906 earthquake and a 1907 bounty on rats.

1980s: The United States averages eighteen cases of plague per year; with the advent of antibiotics, fatalities are only one in seven.

Today, between one thousand and two thousand cases of plague are reported worldwide, mostly in rural areas, and due to infected rats.

THE FLAG AT HALF-MAST

The United States flag may be flown at half-mast to represent the death of a government official, unless otherwise specified by the president. It should first be hoisted to the peak for an instant and then lowered to the half-staff position; it should be raised to the peak again before it is lowered for the day. The flag is never to be displayed with the union down, except as a signal of dire distress in instances of extreme danger to life or property, for instance, if a crew abandons ship. Half-staff etiquette from the federal law known as the Flag Code calls for:

- Thirty days for a president (current or former)

- Ten days for the vice president, chief justice of the Supreme Court (current or former), Speaker of the House

- From day of death until interment for an associate justice of the Supreme Court, secretary of an executive or military department, former vice president, governor of a state, territory, or possession

- On the day of death and the following day for a member of Congress

- On Memorial Day (last Monday of May in the United States), the flag is traditionally displayed at half-mast from dawn until noon and at full mast for the remainder of daylight hours

- Additionally, the flag should be lighted at all times, either by sunlight between dawn and dusk, or by an appropriate light source after dark.

WHEN "WHEN" MAKES THE DIFFERENCE
A Few Words on "When"

Of all cold words of tongue or pen
The worst are these: "I knew him when—"
—ARTHUR GUITERMAN (1871–1943)

When men drink, then they are rich and successful and win
lawsuits and are happy and help their friends.
Quickly, bring me a beaker of wine, so that I may wet my
mind and say something clever.
—ARISTOPHANES (CA. 450–385 BCE)

We are of course a nation of differences.
These differences don't make us weak. They're the source of
our strength. . . . The question is not when we came here . . .
but why our families came here. And what we did after we
arrived.
—JAMES EARL (JIMMY) CARTER JR. (1924–)

I have been here before,
But when or how I cannot tell;
I know the grass beyond the door,
The sweet keen smell,
The sighing sound, the lights around the shore.
—DANTE GABRIEL ROSSETTI (1828–1882)

First Witch: "When shall we three meet again
In thunder, lightning, or in rain?"
Second Witch: "When the hurlyburly's done,
When the battle's lost and won."
—WILLIAM SHAKESPEARE (1564–1616), MACBETH

What never has been, yet may have its when;
The thing which has been, never is again.
—James Thomson (1834–1882)

Where have all the flowers gone?
The girls have picked them, every one.
Oh, when will they ever learn?
—Peter (Pete) Seeger (1919–)

HEAVY-TECH

Adam Osbourne, an ex-publisher turned computer geek, started the short-lived Osbourne Computers and in 1981 produced the Osbourne 1, considered by many to be the first laptop computer. It had a five-inch screen, a modem port, and two floppy drives, weighed in at twenty-four pounds, and cost $1,795.

ALIEN INVASION

Nuremberg, Germany, 1561: The *Nuremberg Gazette* reported a variety of UFOs—a "frightful spectacle," noted observers. Though not, perhaps, what we today think of as an alien invasion, there were reports of a sky filled with "cylindrical shapes from which emerged black, red, orange and blue-white spheres that darted about," and a "black, spear-like object" appeared.

One hundred years ago, 95 percent of all BIRTHS in the United States took place at home.

ONE LEG AT A TIME

In 1872, tailor Jacob Davis contacted dry-goods entrepreneur Levi Strauss about producing a sturdy pair of pants, using metal rivets to hold them together. The two men received a patent for an "Improvement in Fastening Pocket-Openings," put their heads together, and the "waist overall," or modern-day jeans as we know them, was born.

Just over one hundred years ago, in 1904, the five leading CAUSES OF DEATH in the United States were:

1. Pneumonia and influenza
2. Tuberculosis
3. Diarrhea
4. Heart disease
5. Stroke

NUMBER, PLEASE, MR. OSCAR?

Since 1949, starting with the somewhat arbitrary number 501, each Oscar statuette has borne a serial number behind its heels.

DAY IS DONE

The bugle call "Taps" was written by Brigadier General Daniel Butterfield in 1862, and though it is played during funerals and flag ceremonies as well, it is used in the military at the end of every day to signal "lights out," replacing Tatoo, the French bugle call. "Taps" was immediately adopted by both Union and Confederate forces.

In 1851 the first issue of *The New York Times* was published as the NEW YORK DAILY TIMES.

♦

THE FABRIC OF OUR LIVES

In the fourteenth century, hand painting on cotton cloth, both freehand and stencil, became popular in India. Europeans began importing this fabric, mostly an early chintz, because it laundered easily, was lightweight, and featured bright, cheerful colors. Soon both the design and the variety of new fabrics coming out of India reflected European tastes. Countries such as England and France made it illegal to import these Indian goods and began manufacturing their own textiles, cornering the market for both clothing and furniture. By the 1790s, England, France, Germany, Switzerland, and the Netherlands all had busy textile mills of their own.

GOOD EV-EN-INGS

For half a century, Alfred Hitchcock peppered his films with brief and comical cameo appearances: thirty-seven films in all, forty cameos. Hats and musical instruments were often part of his guise, but whether with a familiar prop or skulking in the background, catching a glimpse of the famous director is one of the most enjoyable aspects of many Hitchcock films. Only once did he have a cameo on his TV show, *Alfred Hitchcock Presents*, aside from his onstage introductions. In an episode titled "Dip in the Pool," he is pictured on the cover of a magazine. Following, a list of the forty Hitchcock cameos (some have two) in these thirty-seven films:

Film	Year	Prop
The Lodger	1927	(1) none
		(2) gray cap
Easy Virtue	1927	cane
Blackmail	1929	reading book with a small boy
Murder!	1930	with a female companion
The 39 Steps	1935	tossing litter
Young and Innocent	1937	camera
The Lady Vanishes	1938	cigarette
Foreign Correspondent	1940	hotel
Rebecca	1940	none
Mr. & Mrs. Smith	1941	none
Suspicion	1941	none
Saboteur	1942	none
Shadow of a Doubt	1943	playing cards
Lifeboat	1944	none
Spellbound	1945	violin
Notorious	1946	champagne
The Paradine Case	1947	cello
Rope	1948	(1) none
		(2) none
Under Capricorn	1949	(1) none
		(2) none

Cameo	Minutes into Film
newsroom desk	3
in crowd at arrest	92
walking past tennis court	15
subway car	11
outside murder scene	60
outside theater	7
photographer at courthouse	15
Victoria Station platform	90
outside Johnny Jones' newspaper	11
walking past phone booth	123
outside Smiths' apartment building	41
at village mailbox	45
at newsstand, behind saboteur's car	60
on train to Santa Rosa	17
in newspaper ad in bottom of lifeboat	25
Empire State Building elevator	36
Alex Sebastian's party	64
Cumberland Station train	36
man crossing street	during opening credits
neon silhouette	52
at Sydney parade	3
steps of government house	14

Film	Year	Prop
Stage Fright	1950	none
Strangers on a Train	1951	bass fiddle
I Confess	1953	none
Rear Window	1954	none
Dial M for Murder	1954	none
To Catch a Thief	1955	none
The Trouble with Harry	1955	none
The Man Who Knew Too Much	1956	none
The Wrong Man	1956	none
Vertigo	1958	horn case
North by Northwest	1959	none
Psycho	1960	cowboy hat
The Birds	1963	white terriers
Marnie	1964	none
Torn Curtain	1966	baby on lap
Topaz	1969	in wheelchair
Frenzy	1972	bowler hat
Family Plot	1976	none

Cameo	Minutes into Film
staring at Eve Gill in maid's disguise on street	38
boarding a train	10
top of steps in Quebec	1
repairing clock in musician's apartment	25
class-reunion picture taken off wall	13
sitting near John Robie on bus	10
walking past outdoor art exhibition	21
Morroccan marketplace just before murder	25
onscreen prologue (only onscreen cameo as himself)	film opening
walking across shipyard	10
just missing bus	2
outside Marion Crane's realty office	7
leaving pet shop	2
coming out of hotel room	5
sitting in hotel lobby	8
LaGuardia Airport	28
in crowd at political rally	3
in silhouette outside office	40

WORLD'S OLDEST

When things in our world are *so* old, they're *olde*. A few firsts throughout time . . .

World's Oldest City
Damascus, in Syria, is the world's oldest continuously inhabited city, having been lived in since pre-second millennium BCE.

World's Oldest Backgammon Set
The oldest backgammon board in the world, along with sixty pieces, was unearthed beneath the rubble of the five-thousand-year-old Burnt City in Iran. The intricate board features an engraved serpent coiling around itself twenty times, thus producing twenty slots for game play.

World's Oldest Church
The ruins of the world's most ancient Christian church are from about 350 in Jordan, a few hundred yards from the Red Sea in the Christian community of Ayla, a Roman city damaged by an earthquake.

Oldest City in the United States
Since 1513 St. Augustine, Florida, has been the oldest continuously settled city in the United States. The Spanish explorer Juan Ponce de León, in search of the legendary Fountain of Youth, landed there and took possession of the territory for Spain.

World's Oldest Rodeo
Since July 4, 1888, in Prescott, Arizona, "cowboy tournaments" have had folks saddling up, though the word "rodeo" wasn't actually used until 1916.

World's Oldest Mouse

Yoda, the world's oldest mouse, lived an amazing four years and twelve days, or roughly 136 human years. A dwarf mouse, Yoda's reported that he lived in quiet seclusion with his cage mate, Prin Leia.

World's Oldest Volcanic Rock

Rocks found by geologists in Porpoise Cove on the shores of Canada's Hudson Bay are estimated to be 3.825 billion years old (pl or minus 16 million years). The earth is thought to be 4.6 billion ye old.

World's Oldest Lake

Lake Baikal, or "Sacred Sea," located in southeastern Siberia, is 25–30 million years old, and holds more than 20 percent of the world's fresh water.

World's Oldest Wine Jar

The world's earliest known ancient wine jar dates from ca. 5400–50 BCE and was discovered in 1968 in the "kitchen" of a mud-brick Neolithic building in Hajji Firuz Tepe, Iran.

World's Oldest Insect

The fossilized jaw remains found of the oldest known living insect belong to the winged Rhyniognatha hirsti, which lived between 40€ and 436 million years ago. A professor rediscovered it in a London museum drawer in 2004, where it had been lying, unidentified, sin 1928.

World's Oldest Pet Cat

The remains of a human and a cat were found buried together in 2004 in a 9,500-year-old grave on Cyprus, leading scientists to belie they found the world's oldest known pet cat.

World's Oldest Ice
The oldest ice ever found was taken from a deep hole in Antarctica in 2005; it will help scientists determine the history of the world's climate. The ice dates back 900,000 years, to when modern mammals ruled the earth, but hominids had not yet evolved beyond the *Homo erectus* stage.

World's Oldest Tree
Methuselah, a 4,768-year-old bristlecone pine discovered in 1957, lives in a secret location in the Schulman Grove in California's Inyo National Forest.

World's Oldest Gorilla
Rudy, a lowland gorilla born in 1956 and captured as a baby in Africa, resided in the Erie, Pennsylvania, zoo until March 9, 2005, when he passed away at the age of forty-nine.

World's Oldest Pile of Vomit
Paleontologists discovered mounds of fossilized Jurassic throw-up from ichthyosaurs that swam in the waters of England 160 million years ago. It is believed that these marine reptiles ate shellfish—just as sperm whales do—and then vomited the indigestible shells. The evidence of the dinosaurs' postprandial discomfort is extremely important for scientists' research on their eating habits.

World's Oldest Grapevine
Maribor, Slovenia's second-largest city, is home to an annual grape harvest taken from a four-hundred-year-old grapevine. The grapes are still ripened into wine, bottled in small bottles, and used as special official presents.

World's Oldest Kitchen
In 2003, stone tools between 2.5 million and 2.6 million years

old were discovered in Gona, Ethiopia, in the Awash Valley. The remains from simple knives, and the proximity to a river, plus animals bones found nearby, have scientists believing this to be the site of the oldest known kitchen.

World's Oldest Camp
In 1885, the YMCA opened Camp Dudley, in Westport, New York, making it the oldest continuously running YMCA summer camp for boys.

World's Oldest Wheel
A wooden wheel uncovered in marshes outside of Ljubljana, Slovenia, is between 5,100 and 5,350 years old.

World's Oldest Rice
Archaeologists discovered in Korea a handful of burnt grains of domesticated rice more than 15,000 years old. This find challenges the once-accepted fact that rice cultivation originated in China 12,000 years ago.

World's Oldest Flower
Researchers believe they have discovered fossil evidence of a 142-million-year-old flower. This spindly twig with peapod-shaped fruit and a woody stem was found in the limestone and volcanic ash layers of a rock formation in China.

PUZZLING . . .

European mapmakers were the originators of jigsaw puzzles in the 1760s, pasting maps onto wood and cutting them into small pieces.

THEY'RE HERE . . .

On June 24, 1947, pilot Kenneth Arnold noticed nine disk-shaped objects not far from Mount Rainier in Washington State when he was searching for a lost plane. This is the first reported UFO sighting in the United States, and a journalist's mistake in citing Arnold's description of the event brought about the term "flying saucers." "I said that they flew like they take a saucer and throw it across the water," Arnold later reported to veteran newsman Edward R. Murrow. "Most of the newspapers misunderstood and misquoted that. . . . They said that I said that they were saucer-like; I said that they flew in a saucer-like fashion." No wonder confusion still reigns in the realm of extraterrestrials.

HOW LONG HAS THIS BEEN GOING ON?

An eon is a division of time so long it's, well, timeless. Various definitions include:

the longest unit of geological time, next in order of
magnitude above an era
an immeasurably long period of time
a very long period of time
two or more eras

---◆---

HINDUISM is the world's oldest continuously practiced religion.

DISCO MADNESS

Though many tunes and their new sound paved the way for disco—"The Theme from Shaft" and Love Unlimited's "Love Theme," both from 1971, are often cited—most musical experts agree that 1972's "Soul Makossa" by Manu Dibango is the first real disco song.

By 1974, mixmaster Tom Moulton made two huge contributions to disco. For Gloria Gaynor's first album, "Never Can Say Goodbye," Moulton mixed a medley of three songs into a dance mix that lasted the whole length of one album side. The next year, Moulton and recording engineer José Rodriguez took that one step further, by making the first twelve-inch single as a promotional item for nightclub DJs. By 1976, twelve-inch singles were released for public consumption, and a new kind of disco inferno took over. Yet by the end of the decade, mirror balls were coming down, as the disco era was on its way out.

◆

An EARTHQUAKE on December 16, 1811, in the Mississippi Valley near New Madrid, Missouri, caused parts of the Mississippi River to actually flow backward. It was so severe that it's said the quake made church bells ring in Boston; on the Mississippi, boats were found forty miles upstream of where they had been moored, as the river rushed to fill a depression nearly one hundred miles long from the earthquake. In fact, Arkansas's St. Francis Lake was formed by the New Madrid earthquake.

Recent activity along the New Madrid fault has been much less dramatic. A quake on September 17, 1997, was measured at a magnitude of 3.8 on the Richter scale.

A TIME OF HORROR

"Arbeit Macht Frei" ("Work Makes You Free") was the appalling motto of the Nazi concentration camps that were spread throughout Europe; astonishingly, many existed from the 1930s until their liberation at the end of World War II.

AUSCHWITZ-BIRKENAU (1940–1945)
Poland
Annihilation camp; forced-labor camp
2.1 million–2.5 million killed
Liberated by the Soviet Union
Camp preserved

BELZEC (1942–1943)
Poland
Annihilation camp
500,000–600,000 killed
Liquidated by Germany
Monument

BERGEN-BELSEN (1943–1945)
Germany
Holding center
50,000 killed
Liberated by the United Kingdom
Graveyard

BUCHENWALD (1937–1945)
Germany
Forced-labor camp
56,000 killed
Liberated by the United States
Camp preserved; museum

CHELMNO (1943–1945)
Poland
Annihilation camp
150,000–300,000 killed
Liquidated by Germany
Monument

DACHAU (1933–1945)
Germany
Forced-labor camp
32,000 killed
Liberated by the United States
Camp preserved; museum

DORA/MITTELBAU (1943–1945)
Germany
Forced-labor camp
20,000 killed
Liberated by the United States
Memorial Sculpture Plaza

FLOSSENBÜRG (1938–1945)
Germany
Forced-labor camp
73,000 killed
Liberated by the United States
Buildings; monument

GROSS-ROSEN (1940–1945)
Poland
Forced-labor camp
40,000 killed
Liberated by the Soviet Union
Camp preserved; museum

Janowska (1941–1943)
Ukraine
Forced-labor camp; annihilation camp
40,000 killed
Liquidated by Germany
Not maintained

Kaiserwald (1943–1944)
Latvia
Forced-labor camp
10,000 killed
Liquidated by Germany
Not maintained

Majdanek (1941–1944)
Poland
Annihilation camp
360,000 killed
Liberated by the Soviet Union
Camp preserved; monument

Mauthausen (1938–1945)
Austria
Forced-labor camp
150,000 killed
Liberated by the United States
Buildings; monument

Natzweiler/Struthof (1941–1944)
France
Forced-labor camp
10,000 killed
Liquidated by Germany
Camp preserved

NEUENGAMME (1940–1945)
Germany
Forced-labor camp
56,000 killed
Liberated by the United Kingdom
Used as prison; monument

ORANIENBURG (1930–1935)
Germany
Holding center
105,000 killed
Liquidated by Germany
Not maintained

PLASZOW (1942–1945)
Poland
Forced-labor camp
8,000 killed
Liquidated by Germany
Not maintained

RAVENSBRÜCK (1939–1945)
Germany
Forced-labor camp
92,000 killed
Liberated by the Soviet Union
Buildings; monument

SACHSENHAUSEN (1936–1945)
Germany
Forced-labor camp
30,000–35,000 killed
Liberated by the Soviet Union
Museum; buildings

SOBIBOR (1942–1943)
Poland
Annihilation camp
250,000 killed
Liquidated by Germany
Monument

STUTTHOF (1939–1945)
Poland
Forced-labor camp
85,000 killed
Liberated by the Soviet Union
Buildings; museum

TEREZIN (THERESIENSTADT) (1941–1945)
Czech Republic
Holding center transit ghetto
35,000 killed
Liberated by the Soviet Union
Buildings; monument

TREBLINKA (1942–1943)
Poland
Annihilation camp
265,000 killed
Liquidated by Germany
Monument

WESTERBORK (1939–1945)
Netherlands
Transit camp
Unknown number of deaths
Liberated by Canada
Monument

OLYMPIAN FEATS

In 1936, Jesse Owens ruined Adolf Hitler's grand design to make the Berlin Olympics an Aryan showcase when the African American brought home four gold medals in the 100- and 200-meter dashes, the long jump, and the 4-by-100 relay team. But he was not the first black man to capture an Olympic medal for the United States: In 1904, George Coleman Poage won two bronzes in the St. Louis Olympics for the 220- and 440-yard hurdles.

"THE DEVIL'S ROPE"

By 400 CE, smooth wire was being made, but not until the nineteenth century was it manufactured and available in enough quantity for wide use. On its heels came the invention of barbed wire—and the agricultural future of the United States changed completely. By 1873, Joseph F. Glidden (1813–1906) had applied for a patent for barbed wire, the simple barrier that was perhaps the single most important invention in ranching history. The only drawback? It took some time for livestock to get used to the new fences, and the results were bloody. Protesting religious groups began to call it "The Devil's Rope."

SING!

In 1927, *Show Boat* made its debut as the first Broadway musical play. It was an adaptation of the popular Edna Ferber novel.

INAUGURAL LUNCHEON

It should be the meal of a lifetime for a new president. But apparently, even the leader of the free world can't always get what he wants . . .

Franklin Delano Roosevelt knew exactly what he wanted for his 1945 inauguration luncheon, and on the face of it, the request seemed quite modest: The commander in chief desired chicken à la king. First Lady Eleanor intervened, however, with unfortunate results. Between her lack of culinary taste, and a parsimonious housekeeper, the menu for the two thousand guests looked like this:

Chicken Salad
Rolls, unbuttered
Pound Cake, unfrosted
Coffee

Cut to 2001 and the inaugural luncheon for President George W. Bush—and a Texas-sized menu:

Lobster Pie—Morsels of lobster sautéed with fresh herbs and winter vegetables in a rich cream sauce; served in a flaky pastry crust, topped with fresh lobster, garnished with lemon leaves and lemon wedges

Grenadine of Beef Supreme—Petit filets of prime beef tenderloin individually tied, marinated in garlic and fresh herbs, interlayered with well-seasoned and sautéed vegetables, topped with a turned mushroom cap, and presented over steamed green beans with Madeira demiglace

Chartreuse of Vegetables—A puff pastry ring filled with chestnuts, Brussels sprouts, and parisienne vegetables

304

including carrots, squash, broccoli stems, zucchini, and yellow and red tomatoes

Puree of Small Roots—Celery root, turnips, and parsnips

Sour Cream Drop Biscuits—Served warm

Toffee Pudding—A moist, dense nutmeat pudding loaf served with caramel sauce, surrounded with navel and blood orange slices topped with crystallized ginger and sugared pecans and presented warm with very rich vanilla bean ice cream scoops

Demitasse Cafe and Tea

Chocolate-dipped ginger, candied fruit rinds, fresh strawberries, macaroons, and truffles

◆

THAR SHE BLOWS!

On January 3, 1841, Herman Melville embarked on a whaling voyage from Fairhaven, Massachusetts, aboard the whaling ship *Acushnet*. He jumped ship after eighteen months, finding that the sea was less to his liking than it was to his fictional monomaniac, Captain Ahab. The experience served him well a decade later, however, when he sat down to write his masterpiece, *Moby-Dick*. Incredibly, that literary voyage took him but a year.

UNDER THE KNIFE

In 1787, Austria became the first country to abolish capital punishment. However, it was reinstituted for a time during the reign of Hitler; between 1938 and 1945, 1,377 men and women were guillotined for opposing the Nazis and for treason.

A BRIEF PUBLISHING TIMELINE

The alphabet, the invention of paper, the printing press, the
first potboiler: the written word is unique to the human race—
it is what defines us. Herewith just a few of the many
moments when the written word has changed the world.

1700 BCE: Phoenicians develop the first surviving alphabet,
which consisted of twenty-two consonants and no vowels.

1270 BCE: The first general encyclopedia is written in Syria.

530 BCE: Pisistratus, son of Hippocrates, establishes the first
public library in Athens.

131 BCE: *Acta Diurna (Daily Events)*, a daily gazette comparable
to the modern newspaper. First created for general reading,
then published regularly under Julius Caesar in 59 BCE.

100–200 CE: Lucius Apuleius writes "Cupid and Psyche" and
includes it in *The Golden Ass*; scholars consider this to be the
first literary fairy tale, similar to *Beauty and the Beast*.

105 CE: Ts'ai Lun, an official of the Chinese imperial court,
invents paper—and forever changes the way we learn.

868: The earliest dated printed book is a Chinese translation
of the Diamond Sutra and is printed with plates made from
carved wood blocks.

1007: A Japanese noblewoman, Murasaki Shikibu, writes the
world's first full novel, *The Tale of Genji*.

1450: Johannes Gutenberg invents the first mechanical
printing press, an idea he derived from the olive press.

1452: Gutenberg conceives the idea for a press with movable type, which is individual letters cast on independent metal bodies; this affords easy assembly into blocks for printing, and the type can be constantly rearranged for further usage.

1611: In England, the King's Printer, Christopher Barker, prints the Authorized Version of the King James Bible, a uniform translation in the vernacular for the people, written by the greatest scholars of the day.

1675: John Foster, America's first engraver, sets up the first U.S. press in Boston, Massachusetts.

1709: The Statute of Anne is the first copyright act in the world and introduced the concept of an author being the owner of copyright, and the principle of a fixed term of protection for published works.

1714: Englishman Henry Mill receives the first patent for a typewriter, though his invention won't become popularized for more than a century.

1731: The first American circulating library opens in Philadelphia.

1754: Benjamin Franklin creates the first cartoon published in an American newspaper: a severed snake, representing the states, with the legend "Join, or Die."

1824: Louis Braille creates a method of writing and printing for the blind.

1886: The linotype typesetting machine is patented by Ottmar Mergenthaler; characters can now be cast in metal type as a complete line, rather than as individual characters.

1886: The Berne Convention devises an agreement of mutual recognition among nations, which maintains that a book that is copyrighted in any signatory state is also copyrighted in all the other signatory states under exactly the same conditions as a book first published in that country.

1896: The first comic book, Richard Fenton Outcalt's *The Yellow Kid,* appears in America.

1922: James Joyce's *Ulysses* is published in Paris and is immediately banned in both the United States and England until the 1930s. Though the first edition contained more than two thousand errors, it remains the most accurate edition ever published.

1966: Jacqueline Susann's *Valley of the Dolls* is published, and the steamy blockbuster is born.

2000: Author Stephen King publishes *Riding the Bullet,* the first electronic book to appear exclusively on the Internet. Though it never appeared in printed book form, it was released as a movie in 2004.

FOOD ON THE MOVE

The Pig Stand was the first drive-in restaurant and came on the scene before most Americans even owned cars; it eventually became a local fast-food chain located in Dallas, Texas. Back in 1921, it was a hopping spot—car-hopping, that is. Curb service was available in the parking lot, food production was speedy, and the Pig Stand even had a theme: barbecue, of course.

A fetus develops FINGERPRINTS at twenty-four weeks.

THE LAST NAIL

A great event in transportation occurred at Promontory, Utah, on May 10, 1869, as the Union Pacific tracks joined those of the Central Pacific Railroad, and "The Golden Spike"—the last spike, which would connect the two railroads—was driven. The excitement was so dizzying and the crowd so huge that hardly anyone could see the spike actually being hammered; but a single word went out from the site via Morse code to the rest of the world: "Done."

Then, in 1942, an event few remember: The old rails over the 123-mile Promontory Summit Line were derailed and salvaged for the war effort, and a ceremony marking the "Undriving of the Golden Spike" took place. Since then, Congress has established a Golden Spike National Historic Park. The original Golden Spike, however, is not at the park, but on display at Stanford University, not such an odd destination when one recalls that it was Governor Leland Stanford of California who helped drive the original.

A sentimental aside: Mary Ipsen was the only person in that crowd in 1942 who attended both the Driving and the Undriving of the Spike. She was a waitress on a mess car for the Promontory Mountain crew in May 1869.

TOP FOOD IN TOWN

Gearing up as an icon for the 1962 World's Fair, the Space Needle in Seattle, Washington, opened the previous year with the first revolving restaurant in the United States. It twirled 260 seats in a complete circle in one hour; the needle itself is a six-hundred-foot-high steel and glass tower. The popular Sky City restaurant still twirls and serves fine food in 360-degree splendor today.

A HISTORY OF WORLD'S FAIRS

Year	Venue	Name	Theme
1851	London	Great Exhibition of the Works of Industry of All Nations	
1853	New York		
1853	Dublin, Ireland		
1855	Paris	Exposition Universelle	
1862	London		
1867	Paris	Exposition Universelle	
1873	Vienna, Austria	Weltausstellung	
1874	Dublin, Ireland		
1876	Philadelphia	Centennial Exhibition	
1878	Paris	Exposition Universelle	
1884	New Orleans, Louisiana		
1885	Antwerp, Belgium		
1886	London		
1888	Melbourne, Australia		
1888	Glasgow, Scotland		
1889	Paris	Exposition Universelle	

Year	Venue	Name	Theme
1893	Chicago	World's Columbian Exhibition	
1894	San Francisco		
1895	Atlanta, Georgia		
1897	Brussels, Belgium		
1900	Paris	Exposition Universelle	
1901	Buffalo, New York	Pan-American Exposition	
1904	Saint Louis, Missouri	Louisiana Purchase Exposition	
1905	Liège, Belgium	Exposition Universelle et Internationale	
1906	Milan, Italy		
1907	Dublin, Ireland Hampton Roads, Virginia		
1909	Seattle, Washington		
1910	Brussels, Belgium		
1911	Turin, Italy		
1913	Ghent, Belgium		
1915	San Francisco	Panama-Pacific International Exposition	
1916	San Diego, California		

Year	Venue	Name	Theme
1922	Rio de Janiero, Brazil		
1924	Wembley, United Kingdom		
1925	Paris		
1926	Philadelphia		
1929	Barcelona, Spain		
1930	Seville, Spain		
1930	Antwerp, Belgium		
1930	Liège, Belgium		
1931	Paris		
1933	Chicago	Century of Progress International Exposition	
1935	Brussels, Belgium		
1937	Paris	Exposition Internationale	
1939	New York	New York World's Fair	The World of Tomorrow
1940	San Francisco	Golden Gate International Exposition	
1958	Brussels, Belgium	Expo '58	

Year	Venue	Name	Theme
1962	Seattle, Washington	Century 21 Exposition	Science
1964	New York	New York World's Fair	Peace Through Understanding
1967	Montreal, Canada	Expo '67	
1968	San Antonio, Texas	Hemisfair '68	The Confluence of Civilizations in the Americas
1970	Osaka, Japan	Expo '70	Progress and Harmony for Mankind
1974	Spokane, Washington	Expo '74	Celebrating a Fresh, New Environment
1975	Okinawa, Japan	Expo '75	The Sea We Would Like to See
1982	Knoxville, Tennessee	World's Fair	Energy Turns the World
1984	New Orleans, Louisiana	Louisiana World Exposition	The World of Rivers—Fresh Water as a Source of Life

Year	Venue	Name	Theme
1985	Tsukuba, Japan		Dwellings and Surroundings: Science and Technology for Man at Home
1986	Vancouver, Canada	World in Motion—World in Touch	
1988	Brisbane, Australia	World Expo '88	Leisure in the Age of Technology
1992	Seville, Spain	Expo '92	The Era of Discovery
1992	Genoa, Italy	Genoa Expo '92	Ships and the Sea
1993	Taejon, South Korea	Expo '93	The Challenges of a New Road to Development
1998	Lisbon, Portugal	Expo '98	The Oceans, a Heritage for the Future
2000	Hanover, Germany	Expo 2000	Man, Nature, and Technology

◆

The SHORTEST WAR in history was in 1896, when
Zanzibar took on England for forty-five minutes . . . and lost.

WHO'S CALLING?

In 1878, the world's first telephone book was issued by the New Haven, Connecticut, Telephone Company and contained the names of the company's fifty subscribers.

CUCKOO: EVERY HOUR ON THE HOUR

Around 1740, a certain German clock maker discovered how to echo the cuckoo bird's sound with tiny twin bellows which sent air through small pipes; he decided to make this mellifluous tweet the sound his wall clocks would feature instead of chimes, like everyone else's. As it became a sort of art form, woodworkers began to add tiny details—cut gears, painting, carved decorations and scenery—that made every clock different. After the harsh indoor winters spent carving, these clockmakers put their wares in sacks, put the sacks on their backs, and took them down from the Alps to sell in the villages. They were called *ührschleppers*.

A YEAR OF WEIRD HOLIDAYS

When you're looking for an excuse to celebrate, you can count on somebody to pull through. Whether it's the United Nations or a presidential proclamation, a day sponsored by a corporation or registered by an individual with the Department of Commerce (and a few that are just good-hearted nonsense), every day's a holiday, as the following pages prove.

January

1	2	3	4	5	6	7
Z Day (Go first in line if your last name begins with Z)	Run It Up the Flagpole Day	Drinking Straw Day	Humiliation Day	Organize Your Home Day	Bean Day	Old Rock Day (Find one in your yard)
8	9	10	11	12	13	14
National Man Watcher's Day	Play God Day	Peculiar People Day (Say hello to one)	Rhubarb Day	National Pharmacist Day	Blame Someone Else Day	Dress Up Your Pet Day
15	16	17	18	19	20	21
Get to Know Your Customers Day	National Nothing Day	Judgment Day	Winnie-the-Pooh Day	Popcorn Day	Cheese Day	Squirrel Appreciation Day
22	23	24	25	26	27	28
National Blonde Brownie Day	Handwriting Day (Practice a lost art)	Eskimo Pie Patent Day	Broken Hearts Day	Bubble Wrap Appreciation Day	Thomas Crapper Day	Compliment Day
29	30	31				
National Puzzle Day	Fun at Work Day	Child Labor Day				

February

1	2	3	4	5	6	7
Robinson Crusoe Day	Groundhog Day	Dump Your Significant Jerk Day	Thank a Mailman Day	Weatherman's Day	Lame Duck Day	Charles Dickens Day
8	9	10	11	12	13	14
Kite Flying Day	Toothache Day	Umbrella Day	Satisfied Staying Single Day	Lost Penny Day	Get a Different Name Day	Ferris Wheel Day
15	16	17	18	19	20	21
Susan B. Anthony Day	Do a Grouch a Favor Day	My Way Day	National Battery Day	Chocolate Mint Day	Ember Tart Day	Love Your Pet Day
22	23	24	25	26	27	28
Be Humble Day	International Dog Biscuit Appreciation Day	Pancake Day	Samuel Colt's Pistol Patent Day	Pistachio Day	International Polar Bear Day	Floral Design Day
29						
Leap Day (every four years)						

March

1	2	3	4	5	6	7
Pig Day	Old Stuff Day	Stop the BS Day	Holy Experiment Day (With thanks to William Penn)	Multiple Personality Day (Try one on)	Nothing Day	Babysitters Safety Day
8	9	10	11	12	13	14
Be Nasty Day	Panic Day (Don't)	Barbie's Birthday	Johnny Appleseed Day	Middle Name Pride Day	Jewel Day	Potato Chip Day
15	16	17	18	19	20	21
Act Happy Day	Lips Appreciation Day	Submarine Day	Forgive Mom and Dad Day	Poultry Day	Festival of ET Abduction Day	Memory Day (Don't forget!)
22	23	24	25	26	27	28
Goof Off Day	Chip and Dip Day	Chocolate Covered Raisin Day	Waffle and Pecan Day	Make Your Own Holiday Day	National "Joe" Day	Something on a Stick Day
29	30	31				
Festival of Smoke and Mirrors Day	I Am in Control Day	National Clams on the Half Shell Day				

April

1	2	3	4	5	6	7
International Tatting Day	National Peanut Butter and Jelly Day	Tweed Day	Check your Batteries Day	National Workplace Napping Day	Sorry Charlie Day (For all who've been rejected . . . and survived!)	No Housework Day
8	9	10	11	12	13	14
Vote Lawyers Out of Office Day	Name Yourself Day	Sibling Day	Eight Track Tape Day	Look Up at the Sky Day	Thank Your School Librarian Day	Pecan Day
15	16	17	18	19	20	21
Rubber Eraser Day	Stress Awareness Day	Cheeseball Day	Jugglers Day	Garlic Day	Look Alike Day (Dress like your favorite person)	Kindergarten Day
22	23	24	25	26	27	28
Jelly Bean Day	World Laboratory Animal Day	Pig in a Blanket Day	No Excuse Day	Hug an Australian Day	Tell a Story Day	Kiss Your Mate Day
29	30					
Shrimp Scampi Day	Hairstyle Appreciation Day					

May

1	2	3	4	5	6	7
Save the Rhinos Day	Robert's Rules of Order Day	Paranormal Day	Kite Day	National Hoagie Day	No Homework Day	International Tuba Day
8	9	10	11	12	13	14
Do Dah Day (Hats off to "Camptown Races")	Lost Sock Memorial Day	Clean Up Your Room Day	Eat What You Want to Day	Limerick Day	Leprechaun Day	Dance Like a Chicken Day
15	16	17	18	19	20	21
Chocolate Chip Day	Wear Purple for Peace Day	Pack Rat Day	Youth Against Violence Day	Frog Jumping Jubilee Day	Eliza Doolittle Day	National Waitress/Waiter Day
22	23	24	25	26	27	28
Buy a Musical Instrument Day	Penny Day	Ancestor Honor Day	Tap Dance Day	National Senior Health Day	Body Painting Arts Festival	Hamburger Day
29	30	31				
End of Middle Ages Day	My Bucket's Got a Hole in It Day (Hats off to square dancers)	World No Tobacco Day				

June

1	2	3	4	5	6	7
Dare Day	Rocky Road Day	Repeat Day Repeat Day	Hug Your Cat Day	World Environment Day	Teachers Day	Chocolate Ice Cream Day
8	9	10	11	12	13	14
National Taco Day	Donald Duck Day	Yo-Yo Day	Hug Holiday	Machine Day (Plug it in)	Race Unity Day	Family History Day
15	16	17	18	19	20	21
Smile Power Day	Hollering Contest Day	Eat Your Vegetables Day	Work at Home Fathers Day	Sauntering Day	Vegan World Day	Baby Boomer's Recognition Day
22	23	24	25	26	27	28
Chocolate Éclair Day	Let It Go Day	Swim a Lap Day	Take Your Dog to Work Day	"Happy Birthday" to You Day	Decide to Be Married Day	Paul Bunyan Day
29	30					
Camera Day (Snap something)	Meteor Day (Hats off to Tunguska, Siberia, 1908)					

July

1	2	3	4	5	6	7
Canada Day	I Forgot Day	Compliment Your Mirror Day	Country Music Day	Workaholic Day	Take Your Webmaster to Lunch Day	Strawberry Sundae Day
8	9	10	11	12	13	14
Video Games Day	Lobster Carnival	Don't Step on a Bee Day	National Cheer Up the Lonely Day	Pecan Pie Day	Embrace Your Geekness Day	National Nude Day
15	16	17	18	19	20	21
Respect Canada Day	International Juggling Day	Cow Appreciation Day	Ice Cream Day	Get Out of the Dog House Day	Ugly Truck Contest Day	Tug of War Tournament
22	23	24	25	26	27	28
Rat Catchers Day (Hail to the Pied Piper!)	Vanilla Ice Cream Day	Virtual Love Day	Day Out of Time Day	All or Nothing Day	Take Your Houseplant for a Walk Day	Drive-Thru Appreciation Day
29	30	31				
Parents' Day	Mutts Day	All-American Soap Box Derby Day				

WHEN ?

August

1	2	3	4	5	6	7
Friendship Day	National Ice Cream Sandwich Day	National Watermelon Day	Twins Day	National Mustard Day	Forgiveness Day	National Lighthouse Day
8	**9**	**10**	**11**	**12**	**13**	**14**
Sneak Some Zucchini onto Your Neighbor's Porch Night	National Polka Festival	National S'mores Day	Presidential Joke Day	Middle Child's Day	International Left-Handers Day	National Creamsicle Day
15	**16**	**17**	**18**	**19**	**20**	**21**
Relaxation Day	National Tell a Joke Day	National Thriftshop Day	Bad Poetry Day	Aviation Day	National Radio Day	Hawaii Day
22	**23**	**24**	**25**	**26**	**27**	**28**
Tooth Fairy Day	National Spongecake Day	Knife Day (First Bowie knife, 1838)	Kiss and Make Up Day	Women's Equality Day	Just Because Day	Race Your Mouse Day
29	**30**	**31**				
More Herbs, Less Salt Day	Toasted Marshmallow Day	National Trail Mix Day				

323

September

1	2	3	4	5	6	7
Emma M. Nutt Day (First female telephone operator)	National Blueberry Popsicle Day	Skyscraper Day	Newspaper Carrier Day	Be Late for Something Day	Read a Book Day	Neither Rain nor Snow Day
8	9	10	11	12	13	14
Pardon Day	Teddy Bear Day	Swap Ideas Day	No News Is Good News Day	National Pet Memorial Day	Defy Superstition Day	National Cream-Filled Donut Day
15	16	17	18	19	20	21
Make a Hat Day	Collect Rocks Day	Apple Dumpling Day	National Play-Doh Day	International Talk Like a Pirate Day	National Punch Day	International Peace Day
22	23	24	25	26	27	28
Elephant Appreciation Day	Checkers Day	Rabbit Day	National Comic Book Day	National Pancake Day	Crush a Can Day	Ask a Stupid Question Day
29	30					
Confucius Day	National Mud Pack Day					

324

WHEN

October

1	2	3	4	5	6	7
World Vegetarian Day	Name Your Car Day	Techies Day	National Golf Day	Do Something Nice Day	Universal Children's Day	Bald and Free Day
8	9	10	11	12	13	14
Wallpaper Day	Moldy Cheese Day	National Angel Food Cake Day	Take Your Teddy Bear to Work Day	Farmer's Day	Navy Birthday	National Dessert Day
15	16	17	18	19	20	21
White Cane Safety Day	Dictionary Day	Wear Something Gaudy Day	No Beard Day	Evaluate Your Life Day	Brandied Fruit Day	Count Your Buttons Day
22	23	24	25	26	27	28
National Nut Day	TV Talk Show Host Day	National Bologna Day	Punk for a Day Day	Mule Day	Separation of Church and State Day	Plush Animal Lover's Day
29	30	31				
Hermit Day	National Candy Corn Day	National Magic Day				

325

November

1	2	3	4	5	6	7
National Authors' Day	Deviled Egg Day	Sandwich Day	King Tut Day	Guy Fawkes Day	Saxophone Day	Cook Something Bold Day
8	9	10	11	12	13	14
Dunce Day	Sadie Hawkins Day (First "girls get to ask" dance, 1938)	Forget-Me-Not Day	Air Your Dirty Laundry Day	National Pizza with the Works Except Anchovies Day	National Indian Pudding Day	Young Readers Day
15	16	17	18	19	20	21
Clean Your Refrigerator Day	Button Day	Take a Hike Day	Occult Day	Have a Bad Day Day	Absurdity Day	World Hello Day
22	23	24	25	26	27	28
Go for a Ride Day	You're Welcome Day	Use Even If Seal Is Broken Day	National Parfait Day	Buy Nothing Day	Pie in the Face Day	Red Planet Day
29	30					
Square Dance Day	Stay at Home Because You're Well Day					

December

1	2	3	4	5	6	7
Eat a Red Apple Day	Fritters Day	Roof Over Your Head Day	Wear Brown Shoes Day	Bathtub Day	National Gazpacho Day	Cotton Candy Day
8	9	10	11	12	13	14
Take It in the Ear Day	Pastry Day	Human Rights Day	National Noodle-Ring Day	Ding-a-Ling Day	Violin Day	Bouillabaisse Day
15	16	17	18	19	20	21
Bill of Rights Day	Chocolate-Covered Everything Day	Underdog Day	Roast Suckling Pig Day	Oatmeal Muffin Day	Games Day	Look at the Bright Side Day
22	23	24	25	26	27	28
Date Nut Bread Day	Roots Day	Eggnog Day	National Pumpkin Pie Day	Whiners Day	Fruitcake Day	Card Playing Day
29	30	31				
Tic-Tac-Toe Day	Festival of Enormous Changes Day	Unlucky Day				

THE SUMMER OF LOVE

If you were young and hip and peace was in your heart back in 1967, you wanted to head to San Francisco to celebrate the Summer of Love. But the summer of that year was actually the culmination of events and a way of life that had started long before. The "Summer of Love" was a phrase that meant a time, a feeling, a generation, a counterculture, when the hippie movement came to full fruition. It was the student dissatisfaction of U.S. involvement in Vietnam, civil rights, the murder of JFK, the discovery of LSD, the sexual revolution, and "Free Love," a time in which change was everything, and everything was possible. Youth was out to make the world a better place, and for a short time, everything seemed magical. By the end of 1967—just over the horizon—were political upheaval, the height of the Vietnam War, the Students for a Democratic Society, Kent State University, and more. The Summer of Love truly began long before 1967 . . . and it was the beginning of the end of a carefree time. Herewith a few stops on the road:

1963: LSD first appears on the street in sugar-cube form.

February 1965: The United States begins bombing Vietnam.

November 6, 1965: Appeal I, Bill Graham's first concert at the Fillmore in San Francisco, is held, featuring Jefferson Airplane and the Warlocks (soon to be the Grateful Dead).

December 4, 1965: The Grateful Dead perform their first show in San Jose, California.

1966: Timothy Leary founds the League of Spiritual Development, with LSD as the sacrament.

September 9, 1966: The first issue of the newspaper the *Oracle* appears on the streets of Haight-Ashbury, bringing word of the peace movement to the streets.

October 6, 1966: California outlaws the use of LSD.

November 5, 1966: Ten thousand people join the Walk for Love and Peace and Freedom in New York City.

1967: The original Council for the Summer of Love is created by the Family Dog, the Straight Theatre, the Diggers, the *Oracle*, and about twenty-five other individuals.

January 14, 1967: The Human Be-In in San Francisco's Golden Gate Park is attended by twenty thousand people. It is billed as the Gathering of the Tribes in a "union of love and activism," and is considered the beginning of the Summer of Love.

March 7, 1967: Alice B. Toklas dies.

March 26, 1967: The Be-In in New York's Central Park is held. Ten thousand people attend.

April 5, 1967: Grayline Bus starts "hippie tours" of Haight-Ashbury.

April 15, 1967: An anti–Vietnam War protest is held in New York, with four hundred thousand marchers.

May 1967: Paul McCartney announces that all the Beatles have "dropped acid."

May 19, 1967: The first U.S. air strike on Hanoi is made.

May 20, 1967: Flower Power Day is held in New York City.

June 2, 1967: The Beatles' *Sgt. Pepper's Lonely Hearts Club Band* is released.

June 16, 1967: The Monterey Pop Festival is held.

June 21, 1967: The Summer Solstice Party in Golden Gate Park is held.

July 1967: The Summer of Rioting takes place in the United States. Blacks take to the streets in Chicago, Brooklyn, Cleveland, and Baltimore.

July 24, 1967: Forty-three people die in Detroit—it is the worst rioting in U.S. history.

October 8, 1967: Che Guevara is killed in Bolivia by U.S.-trained troops.

October 21–22, 1967: Antiwar protesters storm the Pentagon.

December 1967: The Beatles release the *Magical Mystery Tour* album.

December 1967: The Stop the Draft movement is organized by forty antiwar groups; nationwide protests ensue.

December 5, 1967: One thousand antiwar protesters try to close a New York City induction center. Allen Ginsberg and Dr. Benjamin Spock are among the 585 arrested.

December 5, 1967: The Beatles open Apple Shop in London.

December 31, 1967: Abbie Hoffman, Jerry Rubin, Paul Krassner, Dick Gregory, and friends pronounce themselves "yippies."

Some Top 40 Hits During the Summer of 1967
"San Francisco (Be Sure to Wear Flowers in Your Hair),"
Scott McKenzie

"Let's Live for Today," Grass Roots

"Groovin'," Young Rascals

"Light My Fire," the Doors

"Society's Child (Baby I've Been Thinking)," Janis Ian

"White Rabbit," Jefferson Airplane

"A Whiter Shade of Pale," Procol Harum

"Somebody to Love," Jefferson Airplane

On the Summer of Love

We are here to make a better world.

No amount of rationalization or blaming can preempt the moment of choice each of us brings to our situation here on this planet. The lesson of the '60's is that people who cared enough to do right could change history.

We didn't end racism but we ended legal segregation.

We ended the idea that you could send half a million soldiers around the world to fight a war that people do not support.

We ended the idea that women are second-class citizens.

We made the environment an issue that couldn't be avoided.

The big battles that we won cannot be reversed. We were young, self-righteous, reckless, hypocritical, brave, silly, headstrong and scared half to death.

And we were right.

—ABBIE HOFFMAN (1936–1989), FORMER HIPPIE
AND POLITICAL ACTIVIST

◆

The word—or concept of—WHEN does not exist in the language of the Moken people, who are sea gypsies of the Andaman Sea living on the islands off the coast of Myanmar.

331

THOSE WERE THE DAYS

When the Dow Jones Industrial Average Hit Some Milestones

May 17, 1792: Buttonwood Agreement signed,
considered initial formation of NYSE
January 12, 1906: First close over 100
March 12, 1956: First close over 500
February 18, 1971: New York Stock Exchange, Inc.,
formed, a not-for-profit corporation
November 14, 1972: First close over 1,000
January 8, 1987: First close over 2,000
April 17, 1991: First close over 3,000
February 23, 1995: First close over 4,000
November 21, 1995: First close over 5,000
October 14, 1996: First close over 6,000
February 13, 1997: First close over 7,000
July 16, 1997: First close over 8,000
April 6, 1998: First close over 9,000
March 29, 1999: First close over 10,000
July 16, 1999: First close over 11,000

HIGHEST VOLUME DAY ON THE NEW YORK STOCK EXCHANGE
July 24, 2002: 2,812,918,977 shares traded

LOWEST NYSE VOLUME DAY
March 16, 1830: 31 shares traded

SOME NYSE TRADING FLOOR TECHNOLOGICAL FIRSTS
Ticker: 1867
Telephones: 1878
Electric lights: 1883
Automated quotation service: 1953

Radio pagers: 1966
Electronic ticker display boards: 1966
Designated Order Turnaround (DOT) system: 1976
Intermarket Trading System (ITS): 1978
Electronic display book: 1983
SuperDot 250: 1984
Integrated technology network: 1994–1996
Wireless data system: 1996

WE'RE HERE, WE'RE QUEER, GET USED TO IT

On June 27, 1969, a police raid at a gay bar called the Stonewall Inn in New York City sparked nationwide controversy and is considered the beginning of the modern gay rights movement.

NEWS FLASH!!

One Times Square has enjoyed a long history as the flagship, at least sentimentally, of New York City's Times Square. At its completion in 1904 as the home of the *New York Times*, it was the second-tallest building in New York City, at twenty-five stories—and immediately became the site for New Year's Eve celebrations. In 1907, the ball-dropping tradition began, followed by more fame in 1928 when the moving headline "zipper" became the most famous electronic billboard in the world. In 1996, new owners found that the building would best be put to use as a sign tower; the 12,048 lightbulbs were changed to LED, and as of 2002, the completely tenantless One Times Square was 99 percent covered in signage.

DECLARATIONS AND CONSTITUTIONALITY

John Hancock and Charles Thomson were the only two people who actually signed the Declaration of Independence on July 4, 1776. Most of the other forefathers signed on August 2, but the signature of Thomas McKean of Delaware did not appear on the printed copy that was authenticated on January 17, 1777. Some historians assert that he didn't affix his, shall we say, "John Hancock" until five years later, as he was serving in the army in 1776.

The United States Constitution is the oldest federal constitution in existence, ratified on June 21, 1788. The Bill of Rights, which codifies Amendments I through X of the Constitution, went into effect on December 15, 1791. At this writing there are twenty-seven amendments (including Amendment XXI, which repeals Amendment XVIII), the last enacted in 1992.

Constitutional Amendments
THE BILL OF RIGHTS (AMENDMENTS I–X)

Amendment I **Freedoms, Petitions, Assembly** (1791)
Freedom of religion, speech, the press, and right of petition

Amendment II **Right to Bear Arms** (1791)
Right of people to bear arms not to be infringed

Amendment III **Quartering of Soldiers** (1791)
No soldier shall be quartered in any house in times of peace without consent of the owner

Amendment IV **Search and Arrest** (1791)
Persons and houses to be secure from unreasonable searches and seizures

Amendment V **Rights in Criminal Cases** (1791)
In general, no person shall be held to answer for a capital
crime, unless on a presentment or indictment of a grand jury

Amendment VI **Right to a Fair Trial** (1791)
Civil rights for a fair and speedy trial

Amendment VII **Rights in Civil Cases** (1791)
In civil cases, the right to trial by jury shall be preserved

Amendment VIII **Bail, Fines, Punishment** (1791)
Excessive bails, fines, and punishments prohibited

Amendment IX **Rights Retained by the People** (1791)
Constitutional rights shall not be construed to deny others
retained by the people

Amendment X **States' Rights** (1791)
Powers not delegated are reserved by state or people

Amendment XI **Lawsuits Against States** (1795)
U.S. judicial power will not extend to suits against a state

Amendment XII **Presidential Elections** (1804)
Election of president and vice president; establishment of
electoral college (*amended by Amendment XX*)

Amendment XIII **Abolition of Slavery** (1865)
Neither slavery nor involuntary servitude shall exist in
the United States

Amendment XIV **Civil Rights** (1868)
Citizenship and its privileges; no state shall make or
enforce any law which shall abridge the privileges or
immunities of citizens, nor deprive any person of life, liberty,
or property, without due process of law

Amendment XV **Black Suffrage** (1870)
Citizens' right to vote shall not be denied on account of race, color, and previous condition of servitude

Amendment XVI **Income Taxes** (1913)
Congress has power to lay and collect taxes on incomes

Amendment XVII **Senatorial Elections** (1913)
Election, vacancies, and qualifications of U.S. senators

Amendment XVIII **Prohibition of Liquor** (1920)
(*repealed by Amendment XXI*)
No manufacture, sale, or transportation of intoxicating liquor

Amendment XIX **Women's Suffrage** (1920)
Citizen's right to vote cannot be denied on account of sex

Amendment XX **Terms of Office** (1933)
Terms for presidents, vice presidents, senators, and representatives; filling the vacancy of office of the president

Amendment XXI **Repeal of Prohibition** (1933)
Repeal of Prohibition Amendment

Amendment XXII **Term Limits for the Presidency** (1951)
President may be elected to serve only two terms

Amendment XXIII **Washington, D.C., Suffrage** (1961)
Appointment of electors for the District of Columbia

Amendment XXIV **Abolition of Poll Taxes** (1964)
Citizens will not be denied the right to vote due to failure to pay a poll tax or any other tax

Amendment XXV **Presidential Succession** (1967)
Succession of vice president to the presidency and subsequent people in line

Amendment XXVI **18-year-old Suffrage** (1971)
Voting age is lowered from twenty-one to eighteen years of age

Amendment XXVII **Congressional Pay Raises** (1992)
No congressional raises may take effect until there has been an intervening election of representatives

The Failed Amendments

Many amendments have been proposed by Congress since the ratification of the Constitution but have failed the second step: acceptance by the states. The language of the bill determines whether or not the amendment has an expiration date by which it has to be passed; some are still outstanding and pending ratification; others have expired.

ARTICLE 1 OF THE ORIGINAL BILL OF RIGHTS
(PROPOSED 1789; STILL OUTSTANDING)

This amendment, proposed in 1789, dealt with the number of persons represented by each member of the House, and the number of members of the House. It provided that once the House had a hundred members, it should not have fewer than a hundred, and once it reached two hundred, it should not have fewer than two hundred. There are more than four hundred members today. It was ratified by ten states, the last in 1791.

THE ANTI-TITLE AMENDMENT
(PROPOSED 1810; STILL OUTSTANDING)

This amendment, submitted to the states in the 11th Congress (in 1810), said that any citizen who accepted or received any title of nobility from a foreign power, or who accepted without the consent of Congress any gift from a foreign power, would no longer be a citizen. Congressional research shows that the amendment was ratified by twelve states, the last being in 1812.

THE SLAVERY AMENDMENT
(PROPOSED 1861; STILL OUTSTANDING)

This amendment, also known as the Corwin Amendment, would prohibit Congress from making any law interfering with the domestic institutions of any state (slavery being specifically mentioned). It was proposed and sent to the states and is still outstanding. Congressional research shows that the amendment was ratified by two states, the last being in 1862.

THE CHILD LABOR AMENDMENT
(PROPOSED 1926; STILL OUTSTANDING)

In 1926, an amendment was proposed that granted Congress the power to regulate the labor of children under the age of eighteen. This amendment has been ratified by twenty-eight states; ratification by thirty-eight states is required for passage.

THE EQUAL RIGHTS AMENDMENT (ERA)
(PROPOSED 1972; EXPIRED UNRATIFIED, AFTER EXTENSION, 1982)

The ERA intended that equality of rights under the law not be denied on account of sex.

THE DISTRICT OF COLUMBIA VOTING RIGHTS AMENDMENT (PROPOSED 1978; EXPIRED UNRATIFIED 1985)

This amendment would have granted the citizens of Washington, D.C., the same full representation in Congress as any state.

UP, UP, AND AWAY

Versailles, France, September 19, 1783: A sheep, a duck, and a rooster become the first passengers launched in a hot-air balloon by a pair of French brothers, Joseph and Ettienne Montgolfier.

Over Paris, November 21, 1783: The first recorded flight with people (instead of livestock) soared for twenty-two minutes in a paper and silk balloon, also built by the Montgolfiers. Aboard were Pilatre de Rozier, who later became the first man killed in an aircraft accident, and the Marquis d'Arlandes, an infantry officer.

English Channel, 1785: French balloonist Jean-Pierre Blanchard and American John Jeffries become the first to fly across the English Channel, considered the first successful trip in long-distance ballooning.

Ballooning in Wartime, 1794–1945: Right through the end of World War II, balloons are used to survey, communicate, and transport.

New Altitude Record Set, 1935: *Explorer II*, a helium gas balloon with a pressurized chamber and two humans aboard, sets the altitude record at 72,395 feet. The record was held for twenty years.

Around the World, March 1–March 20, 1999: Swiss Bertrand Piccard and Brian Jones of England left the Swiss Alps, and nineteen days, one hour, and forty-nine minutes later, floating over Mauritania, North Africa, became the first balloonists to circumnavigate the globe without stopping or refueling.

COFFEE, TEA, OR VITAL SIGNS?

On May 15, 1930, Boeing hired Ellen Church, a nurse, to become the world's first airplane stewardess, flying on the Oakland-to-Chicago route. After being rejected for a position as a pilot, Church approached the airline with the idea that nurses on board commercial flights would allay civilians' fears and attract more passengers.

Stewardesses' careers in the 1930s were less than glamorous. Aside from the duties flight attendants perform today, they loaded luggage, made minor mechanical adjustments, fueled the planes, and even helped push them into the hangars. For this they earned $125 per month. The requirements, besides a nursing degree? Single, under 5 foot 4, and 115 pounds—and many of them were asked to promise to stay single for at least eighteen months.

OVER THE BOUNDING MAIN
Some of History's First Big Voyages

1304–1354:	Ibn Battuta sails to India and China.
1405–1433:	Cheng Ho voyages to Africa and Indonesia.
1419:	Portuguese explorers begin to sail along the west coast of Africa.
1492:	Columbus sails to America.
1497:	Vasco da Gama sails around Africa to reach India.
1519–1522:	Magellan's ship sails around the world (Magellan not so lucky).
1577–1580:	Francis Drake sails around the world.
1642:	Tasman sails to Australia.
1768–1779:	Captain Cook explores the Pacific.

THE MORE-OR-LESS HUNDRED YEARS WAR

The Hundred Years War was an episodic struggle between France and England and actually lasted 116 years—from 1337 to 1453. It began when King Philip VI of France attempted to confiscate the English territories in the duchy of Aquitaine, and ended when the French finally expelled the English from the continent, except for Calais. Much of the time there was no conflict at all: truces and uneasy peace alternated with sudden raids, plundering, and naval battles.

WHAT TH' . . . ?

The first speech bubble is thought to have been drawn by Richard Fenton Outcalt for his comic strip "The Yellow Kid" in 1896.

ALL THAT JAZZ

In about 1895, a group of seven- to twelve-year-old boys in New Orleans got together and formed what some experts call the original jazz band. They advertised themselves as the Razzy Dazzy Spasm Band and, later, the Razzy Dazzy Jazzy Band. It's thought that the word "jazz" originally meant fornication, and it was said, "If the truth was really known about the origins of Jazz, it would certainly never be mentioned in polite society."

◆

The world's oldest continuous LEGISLATIVE BODY is Iceland's official parliament; called the Althingi, it was established in 930 in Iceland by Viking-era settlers.

GREAT MOMENTS IN PIZZA

Since ancient times, flat bread was cooked on a hot stone—and sometimes dates, honey, and olive oil were added. Some food historians say that this was the beginning of pizza, and that the word itself is from an old Italian word meaning "point." But there were thousands of years and many culinary advancements before pizza—as we know it today—came to the table, including the import of the tomato to Italy from Peru in 1522. Throughout the seventeenth and eighteenth centuries, bakers in Naples continued to serve a local dish of bread with tomatoes mixed in, but it wasn't until 1889 that an entrepreneuring Neapolitan concocted the pizza we currently enjoy . . .

1889: Raffaele Esposito created a dish for visiting King Umberto of Italy and his consort, Queen Margherita. In order to impress them, he prepared three kinds of pizza: one with pork fat, cheese, and basil; one with garlic, oil, and tomatoes; and another with mozzarella, basil, and tomatoes—known even today as Margherita pizza.

1905: Naples immigrant Gennaro Lombardi opened the first U.S. Pizzeria in New York City at 53½ Spring Street.

1948: The first commercial pizza-pie mix, Roman Pizza Mix, was produced in Worcester, Massachusetts, by Frank A. Fiorello.

1953: Dean Martin sang, "When the moon hits your eye like a big pizza pie, that's amore."

1957: Frozen pizzas were introduced and found in local grocery stores. The first was marketed by Celentano Brothers. Pizza soon became—and still remains—the most popular of all frozen foods.

A HOLIDAY IN THE MAKING
A Few Things About Turkey Day

Popular history tells us the Pilgrims landed on December 11,
1620 (no Thanksgiving this year).
The first Thanksgiving feast that the Pilgrims hosted, in
1621, lasted three days.
The first time all thirteen original colonies celebrated
Thanksgiving together was in 1777.

VACANCY

In 1925, the first motel—the Motel Inn—opened in San Luis
Obispo, California. The word "motel" was coined by the
architect Arthur Heineman, and just so travelers wouldn't be
confused, a neon sign alternately flashed the words "Hotel"
and "Mo-tel" so that motorists would know that both their
bodies and their automobiles were welcome.

TICK-TOCK

The first version of the sundial appeared somewhere between
5000 and 3500 BCE. It consisted of a stick or pillar placed
vertically; the length of the shadow determined the time of
day. Though there are certainly new variations of the
sundial—analog, and digital, to name a few—they are
essentially the same: a gnomon "shadow-maker" and a dial
face, dependent on the sun rising every day.

◆

In 1908, AIRPLANE ADVERTISING, via a banner
towed behind the plane, was used for the first time, to
promote a Broadway play.

WHEN EMILY POST SPEAKS...

In 1922, people listened when *Etiquette* was first published. Today, Miss Emily Post would surely be horrified with cell phones, e-vites, young ladies with pierced belly buttons, and scores of other undreamt social sins. Herewith a few tips on manners, from back when they meant something:

When to Shake Hands
When gentlemen are introduced to each other they always shake hands.

When a gentleman is introduced to a lady, she sometimes offers her hand—especially if he is someone she has long heard about from friends in common, but to an entire stranger she generally merely bows her head slightly and says, "How do you do!"

What to Say When Introduced
The correct formal greeting is always: "How do you do?"

There are a few expressions possible under other circumstances and upon other occasions. If you have, through friends in common, long heard of a certain lady, or gentleman, and you know that she, or he, also has heard much of you, you may say when you are introduced, "I am very glad to meet you," or "I am delighted to meet you at last!" Do not use the expression "pleased to meet you" then or on any occasion. And you must not say you are delighted unless you have reason to be sure that she, or he, also is delighted to meet you.

When Dinner Is Announced
It is the duty of the butler to "count heads" so that he may know when all the company has arrived. As soon as he has announced the last person, he notifies the cook. The cook being ready, the butler, having glanced into the dining room to

see that windows have been closed and the candles on the table lighted, enters the drawing room, approaches the hostess, bows, and says quietly, "Dinner is served."

Dressing When the Income Is Limited

No one can dress well on nothing a year; that must be granted at the outset. But a woman who has talent, taste, and ingenuity can be suitably and charmingly dressed on little a year, especially at present.

First of all, to mind wearing a dress many times because it indicates a small bank account is to exhibit a false notion of the values in life. Anyone who thinks well or ill of her, in accordance with her income, cannot be too quickly got rid of! But worthwhile people are influenced in her disfavor when she has clothes in number and quality out of proportion to her known financial situation.

It is tiresome everlastingly to wear black, but nothing is so serviceable, nothing so unrecognizable; nothing looks so well on every occasion.

YOU ARE GETTING SLEEPY . . .

At latitude 25° north, the longest day is longer than the longest night, and the shortest day is longer than the shortest night:

Longest Day	13h 42m
Longest Night	13h 25m
Shortest Day	10h 35m
Shortest Night	10h 18m

TITANIC (the 1997 movie) takes forty minutes longer to watch than it took *Titanic* (the ship) to sink.

WONDERS OF THE WORLD LISTS

Since ancient times, people have put together many "seven wonders" lists. The first list is usually attributed to Antipater of Sidon, who listed the structures in a poem around 140 BCE:

> I have set eyes on the wall of lofty Babylon
> on which is a road for chariots,
> and the statue of Zeus by the Alpheus,
> and the hanging gardens,
> and the Colossus of the Sun,
> and the huge labour of the high pyramids,
> and the vast tomb of Mausolus;
> but when I saw the house of Artemis that mounted to the
> clouds, those other marvels lost their brilliancy, and I said,
> "Lo, apart from Olympus, the Sun never looked
> on aught so grand."
> —ANTIPATER, GREEK ANTHOLOGY 9.58

SEVEN WONDERS OF THE ANCIENT WORLD
2680 BCE: The Pyramids of Egypt
600 BCE: The Hanging Gardens of Babylon
550 BCE: The Temple of Artemis (Diana) at Ephesus
ca. 450 BCE: The Statue of Zeus (Jupiter) at Olympia
350 BCE: The Mausoleum at Halicarnassus
280 BCE: The Colossus at Rhodes
Third century BCE: The Pharos (Lighthouse) of Alexandria

With the passage of time, several other lists began to appear, none credited to an author as was the original. Herewith some of the more popular:

THE SEVEN WONDERS OF THE MEDIEVAL MIND
ca. 200 BCE: Stonehenge (England)
70–80 CE: The Colosseum (Rome, Italy)
First century CE: The Catacombs of Kom el Shoqafa
(Alexandria, Egypt)
221–206 BCE and present state **1368–1644:**
The Great Wall of China
Fifteenth century CE: The Porcelain Tower of Nanjing (China)
537 CE: The Hagia Sophia (Constantinople)
1173–1370 CE: The Leaning Tower of Pisa (Italy)

THE SEVEN WONDERS OF THE MODERN WORLD
1930: The Empire State Building (New York City)
1975–1991: The Itaipú Dam (Brazil/Paraguay)
1973: The CN Tower (Toronto, Canada)
1880–1914: The Panama Canal (Panama)
1994: The Channel Tunnel (England/France)
1923: The North Sea Protection Works (Netherlands)
1937: The Golden Gate Bridge (San Francisco, California)

THE SEVEN FORGOTTEN MODERN WONDERS OF THE WORLD
1858: The Clock Tower/Big Ben (London, England)
1889: The Eiffel Tower (Paris, France)
1965: The Gateway Arch (St. Louis, Missouri)
1960: The Aswan High Dam (Egypt)
1935: Hoover Dam (Arizona/Nevada)
1927–1941: Mount Rushmore National Memorial (South
Dakota)
1998: The Petronas Towers (Kuala Lumpur, Malaysia)

THE SEVEN FORGOTTEN WONDERS OF THE MEDIEVAL MIND
1279–1223 BCE: Abu Simbel Temple (Egypt)
1113–1152 CE: Angkor Wat (Cambodia)

1630 CE: Taj Mahal (India)
1023 CE: Mont Saint-Michel (Normandy, France)
100–1650 CE: The Moai Statues/Easter Island (Rapa Nui, Chile)
447–432 BCE: The Parthenon (Athens, Greece)
Unknown: The Shwedagon Pagoda (Myanmar)

THE FORGOTTEN WONDERS
1350 CE: The Aztec Temple (Mexico City, Mexico)
Several centuries BCE: The Banaue Rice Terraces (The Philippines)
750–842 CE: The Borobudur Temple (Indonesia)
1500 CE: The Inca City (Machu Piccu, Peru)
700 CE: The Mayan Temples of Tikal (Northern Guatemala)
100 BCE: The Temple of the Inscriptions (Palenque, Mexico)
550 BCE: The Throne Hall of Persepolis (Iran)
Fourth century BCE: The rock-carved city of Petra (Jordan)
1859–1867: The Suez Canal (Egypt)
1973: The Sydney Opera House (Australia)
1638–1648: The Red Fort in India (Agra)

◆

TRUE OR FALSE?

How does a polygraph know when you're lying? The test simultaneously monitors several of the suspect's physiological functions—breathing, pulse, and galvanic skin response—and prints them on graph paper. The results show when the greatest biological responses occur, which indicate stress and, consequently, lying.

◆

Tropical RAINFORESTS are the world's oldest ecosystems.

GOOD TIMES, BAD TIMES

The theory of biorhythms states that one can determine the physical, emotional, intellectual—and some now say spiritual—cycles that forecast the patterns of a person's critical days and periods of high and low energy. Biorhythms change the behavior or physiology of an organism, which are maintained and generated by a biological clock. The four types of rhythms, which rarely intersect at once, and can greatly affect a person's demeanor and performance are:

Intellectual cycle (32 days)	Affects memory, ability to study, mental activities, clearness of thoughts
Emotional cycle (27 days)	Affects feelings, mood, emotions, and state of mind, as well as sensibility to the surrounding world and to other people
Physical cycle (22 days)	Controls physical and sexual activity, body coordination, resistance to illnesses, and endurance
Intuitive (or spiritual) cycle (37 days)	Controls perception of beauty, creative inspiration, and the reception or apprehension of subconscious impulses, that is, intuition itself; also called spiritual rhythm

◆

Before 1933, the DIME was legal as payment only in transactions of $10 or less. In that year, Congress made the dime legal tender for all transactions.

GREAT MOMENTS IN INVENTING

6500 BCE: Potter's wheel

4000 BCE: Cosmetics (Egypt)

2000 BCE: Toilet flush, Minoan civilization (Crete)

1500 BCE: Scissors (Egypt)

100 BCE: Roller bearing (France or Germany)

1268: Eyeglasses, Salvino D'Armate (Italy)

1540: Artificial limbs, Ambrose Paré (France)

1589: Hosiery-knitting machine, Rev. William Lee (England)

1564: Pencil (England)

1756: Mayonnaise (France)

1816: Phosphorus match, François Derosne (France)

1830: Lawn mower, Edwin Budding, John Ferrabee (England)

1846: Sewing machine, Elias Howe (United States)

1848: Chewing gum, John Curtis (United States)

1849: Bullet, Claude Minie (France)

1849: Safety pin, Walter Hunt (United States)

1853: Condensed milk, Gail Borden (United States)

1859: Oil well, Edwin L. Drake (United States)

1862: Machine gun, Richard J. Gatling (United States)

1866: Lip reading, Alexander Melville Bell (United States)

1877: Concrete, Joseph Monier (France)

1886: Coca-Cola, Dr. John Stith Pemberton (United States)

1891: Zipper, W. L. Judson (United States)

1897: Worm gear, Frederick W. Lanchester (England)

1899: Aspirin, Dr. Felix Hoffman (Germany)

1899: Tape recorder, Valdemar Poulsen (Denmark)

1909: IUD (intrauterine device), R. Richter (Germany)

1910: Airplane autopilot, Elmer A. Sperry (United States)

1926: Aerosol can, Erik Rotheim (Norway)

1929: Scotch tape, Richard Drew (United States)

1933: Cat's eye road reflector, Percy Shaw (England)

1938: Ballpoint pen, Lazlo Biro (Argentina)
1943: Aqualung, Jacques-Yves Cousteau and Emile Gagnan (France)
1945: Tupperware, Earl W. Tupper (United States)
1947: Holograph, Dennis Gabor (England)
1951: Oral contraceptive, Gregory Pincus, Min Chuch Chang, John Rock, Carl Djerassi (United States)
1957: Pacemaker, Clarence W. Lillehie, Earl Bakk (United States)
1972: Prozac, Bryan B. Malloy (Scotland), Klaus K. Schmiegel (United States)
1972: Compact disk, RCA (United States)
1972: Video disk, Philips Company (Netherlands)
1972: Electronic mail, Ray Tomlinson (United States)

◆

LONG LIFE

A Few of Earth's Longest-Living Animals and Plants and Their Recorded Maximum Ages:

giant tortoise: 200 years
human: 122 years
sturgeon: 100 years
blue whale and golden eagle: 80 years
African elephant: 77 years
Amborella: 140 million years
King's Holly (*Lomatia tasmanica*): 43,000 years
creosote plants (*Larrea divaricata*): 11,700 years
bristlecone pine (*Pinus longaeva*): 4,000–5,000 years

◆

A FEMTOSECOND is one quadrillionth of a second, or one millionth of a nanosecond.

"MAZEL TOV—IT'S A BOY!"

Jewish circumcision, *bris milah*, has no meaning when performed before the eighth day of life because kabbalistic writings teach that the child has to transcend the physical—the seven days of creation—to the metaphysical before a covenant joining body and soul can occur.

DOES IT ALL ADD UP?

Though the earliest mention of an abacus is in 190 CE in a Chinese book, *Supplementary Notes on the Art of Figures*, many historians suggest that a Roman version of what might be called the world's first computer preceded the Eastern version. Travel on the Silk Road brought not only social and scientific innovation but commerce, and very likely the introduction of this counting board.

Another view suggests that there is no connection at all between the Roman and Chinese abaci, and that their appearances are the result of convergent evolution—the process by which different and unrelated individuals reached the obvious solution for improving the original adding machine: counting on five fingers while using the fingers of the other hand for place holders.

NICKEL-AND-DIME THEM

Frank Woolworth opened his first five-and-dime store in 1879. A fixture in American downtowns throughout the first half of the twentieth century, Woolworth's was the first store to put its merchandise out for the customers themselves to touch, select, and purchase.

THE FRUIT OF THEIR LABOR

Steven Jobs and Steve Wozniak made nearly as big a splash with their 1984 Apple computer as the serpent did in the Garden of Eden. It changed the world—and yet the specifications below for its debut version are almost laughably inadequate today:

Name: Macintosh
Manufacturer: Apple
Type: Home computer
Origin: United States
Year: January 1984
End of production: October 1, 1985
Keyboard: Full-stroke 59-key
CPU: Motorola MC 68000
Speed: 7.83 MHz
RAM: 128 KB (expandable to 512 KB)
ROM: 64 KB
Text modes: 40 characters x 32 lines bitmapped pseudo-character mode
Graphic modes: 512 x 342 dots
Colors: black-and-white 9-inch monitor
Sound: 4 voices, 12-octave sound @ 22 kHz
Size/Weight: 13.6 inches (H) x 9.6 inches (W) x 10.9 inches (D)/16.5 pounds
I/O ports: Two serial (RS 232/422) for printer and modem, mouse, external floppy drive, sound out
Built-in media: One 400K 3.5-inch internal floppy drive; 400K external drive optional
OS: Macintosh System 1.0
Power supply: Built-in power supply unit
Price: $2,495 (United States, 1984); £1,795 (United Kingdom, 1984)

THE HISTORY OF THE BICYCLE

It seems unimaginable that it took more than five thousand years for man to progress from the invention of the wheel to the bicycle. A short history of a great ride . . .

3500 BCE
The wheel was invented.

1490
Artist, architect, and master inventor Leonardo da Vinci may have sketched an astonishing facsimile of a modern-day bicycle, which apparently never got any further than the drawing board.

c. 1790—The Célérifère
There are reports that Count Mede de Sivrac designed and was seen riding the *célérifère*, a type of rolling machine with two in-line wheels connected by a wooden beam, much more like a hobby horse than anything else. The rider moved by pushing along with his or her feet, as on a scooter.

1817—The Walking Machine
Baron Karl Drais von Sauerbronn improved on de Sivrac's invention by adding an important innovation: steering. His new mode of transportation, which he devised for his own use to get around the royal gardens, allowed the rider to point the front wheel in the direction he or she wanted to go. Unfortunately, the entire machine was made of wood, which made for a rather unsettling ride.

1860s—Pedals and Cranks
Historians say that the father-and-son team of Pierre and Ernest Michaux, French carriage makers, invented the bicycle

sometime in the 1860s, citing the younger Michaux as "the father of the bicycle"; though others disagree and insist that the invention was some years earlier, it is agreed that Ernest added the modern pedal and cranks in 1864—and a brand-new means of propulsion.

1865—The Velocipede

The "fast-foot" was also a two-wheeler . . . but this time with the pedals attached directly to the front wheel. Fast (or faster, anyway) it may have been, but it was also commonly known as "the boneshaker." It was made entirely of wood.

1870—The High-Wheel Bicycle

This is the version associated with the Gay Nineties—men with bowler hats and handlebar mustaches riding head and shoulders above the street traffic—and it is the first version of the bicycle to be made entirely of metal. Previous to this time, metallurgy was not advanced enough to make small, light parts. Hard rubber tires were also added for the first time, affording the rider a much smoother ride. Manufacturers made the radii of the wheel as long as the rider's leg would allow—they had by now realized that the larger the wheel, the further a rider could travel with just one rotation of the pedal.

1871—The Penny Farthing

Engineer James Starley's "ordinary" or "penny farthing" was the first really efficient bicycle, consisting of a small rear wheel and large front wheel pivoting on a simple tubular frame, with tires of rubber.

1880—The High-Wheel Tricycle

Basically, this version was built like the two-wheeler, but the extra wheel made it easy for women in skirts and corsets to balance their cycle alongside those of their male friends.

1880s—The High-Wheel Safety

In one of many new design improvements, a smaller wheel was used in the front in an attempt to prevent tipping over.

1885—The Hard-Tired Safety Bicycle

This version marked a return to the version with two equal-sized wheels, but with a great advancement: metal was now easy enough to work with that a chain and sprocket could be added, so that every turn of the pedal gave the rider both speed and distance.

1888—The Pneumatic-Tired Safety

A Scotsman, John Dunlop, developed the pneumatic to give his son a more comfortable ride on his tricycle. With this cheaper, more comfortable, and now safe version of the bicycle, manufacturers clamored to get in on what had finally made its way beyond a fad.

1899—"Saddle Bags"

The African American inventor Jerry M. Certain patented a parcel carrier for bicycles. It straddled both sides of the wheel, affording the rider two places to stow gear.

1920s–1950s—Kids' Bikes

After World War I, bicycles for children became big sellers, and manufacturers such as Sears, Roebuck and Montgomery Ward, and later Schwinn resized bikes for smaller bodies and added glamorous automobile and motorcycle blandishments, such as chrome and stripes.

1950s–1970s—Three-Speed Bikes

The elegant English bicycles such as Raleigh, on which riders could change gears for the first time, eased topographical challenges.

1970s–1980s—Ten-Speed Bikes

The ten-speed derailleur bike became popular in the 1970s, as both racing and long-distance riding for pleasure became sporting sensations. Though the derailleur had been invented several decades before in Europe, the standard for American bicycles was the "fixed-and-free" gear system, where the hub was threaded for a free wheel on one side and a fixed gear on the other.

1980s–present

Riders took the sport one step further, and mountain bikes joined the rest of the worldwide "extreme sports" boom. Ironically, the construction of today's mountain bikes hearkens back to the Schwinns of the late 1930s, with fore-wheel brakes, cantilever frames, and spring-fork suspension.

"NO BRAIN, NO PAIN"

Scientists now believe that lobsters, crabs, and other creatures without backbones do not feel a thing when popped into a pot of boiling water.

"THE EAGLE HAS LANDED . . ."

At exactly 4:17:40 P.M., Eastern Daylight Time, on July 20, 1969, *Apollo 11* landed on the surface of the moon. That, of course, is Earth time . . . but will we ever know what time it was on the moon?

◆

On Thursday, August 14, 1941, the last EXECUTION in the Tower of London took place. Josef Jakobs, a German spy, was shot by an eight-man firing squad.

HOW DOES YOUR BABY GROW?

The sheer fascination of watching a child in infancy can distract the casual observer from seeing that a child's growth—physical, social, mental, and lingual—proceeds on an extremely smooth schedule (though for parents it may not seem so). A brief look at baby's first months:

First Month
Can recognize parents' voices
Can see objects up to 10 inches away
Oohs and ahhs

Second Month
Begins to understand that crying gets attention
Exhibits emotions
Holds head up for short periods

Third Month
Begins vowel sounds
Discovers hands and feet
Recognizes peoples' scents

Fourth Month
Explores by testing
Laughs hard when tickled
Can bear weight on legs

Fifth Month
Begins to show decision-making behavior
Transfers objects from hand to hand
Recognizes own name

Sixth through Ninth Month

Begins to respond to his or her name
Learns to reach with accuracy
Uses thumb and fingers to pick up
Understands that an object might be behind something
Learns to mimic

Tenth through Twelfth Month

Feels pride when praised
Builds and disassembles
Waves good-bye
Indicates wants with gestures
May learn to scribble

Thirteenth through Fifteenth Month

Plays peekaboo
Eats with fingers
Walks backward
Can identify body parts by pointing
Can draw a line

Sixteenth through Eighteenth Month

Turns pages of a book
Enjoys pretend games
Responds to directions
Can speak in phrases

◆

None of the BRONTË sisters—Anne, Charlotte, or Emily—
lived until their fortieth birthday.

A BRIEF ACCOUNT OF MODERN GAY HISTORY

1533: King Henry VIII began the English common-law tradition of sodomy laws.

1792: France decriminalized sexual acts between men.

1825: Karl Heinrich Ulrichs (d. 1895), considered by many to be the world's first gay activist, was born. He dared to say that homosexuals were natural—not sinners, diseased, or criminal. In 2002, Italian publisher Roberto Massari dedicated a new wine, Rosso Gayardo, to him.

1836: The last known execution for homosexuality in Britain took place.

1869: The term *homosexuality* appeared in print for the first time in a German pamphlet written by Károly Mária Kertbeny (1824–1882), an Austrian-born Hungarian journalist, memoirist, and human rights campaigner. Kertbeny's thesis emphasized that the state should have no part to play in the policing of private sexual behavior. Kertbeny claimed himself to be a "Normalsexualer."

1871: Paragraph 175 (known formally as §175 StGB; also known as Section 175, in English) was a provision of the German criminal code from May 15, 1871, to March 10, 1994. It made homosexual acts between males a crime, and in early revisions the provision also criminalized bestiality.

1892: The word *bisexual* is first used in its current sense in Charles Gilbert Chaddock's translation of Richard von Krafft-Ebing's *Psychopathia Sexualis*.

1897: Sex researcher Magnus Hirschfeld (1868–1935) founded the Scientific Humanitarian Committee to organize for gay rights and the repeal of Paragraph 175.

1903: In New York City, police conducted the first recorded raid on a gay bathhouse, the Ariston on West Fifty-fifth Street. Seven men received sentences ranging from four to twenty years in prison.

1906: The first homosexual periodical, *Der Eigene* ("The Special One"), was published in Germany. Until it ceased publication in 1931, it had an average of fifteen hundred readers per issue.

1908: San Francisco city officials closed the Dash, the city's earliest known gay bar. It was located at 574 Pacific Street, and also offered drag shows.

1910: Anarchist Emma Goldman first began speaking publicly in favor of gay rights.

1924: The Society for Human Rights in Chicago became the earliest known gay rights organization in the United States. Founder Henry Gerber modeled his organization on the homosexual rights movement in Germany.

1937: The pink triangle was first used to identify homosexual prisoners in Nazi concentration camps.

1945: Prisoners interned for homosexuality were not freed from Nazi camps but required to serve out the full term of their sentences under Paragraph 175.

1948: Alfred Kinsey published *Sexual Behavior in the Human Male*, revealing to the public that homosexuality is far more widespread than was commonly believed.

1950: The Mattachine Society, the first openly gay organization in the United States, was founded in Los Angeles by Henry Hay (d. 2002 at the age of ninety) and others, all of whom were associated with the American Communist Party. They were soon ousted in favor of more politically conservative leaders.

1955: The Daughters of Bilitis, a pioneering national lesbian organization, was founded.

1964: *Life* magazine published a path-breaking feature article, "Homosexuality in America."

1969: Patrons at the Stonewall Inn, a gay bar in New York's Greenwich Village, fought back during a police raid, sparking a three-day riot. The widespread protest that ensued is considered the beginning of the modern gay rights movement.

1970: The first gay pride parade in the United States was held in New York City.

1973: The American Psychiatric Association removed homosexuality from its official list of mental disorders.

1974: Kathy Kozachenko became the first openly gay or lesbian American elected to public office, when she won a seat on the Ann Arbor, Michigan, city council.

1977: Anita Bryant led a successful crusade against a Miami gay rights law.

1978: Gay men in the United States and Sweden—and heterosexuals in Tanzania and Haiti—began showing signs of what would later be called AIDS.

1979: On October 14, one hundred thousand gays, lesbians, bisexuals, and straight supporters marched on Washington, D.C., celebrating gay pride and demanding equal rights for homosexuals under the law.

1981: The Moral Majority started its antigay crusade.

Writer Vito Russo published *The Celluloid Closet*, in which he outed and decoded homosexuality in the movies.

Alan P. Bell led a Kinsey study that suggested that homosexuals are born with that predisposition and not influenced by traumatic experiences during childhood.

1982: The term AIDS, for acquired immune deficiency syndrome, was used for the first time. In the United States 853 deaths had been reported. An answering machine in the home of a volunteer for the newly formed Gay Men's Health Crisis, Rodger McFarlane, was the world's first AIDS hotline. It received more than one hundred calls the first night. McFarlane later became the first paid director of the Gay Men's Health Crisis.

1989: The Danish parliament allowed legal marriage among homosexuals.

1993: The World Health Organization removed homosexuality from its list of diseases.

President Bill Clinton instituted the "Don't Ask, Don't Tell" policy for the U.S. military, permitting gays to serve in the military but banning them from any homosexual activity. This policy led to the discharge of thousands of men and women from the armed forces.

1994: Paragraph 175, the 1871 German law criminalizing sex between males, was repealed after the country's reunification.

1996: American gay activists were dealt a double disappointment when the U.S. Senate voted against same-sex marriage with the Defense of Marriage Act; it also rejected a bill that barred job discrimination against gays.

1999: Russell Henderson pleaded guilty to kidnapping and felony murder in the 1998 death of Matthew Shepard, a gay college student, in Laramie, Wyoming.

The Vermont Supreme Court ruled that homosexual couples were entitled to the same benefits and protections as wedded heterosexual couples.

2000: The Vermont legislature approved civil unions.

2003: The U.S. Supreme Court ruled in *Lawrence v. Texas* that sodomy laws in the United States are unconstitutional. Justice Anthony Kennedy wrote, "Liberty presumes an autonomy of self that includes freedom of thought, belief, expression, and certain intimate conduct."

2004: Same-sex marriages became legal in Massachusetts.

HOW LONG?
When "When?" is a complex word:

Semidiurnal	twice a day
Diurnal	daily
Semiweekly	twice a week
Weekly	once a week
Biweekly	every 2 weeks
Triweekly	every 3 weeks
Bimonthly	every 2 months
Trimonthly	every 3 months
Biannual	twice a year
Semiannual	every 6 months

Annual	every year
Perennial	year after year
Biennial	2 years
Triennial	3 years
Quadrennial	4 years
Quinquennial	5 years
Sexennial	6 years
Septennial	7 years
Octennial	8 years
Novennial	9 years
Decennial	10 years
Undecennial	11 years
Duodecennial	12 years
Quindecennial	15 years
Vigennial	20 years
Tricennial	30 years
Semicentennial	50 years
Demisesquicentennial	75 years
Centennial	100 years
Quasquicentennial	125 years
Sesquicentennial	150 years
Terquasquicentennial	175 years
Bicentennial	200 years
Tercentennial or tricentennial	300 years
Quadricentennial	400 years
Quincentennial	500 years
Sexacentennial	600 years
Septuacentennial	700 years
Octocentennial	800 years
Nonacentennial	900 years
Millennial	1,000 years
Bimillennial	2,000 years

A PARTIAL HISTORY OF GLORIOUS FOOD

From the ground to the shelves, the origins, discoveries, and introductions of some of life's greatest gustatory pleasures:

(BCE)	
17,000	Grain
10,000	Almonds
9000	Sheep
8000	Apples and lentils
7000	Pork
7000	Beans
6500	Cattle domestication
6000	Wine
6000	Cheese
6000	Maize
5500	Honey
5000	Olives and olive oil
5000	Potatoes
5000	Milk
4000	Grapes
4000	Citrus fruits
3600	Popcorn
3200	Chicken domestication
3000	Butter
3000	Onions, garlic, and spices
2700	Tea
1500	Chocolate
1200	Sugar
1000	Pickles
500	Sausages
490	Pasta

(CE)

62	Ice cream
2nd century	Sushi
3rd century	Lemons
220	Tofu
7th century	Spinach
9th century	Coffee
9th century	Cod
15th century	Breton and Portuguese fishermen fish off New England
1484	Hot dogs
16th century	Americans begin to export local foods to other continents
1588	Potato arrives in Ireland
1592	Pot luck
17th century	Doughnuts in America
1610	Bagel invented in Poland
1621	Pilgrims host first Thanksgiving
1654	Kosher food introduced in United States
18th century	French fries
1708	Casseroles
1756	Mayonnaise
1762	The Earl of Sandwich invents his eponymous foodstuff
1767	Soda water
1767	Franciscan brothers introduce grapes and vineyards to California
1773	Boston Tea Party
1784	Lollipops
1789	Thomas Jefferson's pasta machine
1794	United States Navy serves up first rations
1811	McIntosh apples

1825	Jean Anthelme Brillat Savarin declares: "Tell me what you eat and I will tell you who you are."
1826	Fondue
1830s	Hopping John
1845	Poland Spring water
1847	Chinese food introduced in America
1853	Potato (or Saratoga) chip
1856	Condensed milk
1867	Synthetic baby food
1868	Fleischmann's Yeast
1869	Campbell's Soup
1869	Thomas Adams invents chewing gum
1876	Heinz Ketchup
1880s	Railroad car dining introduced
1886	Coca-Cola
1891	Quaker Oats
1893	Chili served at the Chicago World's Fair
1894	Hershey bar
1897	Jell-O
1897	Sears & Roebuck prints world's first brownie recipe
1902	Horn & Hardart's Automats
1903	Canned tuna
1904	Ice cream cone
1906	United States: federal pure food and drug law passed
1911	Crisco
1912	First self-service grocery stores open
1915	Kraft processed cheeses
1919	Prohibition begins in the United States
1920	Good Humor Bars
1920	La Choy chinese foods

1921	Wonder Bread
1923	Sanka
1927	Kool-Aid
1927	Oscar Mayer packaged sliced bacon
1928	Twinkie
1929	Clarence Birdseye sells first frozen foods
1930	Wonder Bread sells first sliced bread
1931	Tacos in United States
1931	*The Joy of Cooking* first printed
1933	Waldorf salad invented
1935	Pan Am introduces airline food
1936	First Howard Johnson's opens
1937	First shopping cart
1938	Canned soda
1939	U.S. government offers food stamps
1941	M&Ms
1941	Garbage disposals
1945	Tupperware
1946	Culinary Institute of America opens
1947	Aluminum foil
1949	Electric dishwasher
1953	Welch's Howdy Doody glasses
1957	Tang
1962	Instant mashed potatoes
1963	Julia Child's *The French Chef* appears on TV
1964	Buffalo wings
1965	Gatorade
1991	Salsa outsells ketchup as top condiment in United States
1992	USDA replaces The Four Basic Food Groups with the Food Pyramid

AMERICAN FURNITURE PERIODS

Though a distinct European style accompanied Americans in their furniture design and construction when they crossed the Atlantic in the early seventeenth century, the citizens of the New World soon developed a freer, less constraining style of their own that mirrored their views of living.

Jacobean (1603–1690): English style, medieval in appearance, ornate carvings, and a dark finish; retained many Elizabethan characteristics, but ornamentation became less prominent

Early American (1640–1700): Rudimentary furniture constructed from local woods modeled after European, mostly Jacobean, furniture; mostly oak and pine

William and Mary (1690–1725): After William and Mary of England (r. 1689–1694), often characterized by ball feet and padded or caned seats; Dutch and Chinese influences

Queen Anne (1700–1755): A graceful refinement of William and Mary style; characterized by cabriole and fiddleback chair back.

Colonial (1700–1780): Combined characteristics of William and Mary, Queen Anne, and Chippendale; more conservative than its contemporary European counterparts

Georgian (1714–1760): Named after George I and George II, who ruled England from 1714 to 1760; a more ornate version of Queen Anne; often gilded

Pennsylvania Dutch (1720–1830): A simple, utilitarian country style with Germanic influences; often painted

Chippendale (1750–1790): Named after British cabinet maker Thomas Chippendale; more elaborate development of Queen Anne furniture

Robert Adam (1760–1795): Named for architect Robert Adam, who studied ancient architecture in Italy; reproduced by cabinetmakers in South Carolina; classically designed pieces to match his classically designed homes

Hepplewhite (1765–1800): Named after English designer and cabinetmaker George Hepplewhite; neoclassic and delicate, featuring contrasting veneers and inlays

Federal (1780–1820): Combination of the neoclassic furniture style characteristics of both Hepplewhite and Sheraton; light construction, graceful legs, delicate lines throughout

Sheraton (1780–1820): Named for English designer Thomas Sheraton, the most popular style of the Federal period; a neoclassical style characterized by delicate straight lines, light construction, contrasting veneers, and neoclassical motifs and ornamentation

Duncan Phyfe (1795–1848): Considered by many experts and art historians to be an adaptation of Adam, Sheraton, Hepplewhite, and American Empire rather than a style unto itself

American Empire (1800–1840): A dark, classical style akin to French Empire; closely carved with moderate proportions

Shaker (1820–1860): A utilitarian style produced by the religious group in self-contained communities; characterized by straight tapered legs and woven chair seats

Victorian (1840–1910): Named for Queen Victoria of England, a return to gothic form, heavy proportions, and dark, elaborate ornamentation; the first mass-produced furniture

Arts and Craft (1880–1910): Simple, straight, flat utilitarian design; also referred to as mission furniture

Art Nouveau (1890–1910): A naturalistic style characterized by intricately detailed patterns and flowing, curving lines

Scandinavian Contemporary (1930–1950): A simple, utilitarian design style in natural wood, popularized by Danish and Swedish designers

◆

IT'S SPUTNIK!

The space age began on October 4, 1957, with the launch of a Soviet artificial satellite. Named *Sputnik*, a Russian word for "traveling companion of the world," it was the size of a basketball and weighed only 183 pounds—yet it circled Earth every ninety-eight minutes. It carried a thermometer and two radio transmitters and worked for twenty-one days.

CAN YOU HEAR ME NOW?

While we credit Alexander Graham Bell with the telephone, others contributed the groundwork.

In the nineteenth century, Charles Boursel suggested that a diaphragm making/breaking contact with an electrode might be used to transmit sound electrically. Johann Philipp Reis followed up in 1861 with a device consisting of a metallic strip and vibrating membrane that broke an electrical circuit to transmit a simple tone. In the 1870s Elisha Gray used a set of reeds tuned to different frequencies to induce currents in electric coils as a variation on harmonic telegraphy.

On June 3, 1875, Alexander Graham Bell and Thomas Watson succeeded in transmitting what they called speech-like sounds using electrically connected vibrating membranes. Bell received the patent for his device in 1876.

NATIONAL HOLIDAYS AROUND THE WORLD

There's always something to celebrate somewhere...

Afghanistan:	August 19
Albania:	November 28
Algeria:	November 1
Andorra:	September 8
Angola:	November 11
Antigua and Barbuda:	November 1
Argentina:	May 25
Armenia:	September 21
Australia:	January 26
Austria:	October 26
Azerbaijan:	May 28
Bahamas:	July 10
Bahrain:	December 16
Bangladesh:	March 26
Barbados:	November 30
Belarus:	July 3
Belgium:	July 21
Belize:	September 21
Benin:	August 1
Bhutan:	December 17
Bolivia:	August 6
Bosnia and Herzegovina:	November 25
Botswana:	September 30
Brazil:	September 7
Brunei:	February 23
Bulgaria:	March 3
Burkina Faso:	December 11
Burundi:	July 1

Cambodia:	November 9
Cameroon:	May 20
Canada:	July 1
Cape Verde:	July 5
Central African Republic:	December 1
Chad:	August 11
Chile:	September 18
China, People's Republic of:	October 1
Colombia:	July 20
Comoros:	July 6
Congo:	August 15
Congo, Democratic Republic of:	June 30
Costa Rica:	September 15
Côte d'Ivoire:	August 7
Croatia:	October 8
Cuba:	December 10
Cyprus:	October 1
Czech Republic:	October 28
Denmark:	June 5
Djibouti:	June 27
Dominica:	November 3
Dominican Republic:	February 27
East Timor:	November 28
Ecuador:	August 10
Egypt:	July 23
El Salvador:	September 15
Equatorial Guinea:	October 12
Eritrea:	May 24
Estonia:	February 24
Ethiopia:	May 28
Fiji:	2nd Mon. of October
Finland:	December 6
France:	July 14

Gabon:	March 12
Gambia:	February 18
Georgia:	May 26
Germany:	October 3
Ghana:	March 6
Greece:	March 25
Grenada:	February 7
Guatemala:	September 15
Guinea:	October 2
Guinea Bissau:	September 24
Guyana:	February 23
Haiti:	January 1
Honduras:	September 15
Hungary:	August 20
Iceland:	June 17
India:	January 26
Indonesia:	August 7
Iran:	April 1
Ireland:	March 17
Israel:	April or May*
Italy:	June 2
Jamaica:	August 6
Japan:	December 23
Jordan:	May 25
Kazakhstan:	December 16
Kenya:	December 12
Kiribati:	July 12
Korea (North):	September 9
Korea (South):	August 15
Kuwait:	February 25
Kyrgyzstan:	August 31
Laos:	December 2

*Variable holiday, falling on a different date each year.

Latvia:	November 18
Lebanon:	November 22
Lesotho:	October 4
Liberia:	July 26
Libya:	September 1
Liechtenstein:	August 15
Lithuania:	February 16
Luxembourg:	June 23
Macedonia:	August 2
Madagascar:	June 26
Malawi:	July 6
Malaysia:	August 31
Maldives:	July 26
Mali:	September 22
Malta:	September 21
Marshall Islands:	May 1
Mauritania:	November 28
Mauritius:	March 12
Mexico:	September 16
Micronesia, Federated States of:	May 10
Moldova:	August 27
Monaco:	November 19
Mongolia:	July 11
Morocco:	July 30
Mozambique:	June 25
Myanmar (Burma):	January 4
Namibia:	March 21
Nauru:	January 31
Nepal:	July 7
Netherlands:	April 30
New Zealand:	February 6
Nicaragua:	September 15
Niger:	December 18

Nigeria:	October 1
Norway:	May 17
Oman:	November 18
Pakistan:	March 23
Palau:	July 9
Panama:	November 3
Papua New Guinea:	September 16
Paraguay:	May 14–15
Peru:	July 28
Philippines:	June 12
Poland:	May 3
Portugal:	June 10
Qatar:	September 3
Romania:	December 1
Russia:	June 12
Rwanda:	July 1
St. Kitts and Nevis:	September 19
St. Lucia:	February 22
St. Vincent and the Grenadines:	October 27
Samoa:	June 1
San Marino:	September 3
São Tomé and Príncipe:	July 12
Saudi Arabia:	September 23
Senegal:	April 4
Serbia and Montenegro:	April 27
Seychelles:	June 18
Sierra Leone:	April 27
Singapore:	August 9
Slovakia:	September 1
Slovenia:	June 25
Solomon Islands:	July 7
Somalia:	July 1
South Africa:	April 27

Spain:	October 12
Sri Lanka:	February 4
Sudan:	January 1
Suriname:	November 25
Swaziland:	September 6
Sweden:	June 6
Switzerland:	August 1
Syria:	April 17
Taiwan:	October 10
Tajikistan:	September 9
Tanzania:	April 26
Thailand:	December 5
Togo:	April 27
Tonga:	June 4
Trinidad and Tobago:	August 31
Tunisia:	March 20
Turkey:	October 29
Turkmenistan:	October 27
Tuvalu:	October 1
Uganda:	October 9
Ukraine:	August 24
United Arab Emirates:	December 2
United States:	July 4
Uruguay:	August 25
Uzbekistan:	September 1
Vanuatu:	July 30
Vatican:	April 24
Venezuela:	July 5
Vietnam:	September 2
Yemen:	May 22
Zambia:	October 24
Zimbabwe:	April 18

(source: *CIA World Factbook*)

Where?

Where exactly is Area 51? Where are the world's smallest countries, and holiest religious sites? Exploring new places—be they exotic or comfortable, real or imaginary— is one of life's greatest delights. In this next section, we'll bring you to places you're probably already familiar with (such as the Empire State Building) and others, like the most expensive hotel suite in the world, that you'll wish you could visit but probably never will. You'll also learn the real laws of pretend places, and explore locations and ideas that *sound* fictitious but are all too real. Prepare to be transported.

THE ONLY ROYAL PALACE IN THE U.S.

THE STARS AND STRIPES ALWAYS FLY

A DESERT CALLED ANTARCTICA

THE WORLD'S SMALLEST COUNTRIES

THE WORLD'S LONGEST PLACE NAME

THE HUMAN SKELETON

HOLLYWOOD'S MOST FAMOUS CEMETERY

WHERE GULLIVER TRAVELED

FENG SHUI 101

AREA 51

ALIEN ABDUCTIONS

DEATH VALLEY'S EXTREMES

"HELLISH" SYNONYMS

FICTIONAL TV ADDRESSES

HOLY SHRINES

FAMOUS FINAL RESTING PLACES

WORLD'S RICHEST NATIONS

BUILDING A FOXHOLE

ROMAN CATACOMBS

WORLD'S BEST RESTAURANTS

LIGHTS ATOP THE EMPIRE STATE BUILDING

GHOSTLY HAUNTS

CITY NICKNAMES

ROAD TRIP

The first paved road was seven-and-a-half miles long and six feet wide and was built in Egypt. Made from slabs of sandstone, limestone, basalt, and pieces of petrified wood, experts believe it dates back 4,600 years to the time the great pyramids were built. Ancient Egyptians used the road to transport basalt blocks from the stone quarry to a nearby lake. The blocks were then floated across the lake, which connected to the Nile, where they traveled to a site in Giza.

◆

LETHAL INJECTION

Southern Africa is home to the fastest snake alive—the black mamba, an extremely aggressive reptile that can reach top speeds of up to twelve miles per hour. It moves along flat land with the front third of its body elevated as high as four feet off the ground, which makes it easier to move rapidly. Animals that fall prey to the black mamba die within minutes; a human might last up to four hours. No matter who or what gets bitten, the fatality rate is close to 100 percent.

◆

YEOW!

The United States Postal Service reports that postmen really do get bitten by dogs with some regularity, at a rate of over 3,000 chomps—and at a cost of over $25 million to the USPS—each year. The best advice for postal carriers is either to avoid or transfer out of the Metropolitan Los Angeles area, known as the "Dog Bite Capital" to the cognoscenti.

"WHERE SHALL FREEDOM RING?"
From Dr. Martin Luther King Jr.'s "I Have a Dream" speech

"And if America is to be a great nation this must become true. And so let freedom ring from the prodigious hilltops of New Hampshire. Let freedom ring from the mighty mountains of New York. Let freedom ring from the heightening Alleghenies of Pennsylvania!

"Let freedom ring from the snowcapped Rockies of Colorado! Let freedom ring from the curvaceous slopes of California!

"But not only that; let freedom ring from Stone Mountain of Georgia!

"Let freedom ring from Lookout Mountain of Tennessee!

"Let freedom ring from every hill and molehill of Mississippi. From every mountainside, let freedom ring.

"And when this happens, when we allow freedom to ring, when we let it ring from every village and every hamlet, from every state and every city, we will be able to speed up that day when all of God's children, black men and white men, Jews and Gentiles, Protestants and Catholics, will be able to join hands and sing in the words of the old Negro spiritual, 'Free at last! Free at last! Thank God Almighty, we are free at last!'"

◆

HONOLULU hosts the only royal palace in the United States. The Iolani Palace, built in 1882 by the last king of Hawaii, King David Kalakaua, remained a royal residence until the monarchy was overthrown in 1893—though it served as capitol of the provisional government, republic, territory, and state of Hawaii until 1969. It is now a museum.

LONG DIVISION

A continental divide is a ridge or elevated area that directs the flow of water running into adjacent drainage basins.

- **North America** is one of the only continents with two divides. The Western Continental Divide, often called the Great Divide, runs from British Columbia into the United States along the Rockies, continuing southward into Mexico and Central America. The Eastern Continental Divide runs through the Appalachian Mountains, separating land draining east to the Atlantic Ocean from land to the west, draining to the Mississippi River and Gulf of Mexico.
- **South America** is split by the Andes Mountains, which run nearly the full length of South America, divide land draining west into the Pacific Ocean and east toward the Atlantic.
- **Australia** has fairly indistinct water and mountain boundaries and is surrounded by water, making it difficult to define a single divide.
- **Europe** and **Asia**'s continental divides are equally difficult to distinguish because they both contain a number of large bodies of water into which rain falls and drains, including the North, Black and Baltic Seas, and the Arctic and Atlantic Oceans.

◆

WHERE'S THE GAME?

In May 1874 the first intercollegiate football game under American rules (not soccer or rugby) was played: Harvard vs. McGill in Cambridge, Massachusetts. Home team ruled.

LONG MAY SHE WAVE

According to Presidential Proclamation, or in some cases, U.S. law, the American flag is always displayed at the following locations:

Mount Slover limestone quarry, in Colton, California, by act of Congress. The first flag was raised on July 4, 1917.

Fort McHenry National Monument and Historic Shrine, in Baltimore, Maryland, by Presidential Proclamation, July 2, 1948.

Flag House Square, Albemarle and Pratt Streets in Baltimore, by public law approved March 26, 1954.

United States Marine Corps Memorial (Iwo Jima), Arlington, Virginia, by Presidential Proclamation, June 12, 1961.

Lexington, Massachusetts, Town Green, by public law approved November 8, 1965.

The White House by Presidential Proclamation, September 4, 1970.

The Washington Monument displays fifty U.S. flags around its perimeter; by Presidential Proclamation, July 6, 1971.

United States Customs Service at ports of entry that are continuously open; Presidential Proclamation, May 5, 1972.

National Memorial Arch, Valley Forge State Park, Valley Forge, Pennsylvania, by public law approved July 4, 1975.

In addition, the American flag is presumed to be on continuous display on the surface of Earth's Moon, having been placed there by the astronauts of *Apollo 11*. The first flag was replaced because the force of *Apollo 11*'s return to lunar orbit knocked the flag down.

FORECAST: DRY

Antarctica is the world's largest desert, covering over 5.5 million square miles. Deserts are generally described as an arid region that either receives less than ten inches of rain per year or where the potential evaporation rate is twice as great as the precipitation. The world's largest deserts:

Desert	Square Miles	Rainfall/Year (inches)	Temp (°F)
Antarctica	5,500,000+	<2	-129–58+
Sahara	3,500,000+	< 5	55–135+
Arabian	1,000,000+	4–20	30–129+
Gobi	500,000	<2.7–8	40–113+

LESS—AND MORE—THAN ZERO

The equator is at 0 degrees latitude and is 24,901.55 miles long. The Tropic of Cancer and the Tropic of Capricorn each lie at 23.5 degrees latitude—the Tropic of Cancer is located at 23.5° north of the equator and Tropic of Capricorn lies at 23.5° south.

Brazil is the only country that passes through both the equator and a tropic. The word *tropics* is most commonly used to describe the area bound by the Tropic of Cancer on the north and Tropic of Capricorn on the south.

◆

ISRAEL is ineligible to sit in on the United Nations Security Council because it is the only member nation that is not a member of any regional UN grouping.

TINY TERRITORY
The 10 smallest countries in the world...

Country	Land Mass/ Location	Type of Government
Vatican City	0.17 sq. mi. Holy See, Rome, Italy	Pope has executive power
Monaco	0.75 sq. mi. French Mediterranean, near Nice, France	Constitutional monarchy
Nauru	8.2 sq. mi. Pacific island	Republic
Tuvalu	10 sq. mi. Nine small islands scattered in Western Pacific	Constitutional monarchy with parliamentary democracy
San Marino	24 sq. mi. Surrounded by Italy	Republic
Liechtenstein	62 sq. mi. Between Austria and Switzerland	Hereditary constitutional monarchy
Marshall Islands	70 sq. mi. North Pacific	Constitutional government in free association with the U.S.
St. Kitts and Nevis	104 sq. mi. Caribbean Sea	Constitutional monarchy

Country	Land Mass/ Location	Type of Government
Seychelles	107 sq. mi. Indian Ocean	Socialist multiparty republic
Maldives	115 sq. mi. Indian Ocean	Republic

◆

"EVERY MAN A REMBRANDT!"

This was the promise from the team that created one of the biggest fads of the 1950s: paint-by-numbers. Its invention is attributed to Max S. Klein, owner of the Palmer Paint Company of Detroit, Michigan, and his partner, artist Dan Robbins, who also conceived the idea and actually designed many of the early paintings. The first kits appeared in 1951 under the CraftMaster name, and by 1954 it had become a full-blown craze, with twelve million kits sold.

Robbins said the idea had come to him from something a high school teacher had mentioned: Michelangelo often mapped out portions of a work-in-progress (including the Sistine Chapel), numbering the parts so he could remember the colors later. Robbins proposed abstract art for the debut kit, as was the fashion of the day, but America's new *artistes* preferred landscapes, seascapes, animals, and, yes, clowns.

◆

BOSTON LIGHT was the first lighthouse in America, and the last one to be automated.

WHERE'S THE WINNER?

There's a long-standing argument about the world's longest place name. Here are the choices:

Llanfairpwllgwyngyllgogerychwyrndrobwllllantysiliogogogoch

This Welsh town's name means "Saint Mary's Church in the hollow of white hazel near a rapid whirlpool and the Church of Saint Tysilio near the red cave." Though often called simply Llanfair PG, natives point out that the railway station, which opened in 1848, has a fifteen-foot sign sporting all 58 letters.

Tetaumatawhakatangihangakoauaotamateaurehaeaturipukapi-
himaungahoronuku pokaiwhenuaakitanarahu (92 letters)

This is a hill on New Zealand's South Island. The name is said to mean "the place where Tamatea, the man with the big knees, who slid, climbed, and swallowed mountains, known as land eater, played his flute to his loved one." This is featured as the world's longest place name in *The Guinness Book of World Records*, but Welsh proponents say it's not commercially used, and is, after all, only a hill.

And Thailand has entered the fray with the 167-letter "poetic name" of Bangkok:

Krung thep mahanakhon bovorn ratanakosin
mahintharayutthaya mahadilok pop noparatratchathani
buriromudomratchanivetmahasathan amornpiman
avatarnsathit sakkathattiyavisnukarmprasit

This is considered by many to be an unfair addition to the

contest, as it is more of a lengthy description of Bangkok from a loving resident's eye, and is not in popular use; most often it is abbreviated to Krung Thep, or "City of Angels." The translation is:

The land of angels, the great city of
immortality, various of devine gems,
the great angelic land unconquerable,
land of nine noble gems, the royal city, the pleasant capital,
place of the grand royal palace,
forever land of angels and reincarnated spirits,
predestined and created by the highest devas.

◆

WHO ARE YOU CALLIN' YANKEE?

Astronomer Charles Mason and surveyor Jeremiah Dixon were hired by the British courts to settle a property dispute in the colonies about two pieces of land: one which Charles I of England had given to Lord Baltimore, and the other that Charles II had gifted to William Penn. From 1763 through 1767, the surveyors undertook this enormous feat, and finally the Mason-Dixon Line was defined as the boundary between Pennsylvania and Maryland running between latitude 39°43'26.3"N and latitude 39°43'17.6"N. The survey was completed to the western limit of Maryland in 1773; in 1779 the line was extended to mark the southern boundary of Pennsylvania with Virginia (now West Virginia). It was only during debates over the Missouri Compromise in 1820 that Congress began to popularize the Mason-Dixon Line as the boundary dividing "free states" from "slave states." Today it remains a colloquialism for dividing the North from the South.

A WORLD OF ITS OWN
Where everything isn't as it should be . . . or is it?

Bizarro World is a place populated by accidental, imperfect duplicates of Superman, Lois Lane, and their friends. Back in a 1959 edition of DC Comics, Superman's archenemy Lex Luthor botched an experiment with a duplicator ray, producing a chiseled, chalk-faced version of Superman. Complete with superpowers, he was not evil, but due to his lack of intelligence, he was somewhat dangerous. Feeling rejected, Bizarro, as he was called, moved to his own planet, Htrae, which is shaped like a cube and is, of course, the word Earth spelled backward. Superman constructed an ugly, chalk-faced Bizarro Lois mate for him, and Bizarro used an "ancient advanced technology" to populate his planet with countless replicas of himself and his lady love. They lived according to the strict, backward Bizarro Code:

Us do the opposite of all Earthly things!
Us hate beauty! Us love ugliness! Is a big crime to make anything perfect on Bizarro World!

U.S. AIR BASES AROUND THE WORLD

U.S. military establishments can be found in these cities:

Aviano, Italy	Mildenhall, United Kingdom
Incirlik, Turkey	Misawa, Japan
Kadena, Japan	Osan, South Korea
Kunsan, South Korea	Ramstein, Germany
Lajes, Azores	Spangdahlem, Germany
Lakenheath, United Kingdom	Yokota, Japan

PASSION ON STAGE

The original and most famous Passion play began in the Bavarian Alps in Oberammergau as a promise to God in 1633. The townspeople were besieged by both the Thirty Years' War and plague, and swore an oath that they would perform the "Play of the Suffering, Death and Resurrection of Our Lord Jesus Christ" every ten years. The following year they began to fulfill that pledge—in a nearby cemetery surrounded by the graves of plague victims. In 2000, the Oberammergauers performed the Passion play for the fortieth time. Passion plays have become increasingly popular over the years; other large productions currently staged around the world include those in Iztapalapa, Mexico; Eureka Springs, Arkansas; and Canada's Badlands, in Alberta.

THE TRAVELS OF TARZAN

Edgar Rice Burroughs's jungle hero really got around. Here are some of the fictional spots where Tarzan swung in his twenty-five novels, which have subsequently been translated into more then fifty languages:

Ashair
Castra Sanguinarius & Castrum Mare
London-on-Thames
Opar
Pellucidar
Pal-ul-Don
Xujan Kingdom

THE SHINBONE'S CONNECTED TO . . .

A typical adult human skeleton consists of these 206 bones:

Axial skeleton

SKULL (22)
Cranial bones (8)
- frontal bone (1)
- parietal bone (2)
- temporal bone (2)
- occipital bone (1)
- sphenoid bone (1)
- ethmoid bone (1)

Facial bones (14)
- zygomatic bone (2)
- superior and inferior maxilla (2)
- nasal bone (2)
- palatine bone (2)
- lacrimal bone (2)
- vomer bone (1)
- inferior nasal conchae (2)
- mandible (1)

Middle ear bones (6)
- malleus (2)
- incus (2)
- stapes (2)

Throat (1)
- hyoid bone (1)

Vertebral column (26)
- cervical vertebrae (7) incl. atlas & axis
- lumbar vertebrae (5)
- thoracic vertebrae (12)
- sacrum (1)
- coccyx (1)

Thoracic cage (25)
- sternum (1)
- ribs (2 x 12)

Appendicular skeleton

Pectoral girdle (4)
- clavicle or collarbone (2)
- scapula or shoulder blade (2)

Pelvic girdle (2)
- coxal bone (2)

Upper limbs (60)
- humerus (2)
- radius (2)
- ulna (2)
- carpal (16)
- metacarpal bones (10)
- phalanx (28)

Lower limbs (60)
- femur (2)
- tibia (2)
- fibula (2)
- patella (2)
- tarsal (14)
- metatarsal (10)
- phalanx (28)

The infant skeleton has the following additional bones:

Sacral vertebrae (4 or 5), which fuse in adults to form the sacrum

Coccygeal vertebrae (3 to 5), which fuse in adults to form the coccyx

Ilium, ischium, and pubis, which fuse in adults to form the pelvic girdle

To recap:

- Skull and upper jaw (21 bones)
- Tiny ear bones, 3 each (6 bones)
- Lower jaw, or mandible (1 bone)
- Front neck bone, or hyoid (1 bone)
- Backbone or spine (26 bones or vertebrae)
- Ribs, 12 pairs—same for men and women (24 bones)
- Breastbone (1 bone)
- Each upper limb has 32 bones: 2 in shoulder, 3 in arm, 8 in wrist, 19 in hand and fingers (64 bones)
- Each lower limb has 31 bones: 1 in hip (one side of pelvis), 4 in leg, 7 in ankle, 19 in foot and toes (62 bones)

Total = 206 bones

FOREST LAWN RESIDENTS

One of the world's most famous cemeteries is where some of
Hollywood's greatest were laid to rest; the Glendale location is the
hillside where D. W. Griffith filmed *The Birth of a Nation* in 1915.

Forest Lawn—Glendale

Gracie Allen	Jean Harlow
L. Frank Baum	Jean Hersholt
Wallace Beery	Edward Everett Horton
Humphrey Bogart	Ted Knight
William ("Hopalong	Alan Ladd
Cassidy") Boyd	Louis L'Amour
Joe E. Brown	Carole Lombard
George Burns	Chico Marx
Jack Carson	Aimee Semple McPherson
Lon Chaney	Tom Mix
Nat King Cole	Jack Oakie
Sam Cooke	Mary Pickford
Robert Cummings	Dick Powell
Dan Dailey	Norma Shearer
Sammy Davis Jr.	Red Skelton
Dorothy Dandridge	Casey Stengel
Walt Disney	Jimmy Stewart
Theodore Dreiser	Robert Taylor
Marie Dressler	Irving Thalberg
W. C. Fields	Spencer Tracy
Larry Fine	Ethel Waters
Errol Flynn	Mary Wells
Clark Gable	Ed Wynn
Sid Grauman	Robert Young
Sydney Greenstreet	

Forest Lawn—Hollywood Hills

Steve Allen	Stan Laurel
Gene Autry	Liberace
Lucille Ball	Ozzie, Harriet, and
Albert "Cubby" Broccoli	Ricky Nelson
Bette Davis	Freddie Prinze
Andy Gibb	George Raft
Rick James	John Ritter
Buster Keaton	Isabel Sanford
Charles Laughton	Telly Savalas

◆

MONDO MONOLITH

Uluru is the Australian Aboriginal word for "great pebble."
Also called Ayers Rock, it is the world's biggest monolith.
Made of arkose, a course-grained sandstone, it rises 1,043 feet
above the ground, with a circumference of nearly five miles,
and extends down over 3½ miles beneath the surface.

'TWAS NOTHING TO SNEEZE AT

Though Clement C. Moore's 1822 "A Visit from St.
Nicholas" seems to take place in the country, he could have
been describing his New York City home. Moore lived in a
mansion on a huge estate, stretching from 18th to 24th Streets
between Eighth and Tenth Avenues, in a Manhattan
neighborhood now called Chelsea.

WHERE COUNTRIES GET HELP

Much of the generosity of countries around the world comes from money donated by member nations of the Organization for Economic Cooperation and Development to developing countries. The thirty funding democracies of the Organization for Economic Cooperation and Development work together to address the economic, social, environmental, and governance challenges of the world economy. Exchanges between OECD governments flow from information and analysis provided by the Secretariat in Paris. The Secretariat collects data, monitors trends, forecasts economic developments, and researches social changes. Each member country's contribution to the OECD annual budget is based on a formula related to the size of each member's economy. The budget for 2005 is 327 million euros (over 412 million U.S. dollars).

Country by rank	Contribution (%)
1. United States	24.975
2. Japan	23.128
3. Germany	9.467
4. United Kingdom	6.885
5. France	6.382
6. Italy	5.182
7. Canada	3.181
8. Spain	2.771
9. Mexico	1.996
10. Korea	1.932
11. Netherlands	1.876
12. Australia	1.736
13. Switzerland	1.454
14. Belgium	1.165

Country by rank	Contribution (%)
15. Sweden	1.083
16. Austria	0.926
17. Norway	0.784
18. Denmark	0.747
19. Turkey	0.706
20. Poland	0.651
21. Finland	0.583
22. Greece	0.546
23. Portugal	0.495
24. Ireland	0.399
25. Czech Republic	0.238
26. New Zealand	0.231
27. Hungary	0.181
28. Iceland	0.100
29. Luxembourg	0.100
30. Slovak Republic	0.100

◆

STROLL DOWN SEÑOR WENCES WAY

He was one of the most beloved acts on TV's *The Ed Sullivan Show*. A little man with a thick Spanish accent born Wenceslao Moreno, he was a ventriloquist without a dummy—he used his fist, a pen, and a little lipstick to make his character come alive. And when Señor Wences died just days after his 103rd birthday, New York City applauded him one more time, naming 54th Street between Sixth and Seventh Avenues "Señor Wences Way."

◆

PAJAMAS, a word that has a mysterious, luxurious sound, is from the Persian, *pa* (leg) and *jamah* (garment).

NO TRESPASSING

Schoolchildren in Massachusetts like to show off at being able to pronounce the name of a local lake (which is also the longest name for a lake in the United States):
Chargoggagoggmanchauggagoggchaubunagungamaugg

UNDERWATER VACANCY

At the bottom of Emerald Lagoon in Florida's Key Largo Undersea Park lies Jules' Undersea Lodge, an authentic underwater research lab that is also a hotel to scuba divers. In deference to the protected environment, the entire structure sits on five-foot legs. Guests trade Florida's renowned sunsets for its interior, filled with compressed air, two bedrooms (complete with sheets sporting an underwater theme), air conditioning, TV, and all the usual amenities of aboveground living, complete with gorgeous porthole undersea views. This unusual hostelry takes its name, of course, from the world's first science-fiction writer, Jules Verne.

BAD ADDRESS

A really bad place to live is 323 E. 107 Street in New York City—so bad that when Black Hand leader Ignatius "Lupo the Wolf" Lupo lived at the former horse lodgings in the early 1900s, it was called "The Murder Stable." Apparently Lupo didn't even bother to dump the victims he whacked: Reports were that when the place was finally demolished, the dead had been buried right there, underneath the stable.

WHERE GULLIVER TRAVELED

The strange lands and less-than-perfect societies Lemuel Gulliver visited in Jonathan Swift's 1726 novel, Gulliver's Travels

Balnibarbi: The island below Laputa, where things are done contrary to their natural order

Brobdingnag: A country of giants whose views and culture mock those of eighteenth-century Europe

Glubbdubdrib: An island of sorcerers and magicians, who are served by people from beyond the grave

Laputa: A flying island of brilliantly scientific, yet extremely impractical, people

Lilliput and Blefuscu: An island where everything is half the size (Lilliput) and its neighbor (Blefuscu) have an ongoing, pointless war about which end of eggs should be broken

Luggnagg: A land of prideful yet polite and generous people, and home to the Struldbrugs, a small tribe of immortal people

Land of the Houyhnhnms and Yahoos: Where intelligent horses rule over primitive, base humans

BILLED GATES

As final plans were laid in place for Central Park, architect Frederick Law Olmsted and landscape architect Calvert Vaux met opposition about their idea to make some of the park entrances special. New York City's café society suggested ornate gates for grand entrances in their carriages, which was anathema to the architects, prompting Olmsted to declare that "an iron railing always means thieves outside or bedlam inside." In 1862, the architects persuaded the park's commissioners to carve names into the stone walls near many of the entrances—or gates—instead. The commissioners chose the types of people and professions that they thought would most be enjoying the park. Clockwise, from Columbus Circle:

Merchants' Gate:	Columbus Circle
Women's Gate:	Central Park West at West 72nd Street
Explorers' Gate:	Central Park West at West 77th Street
Hunters' Gate:	Central Park West at West 81st Street
Mariners' Gate:	Central Park West at West 85th Street
All Saints' Gate:	Central Park West at West 97th Street
Boys' Gate:	Central Park West at West 100th Street
Strangers' Gate:	Central Park West at West 106th Street
Warriors' Gate:	Central Park North at Adam Clayton Powell Blvd. (Seventh Avenue)
Farmers' Gate:	Central Park North at Malcolm X Blvd. (Lenox Ave.)
Pioneers' Gate:	Duke Ellington/James Frawley Circle at Fifth Avenue
Vanderbilt Gate:	Fifth Avenue at East 106th Street
Girls' Gate:	Fifth Avenue at East 102nd Street
Woodmen's Gate:	Fifth Avenue at East 96th Street
Engineers' Gate:	Fifth Avenue at East 90th Street

Inventors' Gate:	Fifth Avenue at East 72nd Street
Scholars' Gate:	Fifth Avenue at East 60th Street
Artists' Gate:	Central Park South at 6th Avenue
Artisans' Gate:	Central Park South at 7th Avenue

OTHER OSCARS

Awards in other countries comparable to the
United States' Academy Awards:

Canada: Genie
France: César
Great Britain: British Academy Film Award, the "BAFTA"
Italy: David di Donatello
Mexico: Ariel
Spain: Goya
Sweden: Guldbagge ("Golden Ram")
Taiwan: Golden Horse

HE YAM WHERE HE YAM

Popeye pops up as town mascot in three places in the United
States: There are oversized statues of the sailor man in Alma,
Arkansas, and Crystal City, Texas (Crystal City has two).
Alma and Crystal City have had a rivalry since the 1980s,
when each laid claim to the title "Spinach Capital of the
World." Both have Spinach Festivals, and Alma is also home
to Popeye Brand Spinach. Yet Zavala County's Crystal City
has billed itself "Spinach Capital" since 1937, having been
one of the nation's premier spinach growers since the 1920s.
But perhaps Popeye himself would feel most at home in
Chester, Illinois, birthplace of Popeye creator Elzie Segar.

WHERE DID THAT SONG COME FROM?
Odd stories and legends about some of our favorite tunes

"Kid Charlemagne" by Steely Dan: All about Stanley Owsley III, a major presence in the early Haight-Ashbury scene in San Francisco, and the first "underground" chemist to mass-produce high-quality LSD in the 1960s.

"California Dreamin'" by the Mamas and the Papas: John and Michelle Phillips wrote this on a cold night in New York City when Michelle was longing to be back in California.

"Big in Japan" by Alphaville: Many rock bands, like many Hollywood stars, find they continue to be "big in Japan" long after they cannot draw a large audience in the U.S. and U.K.

"Billie Jean" by Michael Jackson: Jackson wrote this song about a woman who used to stalk him and write him letters about a son she claimed was his.

"The House of the Rising Sun" by the Animals: An homage to a brothel in New Orleans that took its name from its proprietor, Madame Marianne LeSoleil Levant (hence, the "Rising Sun" moniker). Open from 1862 to 1874, it was located at 826-830 St. Louis Street. Leadbelly wrote the lyrics for this tune in 1945. The song was first recorded in the 1920s by Texas Alexander, then by other artists.

"Carry That Weight" by the Beatles: Paul McCartney wrote this about his struggle to keep the Beatles together after Brian Epstein's death from a sleeping pill overdose in 1967. It is recorded as one song with "Golden Slumbers" as part of a suite of unfinished songs at the end of *Abbey Road*.

"Cold Blooded" by Rick James: Written by the performer about his scary girlfriend of the moment, Linda Blair, who starred in *The Exorcist*.

"Lola" by the Kinks: Band member Ray Davies wrote this number after their manager got drunk at a club and started dancing with a transvestite he mistook for a woman. Toward the end of the night, "Lola's" stubble began to show, but by then the manager was too far gone to notice, or apparently care.

"Mama Told Me Not to Come" by Three Dog Night: Randy Newman wrote this about a party that was a little bit wilder than he expected; the drug scene was fairly new to American middle-class youth at that time.

"Pass the Dutchie" by Musical Youth: Originally the song was titled "Pass the Kutchie," meaning a marijuana pipe, but because all the band members were minors, the group's manager demanded a slight lyrical change.

"Philadelphia Freedom" by Elton John: A huge rugby fan himself, Elton dedicated this to friend and tennis star Billie Jean King, who coached the burgeoning World Team Tennis team from Pennsylvania called the Philadelphia Freedoms.

◆

YUMMY

The human tongue detects only four fundamental tastes—or a combination thereof: sweet, sour, salty, and bitter. The taste buds that are sensitive to salt are spread evenly over the tongue. Sweet tastes are experienced at the tip of the tongue, sour flavors on each side, and bitter ones toward the back.

DANTE'S NINE CIRCLES OF HELL

The Divine Comedy (1308–1321), Dante Alighieri's great epic poem, takes the reader through Dante's Inferno:

Circle 1: Limbo—unbaptized yet virtuous pagans

Circle 2: The Lustful—those overcome by carnal desires

Circle 3: The Gluttonous—overindulgers and obsessive consumers

Circle 4: Hoarders and Spendthrifts—the greedy, hoarders, and indulgers

Circle 5: The Wrathful—the gloomy who can find no joy

Circle 6: Heretics—religious dissenters

Circle 7: The Violent—those who commit sins against people and property, suicides, blasphemers, sodomites, and usurers

Circle 8: The Fraudulent—those guilty of deliberate evil: panderers, seducers, flatterers, false prophets, sorcerers, corrupt politicians, thieves, perjurers, counterfeiters, impersonators

Circle 9: Traitors—betrayers, either to relatives, country, guests, or lord; Satan himself resides in the Ninth Circle

TALK ABOUT TURNOVER . . .

Two countries have been through more than the usual number of regimes: Since gaining its independence from Spain in 1825, Bolivia has had nearly 200 different governments. And since the end of World War II in 1945, Italy has been through 57 governments.

CHUNNELING

The Eurostar Train connects the cities of Paris, London, and Brussels and creates a link—an underground channel tunnel popularly called the Chunnel—between Great Britain and continental Europe for the first time since they were geographically connected during the Ice Age. Traveling 23 miles at 150 feet under the English Channel, at a speed of about 100 miles per hour, the crossing now takes only about twenty minutes, and travelers can choose whether to ride as a passenger or bring their own cars on board.

The Chunnel, completed in 1994 after seven years of labor by 13,000 engineers and workers, was not a new idea. In 1802, French engineer Albert Mathieu-Favier put forth a proposal for a tunnel between England and France, in which passengers would ride in horse-drawn carriages. In 1875, both English and French parliaments passed bills for such a project—but the deadline passed before the necessary funds were raised. The $15 billion tunnel, one of Europe's largest infrastructure projects ever, was made financially possible by the Anglo-French TransManche Link, a consortium of ten construction companies and five banks from the two countries. Ironically, the Eurostar Train leaves from London's Waterloo Station—named for England's defeat of the French general Napoleon.

INTERROGATION TIME

The phrase "being given the third degree" most likely originated from the deep secrets of the Masonic organization. When a Freemason advances to the third level, or degree—referred to as master Mason—there is a careful examination of the person's background and qualifications.

THE LONG, LONG ROAD

The Appalachian Trail runs from Springer Mountain, Georgia, to Katahdin, Maine—a distance of 2,174 miles—and was the vision of forester Benton MacKaye. Since its inception in 1937, more than 8,000 people have reported hiking the entire trail. Many quit at the first town, about 20 miles up the trail; 15 percent quit in the first week, and only about 20 percent of hikers make it the whole way. The entire trip generally takes four to eight months.

The Canadians have added a 675-mile addition from Maine into Quebec called the International Appalachian Trail, though it is separate and not an official extension.

State	Miles of Trail
Maine	281.4
New Hampshire	161.0
Vermont	149.8
Massachusetts	90.2
Connecticut	51.6
New York	88.5
New Jersey	72.4
Pennsylvania	229.3
Maryland	40.8
West Virginia	4.0
Virginia	549.9
North Carolina	88.1
Tennessee	292.7
Georgia	75.2

In PARAGUAY, dueling is still legal—as long as both parties are registered blood donors.

THE TOWN THAT BOOKS BUILT

There is a very small village in Wales in the Black Mountains near England called Hay-on-Wye. In the early 1960s a young man named Richard Booth opened a secondhand bookshop, eventually bought an old castle for the same purpose, and soon other entrepreneurs did the same. By 1988 the Annual Hay Festival began to showcase the wares of the town's booksellers, primarily antiquarian and used-book dealers. Today it is known worldwide as "The Town of Books," and it's no wonder: this little hamlet of 1,300 people currently boasts 39 bookshops.

WORLD POLLUTION

Mexico City has the worst smog levels of any city on earth, followed by Beijing and Xian in China, and New Delhi, India. The U.S. cities most polluted by smog are:

1. Los Angeles (CA)
2. Visalia-Porterville (CA)
3. Bakersfield (CA)
4. Fresno (CA)
5. Houston (TX)
6. Merced (CA)
7. Sacramento (CA)
8. Hanford (CA)
9. Knoxville (TN)
10. Dallas–Fort Worth (TX)

The CITY OF LOS ANGELES's full name is El Pueblo de Nuestra Senora la Reinade los Angeles de Porciuncula, which translates from the Spanish to "The Town of Our Lady the Queen of Angels of the Little Portion." ("Little Portion" referred to a small parcel of land.)

IT'S ALL ABOUT THE WHERE
A little bit of feng shui

Basic Tools
THINGS THAT WILL HELP FREE UP BLOCKAGES OF
ENERGY IN BOTH A HOME OR BUSINESS

Color: adds emotional, physiological, and
cultural content to life

Sound: connects us with others in our environment

Lighting, including fireplaces and garden lighting: brings
more life energy into the environment

Art: any kind that pleases you

Growing things: both plants and flowers

Water features: such as fountains, aquariums, and waterfalls

Wind-sensitive objects: wind chimes and other movement-
sensitive objects

Mirrors and crystals: circulate energy

THE BAGUAS, OR LIFE AREAS, AND THEIR
CORRESPONDING COLORS

Area	*Color*
Career	Black, Blue & Brown
Wisdom	Black, Blue & Green
Health & Family	Blue & Green
Wealth	Blue, Red & Purple
Reputation & Fame	Red

Area	Color
Love & Marriage	Red, Pink & White
Creativity & Children	White & Pastels
Helpful People	White, Gray & Black
Center or Chi	Yellow & Earth Tones

MEANING OF COLORS

Color	Meaning
Red	Attraction, Warmth, Strength
Green	Health, Potential
Purple	Spiritual guidance
Yellow	Energy, Life
Black	Mood, Perception
Pink	Love, Romance

AND A FEW FENG SHUI TIPS YOU SIMPLY
MAY NOT BE ABLE TO FOLLOW:

Your apartment should not be on the top floor.

The main door should not be in front of the toilet.

Pictures showing cruelty or war scenes should
not be hanging on the walls.

The dining room should have a fruit or vegetable
picture on the wall.

Articles that cannot be repaired, especially watches,
should not be kept in the house.

Oven burners should be kept clean.

BAD REPORT

The Committee to Protect Journalists is a nonprofit organization that promotes press freedom worldwide by defending the right of journalists to report the news without fear of reprisal. In their mission to publicly reveal journalistic abuses, the CPJ has released a list of its choices of the ten worst places in the world to be a journalist. These assignments are dangerous for a number of reasons, primarily lack of local journalistic freedoms, crackdowns from political regimes, and violent assaults on journalists:

West Bank	Burma
Columbia	Zimbabwe
Afghanistan	Iran
Eritrea	Kyrgyzstan
Belarus	Cuba

◆

SHOVELFESTS
Best North American Sandcastle Contests,
According to The Travel Channel

1. Myrtle Beach Open Sand Sculpting Competition, South Carolina (May)
2. World Championship Sand Sculpture, Harrison Hot Springs, British Columbia, Canada (September)
3. The Pizza Expo Sandtennial, Las Vegas, Nevada (April)
4. ExpoCité, Quebec, Canada (August)
5. Annual Port Aransas Sand Sculpture Contest, Texas (April)
6. U.S. Open Sandcastle Competition, Imperial Beach, California (July)
7. Annual Cannon Beach Sandcastle Contest, Oregon (June)

NOW BOARDING

Exactly where—and what—is Area 51?

Anything we suspect about Area 51 is just that: suspicion. Herewith, some of the more reliable ruminations on the tract of land we associate with aliens, UFOs, and secrecy.

- North of Las Vegas (at approximately longitude 115°45' and 115°56', and latitude 36°12.5' and 37°17.5') is a federally protected territory that covers an area equal to Rhode Island and Connecticut which is officially designated the Nellis Air Force Bombing and Gunnery Range.

- The draft version of the Environmental Impact Statement for the Nevada Test Site describes the origin of the block of land we know as Area 51: "Under Public Land Order 1662 (June 20, 1958), approximately 38,400 acres were reserved for the use of the Atomic Energy Commission in connection with the NTS. Management of this land has since been delegated to the U.S. Air Force." (Pages 4–9 to 4–11 of volume 1 of the EIS.)

- Area 51 is a tract of land six miles (north-south) by ten miles (east-west) bordered by the Nellis Bombing and Gunnery Range on the northwest, north, east, and south, and by the Nevada Test Site on the southwest. Area 51 is bounded, approximately, by longitude 115°45' and 115°56', and latitude and 36°12.5' and 37°17.5'.

- Reports are that more than 500 employees arrive at a guarded terminal at Las Vegas's McCarran Airport each day, where they board a small fleet of Boeing 737s that shuttle back and forth to Area 51.

IF YOU LIVED HERE

The most and least expensive cities from nearly 150 surveyed around the world

Most Expensive Cities

1. Tokyo, Japan
2. London, UK
3. Moscow, Russia
4. Osaka, Japan
5. Hong Kong
6. Geneva, Switzerland
7. Seoul, South Korea
8. Copenhagen, Denmark
9. Zürich, Switzerland
10. St. Petersburg, Russia

Least Expensive Cities

1. Asunción, Paraguay
2. Montevideo, Uruguay
3. Santo Domingo, Dominican Republic
4. Buenos Aires, Argentina
5. Harare, Zimbabwe
6. Bogotá, Colombia
7. Manila, Philippines
8. Bangalore, India
9. Quito, Ecuador
10. Blantyre, Malawi

◆

NORTH BY NORTH BY NORTH

Grid north is a navigational term referring to the direction northward along the grid lines of a map projection.

Magnetic north is the end of the planet where the earth's magnetic intensity is the greatest.

True north is a navigational term referring to the direction of the North Pole, relative to the navigator's position.

WATCH IT!

No matter how much time you think you're wasting in front of the television, chances are someone in the world has got you beat:

Location	TV Sets per Capita
1. Christmas Island	1,385.68 per 1,000 people
2. Bermuda	1,023.54 per 1,000 people
3. Monaco	778.08 per 1,000 people
4. United States	754.28 per 1,000 people
5. Malta	699.26 per 1,000 people
6. Japan	679.95 per 1,000 people
7. Canada	667.55 per 1,000 people
8. Norfolk Island	647.59 per 1,000 people
9. Guam	646.57 per 1,000 people
10. Luxembourg	627.53 per 1,000 people

Source: CIA World Factbook, December 2003

◆

THE MONEY MEN

The origin of the Medici family crest is also part of a familiar symbol seen around the world: a pawnbroker's sign. The Medicis, wealthy merchants and bankers in Florence from the fifteenth through the eighteenth centuries, were the largest moneylenders in Europe, and their crest is said to refer to a family story wherein a Medici fought a giant and killed him with a sack of three rocks. Those rocks became the three spheres in their emblem, and were subsequently immortalized as the trio of golden balls hanging outside the shops of moneylenders worldwide.

"THEY'RE HEEEERE"

An alien abduction is the forced removal of a person from his or her physical location to an unknown destination, presumably not on planet Earth. After the abduction, the person is returned to the original location and frequently has little or no recollection of the experience, and no idea where he or she might have been.

Common features of alien abductions include the feeling of paralysis; the perception of having been transported immaterially, frequently through a light beam; the sense of having been surgically probed or implanted with devices; the sense of freezing or slowing of time; and sexual or reproductive contact or manipulation by the aliens.

Alien and UFO believers cite indicators for those wondering whether or not they may be abductees. Some questions you might ask yourselves:

Have you lost time of any length, especially an hour or more?

Have you been paralyzed in bed with a being in your room?

Have you any unusual scars or marks with no explanation of how you received them (e.g., small scooplike indentations, scars in roof of mouth, nose, behind or in ears, genitals, etc.)?

Do you have a memory of flying through the air which you believe is not a dream?

Have you seen beams of light outside your home, or beams that enter your room through a window?

Have you had a strong sense of having a mission or an important task to perform, without knowing from where this compulsion comes?

Have you had a dream of eyes, such as animal eyes (like an owl's or deer's), or do you remember seeing an animal looking in at you from outside? Do you have a fear of eyes?

Do you have puzzling insomnia or sleep disorders?

Have you awoken in a place other than where you went to sleep—for example, in your car?

Have you seen someone become paralyzed, motionless, or frozen in time, especially someone you sleep with?

Have you known someone who claims to have witnessed a UFO or alien near you, or has said you have been missing?

Have you ever had the feeling of being watched, especially at night?

Have electronics around you gone haywire with no explanation, such as streetlights, televisions, and radios?

Do you believe that you have channeled telepathic messages from extraterrestrials?

Have you seen a hooded figure in or near your home, especially next to your bed?

According to the National UFO Reporting Center*, these are the places to keep your eyes on the skies:

Location	Reported Count
Unspecified/International	3,135
Alabama	236
Alaska	142
Alberta, Canada	167
Arizona	1,159

Location	Reported Count
Arkansas	313
British Columbia, Canada	553
California	3,950
Colorado	632
Connecticut	288
District of Columbia	46
Delaware	59
Florida	1,332
Georgia	439
Hawaii	121
Idaho	197
Illinois	1,007
Indiana	525
Iowa	247
Kansas	247
Kentucky	314
Louisiana	213
Maine	227
Manitoba, Canada	72
Maryland	305
Massachusetts	450
Michigan	766
Minnesota	394
Mississippi	166
Missouri	615
Montana	192
Nebraska	160
Nevada	426
New Brunswick, Canada	34
Newfoundland, Canada	11

Location	Reported Count
New Hampshire	176
New Jersey	536
New Mexico	326
New York	1,259
North Carolina	543
North Dakota	60
Northwest Territory	13
Nova Scotia, Canada	58
Ohio	928
Oklahoma	294
Ontario, Canada	662
Oregon	853
Pennsylvania	860
Prince Edward Island	8
Puerto Rico	36
Quebec, Canada	101
Rhode Island	87
Saskatchewan, Canada	39
South Carolina	252
South Dakota	66
Tennessee	455
Texas	1,456
Utah	285
Vermont	78
Virginia	454
Virgin Islands	2
Washington	2,088
West Virginia	179
Wisconsin	528
Wyoming	100

*As of June 2005

DIVE IN

The world's largest lake is actually the Caspian Sea, a saltwater lake measuring 143,200 square miles. It is surrounded by Russia, Azerbaijan, Iran, Turkmenistan, and Kazakhstan. The world's second-largest lake is also the world's largest freshwater lake: North America's Lake Superior, at 31,700 square miles.

Pirate stories and old salts often mention "The Seven Seas," which are actually the oceans of the worlds:

The Seven Seas
Northern Atlantic Ocean
Southern Atlantic Ocean
Northern Pacific Ocean
Southern Pacific Ocean
Indian Ocean
Southern Ocean
Arctic Ocean

◆

A PEACENIK IN THE OVAL OFFICE

The rumor has long been that the rug in the White House Oval Office changes depending on the state of the nation: that the eagle faces the arrows in his claw in times of war, and the olive branches in peacetime. There have been several rugs over the years, but in 1945 President Harry Truman had both the Presidential Seal and Flag redesigned for good. Truman felt that the eagle's head should never face the arrows of war. He believed that although the president should be prepared for war, he should always look toward peace, and had the head turned toward the olive branches.

ROUTE 66 REDUX

"The Mother Road." "The Main Street of America." "The Will Rogers Highway." These are all monikers for the road-tripper's paradise, Route 66. Today a traveler won't find a single original sign with that number—the last original Route 66 road sign was taken down in Chicago on January 17, 1977. The Mother Road (a term first used by John Steinbeck in *The Grapes of Wrath*) was decommissioned as a federal highway, with the last stretch disappearing from the records in 1984, replaced by interstates I-55, I-44, I-40, I-15, and I-10. Commissioned in 1926, this long and sometimes lonesome highway stretched for 2,448 miles across eight states (Illinois, Missouri, Kansas, Oklahoma, Texas, New Mexico, Arizona, and California) and three time zones, starting in Chicago and ending in Santa Monica; this was also the site of the eponymous TV series that ran from 1960 to 1964. When Route 66 was bypassed by superhighways in the 1960s, entire towns closed down, and businesses that had thousands of vehicles pass their way every day saw traffic dwindle to fewer than ten cars. About 85 percent of the original Route 66 can still actually be driven on. Today, Route 66 lives on in several books and Web sites.

◆

WHERE TO LAY ONE'S WEARY HEAD

The most expensive hotel room in the world is the Imperial Suite at the President Wilson Hotel in Geneva, Switzerland. Four bedrooms, a study, a dressing room, a library, cocktail lounge, billiards, a dining room that seats 26, and bulletproof windows throughout add up to $33,000 a night. And yet you still have to check out at 11 A.M.

WHERE AM I?

Accident, Maryland
Aimwell, Alabama
America, Cambridgeshire, England
Arab, Alabama
Arabia, Finland
Arsenic Tubs, New Mexico
Atomic City, Idaho
Bat and Ball, Sevenoaks, Kent, England
Bat Cave, North Carolina
Beans Corner Bingo, Maine
Beer, Devon, England
Beer Bottle Crossing, Idaho
Big Arm, Montana
Big Ugly, West Virginia
Bird-in-Hand, Pennsylvania
Bitey Bitey, Pitcairn Island
Blow Me Down, Newfoundland, Canada
Bob, Canada
Bobo, Alabama
Bong Bong, New South Wales
Bottom, North Carolina
Bowlegs, Oklahoma
Bread Loaf, Vermont
Bucksnort, Tennessee
Bug, Kentucky
Bugscuffle, Tennessee
Bumble Bee, Arizona
Bumpass, Virginia
Bunlevel, North Carolina
Burnt Corn, Alabama

Cabbage Patch, California
Camel Hump, Wyoming
Carefree, Arizona
Cat Elbow Corner, New York
Chicken, Alaska
Chugwater, Wyoming
Clam, Virginia
Climax, Pennsylvania
Cold Christmas, Hertfordshire, England
Cool, California
Cuckoo, Virginia
Cut n' Shoot, Texas
Cut Off, Louisiana
Diagonal, Iowa
Difficult, Tennessee
Dildo Key, Florida
Dinosaur, Colorado
Disco, Tennessee
Dismal, Tennessee
Doghouse Junction, California
Do Stop, Kentucky
Double Trouble, New Jersey
Ecce Homo, Schwyz, Switzerland
Economy, Indiana
Eek, Alaska
Egg, Austria
Eighty Eight, Kentucky
Eighty Four, Pennsylvania
Elephant Butte, New Mexico
Eyebrow, Saskatchewan, Canada
Fear Not, Pennsylvania
Fertile, Minnesota
Flippin, Arkansas

Frankenstein, Missouri
Frostproof, Florida
Frying Pan, California
Gas, Kansas
Gay, Michigan
Grand Detour, Illinois
Gravity, Iowa
Hardup, Utah
Held For Certain, Kentucky
Hell, Michigan
Hellhole Palms, California
Hi Hat, Kentucky
HooHoo, West Virginia
Hot Coffee, Mississippi
How, Wisconsin
Humptulips, Washington
Hurt, Virginia
Hygiene, Colorado
Index, Washington
Intercourse, Pennsylvania
Jinks, Kentucky
Keg, California
Knockemstiff, Ohio
Last Chance, California
Latex, Louisiana
Left Hand, West Virginia
Lickskillet, Ohio
Little Penny, California
Lizard Lick, North Carolina
Looneyville, West Virginia
Lost Nation, New Hampshire
Loveladies, New Jersey
Manly, Iowa

Mars, Pennsylvania
Mary's Igloo, Alaska
Matching Tye, Essex, England
Meat Camp, North Carolina
Medicine Hat, Alberta, Canada
Metropolis, Illinois
Mexican Hat, Utah
Monkey's Eyebrow, Kentucky
Monster, Netherlands
Moose Factory, Ontario, Canada
Moose Jaw, Saskatchewan, Canada
Moron, Mongolia
Mosquitoville, Vermont
Mudsock, Ohio
Nasty, Hertfordshire, England
Needmore, Virginia
New Invention, West Midlands, England
Newtwopothouse, Ireland
Nightcaps, Southland, New Zealand
Nimrod, Minnesota
Ninety Six, South Carolina
No Guts Captain, Pitcairn Island
No Name Key, Florida
No Place, County Durham, England
Nothing, Arizona
Oblong, Illinois
Okay, Arkansas
Ordinary, Kentucky
Oven Fork, Kentucky
Paint Lick, Kentucky
Peculiar, Missouri
Peep-o-Day, near Wanganui, New Zealand
Pinch, West Virginia

Pity Me, County Durham, England
Police, Poland
Polkadotte, Ohio
Porcupine, South Dakota
Possum Grape, Arkansas
Pukë, Albania
Punkeydoodles Corners, Ontario, Canada
Purgatory, Maine
Pussy, Savoie, France
Puzzletown, Pennsylvania
Quick, West Virginia
Rabbit Hash, Kentucky
Rectum, The Netherlands
Rest and Be Thankful, Argyll and Bute, Scotland
River Styx, Ohio
Rottenegg, Upper Austria, Austria
Rough and Ready, California
Rum Jungle, Australia
Saddam Hussein, Sri Lanka
Saint-Louis-du-Ha! Ha!, Quebec, Canada
Sanatorium, Mississippi
Santa Claus, Georgia
Satan's Kingdom, Vermont
Secretary, Maryland
Secret Town, California
Seldom Seen Roadhouse, Victoria, Australia
Semen, Indonesia
Silly, Belgium
Skidoo, California
Sleepy Eye, Minnesota
Snafu Creek, Yukon, Canada
Snapfinger, Georgia
Soso, Mississippi

Spasticville, Kansas
Spit Junction, New South Wales, Australia
Splatt, Devon, England
Squabbletown, California
Sugar Tit, South Carolina
Surprise, Arizona
Swastika, Ontario, Canada
Sweet Lips, Tennessee
Thong, Kent, England
Tick Bite, North Carolina
Tincup, Colorado
Toadsuck, Perry County, Arkansas
Toast, North Carolina
Tombstone, Arizona
Twopothouse, Ireland
Useless Loop, Western Australia, Australia
Virgin, Utah
Wahoo, Nebraska
Wankers Corner, Oregon
Westward Ho!, Devon, England
Where Freddie Fall, Pitcairn Island
Where Minnie Off, Pitcairn Island
Where Reynolds Cut the Firewood, Pitcairn Island
Who'd Thought It, Texas
Why, Arizona
Whynot, North Carolina
Wide Open, Tyne and Wear, England
Wigtwizzle, South Yorkshire, England
Wink, Texas
Worms, Nebraska
You Bet, California
Zig Zag, Oregon
Zzyzx, California

SOME KIND OF HOT

A Land of Extremes: Death Valley days, nights, and other facts about one of the hottest, lowest, driest places on earth

TOTAL AREA: 3,372,402 acres

HIGHEST POINT:
Telescope Peak, 11,049 feet

LOWEST POINT:
Badwater: 282 feet below sea level, it is also the lowest point in the Western Hemisphere. During the Pleistocene era, the floor of Death Valley was the bottom of a vast lake.

HIGHEST TEMPERATURE:
134°F. In 2001, a new record was set when temperatures of over 100°F were recorded for 153 consecutive days.

LOWEST TEMPERATURE:
15°F, recorded January 8, 1913

ANNUAL RAINFALL:
1.96 inches

WATER SOURCES
Darwin Falls provides year-round water for plants and wildlife; Salt Creek, Travertine Springs, and other springs provide pockets of water in other parts of Death Valley.

ANIMALS & PLANTS:
Mammals: 51 species
Reptiles: 36 species
Amphibians: 5 species
Fish: 5 species
Birds: 346 species
Plants: 1,042 species

TAKING IT ON THE ROAD

*The stops around the world where Bing Crosby and Bob Hope
traveled in the "Road Pictures":*

Road to Singapore (1940)
Road to Zanzibar (1941)
Road to Morocco (1942)
Road to Utopia (1946)
Road to Rio (1947)
Road to Bali (1952)
Road to Hong Kong (1962)

OH COME, ALL YE FAITHFUL

In 1995, the Supreme Court turned down an appeal by the
Jennings Osborne family of Little Rock, Arkansas, who
claimed that the state violated their religious beliefs when
complaints from neighbors forced the Osbornes to drastically
reduce the number of lights in their home's Christmas display.
After losing the appeal, the Osbornes donated their collection,
thought to be the largest in the world with three million lights,
to Walt Disney World, where it has now grown to over five
million lights, and has become the theme park's third-largest
attraction. The Osbornes haven't lost that love-thy-neighbor
feeling, though: They still sponsor light displays in 32 cities
throughout Arkansas.

◆

The very FIRST BOMB dropped by the Allies on Berlin in
World War II was just that—a bomb. The only thing it hit
was an elephant in the Berlin Zoo.

FOLLOWING IN HIS FOOTSTEPS

In the early days after the crucifixion of Jesus Christ, people came to Jerusalem to see the holy sites connected with Jesus' death. Distance and the ravages of time eventually made it difficult for visits to continue for these pilgrims; consequently, the Stations of the Cross were developed in the Middle Ages as a Lenten devotion for Catholics around the world. It is a reenactment of the route in Jerusalem, the Via Dolorosa, that Jesus Christ followed to Calvary and his crucifixion. Traditionally, fourteen small shrines are set up in churches, and the supplicant follows the story of the Passion of the Christ—virtually in his footsteps.

The First Station:
Jesus Is Condemned to Die

The Second Station:
Jesus Carries His Cross

The Third Station:
Jesus Falls the First Time

The Fourth Station:
Jesus Meets His Mother

The Fifth Station:
Simon Helps Jesus Carry His Cross

The Sixth Station:
Veronica Wipes Jesus' Face

The Seventh Station:
Jesus Falls the Second Time

The Eighth Station:
Jesus Meets the Women of Jerusalem

The Ninth Station:
Jesus Falls the Third Time

The Tenth Station:
Jesus Is Stripped

The Eleventh Station:
Jesus Is Nailed to the Cross

The Twelfth Station:
Jesus Dies on the Cross

The Thirteenth Station:
Jesus Is Taken Down from the Cross

The Fourteenth Station:
Jesus Is Laid in the Tomb

FANCY FOOTWORK

Tap dancing is a type of American theatrical dance, thought to be rooted as far back as the 1600s in the Irish jig and step dancing, English wooden shoe clog dancing, and African dance movements echoed and improvised upon by American slaves in the 1800s. Percussive footwork with precise rhythmic patterns is at the heart of tap dance, as its descriptive step names show—brush, flap, shuffle, ball change, cramp roll. By the 1920s the dancing became jazz-driven, and performers began to experiment with different types of metal plates, or taps, on their leather soles—and tap dancing became a true art form at last.

The word PANDEMONIUM, first used by John Milton in *Paradise Lost*, means the place of all demons. Other words for hell:

Abaddon
abyss
Apollyon
barathrum
blazes
everlasting fire
exterior darkness
furnace of fire
Gehenna
Hades
Hell
infernal region
inferno
netherworld
the pit
perdition
place of torments
pool of fire
Scheol
Tophet
underworld
unquenchable fire

The Five Rivers of Hell

Acheron—River of Woe
Cocytus—River of Lament
Lethe—River of Forgetfulness
Phlegethon—River of Fire
Styx—River of Oath

OLD IVY

The origin of the term Ivy League, though certainly referring to vine-covered college campuses, had nothing to do with the halls of education, and everything to do with their playing fields. Sportswriter Caswell Adams, from the *New York Herald-Tribune*, first used it in 1937 in reference to the conference of teams that was also known as the Old Ten: Army, Brown, Columbia, Cornell, Dartmouth, Harvard, Navy, Pennsylvania, Princeton, and Yale. In 1940, Navy and Army dropped out of the conference, but the rest had common athletic programs. The phrase soon began to cross over to represent the educational philosophies of the schools as well.

In 1927, a small group of women's colleges came together to promote the cause of all-women's education, and soon became known as the Seven Sisters:

Barnard
Bryn Mawr
Mount Holyoke
Radcliffe
Smith
Vassar
Wellesley

Vassar became coeducational in 1969, and Radcliffe has merged with Harvard; otherwise, the rest remain women's colleges.

◆

The Bronx, Brooklyn, Manhattan, Queens, and Staten Island were incorporated into one single entity—NEW YORK CITY—in 1898.

THE SMITHSONIAN MUSEUMS

The Smithsonian Institution, founded in 1826 by British scientist James Smithson, is the parent institution of the Smithsonian Museums, the largest museum complex in the world. The museums include:

- African Art Museum
- Air and Space Museum and the Steven F. Udvar-Hazy Center (Chantilly, Virginia)
- American Art Museum and its Renwick Gallery
- American History Museum
- American Indian Museum
- Anacostia Museum (African-American history and culture)
- Arts and Industries Building
- Cooper-Hewitt, National Design Museum (New York City)
- Freer and Sackler Galleries (Asian art)
- Hirshhorn Museum and Sculpture Garden (modern and contemporary art)
- National Museum of African-American History and Culture (in development)
- National Zoo
- Natural History Museum
- Portrait Gallery
- Postal Museum
- Smithsonian Institution Building, the Castle (visitor information)

All museums are in Washington, D.C., except where noted.

◆

RIKERS ISLAND, in New York City, is the largest penal colony in the world, with the population consistently around 13,000.

CRIMSON TIDE

On August 3, 1852, Yale and Harvard met for the nation's very first intercollegiate sporting event: a rowing contest at Lake Winnepesaukee, New Hampshire. The Cambridge crew prevailed over Yale by two lengths over a three-mile course. This set in motion a rivalry that thrives to this day. The Harvard and Yale crews now hold an annual four-mile race on the Thames River in New London, Connecticut, the longest of its kind in the country.

MURDER BY GEOGRAPHY

Countries throughout the world with the most intentional homicides per capita:

Rank	Country	Rate
1.	Colombia	0.62 per 1,000 people
2.	South Africa	0.51 per 1,000 people
3.	Jamaica	0.33 per 1,000 people
4.	Venezuela	0.33 per 1,000 people
5.	Russia	0.19 per 1,000 people
6.	Mexico	0.14 per 1,000 people
7.	Lithuania	0.10 per 1,000 people
8.	Estonia	0.10 per 1,000 people
9.	Latvia	0.10 per 1,000 people
10.	Belarus	0.10 per 1,000 people

MONT BLANC, on the French-Italian border, is the highest mountain in the Alps at 15,771 feet.

OUR HOMES AWAY FROM HOME
Some of the world's best addresses—and all of them fictional

The Addams Family, 001 Cemetery Lane, USA

The Anderson family from *Father Knows Best*,
607 South Maple Street, USA

Batman (aka Bruce Wayne), Wayne Manor, Gotham City, USA

The Baxter family and their maid, Hazel,
123 Marshall Road, Hydsberg, NY

The Brady Bunch, 4222 Clinton Way, Los Angeles, California

The Bunker family from *All in the Family*,
704 Hauser Street, Queens, NY

Montgomery Burns, Homer's boss on *The Simpsons*,
1000 Mammon Street, Springfield, USA

Blake Carrington from *Dynasty*, 173 Essex Drive,
Denver, CO

The Clampett family from *The Beverly Hillbillies*, 518
Crestview Drive, Beverly Hills, CA

The Cleaver family from *Leave It to Beaver*, 485 Maple Drive
(later 211 Pine Street), Mayfield, USA

The Ewing family from *Dallas*, Southfork Ranch,
Braddock County, TX

Jessica Fletcher (aka J. P. Fletcher) from *Murder, She Wrote*, 698
Candlewood Lane, Cabot Cove, ME

Dr. Frasier Crane from *Frasier*, Apartment 1901, Elliot Bay
Towers, Seattle, WA

WHERE

Sherlock Holmes, 221B Baker Street, London, UK

Ralph and Alice Kramden from *The Honeymooners*,
328 Chauncey Street, Brooklyn, NY

Leopold Bloom from the James Joyce novel *Ulysses*,
7 Eccles Street, Dublin, Ireland

Agent Fox Mulder from *The X-Files*, 42-2630 Hegal Place,
Alexandria, VA

The Munsters, 1313 Mockingbird Lane,
Mockingbird Heights, USA

Oscar Madison and Felix Unger from *The Odd Couple*,
1049 Park Avenue, New York, NY

The Partridge Family, 698 Sycamore Road,
San Pueblo, CA

The Petrie family from *The Dick Van Dyke Show*, 448 Bonnie
Meadow Road, New Rochelle, NY

The Ricardo family from *I Love Lucy*, Apartment 4A (later
3D), 623 East 68th Street, New York, NY

Mary Richards from *The Mary Tyler Moore Show*, Apartment D,
119 North Weatherly Avenue, Minneapolis, MN

Jerry Seinfeld, Apartment 5A, 129 West 81st Street,
New York, NY

The Simpsons, 742 Evergreen Terrace, Springfield, USA

The Stephens family from *Bewitched*,
1164 Morning Glory Circle, Westport, CT

Buffy Summers from *Buffy the Vampire Slayer*,
1630 Revello Drive, Sunnydale, CA

WHEEE!

The oldest amusement park in the world is in Bakken, Denmark, dating back to 1583. It was one of the premier "pleasure gardens" of medieval Europe, the forerunner of what we think of today as the amusement park, featuring entertainment, fireworks, games, and even primitive rides. Originally these sites were often a town's public garden, and ball games and shooting galleries started springing up, commercializing them. They continued to be popular into eighteenth-century Europe, when political unrest brought the end to such frivolity. By the late 1800s, the growth in interest in these parks switched from Europe to the United States, with a little help from newly formed trolley companies that were looking for ways to encourage ridership. The parks offered picnic facilities, dance halls, restaurants, games, and a few amusement rides—often on the shores of a lake or river, and at the end of the trolley line.

The Chicago World's Fair brought the modern amusement park into its golden age, with the introduction of both the Ferris wheel and the midway, a long stretch of food and game concessions and rides.

Soon the parks were known more for the excitement of their rides rather than their pastoral locations, and in 1895 the twain met in the development of perhaps the world's most famous amusement park of all: Coney Island. Then, in 1955, "The Happiest Place on Earth" opened: Walt Disney produced his dream park at Disneyland, taking the genre a step further by developing the theme park, eschewing typical rides for the fantasy of different "worlds" for guests to visit. Ironically, the success of the theme park has spread across the Atlantic and around the world, bringing the "pleasure gardens" back home again.

PARADISES FOUND

A selection of beaches most often mentioned as the best in the world

Anse Source d'Argent, La Digue, Seychelles
Cancun, Mexico
Clifton Beach, Cape Town, South Africa
Copacabana, Brazil
Crete, Greece
Datai Beach, Langkawi, Malaysia
Fraser Island, Australia
Grand Cul-de-Sac, St. Bart's
Ipanema, Rio de Janeiro, Brazil
Kuta Bali, Indonesia
Larvotto Beach, Monte Carlo, Monaco
The Maldives Islands
Maroma Beach, Mexico
Mauna Kea, Hawaii
Natadola Beach, Fiji
Negril, Jamaica
Paradise Beach, Mykonos Island, Greece
Paradise Island, Bahamas
Patong Beach, Phuket Island, Thailand
Phi Phi Island, Langkawi, Thailand
Pink Sands, Bahamas
Poipu Beach, Kauai, Hawaii
South Beach, Florida
Surfers Paradise, Australia
Tenerife, Canary Islands
Waikiki, Hawaii

◆

Every continent has a city named ROME.

LEFT-HANDERS
Places around the world where you must drive on the left

Anguilla
Antigua and Barbuda
Australia
Bangladesh
Barbados
Bhutan
Brunei
Bahamas
Bermuda
Botswana
Caymen Islands
Christmas Island (Australia)
Cook Islands
Cyprus
Dominica
East Timor
Falkland Islands
Fiji
Grenada
Guernsey (Channel Islands)
Guyana
Hong Kong
India
Indonesia
Ireland
Isle of Man
Jamaica
Japan
Jersey (Channel Islands)
Kenya

Kiribati
Kneeling (Cocos) Islands (Australia)
Lesotho
Macau
Malta
Malawi
Malaysia
Maldives
Mauritania
Montserrat
Mozambique
Namibia
Nauru
Nepal
New Zealand
Niue
Norfolk Island (Australia)
Pakistan
Papua New Guinea
Pitcairn Islands (Britain)
Saint Helena
Saint Kitts and Nevis
Seychelles
Singapore
Solomon Islands
South Africa
Sri Lanka
St. Lucia
St. Vincent and Grenadines

Suriname
Swaziland
Tanzania
Thailand
Tokelau (New Zealand)
Tonga
Trinidad and Tobago
Turks and Caicos

Tuvalu
Uganda
United Kingdom
Virgin Islands (U.S. and British)
Zambia
Zimbabwe

◆

BRIDGES OVER SEVERAL WATERS
Where to see some of the most fascinating connectors in the world

- The very short Baily Bridge, 98 feet long, is the highest bridge in the world at 18,379 feet above sea level. Built by the Indian Army in 1982, it spans the Ladakh Valley, between the Dras and Suru Rivers, in the Himalayas.
- The longest bridge in the world that is built completely over water is the Pontchartrain Causeway in New Orleans, constructed in 1956 with a total length of 24 miles.
- The world's largest natural bridge is also a natural wonder: the Rainbow Bridge, at the base of Navajo Mountain, at the edge of Lake Powell in Utah. It reaches 290 feet from its base to the top of the arch, and spans 275 feet across the Colorado River. The top of the arch is 42 feet thick and 33 feet wide.

NOT IN THE USSR
The USSR broke into fifteen new countries in 1991:

Armenia * Azerbaijan * Belarus * Estonia * Georgia * Kazakhstan * Kyrgyzstan * Latvia * Lithuania * Moldova * Russia * Tajikistan * Turkmenistan * Ukraine * Uzbekistan

ABC'S AROUND THE WORLD
Where children stay in school the longest

Rank	Country	Years Educated
1.	Norway	16.9
2.	Finland	16.7
3.	Australia	16.6
4.	United Kingdom	16.4
5.	New Zealand	16.2
6.	Sweden	16.0
7.	Netherlands	15.9
8.	Belgium	15.8
9.	Iceland	15.8
10.	Denmark	15.6
11.	France	15.4
12.	Germany	15.3
13.	Spain	15.3
14.	United States	15.2
15.	Portugal	15.2
16.	Switzerland	15.0
17.	Ireland	14.9
18.	Canada	14.8
19.	Austria	14.7
20.	Italy	14.7

Source: UNESCO Institute for Statistics

◆

The most SENSITIVE parts of the body have the most touch receptors—like the lips, tongue, fingertips, and soles of the feet. One of the least sensitive areas of the body is the middle of the back.

WHERE AM I?

A maze is predominantly a horticultural puzzle commonly found in landscape gardening and based on the Greek labyrinth in Crete—the home of the minotaur killed by Theseus, who found his way out of the labyrinth by following a string. Over time, a maze has taken on a different connotation than a labyrinth; the former is designed to be a puzzle, while the latter is an unambiguous through-route and is not designed to be difficult to navigate. Built with complex branching passages often made of high hedges, a maze is designed so that both the center and the exit are difficult for the walker, or solver, to find. A prominent feature of the formal English gardens of the seventeenth and eighteenth centuries—most notably Hampton Court Palace, London—mazes are presently enjoying a renaissance as a meditative and spiritual tool.

Mathematician Leonhard Euler was one of the first to analyze mazes, and in doing so founded the science of topology. The best rule for traversing mazes is the Wall Follower, also known as either the "left-hand rule" or the "right-hand rule." By consistently keeping a hand in contact with the maze's wall, one is guaranteed not to get lost, and either reach the exit, if there is one, or return to the entrance. Other options, including the Pledge Algorithm (which utilizes a compass) or Tremaux's Algorithm (a version of Theseus's escape plan), are more complex methods of escape. The last rule, called Random Mouse, is nearly self-explanatory: If at first you don't succeed...

SPELL IT OUT

The "ABC Islands" is the nickname given to the Caribbean resort spots of Aruba, Bonaire, and Curacao.

WORLD RELIGIOUS SITES
Some holy destinations, shrines, and pilgrimages

Amritsar, India: site of the Golden Temple of the Sikhs

Axum, Ethiopia: Ethiopian Orthodox believe the Ark of the
Covenant is kept here

Bethlehem, Israel: birthplace of Jesus Christ

Black Hills, South Dakota: Lakota Indians' site
for sacred vision quests

Bodhi Gaya, India: where Buddha reached enlightenment

Canterbury, England: seat of the Anglican archbishop

Dharamsala, India: seat of the Dalai Lama in exile

Fatima, Portugal: Catholics believe this to be the site of
1917 visions of the Virgin Mary

Ganges River, India: Hindus immerse themselves
here for spiritual purification

Haifa, Israel: seat of the Baha'i faith

Istanbul, Turkey: Eastern Orthodox seat of the
patriarchate of Constantinople

Jerusalem, Israel: world's only holy site for Judaism,
Christianity, and Islam

Kusinagar, India: site of the Buddha's death

Lhasa (Zhangmu), Tibet: sacred site for Tibetan Buddhists of
Potala Palace, historical abode of the Dalai Lama

Lourdes, France: Catholics believe springs have been curative
here since St. Bernadette's visions in 1858

Lumbini, Nepal: birthplace of Buddha

Mecca, Saudi Arabia: the center of Islam, birthplace of Muhammad, and destination of the *hajj*, the Muslim pilgrimage

Medina, Saudi Arabia: the Muslim holy city, home of Muhammad after his escape from Mecca in 622 C.E.

Palitana, India: Shatrunjaya Hill, home to 863 temples, is the pilgrimage destination for Jains

Salt Lake City, Utah: seat of the Church of Jesus Christ of Latter-Day Saints

The Vatican: seat of Catholicism and home to the pope

ANOTHER RAINY DAY IN PARADISE

The Tumucumaque Mountains National Park in Brazil is the world's largest rain forest state park, covering 9,562,770 acres of remote, unexplored forests in Amapá. Bordered by the northern Amazon River and French Guyana, the park is larger than Massachusetts and Connecticut combined. At least eight primate species, 350 bird species and 37 lizard species live in these forests. Several other species represent endangered populations, including the jaguar, giant anteater, giant armadillo, harpy eagle, the black spider monkey, the brown-bearded saki monkey, and the white-faced saki monkey.

The oldest working LIGHTHOUSE in the world is at La Coruña in northwestern Spain, near the town of Ferol. A lighthouse has been on this site since the time of the Roman emperor Trajan (98–117 C.E.). The current lighthouse was renovated and altered in 1682 and again in 1778.

ACTION!

Labor law describes a movie studio as any location where movies are made and also the company that produces, promotes, and distributes them. If this is so, the ramshackle tar structure Thomas Edison built in West Orange, New Jersey, in 1892 fits the bill. It cost $637.67, the roof opened so the sun could shine on the twelve-foot stage, and they called it the "Black Maria." Within a few years, companies began to move west to California—not only for the good weather, but because Edison's Motion Picture Patents Company couldn't keep an eye on their work as easily out west. The inventor owned almost every patent relevant to movie production at the time.

Nestor Studios opened in 1911 in the area soon to be called Hollywood, and as soon as the talkies took over, the mergers began (and haven't stopped since). Five large companies, Fox (later 20th Century Fox), Loew's Incorporated (later Metro-Goldwyn-Mayer), Paramount Pictures, Warner Bros., and RKO (Radio-Keith-Orpheum), began functioning as producers, promoters, distributors, and exhibitors, and the studio system took off.

◆

I, ROBOT

Robots were a literary conceit before they were real. Webster defines robot as "an automatic device that performs functions normally ascribed to humans, or a machine in the form of a human." In 1921, acclaimed Czech playwright Karel Capek (1890–1938) introduced the word in *R.U.R.* (Rossum's Universal Robots). *Robot* was a Czech word for forced laborer or serf; Capek's play presents robots initially as a boon to people, but they become the cause of unemployment and social unrest.

EAGLES, BIRDIES, AND JASMINE

Each hole of the famed Augusta National Golf Club, home of the renowned Masters tournament, is named after flora found on the course. Here's where to catch a "birdie's eye view."

1st	Tea Olive
2nd	Pink Dogwood
3rd	Flowering Peach
4th	Flowering Crabapple
5th	Magnolia
6th	Juniper
7th	Pampas
8th	Yellow Jasmine
9th	Carolina Cherry
10th	Camellia
11th	White Dogwood
12th	Golden Bell
13th	Azalea
14th	Chinese Fir
15th	Firethorn
16th	Redbud
17th	Nandina
18th	Holly

WHERE DID YOU HEAR THAT?

Though foul words, dialects, and vernacular are likely as old as language itself, the first volume that recorded "English slang" was Captain Francis Grose's *A Classical Dictionary of the Vulgar Tongue*. It was first published in 1785; today the U.S. Library of Congress lists 169 slang dictionaries.

BLAST OFF!

Troposphere, stratosphere, mesosphere—and you're out of here!

Outer space is out there all right—but where? The atmosphere thins with increasing altitude, even on terra firma, but the actual place where atmosphere turns into space is vague. The Fédération Aéronautique Internationale uses 62 miles (100 km)—known as the Karman Line—as the boundary between atmosphere and space, but there are other steps along the way:

1.86 miles (3 km)	U.S. Federal Aviation Administration requires supplemental oxygen for aircraft pilots and passengers
9.94 miles (16 km)	pressurized cabin or pressure suit required
11.18 miles (18 km)	troposphere ends
14.91 miles (24 km)	aircraft pressurization systems no longer function
19.88 miles (32 km)	turbojets no longer function
27.96 miles (45 km)	ramjets no longer function
31.07 miles (50 km)	stratosphere ends
49.71 miles (80 km)	mesosphere ends
62.14 miles (100 km)	aerodynamic surfaces no longer function
75.81 miles (122 km)	reentry from orbit begins

In the United States, persons who travel above an altitude of 50 miles (80 km) are designated as astronauts.

◆

Siberia's LAKE BAIKAL is the only lake in the world that is deep enough to have deep-sea fish.

THE MYSTERY OF THE GIRL SCOUT COOKIE

Like Santa Claus, they come once a year. A strange and unique variety of cookies, hand-sold by Girl Scouts. Where *do* they come from? Currently only two licensed bakers supply local Girl Scout councils:

ABC/Interbake Foods (40 percent of cookies) bill themselves in their company literature as "the oldest and most experienced licensed Girl Scout Cookie baker. We became 'Official Girl Scout Cookie Bakers' in 1939, just two years after the first sale of commercially baked Girl Scout cookies took place. ABC is part of Interbake Foods LLC, a Richmond, Virginia–based manufacturer that has been baking cookies and crackers for 100 years." ABC makes Thin Mints, Peanut Butter Sandwiches, Shortbread, Caramel deLites, Peanut Butter Patties, Reduced Fat Lemon Pastry Cremes, Animal Treasures, and Iced Berry Piñatas for the Girl Scouts.

Little Brownie Bakers (60 percent of cookies) have been baking Girl Scout cookies for over twenty-five years and provide eight varieties of cookies for the annual Cookie Sale, including Samoas, Thin Mints, Tagalongs, Do-si-dos, Trefoils, and All Abouts.

REPTILIAN MALARKEY

It's a nice legend, but full of blarney: St. Patrick didn't drive the snakes out of Ireland—ice did. No snakes survived the glaciers that covered the Isle of Erin after the last Ice Age, about 15,000 years ago. The island is isolated far enough away across the Irish Sea from England that the snakes have never been able to return. Or maybe St. Patrick just asked politely . . .

HIGH-LOW: THE TOP AND BOTTOM OF THE WORLD

Mount Everest
It's approximately 5.5 miles high, and though the exact height is disputed, current readings count Everest at 29,035 feet.

Dead Sea
Bordering Jordan and Israel, it is the lowest point on earth that is on land, at 1,312 feet below sea level.

Marianas Trench
The lowest underwater point on earth is in the Pacific Ocean near Guam—it is 36,201 feet deep.

EARLY AMERICAN VITICULTURE

"The birthplace of American viticulture" isn't Sonoma or Napa, or even Long Island's North Shore. It's a spot in New York's Hudson River Valley—a planting in 1827 at Croton Point, to be exact—where the nation's oldest continually operating vineyard started. Wine was made from grapes from this region by the French Huguenots in the seventeenth century (Huguenots also helped early Americans in St. Augustine, Florida, grow the hearty muscadine in the late sixteenth century). In the early 1800s, Andrew Jackson Caywood bought and planted a piece of land that had been growing grapes since 1772; it was later incorporated as the Village of Marlborough. Cayman created hearty hybrids that anticipated some French varieties by nearly a dozen years. In 1957, the property was sold and renamed Benmarl—and the new owners carry on Caywood's legacy of experimental winemaking.

ALL OVER YOUR BODY
Odd places you may not know you even have

Glabella: The space between the eyebrows, just above the nose.

Uvula: The pendent fleshy lobe in the middle of the posterior border of the soft palate.

Canthus: The corner where the upper and under eyelids meet on each side of the eye.

Axilla: The armpit, or the cavity beneath the junction of the arm and shoulder.

Frenum: A connecting fold of membrane serving to support or restrain any part, as of the tongue.

Lunula: The crescent-shaped area at the base of the human fingernail.

A SEA THAT IS AT SEA

The Sargasso Sea is the only body of water in the world without a shoreline; it's completely surrounded by the North Atlantic. Oval-shaped and filled with vast amounts of seaweed, it encompasses thousands of square miles and slowly rotates clockwise. It's considered a sea because it is essentially a body of water completely different than the Atlantic in which it lies: It has its own unique ecosystem, with organisms that are specially adapted to live among the unusual Sargassum seaweed, and has currents that move at a different rate than those around it—giving it an all-water "shoreline" of its own. It appears as a floating lens of warm, exceptionally clear water, and it drifts, its location determined by the changing ocean currents.

THE VAGUE HAGUE

The Hague: What exactly is it? A few facts . . .

The Hague is the administrative capital and the third-largest city in the Netherlands after Amsterdam, its capital, and Rotterdam. Amsterdam is the nominal national capital; the Dutch government, the seat of the Crown (Queen Beatrix), and the supreme court are located in The Hague.

The Hague is located in the western part of the country, in the province South Holland, of which it is also the capital.

Founded in 1248 by William II, Count of Holland and King of Germany, The Hague had a population of nearly 475,000 in 2004.

The Hague Conventions of 1899 and 1907 were, along with the Geneva Conventions, among the first formal statements of the laws of war and war crimes in the body of international law.

The United Nations names The Hague as one of its capitals; thus it is host to several institutions of the UN:

The International Court of Justice, located in the Peace Palace, Vredespaleis (its construction was financed by Andrew Carnegie)

The International Criminal Tribunal for the Former Yugoslavia

The International Criminal Court

The Organization for the Prohibition of Chemical Weapons

The Model United Nations

Other famous institutions in The Hague are:

Permanent Court of Arbitration

Organization for Prohibition of Chemical Weapons (OPCW)

European Patent Office

Europol

In the near future the city will also welcome the Organization for Prohibition of Biological Weapons.

◆

YO! HO! HO! AND NO BOTTLE OF RUM

A major change in U.S. naval regulations came down with the appointment of Secretary of the Navy Josephus Daniels in 1913. He prohibited alcohol aboard all naval vessels—making strong coffee the strongest quaff around. In a mock salute, sailors began to call it "a cup of Joe." Current regulations state that if a ship is at sea for forty-five consecutive days the captain can authorize a special ration of two cans of beer per crew member. Otherwise, navy ships still remain dry.

GROUND ROUTE
Freedom in a box

Henry "Box" Brown was born a slave in Louisa County, Virginia, in 1815. He married and had children, but when his family was sold to a plantation owner in North Carolina in 1849, he decided to escape, and procured the help of a southern shoemaker. The sympathetic friend arranged for him to be shipped to Philadelphia in a box. Brown not only survived, but became a renowned anti-slavery speaker and wrote his autobiography, *Narrative of the Life of Henry Box Brown*.

R. I. P.

Final resting places of the famous, infamous, or unknown, and some of the world's renowned burial sites

Basilica di Santa Croce di Firenze, Florence, Italy: Galileo, Machiavelli, Michelangelo, Gioacchino Rossini, and many other notables are laid to rest here, perhaps opened by St. Francis himself in 1294.

Cimetière du Père Lachaise, Paris, France: Founded in 1805, this famous resting place is the final home to many French Holocaust victims; also the resting place of Oscar Wilde, Jim Morrison, and Frederic Chopin.

Cimitero Monumentale, Milan, Italy: On the grounds of this vast cemetery founded in 1860 is the *Famedio,* or Temple of Fame, where Giuseppe Verdi, Vladimir Horowitz, Alessandro Manzoni, and Arturo Toscanini are interred.

Fairview Cemetery, Fairfax, Nova Scotia: Though founded in 1832, this cemetery made history in 1912 when it became the Titanic Cemetery, where 121 victims of the maritime disaster were laid to rest. Each grave says the same thing: Besides the victim's name, it reads only "Died April 15, 1912."

The Great Pyramid of Giza: This is the last of the Seven Wonders of the World (allegedly 2570 B.C.E.), and probably the most renowned cemetery in the world. It presumably serves as the tomb of the Fourth Dynasty Egyptian Pharaoh Cheops.

Catholic Cemetery, Mount Zion, Jerusalem, Israel: In almost continual use from the time of the First Temple (ca. 850 to 586 B.C.E.) until the present. Oskar Schindler is buried here.

Novodevichy Cemetery, Moscow, Russia: Many famous Russians and citizens of the former Soviet Union have been buried here since its founding in 1524, including Nikita Khrushchev, Anton Chekhov, and composers Sergei Prokofiev and Dmitri Shostakovich.

Peter and Paul Fortress, St. Petersburg, Russia: All Russian czars since Peter the Great are buried in the cathedral, built between 1703 and 1728.

Rockwood Cemetery, Sydney, Australia: The largest burial site in the Southern Hemisphere, founded in 1867, is the final resting place of approximately one million souls.

Westminster Abbey, London, England: Eighteen monarchs and England's most notable statesmen and distinguished subjects have been laid to rest in the Abbey since Henry III began its rebuilding in 1245. Since the fourteenth century, the Abbey has become a burial place for notables such as Charles Darwin, Sir Isaac Newton, Robert Browning, Geoffrey Chaucer, Charles Dickens, George Frederick Handel, Thomas Hardy, Rudyard Kipling, Laurence Olivier, and Alfred, Lord Tennyson.

◆

AN EVERYMAN FOR EVERYWHERE

On June 20, 1970, David Kunst set out from Waseca, Minnesota, to walk 14,450 miles around the world. He made it— four years, three months, sixteen days, and 21 pairs of shoes later. It is to date the only certified walk around the world (he flew across the oceans) and is listed in *The Guinness Book of World Records*.

THINKING GLOBALLY

The Greeks are considered to be the founders of geography as a scientific discipline. In 140 B.C.E., a Greek named Crates is said to have created the first globe, a spherical representation of Earth; today the globe is still considered to be the most spatially accurate depiction of Earth.

The world's largest globe is the Unisphere, built for the 1964 New York World's Fair at Flushing Meadows, New York. This stainless steel globe is 120 feet across and weighs 900,000 pounds. The three rings around it trace the orbits of Yuri Gagarin, the first man in space; John Glenn, the first American to orbit Earth; and Telstar, the first communications satellite. Its motto: "Peace Through Understanding."

LOST WEEK-AND-A-HALF

On September 2, 1752, time flew like never before in both England and its American colonies, when the Gregorian calendar replaced the Julian calendar. On the day calendars changed, the world was suddenly eleven days ahead of where it had been. People went to bed on September 2 . . . and woke up on September 14.

PENNSYLVANIA CRUDE

The first successful oil well in the world gushed on an August day in 1859, and in a rather surprising spot: Titusville, in northwestern Pennsylvania. Colonel Edwin L. Drake was certain that extracting oil from the earth by drilling was the way of the future, and set aside enough money to drill 1,000 feet. He struck black gold at 69½ feet.

HANGAR STAKES

Everett, Washington, is home to the Boeing Aircraft Plant, a major aircraft manufacturing location that offers visitors factory tours that showcase Boeing and invites visitors to enter what the company claims is the largest building in the world: 472 million cubic feet of space, almost 100 acres. Guests—and there are 120,000 of them a year—see airplanes in various stages of flight tests and how the company tailors its aircraft for different countries and carriers around the world.

◆

BUT THEY'RE NOT MADE OF HAM

"Hamburgers, hamburgers, hamburgers hot; onions in the middle, pickle on top. Makes your lips go flippity flop."

There are several claims to the origin of the hamburger in the United States, from Charlie Nagreen of Seymour, Wisconsin, who composed the haunting melody above for the 1885 Outagamie County Fair, to the traveling Menches Brothers from Akron, Ohio, who claim they invented the patty sand- wich in the same year. There is even a mention of a "hamburg steak" on the 1827 menu of Delmonico's in New York, though exactly what it was remains unknown. But the earliest refer- ences seem to come from the days of Genghis Khan, when his army would carry pieces of lamb or beef under their saddles to soften the meat, then grind it and eat it one-handed while riding horseback. When Ghengis's grandson, Kublai Khan, invaded Moscow in 1238, the Russians began to make their own changes to the recipe, adding chopped onion, raw eggs, and spices and naming it after the invaders: Steak Tartare.

SAIL AWAY
The inhabited islands of the Caribbean

Anguilla (UK)

Antigua and Barbuda
Antigua
Barbuda

Aruba (Netherlands)

Barbados
Barbados
Culpepper Island
Pelican Island (now
absorbed into Barbados)

Belize
Ambergris Caye
Caye Caulker
Glover's Reef
Lighthouse Reef
South Water Caye
Turneffe Islands

British Virgin Islands (UK)
Anegada
Beef Island
Bellamy Cay
Cooper Island
Frenchman's Cay
Great Camanoe
Guana Island
Jost Van Dyke
Little Thatch
Marina Cay

Mosquito Island
Nanny Cay
Necker Island
Norman Island
Peter Island
Prickly Pear Island
Saba Rock
Salt Cay
Tortola
Virgin Gorda

Cayman Islands (UK)
Cayman Brac
Grand Cayman
Little Cayman

Colombia
San Andrés and Providencia

Cuba
Cuba
Isla de la Juventud

Dominica

Grenada
Carriacou
Grenada
Petit Martinique

Guadeloupe (France)
Basse-Terre
La Désirade

Grande-Terre
Marie-Galante
Iles de la Petite-Terre
Saint-Barthélemy
Terre-de-Bas (Les Saintes)
Terre-de-Haut (Les Saintes)
Saint-Martin (same island as Sint Maarten)

Hispaniola (Haiti and the Dominican Republic)

Honduras
Barbaretta (Islas de la Bahía Department)
Cayos Cochinos (Islas de la Bahía)
Guanaja (Islas de la Bahía)
Roatán (Islas de la Bahía)
Swan Islands
Útila (Islas de la Bahía)

Jamaica

Martinique (France)

Mexico
Cancún
Isla Contoy
Isla Cozumel
Isla Mujeres

Montserrat (UK)

Netherlands Antilles (Netherlands)
Bonaire

Curaçao
Saba
Sint Eustatius
Sint Maarten (same island as Saint-Martin)

Nicaragua
Corn Islands
Cayos Miskitos

Panama
San Blas Islands
Bocas del Toro

Puerto Rico (U.S.)
Culebra
Mona
Puerto Rico
Vieques

Saint Kitts and Nevis
Nevis
Saint Kitts

Saint Lucia

Saint Vincent and the Grenadines
Bequia
Canouan
Mayreau
Mustique
Palm Island
Petit Saint Vincent
Saint Vincent
Union Island
Young Island

Trinidad and Tobago
Tobago
Trinidad

Turks and Caicos (UK)
Grand Turk
Middle Caicos
North Caicos
Parrot Cay
Pine Cay
Providenciales
Salt Cay

South Caicos

U.S. Virgin Islands
Hassel Island
Saint Croix
Saint John
Saint Thomas
Water Islan

Venezuela
Isla Margarita
Los Roques
Los Testigos

NO MAN'S LAND?

In 1861, the British government defined "island": If it was inhabited, then the size of the piece of land was of no import. If no one lived on the land, it had to be the size of "the summer's pasturage of at least one sheep"—which is about two acres.

Bishop Rock is commonly considered the smallest island in the world. Off the Scilly Islands in Cornwall, UK, it has only a lighthouse and takes perhaps the worst buffeting by the ocean on earth (the first tower, erected in 1847, was swept away before it was even operable).

"Where all the women are strong, all the men are good-looking, and all the chidren are above average."

—GARRISON KEILLOR'S DESCRIPTION OF THE FICTIONAL
LAKE WOEBEGON, MINNESOTA, ON RADIO'S
Prairie Home Companion

KITTY HEAVEN

In Key West, Florida, the streets are filled not only with loose chickens and roosters, but countless six-toed cats. Many of them are believed to be descendants of a feline given to the writer Ernest Hemingway. Local legend has it he was penning *The Old Man and the Sea* at the time, and a drinking buddy, who was also a sea captain, gave him a polydactyl cat. Sea lore has it that six-toed cats are good luck for sailors (and are superior mousers). Hemingway brought the kitty home, and his Key West house, which is now a museum, cares for more than sixty "Hemingway cats" to this very day. Most of the family are six-toed, and many of them are named after other writers or movie stars. Presently on location are Somerset Maugham, Emily Dickinson, Archibald MacLeish, Simone de Beauvoir, Zelda Fitzgerald, Trevor Howard, Marilyn Monroe, Joan Crawford, Charlie Chaplin, and Ava Gardner—to name just a few.

THIS OLD HOUSE

Outside of Tokyo, Japanese archaeologists have recently discovered ten post holes forming two irregular pentagons: They are mostly likely the remains of two huts, and what seem to be the world's oldest artificial structures. Thought to be built by *Homo erectus*, who were known to use simple tools, the site is about 500,000 years old.

◆

REYKJAVIK, ICELAND, is the world's northernmost capital, with a population of approximately 180,000 people. The city was settled in the year 874.

THE RICHEST OF THE RICH

A country's wealth is defined by its gross domestic product (GDP), or value of all final goods and services produced within that nation in a given year. These estimates are derived from purchasing power parity calculations.

Country	Amount
1. Luxembourg	$58,900 per person
2. United States	$40,100 per person
3. Guernsey	$40,000 per person
4. Norway	$40,000 per person
5. Jersey	$40,000 per person
6. British Virgin Islands	$38,500 per person
7. Bermuda	$36,000 per person
8. San Marino	$34,600 per person
9. Hong Kong	$34,200 per person
10. Switzerland	$33,800 per person
11. Cayman Islands	$32,300 per person
12. Denmark	$32,200 per person
13. Ireland	$31,900 per person
14. Iceland	$31,900 per person
15. Canada	$31,500 per person
16. Austria	$31,300 per person
17. Australia	$30,700 per person
18. Belgium	$30,600 per person
19. United Kingdom	$29,600 per person
20. Netherlands	$29,500 per person
21. Japan	$29,400 per person
22. Finland	$29,000 per person
23. France	$28,700 per person
24. Germany	$28,700 per person
25. Isle of Man	$28,500 per person

Source: CIA World Factbook 2005

NO SMALL MALL

It's not "the mall" most of us think of when we hop in the car to hit the movies and run a few errands. The West Edmonton Mall, in Alberta, Canada, is not only the world's largest mall, but also bills itself as the world's largest shopping, amusement, and recreation center, attracting millions of tourists every year; the mall's economic impact on the Province of Alberta surpasses that of even Banff National Park. It employs over 23,000 people, covers over 5.2 million square feet, has more than 80 restaurants, an amusement park, a seven-acre water park, an NHL-size ice arena, submarines, an exact replica of the Santa Maria ship, a lagoon featuring special aquatic attractions, aquarium facilities, a miniature golf course, 26 movie theaters, a hotel, and a casino. And, of course, parking for 20,000 cars.

ESCAPE TO PARADISE

Until the beginning of the fifth century, the Venetian Lagoon was more of an escape hatch than anything else. As the Roman Empire began to crumble, people began to move to the Lagoon from the Italian mainland to escape the constant danger of invaders, especially Attila the Hun. Though tradition has it that Venice—which is actually 118 tiny islands connected by both bridges and canals—was founded as a city in 421 C.E., people continued to return to their cities and former lives until about 450 C.E. It became clear to them at last that life in the sanctuary of the canals was not only safer, but in fact quite pleasurable as well.

◆

The JAPAN Sherlock Holmes Club is the largest of the 375 such organizations worldwide, with 1,200 members.

BEFORE "FORE!"

No doubt that Scotland is the birthplace of golf—this compact-sized country, with more than 400 courses for five million inhabitants, is truly heaven on earth for the linksman. But the word *golf* did not stem from "Gentlemen Only, Ladies Forbidden!" as the old acronymal anecdote goes—most likely the name is derived from an Old Dutch word *kolf* or *kolve*, meaning club. Scottish dialect eventually transformed it into *gouf* or gowf.

Exactly when golf began to be played, however, is an even bigger mystery. Oddly, the first recorded mention of the sport, in 1457, was when King James II banned play, demanding that "fute-ball and golfe be utterly cryed down and not to be used." In 1502, this ban was repealed by King James IV of Scotland (1473–1513), a most learned monarch, who also practiced dentistry, founded the Royal College of Surgeons in Scotland, and introduced compulsory education. He became the first recorded golfer as we know it, playing on the North Inch (which still has a golf course today), and around Scone Palace, to the North of Perth.

As for the number of holes: on May 5, 1858, new rules were issued by the Royal and Ancient Golf Club at St. Andrews, Scotland. Among these was the stipulation that "one round of the links or eighteen holes is reckoned a match." At that time the course at St. Andrews happened to have eighteen holes, and that became the standard for golf courses around the world.

◆

INDONESIA is unique among all other countries, having a landmass composed completely of islands—17,508 of them—only 6,000 of which are inhabited.

WORLD'S LARGEST SUBWAY SYSTEMS
By annual ridership

City	Date Completed	Ridership Annually	Length (km)
Moscow	1935	3.3 billion	340
Tokyo	1927	2.6 billion	281+
Seoul	1974	2.2 billion	278+
Mexico City	1969	1.4 billion	202
New York City	1904	1.4 billion	371
Paris	1900	1.2 billion	211
London	1863	970 million	415
Osaka	1933	957 million	114
St. Petersburg	1955	821 million	110
Hong Kong	1979	786 million	82

Source: 2002 statistics, www.infoplease.com

THE THING FROM OUTER SPACE

The world's largest meteorite is located in Namibia, South Africa, and can be found on the Hoba farm near Grootfontein. It was discovered and first described by J. Brits in 1920 and weighs approximately 60 tons. Scientists estimate that the Hoba fell to Earth approximately 80,000 years ago. It is composed of 82% iron, 16% nickel, and 1% cobalt, as well as various trace elements.

◆

The WORLD'S current population growth rate is about 1.3 percent, with a doubling time of 54 years. The greatest recorded growth rate to date was in the 1960s at 2 percent, with a doubling time of 35 years.

WORLD JEWISH POPULATION
Countries with 100,000 or more Jewish residents:

United States	5,800,000
Israel	4,847,000
France	600,000
Russia	550,000
Ukraine	400,000
Canada	360,000
United Kingdom	300,000
Argentina	250,000
Brazil	130,000
South Africa	106,000
Australia	100,000

◆

From the 1920s to the 1960s, BURMA-SHAVE signs were as much a part of the American landscape as diners and gas stations. At the height of their popularity, there were 7,000 of them on the road, in every state except Arizona, Nevada, Massachusetts, and New Mexico; traffic was so sparse in these states at the peak of Burma-Shave Nation that the company didn't bother to post them there.

◆

CHINA is the country with the largest population: about 1.306 billion people. At the other end of the spectrum is The Vatican, the country with the world's smallest population, which hovers somewhere between 900 and 1,000 residents.

AN INSTRUMENT FOR WHERE

Although a rudimentary compass most likely appeared in China during the Han Dynasty (second century B.C.E. to the second century C.E.), it was not a navigational tool, but more of a divinational device for use in the art of feng shui. These first versions used a piece of lodestone floating on water, which pointed south. A flat piece of iron was then used as a pointer, eventually replaced by a needle; needles were magnetized by stroking them with a lodestone.

Magnetic compasses of a very simple kind were in use in the Mediterranean as early as the twelfth century, although little was known about how they worked. (Its evolution was so slow, in fact, that for some time superstitious sea captains believed if their crew ate onions, it would influence the compass's magnetism.) The compass is the first instrument to play a large part in modern scientific observation; the sundial and the wind vane were all that preceded it. The journeys of famous Chinese navigator, Zheng He (1371–1435), were the first recorded instances of the use of the compass as a navigational aid.

PLAY THAT PLUCKY MUSIC

Though it has long been held that the banjo is the only musical instrument indigenous to the United States, it is more likely that the earliest banjos were introduced in countries that were engaged in the slave trade. It is quite possible that the Arabs brought the instrument to the West African Coast, and it was then carried into America along with the Negro slaves. Thomas Jefferson wrote of its introduction in his *Notes on the State of Virginia* (1781), *"The instrument . . . is the banjar, which they brought hither from Africa."*

THE MAKING OF A FOXHOLE

Choose a piece of flat land, away from a water source.

For foxhole depth, measure height of soldier plus 6 to 8 inches, adding a few inches if foxhole is going to be covered.

If foxhole will be used for some duration, procure chicken wire, string, and stakes.

Put the chicken wire around the inner diameter of foxhole and tie it.

Place the stakes into the center of the parapet encircling foxhole, tying the top of the chicken wire to the stakes.

The firestep is where a soldier stands when in firing position. Off the step, there should still be sufficient room to receive head-level protection.

The water sump is located at one end of the emplacement to collect water.

The grenade sump is a small tunnel about 18 inches long, sloped downward at an angle of about 30 degrees, and is dug at the lowest level away from the firing position. Hand grenades thrown into the emplacement are disposed of here, and the fragments absorbed by the surrounding soil.

Excavated soil around the foxhole forms the parapet and is piled 3 feet wide and 6 inches high. This provides an elbow rest and extra protection from small arms fire.

A foxhole can be effectively camouflaged with available branches and foliage. Simple frames, with ponchos when available, create overhead cover.

RIDING THE RITZY RAILS

If the idea appeals to you, and you are not afraid to embark on a 2,000-kilometer journey powered only by steam, we would be happy to have you join us.... We are leaving Paris on Tuesday, 10th October, and we will be in Vienna Wednesday night.

Announcements like the one in the advertisement above inaugurated the newest way to travel for wealthier Europeans in 1883—and soon the Orient Express became the most fashionable way to go. Though the train's original route was from Paris through Munich, Vienna, and Sophia to Constantinople (Istanbul)—1,980 miles—passengers could continue the journey, traveling by boat across the Bosphorus to the Haydarpasa Railway Station to join the Taurus Express to Baghdad.

In the 1980s investors had many of the original cars refurbished and reintroduced the Orient Express, running from Paris to Vienna (864 miles) and from Stuttgart to Prague (779 miles). American Orient Express also presently offers ten deluxe train tours, ranging from National Parks of the West to an Antebellum South Train Holiday. Agatha Christie has yet to make a reservation.

HOW NOW HOCKEY?

Though there's some question as to how and where ice hockey came to be, most agree that its beginnings lie in Canada. One popular theory has the sport originating around 1800 in Windsor at Canada's first college, King's College School, when the students began to play hurley, a field game, on nearby skating ponds. A new winter version, "ice hurley," developed, which eventually became ice hockey.

STARRY SKIES

A *zodiac*, from the Greek for animal, is an imaginary band in the heavens extending approximately 8 degrees on either side of the apparent path of the sun, moon, and planets. It is divided into twelve parts of 30 degrees each—astrological signs each named for a constellation.

The Twelve Zodiacal Constellations
Aquarius, the Water-Bearer
Aries, the Ram
Cancer, the Crab
Capricorn, the Goat
Gemini, the Twins
Leo, the Lion
Libra, the Scales
Pisces, the Fishes
Sagittarius, the Archer
Scorpio, the Scorpion
Taurus, the Bull
Virgo, the Virgin

Twenty-nine Constellations North of the Zodiac
Andromeda, the Chained Lady
Aquila, the Eagle
Auriga, the Charioteer
Bootes, the Wagoner
Camelopardalis, the Camelopard (Giraffe)
Canes Venatici, the Hunting Dog
Cassiopeia, the Lady in the Chair
Cepheus, the King
Coma Berenices, Berenice's Hair
Corona Borealis, the Northern Crown

Cygnus, the Swan
Delphinus, the Dolphin
Draco, the Dragon
Equuleus, the Colt
Hercules (Kneeling)
Lacerta, the Lizard
Leo Minor, the Lesser Lion
Lynx, the Lynx
Lyra, the Lyre or Harp
Ophiuchus, the Serpent Holder
Pegasus, the Winged Horse
Perseus, the Hero (with Medusa's head)
Sagitta, the Arrow
Scutum, the Shield
Serpens, the Serpent
Triangulum, the Triangle
Ursa Major, the Greater Bear
Ursa Minor, the Lesser Bear
Vulpecula, the Fox (and the Goose)

Forty-nine Constellations South of the Zodiac
Antila, (Pneumatica), the Air Pump
Apus (Avis Indica), Bird of Paradise
Ara, the Altar
Caelum (Sculptorium), the Engraver's Tool
Canis Major, the Greater Dog
Canis Minor, the Lesser Dog
Carina, the Keel (Argo Navis)
Centaurus, the Centaur
Cetus, the Whale
Chamaeleon, the Chameleon
Circinus, the Pair of Compasses
Columba (Noachi), (Noah's) Dove

469

Corona Australis, the Southern Crown
Corvus, the Crow
Crater, the Bowl
Crux Australis, the Southern Cross
Dorado (Xiphias), the Gilthead or Swordfish
Eridanus, the River Po
Fornax (Chemicae), the Chemist's Furnace
Grus, the Crane
Horologium, the Clock
Hydra, the Water Serpent (feminine)
Hydrus, the Water Snake or Sea Serpent (masculine)
Indus, the Indian
Lepus, the Hare
Lupus, the Wolf
Pyxis Nautica, the Compass
Mensa (Mons Mensae), the Table Mountain
Microscopium, the Microscope
Monoceros, the Unicorn
Musca (Apis), the Fly or Bee
Norma, the Square or Rule
Octans, the Octant
Orion, the Hunter
Pavo, the Peacock
Phoenix, the Fabulous Bird
Pictor (Equuleus Pictorius), the Painter's Easel or Little Horse
Piscis Austrinus, the Southern Fish
Puppis, the Stern (Argo Navis)
Pyxis (Nautica), the Ship's Compass
Reticulum, the Reticule or Net
Sculptor (Apparatus Sculptorius), the Sculptor's Tool
Sextans, the Sextant
Telescopium, the Telescope
Triangulum Australe, the Southern Triangle

Tucana, the Toucan
Vela, the Sails (Argo Navis)
Volans, the Flying Fish

Asterisms are recognizable patterns of stars that have names, but are not constellations. These include the Big Dipper, which lies within the Ursa Major constellation; the Little Dipper; the Sickle, which forms Leo's mane; the Great Square, or Baseball Diamond, within Pegasus's body; and the Circlet, which lies within Pisces

◆

CHEERS!

Brewing is perhaps the most ancient manufacturing art known to man, though its exact origin remains uncertain. Records from 6,000 years ago show evidence that the Sumerians discovered fermentation, though perhaps by chance. The Chinese were brewing a beer called *kui* 5,000 years ago, and seven hundred years later, clay tablets of the Babylonians were found with beer recipes, citing brewing as a highly respected profession—one in which the master brewers were women.

BROADCAST NEWS

South Dakota may have Mount Rushmore, but that's nothing compared to what Blanchard, North Dakota, has to offer: the largest man-made structure in the world. It's the KVLY-TV tower, and at 2,063 feet high, the steel structure is taller than the Great Pyramid at Giza, the Eiffel Tower, and the Washington Monument combined.

"HELLO, SANTA?"
Important phone numbers at the North Pole*

Recorded local events
(907) 456-INFO

Federal Aviation Administration
(907) 474-0137
or (800) 992-7433

Highway and Travel Conditions
(907) 456-7623
or (800) 478-7675

Time & Temperature
(907) 488-1111

Weather
Recorded Weather (907) 458-3745
Forecast (800) 472-0391

* North Pole, Alaska

◆

C'MON-A MY HOUSE

Levittown, Pennsylvania, was the largest planned community constructed by a single builder in the United States. Begun in 1951 under the direction of Abraham Levitt and his sons, William and Alfred, the development occupied over 5,500 acres in lower Bucks County by the time it was completed in 1958, and included churches, schools, swimming pools, and shopping centers. And, of course, 17,311 single-family homes.

ROMAN CATACOMBS

Though it has long been rumored that the catacombs were used extensively as hiding places for Christians from invaders of Rome, this is a fallacy: When Peter and Paul preached to early Christians, pagan and Jewish catacombs already existed. As burial places, they were considered sacred and protected by Roman law.

As a rule, a stairway leads below ground to a depth of about 30 to 50 feet; from this point diverge the galleries, which are from 10 to 13 feet in height, and seldom broader than necessary for two gravediggers, one behind the other, to carry a bier. In the side walls of the galleries horizontal tiers of graves are cut out of the rock from floor to ceiling. The number of graves in the Roman catacombs is estimated at two million. Burial continued in the catacombs until 410 C.E.

Over time, landslides and vegetation hid the entrances to the other catacombs, so that all traces of their existence were lost until 1578, when they were rediscovered. One of the most famous sites, the Crypt of the Popes, is in the Catacombs of Saint Callixtus and was discovered in 1854 by archaeologist Gian Battista de Rossi. Nine of the Catholic Church's early pontiffs were buried there:

St. Pontianus (230–235)
St. Antherus (235–236)
St. Fabian (236–250)
St. Lucius (253–254)
St. Stephen (254–257)
St. Sixtus II (257–258)
St. Dionysius (259–268)
St. Felix (269–274)
St. Eutichian (275–283)

WORLD-CLASS FOOD
The 50 best places on earth to dine

1. The Fat Duck, Bray, Berkshire, UK
2. El Bulli, Montjoi, Spain
3. French Laundry, Yountville, CA
4. Tetsuya's, Sydney
5. Restaurant Gordon Ramsay, Royal Hospital Road, London
6. Pierre Gagnaire, Rue Balzac, Paris
7. Per Se, New York
8. Tom Aikens, London
9. Jean Georges, New York
10. St. John, London
11. Michel Bras, Laguiole, France
12. Le Louis XV, Monaco
13. Chez Panisse, California
14. Charlie Trotter, Chicago
15. Gramercy Tavern, New York
16. Guy Savoy, Rue Troyon, Paris
17. Restaurant Alain Ducasse, Paris
18. The Gallery at Sketch, London
19. The Waterside Inn, Bray
20. Nobu, Park Lane, London
21. Restaurante Arzak, San Sebastian, Spain
22. El Raco de Can Fabes, San Celoni, Spain
23. Chessino dal 1887, Rome
24. Le Meurice, Paris
25. L'Hotel de Ville, Crissier, Switzerland
26. L'Arpege, Paris
27. Angela Hartnett at the Connaught, London
28. Le Manoir Aux Quat' Saisons, Oxford
29. Le Cinq, Paris, France
30. Hakkasan, London

31. Cal Pep, Barcelona
32. Masa, New York
33. Flower Drum, Melbourne
34. WD50, New York
35. Le Quartier Francais, Franschhoek, South Africa
36. Spice Market, New York
37. Auberge de Auberge de l'Ill, Illhauseern-Alsace, France
38. Manresa, California
39. Restaurant Dieter Muller, Bergisch Gladbach, Germany
40. La Masion Troisgros, Roanne, France
41. The Wolseley, London
42. Rockpool, Sydney
43. Yauatcha, London
44. The Ivy, London
45. Gambero Rosso, San Vincenzo, Italy
46. The Cliff, St. James, Barbados
47. Le Gavroche, London
48. Enoteca Pinchiorri, Florence, Italy
49. Felix, The Peninsula, Hong Kong
50. La Tupina, Bordeaux, France

Source: Restaurant Magazine, 2005

BY ANY OTHER NAME

The Bermuda Triangle—if you believe in it at all—is said to cover 440,000 square miles of ocean, with its points on the Bermuda Islands; Miami, Florida; and San Juan, Puerto Rico. It's also known as Devil's Triangle, Hoodoo Sea, Triangle of Death, and Jinx.

◆

VENUS is the only planet in the solar system that rotates clockwise.

WHAT A WAY TO GO

It was bound to happen: Since 1997, more than 150 people have been "buried" in space. Though seemingly a contradiction in terms, "space burial" is now available for the dearly departed—or at least part of them. A small amount (about 7 grams) of cremains can be placed in a lipstick-sized capsule and launched into space.

Some funerary missions are sent far enough only to orbit the Earth, finally reentering the Earth's atmosphere when the capsule slows down and burns up like a shooting star. The first space burial returned from orbit after only five years: it was launched on April 21, 1997, carrying the remains of twenty-four people, including *Star Trek* creator and science fiction writer Gene Roddenberry, and LSD proponent and guru Timothy Leary. The rocket circled Earth every ninety-six minutes, finally reentering in 2002 northeast of Australia. Future missions promise voyages to Jupiter and deep space—and though they leave our planet only intermittently, the price is currently an affordable $1,000—as long as you don't mind traveling with a few new friends.

Roddenberry's intergalactic presence is more extensive than most peoples': He has both a crater on Mars and an asteroid, 4659 Roddenberry, named after him.

PLAYING AROUND

The oldest board game in the world still being played is Go, which originated in ancient China more than 2,000 years ago; archaeologists have found a porcelain playing board from the Western Han Dynasty (206 B.C.E.–24 C.E.). The name for the strategic game-for-two is roughly translated from the Chinese as "Board Game of Surrounding One's Opponent."

MEETING MARY JANE

We can't really say whether they inhaled, but these countries have reported that more than 5 percent of their teenage and adult population has had at least one experience smoking marijuana:

Rank	Country	Percentage
1.	New Zealand	22.23
2.	Australia	17.93
3.	United States	12.30
4.	United Kingdom	9.00
5.	Switzerland	8.50
6.	Ireland	7.91
7.	Spain	7.58
8.	Canada	7.41
9.	Netherlands	5.24
10.	Belgium	5.01

THRILL ON THE HILL

"Blueberry Hill" was not first sung by "Fats" Domino but Gene Autry, in the 1940 western, *The Singing Hill*. Lyricist Larry Stock recalled that one important music publisher turned it down, saying "blueberries don't grow on hills," contrary to Stock's memories. A very wrong, very sorry music publisher, as it turned out—"Blueberry Hill" became a #1 hit.

◆

The estimated weight of the planet EARTH is 6,000,000,000,000,000,000,000 metric tons—or six sextillion.

WAY TO GO

War heroes, life-or-death messengers, newspaper reporters—
for centuries, "homers" have gone where and when others
could not go. Homing pigeons, also called rock doves, are
domesticated pigeons, *Columba livia*. There are reports that
during the Olympic games of 776 B.C.E., they carried news of
the winners to the different city-states of Greece, and were
used by the Egyptian pharaohs to relay news as far back as
2900 B.C.E.

Homers are bred to be able to find their way back home
over extremely long distances; this is relatively easy, as they
instinctively return to their own nests, food, and the mates
they have chosen for life. "Rookies"—birds less than a year
old—are trained to fly between one hundred and three
hundred miles a day, so that they can eventually join the "old
birds," who can easily fly six hundred or more miles a day.
Before a trip, homing pigeons are fed like marathon racers on a
special diet of high-protein grain mixture with extra carbo-
hydrates. Motivated by food, water, and the prospect of
returning to the nest, they will fly at speeds of forty to sixty
miles per hour.

Recently, researchers at Oxford University completed a
ten-year study on the birds and how it is they know their routes.
When learning a route for the first time, or on a long-distance
trip, homing pigeons use their own, mysterious navigational
system. But when they're taking a trip they're used to, they do
what humans do—go the way they know. GPS satellites used in
the Oxford study found the birds actually flying above major
highways, turning at stop lights, even circling roundabouts and
adding extra mileage—just because it's the route they recognize, and it is mentally easier for them.

There is, by the way, a celebrity in the world of homing

pigeons in one Cher Ami, a World War I flying ace who was awarded the French Croix de Guerre for heroic service, delivering a dozen top secret messages—once despite being shot in the line of duty.

◆

ON THE ROCK
What Life Is Like on the Rock of Gibraltar

0 percent arable land
0 percent permanent crops
0 oil production
More than ten thousand cell phones for a country that is eleven times the size of . . . the Washington Mall
1 television station
1 AM and 5 FM radio stations
18 miles of highway
7.5 miles of coastline

GROUND WORK

The Bingham Canyon Copper Mine in Utah is the biggest man-made hole on Earth. It is three-quarters of a mile deep and 2½ miles across. It has a couple of additional superlatives to its credit: Not only has it produced more copper than any other mine in history—about 17 million tons of the metal— but it bears the nickname of the "Richest Hole on Earth."

WHEN YOU HAVE TO GO . . .

Leave it to the Swiss: Travel experts say that the world's best rest stop is on highway M-1 in Deitingen. The bathroom, designed by architect Heinz Eisler, is cleaned every hour on the hour, without fail.

EMPIRE STATEMENTS

It is probably the most famous building in the world; it has twice been the tallest building in New York City (before and after the World Trade Center); it is the lead character in hit movies (*An Affair to Remember* and *Sleepless in Seattle*, to name two); an Irish governor broke ground for it on St. Patrick's Day; and it now shows streaming video of all it surveys, twenty-four hours a day, seven days a week, on its ESB TowerCAMS/TowerVISION.

So there are a lot of reasons to love the Empire State Building—but perhaps the most delightful is the lights atop the building, which are a daily looking glass into New York City life. Their colors honor national holidays, seasons, myriad ethnic groups living in the area, and worthy causes. Occasionally during spring and fall bird migration seasons and on cloudy or foggy nights, the lights are turned off. The first light shone on Election Day 1932 to let everyone within fifty miles know that Franklin Delano Roosevelt had been elected president. After special lighting for the 1964 World's Fair, the country's bicentennial, and the Yankees winning the World Series in 1977, a more permanent setup was designed in 1984. At this time, designer Douglas Leigh constructed an elaborate system of automated, fluorescent, color-changing apparatus in the uppermost mooring mast, which can be changed by just flipping a switch. And though the day's lighting extravaganza shuts off every night at midnight, Leigh also added thirty-two high-pressure sodium-vapor lights of just seventy watts each above the 103rd floor that create a golden "halo" effect around the top of the mast from dusk to dawn—a little nightlight for the city that never sleeps.

Here are just some of the reasons the Tower Lights celebrate (colors are listed from bottom to top):

480

Colors	Special Significance
Black/Green/Gold	Jamaica Independence
Black/Red/Yellow	German Reunification Day
Blue	Child Abuse Prevention Muscular Dystrophy Police Memorial Day
Blue/Blue/Red	Equal Parents Day
Blue/Blue/White	Colon Cancer Awareness Greek Independence
Blue/White/Blue	Americans with Disabilities First Night of Hanukkah Israel Independence Day Juvenile Diabetes Awareness Last Night of Hanukkah Tartan Day/Scotland
Blue/White/Red	Bastille Day
Blue/White/White	United Nations Day
Blue/Yellow/Black	Bahamas Independence
Gold	Oscar Week in New York City
Green	March of Dimes Organ Donor Awareness St. Patrick's Day
Green/Blue/Blue	Earth Day
Green/Green/White	Pakistan Independence
Green/Red/White	Wales/St. David's Day

Colors	*Special Significance*
Green/White/Orange	India Independence
Green/White/Red	Anniversary of Mexico's Independence
Green/Yellow/Blue	Brazil Independence
Lavender/Lavender/White	Stonewall Anniversary
No Lights	"Day without Art/Night without Lights" AIDS Awareness National Day of Mourning
Orange/Blue/Blue	New York Knicks Opening Day
Orange/Orange/Blue	Celebrate New York City New York City Marathon
Orange/Orange/White	Netherlands' Queens Day Walk to End Domestic Violence
Orange/White/Green	India Independence
Pink/Pink/White	Breast Cancer Awareness Month Race for the Cure
Purple/Purple/Gold	Westminster Dog Show
Purple/Purple/White	Alzheimer's Awareness Alzheimers' "Walk to Remember"
Purple/Teal/White	National Osteoporosis Society
Red	"Go Red for Women" Big Apple Circus Big Apple Fest/NYC&Co. Diabetes Awareness

Colors	Special Significance
Red	Fire Department Memorial Day Multiple Sclerosis Society Red Hot Summer Charity Event Valentine's Day
Red/Black/Green	Dr. Martin Luther King Jr., Day
Red/Blue/Blue	Haitian Culture Awareness
Red/Blue/White	New York Rangers
Red/Blue/Yellow	Colombia Independence Philippines/Manila Day
Red/Gold/Green	Grenada Independence
Red/Gold/Red	Lunar New Year
Red/Red/Green	Holiday Season
Red/Red/White	Pulaski Day Red Cross Month Swiss National Day
Red/Red/Yellow	Autumn Colors Ringling Bros. and Barnum & Bailey Circus
Red/White/Blue	Armed Forces Day Election Day Flag Day Fleet Week/Memorial Day Independence Day Labor Day Presidents' Day Veterans Day

Colors	*Special Significance*
Red/White/Green	Feast of San Gennaro Columbus Day
Red/White/Red	Peru Independence Poison Prevention Month
Red/White/White	Leukemia and Lymphoma "Light the Night"
Red/Yellow/Green	Portuguese Independence
White	ESB Lighting
White/Blue/Blue	Jackie Robinson Day
White/Red/Red	Qatar Independence
Yellow	Broadway on Broadway U.S. Open
Yellow/Blue/Blue	Ukrainian Independence
Yellow/Orange/Yellow	Corporate Philanthropy Day
Yellow/White/Yellow	Spring/Easter

For several months after the events of September 11, 2001, the Empire State Building lights glowed red, white, and blue twenty-four hours a day at the request of the men and women working at the World Trade Center site.

◆

A SNOOD, an ornamental net in the shape of a bag, confines a woman's hair on the nape of the neck.

484

BOOK STORE

Though its original purpose was to serve as the research arm of the U.S. Congress, the Library of Congress has grown to be the largest library in the world. It holds more than 130 million items, which require more than 530 miles of shelving. The collections include more than

- 29 million books and other printed materials
- 2.7 million recordings
- 12 million photographs
- 4.8 million maps
- 58 million manuscripts

THAT REINDEER SONG

Where did Rudolph come from? There were "eight tiny reindeer"—and Rudolph was *not* one of them. So how did Rudolph get to be part of Santa Claus's Christmas Eve crew?

Rudolph the Red-Nosed Reindeer was born in 1939 in Chicago, Illinois, and before he went to work for Santa, he held a job at the Montgomery Ward Department Store. During Christmas seasons in the past, the store had bought coloring books for kids; this year they decided to save some money and write and produce a story of their own. Store copywriter Robert L. May got to work, and 2.4 million books were given away that season; by 1946, 6 million children knew the story of Rudolph, thanks to the giveaway. Eventually May's brother-in-law, songwriter Johnny Marks, developed the music and lyrics to the famous song, and in 1949 Gene Autry, of "Singing Cowboy" fame, recorded it, selling 2 million copies the very first year.

ROUTES TO FREEDOM

Its existence was an open secret, but from its inception, the routes and locations that made up the Underground Railroad remained one of the best-kept secrets of American history. Its mission—to help Southern American slaves escape to freedom in the North or Canada—was of such import, and was fraught with such grave consequences, that even today the actual routes American slaves traveled are generally a matter of speculation, or remnants of oral history.

The Underground Railroad was more a loose association of people rather than an actual mode of transportation or even a systematic route of escape. Reports as early as the 1700s tell of slaves escaping, but by the passage of the Fugitive Slave Bill of 1850, it became considerably more dangerous for runaway slaves to stay in urban areas in the North. Therefore, more slaves—there are reports of more than thirty thousand—continued on to Canada, or fled south to the Caribbean. Earlier in the nineteenth century, organized flights through Pennsylvania and New Jersey were aided by Quaker abolitionists. At its height between 1810 and 1850, nearly one hundred thousand people escaped enslavement via the Underground Railroad, a fraction of the estimated 4 million slaves who would eventually escape. Historians do know that flights to freedom took place mostly at night on routes more well known and easy to travel, such as the Mississippi River; the Appalachian Mountains; from Washington, D.C., to Frederick County, Maryland; and to ports such as New Bedford, Massachusetts, where the labor-hungry whaling industry assured that men of color would disappear virtually overnight for sea voyages of several years.

Perhaps the most amazing and yet little-known aspect of the Underground Railroad has come to light only in the last few decades. Folkloric reports and oral history tell of sympathizers in homes both north and south of the Mason-Dixon Line who aided the refugee slaves with a series of signals given by the placement of quilts in and around their homes. According to some, both the patterns of the quilts and the way and place in which they were hung directed the travelers to the next safe haven along the route.

COUNTRIES WITH LESS THAN ONE PERCENT UNEMPLOYMENT*

Andorra	0.00	Isle of Man	0.60
Norfolk Island	0.00	Uzbekistan	0.60
Guernsey	0.50	Jersey	0.90
Aruba	0.60		

*CIA World Factbook 2005.

HOLD ON TO YOUR HAT

On the planet Jupiter, winds regularly whip around at an average of 225 miles per hour. But Saturn is by far the windiest planet, though photos taken in the 1980s vary greatly with more recent pictures sent back from the Hubble Space Telescope from 1996 to 2002, which indicate that winds have slowed by about 40 percent at Saturn's equator. Where wind speeds formerly peaked at 1,000 miles per hour, now 600 miles per hour is the norm.

But Earth can't really compare: The highest surface winds ever recorded on this planet are said to have been a gust of 231 miles per hour, clocked on New Hampshire's Mount Washington on April 12, 1934, and tornado winds of 318 miles per hour measured during a 1999 tornado in Oklahoma.

THE GREATEST SHOW ON EARTH

It may seem that a form of entertainment so simple would be many thousands of years old—but the circus is quite a modern event. Though the way the circus is constructed and the way the audiences assemble are reminiscent of ancient Roman amphitheaters and coliseums, those ancient venues were used as racecourses or devoted to gladiatorial combat.

Entertainment display that took to the road has existed since some man found out he had a talent others did not, but the modern circus was created in 1768 by Philip Astley (1742–1814). Originally the owner of a horseback-riding school in London, Astley used a circular performance ring for two reasons: It was easier for the riders to balance on a moving horse, and an audience could see everything. The trick-riding display soon grew to include clowns, acrobats, jugglers, musicians, tumblers, tightrope walkers, and dancing dogs, and what we know as the circus was born. Astley's circus was so popular that soon he opened another in Paris, and other performers with their various acts followed suit around the world.

Astley's original space was sixty-two feet in diameter, and later he made it smaller, forty-two feet, which became an international standard for circuses. It wasn't until 1825 that American J. Purdy Brown began putting the circus under a tent. Brown realized that most large American cities lacked buildings a traveling show could move into and out of for short periods of time. At first the tents weren't exactly "big tops"— they were very small, containing only one ring and a few hundred seats. At the height of their popularity, however, circuses exhibited simultaneously in two rings (1872) and then three (1881), and the great American tented circuses became the stuff of legend.

"THE 400"

It was socialite Ward McAllister who said there were only about four hundred people in New York who were at ease in a ballroom. So in the late 1880s, he and Caroline Schermerhorn Astor went so far as to make a list. To be more exact, to be included in "Mrs. Astor's Four Hundred," one had to be from a family who had money, and for three generations, one's ancestors could not have worked in the trades. Reports are that Mrs. Astor's parties were apparently quite dull.

SILVER SERVICE

Everyone knows where the gold is: Fort Knox, Kentucky, is the home of the U.S. gold depository. There are nearly 150 million ounces there today, worth about $60 billion—pretty hefty for a storage facility constructed in 1936 of granite, steel, and concrete at a cost of only $560,000. (It sounds insecure, but rest assured: The vault door alone weighs more than twenty tons—and no one person is entrusted with the entire combination.)

But since 1939 there's been a little-known silver depository as well—in West Point, New York. The "Fort Knox of Silver," as it's nicknamed, is actually the West Point Bullion Depository. It presently houses both silver and gold, and it is even used occasionally as a mint. In the 1970s, a severe shortage of pennies (if one can even imagine such a thing) moved the government to produce "mintmarkless" one-cent coins at West Point, and over the years the depository has also manufactured gold and silver commemorative coins, and American Eagle Bullion coins in proof and uncirculated condition. In 2000, it struck the first-ever gold and platinum bimetallic coin.

IF YOU BELIEVE . . .

Who ghost there? If the spirit world is a place as real to you as your own home, you know that ghosts make their homes all over the world, and in the strangest places . . .

The *azeman* is a ghostly woman who haunts the villages of Surinam in South America. The unwelcome phantom bites a piece of flesh from the big toe of sleeping persons, sapping their blood.

Canada has many haunted sites, a recent example being the Firkins' House in Heritage Park in Fort Edmonton, Alberta. Many claim that it is haunted by the presence of Dr. Firkins' son, upset that the house itself was moved to a new site. Tour guides have been pushed while going down the stairs, visitors report the smell of lilacs, and some hear singing in one of the bedrooms.

The posh ocean liner *Queen Mary I* may have retired to Long Beach, California, in 1967, but some say she hasn't exactly settled down. Since the ship's doors opened as a museum and hotel, there have been several ghostly sightings, including one near a doorway marked number 13, where a young crewman was crushed to death during a 1966 safety drill.

The City Cemetery in Port-au-Prince, Haiti, is haunted by ghastly apparitions of decomposing bodies.

In Brisbane, Australia, ghosts are quite political: They're found in the Old Government House, the Parliament House, and especially City Hall, where at least three ghosts haunt the hallways. One is an elegant woman in period clothes seen on the main staircase, the second a maintenance man who rides the elevator that killed him as he installed it in the 1930s. The last is an American sailor in the Red Cross Tea Room, stabbed to death by another sailor over a young Australian woman.

A ghost has been walking along the battlements of the Cape Town Castle in South Africa for more than three hundred years. The tall, luminous figure disappears over the edge at the approach of a human.

South Africa's Port Elizabeth Highway (between the Hex River Mountains and Drakensberg) is haunted by a phantom automobile that is blamed for several accidents.

Asia considers Singapore its most haunted city. Strange lights are not uncommon, and people are slapped by an unseen presence at the Changi Beach Houses. Specters also beg for food along the coast near Lor Halus—one spot even has a spirit that calls for help and then runs away.

Security cameras at the Parliament House in Suva, Fiji, recorded their ghost for five minutes. The footage was so clear that it was shown on national television, and the prime minister is said to have called for an exorcism.

Mount Everest claims to have its own spirit in climber Andrew Irvine, who died there in 1924. His ghost shares tents with climbers and encourages them to make the final ascent. First reported by climbers Dougal Haston and Doug Scott in 1975, he has been seen several times since.

There is an angry specter in Tasmania—a settler from England who hanged himself over a broken heart. He spent three years building a new house for his wife-to-be back home; when he sailed back to wed her, he found that she had gotten lonely and married another. Grief-stricken, he returned to Australia and killed himself in the courtyard of the house he had prepared for his love. Even today, cattle and horses become unnerved around the house called Garth, and the cries of the Englishman are still often heard.

Ghosts are so pesky in Iceland that there used to be a law that enabled people to legally summon to court a ghost that had been tormenting them, and have it bound over to authorities.

In Germany, the White Lady of Hohenzollerns is more mobile than most. She visits castles all over Germany, including Neuhaus, Berlin, Bechin, Tretzen, and Raumleau. Believers say she is Princess Perchta von Rosenberg, who haunts descendents of her cruel husband.

Austrian Baroness Russlein von Altebar seeks her revenge against any descendants of Count Johannes Rathenau, who slaughtered her family during the Middle Ages. She first appears as a beautiful courtesan before turning into a rotting corpse. In Vienna, she once boarded the cab of Walther Rathenau, who immediately died of fright. One Major Helmut Rathenau met much the same demise.

Russians are not at all surprised to have ghosts in their homes. In fact, they're so common that they have classifications. *Domovoi* are domestic ghosts that tend to be nuisances or poltergeists, but help with chores if treated with respect. *Domovikha* are quiet, but their presence can be sensed in certain rooms.

Scottish lore stars the *bean-nighe*, an ugly Scottish banshee that shows up to wash the blood from the clothes of those who are about to die. Picture this for scary: one nostril, one big, protruding tooth, webbed feet, and long, hanging breasts.

In England, the ghosts go straight to the top: 10 Downing Street. The resident phantom there is a man dressed in Regency-style clothes who appears in several rooms. Speculation is that he may be a former prime minister, especially as he appears only during a national crisis.

WHENCE THE WEB?

The World Wide Web is so ephemeral, so beyond most people's ken, that it's hard to believe that it started in a *place*. But it did. Tim Berners-Lee (the son of two people who met designing a computer) designed it alone, in 1989, while he was working at CERN (the European Organization for Nuclear Research) in Switzerland. Basically, Berners-Lee took everything on the Internet and wove it into a web. The very first Web site, by the way, was nxoc01.cern.ch, and the very first Web page was http://nxoc01.cer n.ch/hypertext/WWW/TheProject.html.

❖

JUST A HOLE IN THE GROUND

About 150 meteor collision sites have been identified on Earth. Ten of the largest visible craters—by their diameters—are:

Meteor Crater, Arizona: 4,150 feet
Wolf Creek, Australia: 2,789 feet
Henbury, Australia: 722 feet
Boxhole, Australia: 574 feet
Odessa, Texas: 558 feet
Tswainga, South Africa: 433 feet
Wabar, Saudi Arabia: 381 feet
Oesel, Estonia: 328 feet
Campo del Cielo, Argentina: 246 feet
Dalgaranga, Australia: 230 feet

"HAPPINESS NET"

Don't be so sure you can't quantify happiness. This survey shows the countries that lead in what's called "Happiness Net." Samples of various populations were questioned as to how happy they were—very happy, quite happy, not very happy or not at all happy. The net was determined by taking the percentage of the first two (the happy people) and subtracting the percentage of the last two (the unhappy people). Maybe it's the politics, the scenery, or just the way of life, but in general it looks like if you're not happy, it's time to move north.

Rank	Country	Happiness Net
1.	Iceland	94%
2.	Netherlands	91%
3.	Sweden	91%
4.	Denmark	91%
5.	Australia	90%
6.	Switzerland	89%
7.	Ireland	89%
8.	Norway	88%
9.	Venezuela	87%
10.	United Kingdom	87%
11.	Belgium	86%
12.	Philippines	85%
13.	United States	84%
14.	France	84%
15.	Finland	83%
16.	Austria	81%
17.	Canada	75%
18.	Poland	74%

19.	Japan	72%
20.	Turkey	71%
21.	Bangladesh	70%
22.	Spain	68%
23.	Italy	64%
24.	Uruguay	60%
25.	Argentina	59%

Source: Nationmaster.com

◆

TRULY THE "SHOW ME" STATE

Though its true and exact location may forever remain a mystery, most scientists and historians believe that the Garden of Eden—if it existed at all—lay somewhere in what was Mesopotamia, between the Tigris and Euphrates rivers. There are followers of Joseph Smith, founder of the Church of Jesus Christ of Latter-Day Saints, who say Smith came upon a mountaintop, surveyed all below him, and declared that Missouri was indeed the original Garden of Eden.

"THE GREAT INDIAN WAY"

One old Algonquin Indian trade route lasted throughout the centuries and became perhaps one of the most successful streets of commerce in history. It was originally called the Wiechquaekeck Trail. Today, people simply call it Broadway.

◆

The GREAT CHICAGO FIRE gets all the attention, but a more destructive fire took place the same day, October 8, 1871, in Peshtigo, Wisconsin.

AKA

Some people—and some places—have big ideas about themselves. All around the world, places give themselves nicknames, and not too surprisingly, they're often self-aggrandizing. How many places can actually *be* "The Garden Capital of the World," after all? But very often these nicknames are an insight to culture, agriculture, history, pride, geography, and humor. Here are some secret personalities from around the world:

Aberdeen, Scotland	The Granite City
Albany, Georgia	Good Life City
Albany, Oregon	Home of the Timber Carnival
Alexandria, Egypt	Pearl of the Mediterranean
Alpine, Texas	Gateway to the Big Bend
Annapolis, Maryland	Crabtown
Atlanta, Georgia	The City Too Busy to Hate
Auckland, New Zealand	City of Sails
Baltimore, Maryland	Charm City
Banaras, India	Luminous City
Bandon, Oregon	Storm Capital of the World
Bangkok, Thailand	Venice of the East
Bardstown, Kentucky	Bourbon Capital of the World
Beaver, Oklahoma	Cow Chip Throwing Capital of the World
Bemidji, Minnesota	Home of Paul Bunyan and Babe, the Blue Ox
Berrien Springs, Michigan	Christmas Pickle Capital of the World
Bickleton, Washington	Bluebird Capital of the World
Birmingham, Alabama	Pittsburgh of the South
Boston, Massachusetts	The Cradle of Liberty

Bristol, Tennessee	Food City
Bucharest, Romania	The Little Paris
Budapest, Hungary	The Pearl of the Danube
Buffalo, New York	The City of Good Neighbors
Burlington, Iowa	Loader/Backhoe Capital of the World
Butte, Montana	Copper City
Byron, Ohio	The Fountain City
Calgary, Alberta, Canada	The Stampede City
Cape Girardeau, Missouri	Rose City
Cape Hatteras, North Carolina	The Graveyard of the Atlantic
Castroville, California	Artichoke Center of the World
Charleston, South Carolina	Palmetto City
Chicago, Illinois	Hog Butcher to the World
Christchurch, New Zealand	The Garden City
Cincinnati, Ohio	Queen City
Cleveland, Ohio	Mistake on the Lake
Cody, Wyoming	Rodeo Capital of the World
Columbus, Ohio	The Crossroads of Ohio
Coober Pedy, Australia	Opal Capital of the World
Cooperstown, New York	Birthplace of Baseball
Council Bluffs, Iowa	Iowa's Leading Edge
Cozad, Nebraska	Alfalfa Capital of the World
Cuernavaca, Morelos, Mexico	The City of Eternal Spring
Dallas, Texas	Big D
Dayton, Ohio	Birthplace of Aviation
Detroit, Michigan	Motown
Dipolog City, Philippines	Orchid City
Douglas, Wyoming	Jackalope Capital of the World
Drumheller, Albert, Canada	Dinosaur Capital of the World
Durham, North Carolina	City of Medicine
Edinburgh, Scotland	Athens of the North

Erie, Pennsylvania	The Gem
Fallbrook, California	Avocado Capital of the World
Florence, Italy	The City of Lilies
Fort Myers, Florida	The City of Palms
Franklin County, Virginia	Moonshine Capital of the World
Frannie, Wyoming	Biggest Little Town in Wyoming
Gainesville, Florida	Hogtown
Gallup, New Mexico	Drunk Driving Capital of America
Gilroy, California	Garlic Capital of the World
Gotland, Sweden	Pearl of the Baltic
Grants Pass, Oregon	Where the Rogue River Runs
Greenfield, California	Broccoli Capital of the World
Hammondsport, New York	Cradle of Aviation
Hammonton, New Jersey	Blueberry Capital of the World
Hatch, New Mexico	Chili Capital of the World
Hershey, Pennsylvania	Chocolate Town, USA
Hollywood, California	Tinseltown
Holtville, California	Carrot Capital of the World
Hong Kong, China	Pearl of the Orient
Hood River, Oregon	Windsurfing Capital of the World
Hoople, North Dakota	Tater Town
Houston, Texas	Magnolia City
Indianapolis, Indiana	Circle City
Indio, California	Date Capital of the World
International Falls, Minnesota	The Icebox of the United States
Isleton, California	Crawdad Town, USA
Jackson, Mississippi	Chimneyville

Jerusalem, Israel	City of David
Kalamazoo, Michigan	Celery City
Kansas City, Kansas	Heart of America
Kokomo, Indiana	City of Firsts
Keizer, Oregon	Iris Capital of the World
Lacrosse, Wisconsin	Barbed Wire Capital of the World
Laramie, Wyoming	Gem City of the Plains
Letchworth, England	The First Garden City in the World
Lodi, California	The [Tokay] Grape Capital of the World
London, Ontario, Canada	The Forest City
Los Angeles, California	The Big Orange
Louisville, Kentucky	City of Beautiful Churches
Lowell, Wyoming	The Rose City of Wyoming
Madison, Wisconsin	Four Lake City
Manila, Philippines	Pearl of the Orient
Mar del Plata, Argentina	Queen of the Coast
Marysville, California	Gateway to the Gold Fields
Mattoon, Illinois	Bagel Capital of the World
Medellin, Colombia	Orchid City
Meeteetse, Wyoming	Where Chiefs Meet
Memphis, Tennessee	Bluff City
Miami, Florida	Little Cuba
Milwaukee, Wisconsin	Cream City
Minneapolis, Minnesota	Flour City
Mobile, Alabama	City of Five Flags
Montreal, Quebec, Canada	The City of Saints
Mountain Iron, Minnesota	Taconite Capital of the World
Mountain View, Arkansas	Folk Music Capital of the World

Moyobamba, Peru	Orchid City
Nashville, Tennessee	Music City, USA
Newark, New Jersey	Brick City
New Haven, Connecticut	Elm City
New Orleans, Louisiana	The Crescent City
New York, New York	Gotham
Oakdale, California	Cowboy Capital of the World
Oroville, California	City of Gold
Oxford, England	City of Dreaming Spires
Palatka, Florida	Bass Capital of the World
Paris, France	City of Light
Pasadena, California	City of Roses
Patterson, California	Apricot Capital of the World
Pearsonville, California	Hubcap Capital of the World
Petaluma, California	Egg Basket of the World
Philadelphia, Pennsylvania	Rebel Capital
Pittsburgh, Pennsylvania	Steel City
Placerville, California	Hangtown
Portland, Maine	Forest City
Prague, Czech Republic	The Golden City
Providence, Rhode Island	Beehive of Industry
Quebec City, Quebec, Canada	The Gibraltar of North America
Queenstown, New Zealand	Extreme Sports Capital of the World
Reno, Nevada	The Biggest Little City in the World
Rigby, Idaho	Birthplace of TV
Rochester, New York	Snapshot City
Rockport, Massachusetts	The Mendocino of the East
Rome, Italy	The Eternal City
Rye, New York	Border Town

Sacramento, California	River City
St. Louis, Missouri	Gateway to the West
St. Petersburg, Russia	Venice of the North
Salem, Massachusetts	City of Witches
San Antonio, Texas	Alamo City
San Diego, California	America's Finest City
North San Jose, California	The Golden Triangle
Santa Fe, New Mexico	The City Different
Santa Rosa, New Mexico	The SCUBA Diving Capital of New Mexico
Saratoga Springs, New York	Spa City
Savannah, Georgia	Garden City
Sault Ste. Marie, Michigan	The SOO
Seattle, Washington	The Emerald City
Selma, California	Raisin Capital of the World
Shah Alam, Malaysia	Orchid City
Sonora, California	The Queen of the Southern Mines
Stockholm, Sweden	Venice of the North
Stockton, California	California's Sunrise Seaport
Sturgis, Michigan	Curtain Rod Capital of the World
Syracuse, New York	Salt City
Taxco, Mexico	Silver Capital of the World
Thousand Oaks, California	T.O.
Tijuana, Mexico	Television Capital of the World
Toledo, Ohio	Corn City
Toronto, Ontario, Canada	Hogtown
Tulelake, California	Horseradish Capital of the World
Umeå, Sweden	Björkarnas Stad (The City of the Birches)

Vancouver, British Columbia, Canada	Gastown
Venice, Italy	Bride of the Sea
Värnersborg, Sweden	Lilla Paris (Little Paris)
Västerås, Gurkstan	The Cucumber City
Vicksburg, Mississippi	The Gibraltar of America
Victoria, Australia	The Cabbage Patch
Victoria, British Columbia, Canada	Little England
Walla Walla, Washington	The Town So Nice They Named It Twice
Washington, D.C.	Capital City
Waterbury, Connecticut	Brass City
Waynesboro, Georgia	Bird Dog Capital of the World
Wenatchee, Washington	Apple Capital of the World
West Hollywood, California	Boystown
Wheeling, West Virginia	Nail City
Wichita, Kansas	Emerald City
Windsor, Ontario	Tijuana North
Yates Center, Kansas	Hay Capital of the World

◆

COLLEGE HONORS

Landmark College takes the honors as the most expensive college in the world. This specialized institution, located in Putney, Vermont, is an accredited college that caters to students with learning disabilities such as dyslexia and attention deficit hyperactivity disorder.

Why?

"Why" is almost never the question that peacefully ends wars or sends a guilty man to prison; black-and-white questions like these are usually in the form of "what" or a "how." But aren't the "whys" our favorite questions to ask, and have answered? The reasons things are the way they are, and why we follow the customs we do, feed our intellects and souls, and tickle our funny bones in ways that little else will. Why do people lie? Why did the Ancient Greeks begin the tradition of toasting to one's health? Your curiosity is about to be satisfied!

PRESIDENT LINCOLN'S ASSASSINATION

ORIGIN OF THE TERM "LYNCHING"

FAILING MARRIAGES

STATES AND COUNTRY NAMES

THE RISE OF "HANKY PANKY"

DREAMS AND COLORS

HISTORICAL SIGNIFICANCE OF NURSERY RHYMES

MEANINGS OF FLOWERS

NEW YEAR'S MEALS

EPONYMS

MOVIE RATINGS

COMAS

DREAM INTERPRETATIONS

BURIAL CUSTOMS

PSYCHIATRIC DISORDERS

ESTATE PLANNING

CHEERS! AROUND THE WORLD

ANIMAL ADJECTIVES

EMOTICONS

THE TURKEY CITY LEXICON

DINER SLANG

BLUE SKIES SMILIN' AT ME

Sunlight passes through the earth's oxygen- and nitrogen-rich atmosphere on its way to the planet's surface. Blue light— one component of the sun's light, which looks white because it is made up of all the colors of the spectrum—has a wave- length that's roughly the size of an atom of oxygen, and so it is continuously redistributed, or scattered, by the oxygen atoms in the atmosphere. The blue light enters our eyes from all sorts of angles, and so we see the sky as blue. (The atmosphere scatters violet light even better, but our eyes are more sensitive to blue.) If the earth had no atmosphere, light would travel directly from the sun to our eyes, and all we would see is bright white light against a black sky. And if the earth's atmosphere contained different gases, we might be looking at a different color of sky.

POINTS OF LIGHT

He may have been gearing up to be first president of the United States, but George Washington lost his battle with Betsy Ross when it came to designing the nation's new flag. Washington wanted a six-pointed star on the new banner, but Ross voted for a five-pointed star, knowing that it would be easier and faster to make. She won, and we have Betsy Ross to thank for the five-pointed stars on the U.S. flag today.

◆

The ice cream company BASKIN-ROBBINS regularly draws from its library of nearly 1,000 recipes to rotate their signature 31 flavors. Why 31? No month in the year has more than 31 days, which means Baskin-Robbins offers a new fla- vor for every day of the month.

IS IT A HAPPY PUPPY?

Tail wagging is not necessarily the sign of a happy dog. When standing before human beings, dogs will often keep their bodies still, their tails wagging in a rhythmic back-and-forth motion. According to many canine behavioral experts, this combination of body stance and tail motion expresses the internal conflict between dogs' attraction to people and their instinctive caution, suggesting conflict or confusion.

Different tail-wagging and body stance patterns express other emotions: Tail wagging back and forth along with vigorous body movement signals friendly or excited behavior; a tail held high with the tip wagging in jerking movements and a taut, alert torso demonstrate aggression; a low, stiff wagging tail and crouched body represent submission and/or fear.

ORDER IN THE COURT

Oyez is a Middle English word shouted three times in succession in the United States to call a courtroom to order. Pronounced "oh-yay" or "oh-yez," it is derived from the Latin verb *audire*, "to hear," and entered our language—and our court system—through Middle English via Anglo-Norman French. It first appeared in 1425 in English, when French was used as the language of the English courts.

◆

The 1999 JAMES BOND movie *The World Is Not Enough* takes its name from the Bond family motto, *Orbis non sufficit*. The motto appeared in 1969's *On Her Majesty's Secret Service*, where it was seen on a plaque.

A COOLING-OFF PERIOD

One early attempt at air-conditioning worked reasonably well but was too high-maintenance, even for a world leader. In July 1881, President James Garfield, mortally wounded by an assassin's bullet, lay in Washington, D.C.'s sweltering heat (ironically, he was shot in Union Station as he was leaving town to escape the summer's unbearable heat and humidity). In a futile attempt to improve his condition—or at least make him comfortable—naval engineers designed a box to vent cool air, produced by suspending ice-water-saturated cloths in front of a fan, into Garfield's room. Although it did lower the room temperature considerably, it was impractical, and in the two months Garfield lay dying, the early air conditioner used more than half a million pounds of ice.

A modern, more practical air-conditioning system didn't appear until 1906, when Willis Carrier introduced his "apparatus for treating air," which cooled, filtered, and redirected air. Carrier's first system was expensive and often impractical. By 1960, technology had advanced enough to make air-conditioning inexpensive, and it quickly became as important as central heating. Not surprisingly, the 1960s were also the first decade to see more people move into the South than leave since the Civil War.

◆

DOWN AND OUT

The most common reasons for filing for bankruptcy include:
- Extended periods of unemployment
- Large and often unanticipated medical expenses
- Overextended credit
- Marital problems leading to financial hardship

"WITH THIS GARTER . . ."

Brides throw their bouquet to all the single women at a wedding reception, the age-old belief being that the one who catches it will be the next to marry. The removal and tossing of the bride's garter is a slyer and more lascivious reference to the groom's good fortune, and demonstrates a bit of his generous and sharing nature.

ROAD FOOD

Even in the days of Pompeii, people were in a hurry. Or perhaps they lived in small quarters without a kitchen of their own. Believe it or not, early fast-food dining was available down at the corner *thermopolium*, a little neighborhood stand that served hot food and mulled wine from earthenware jars set into a counter. Food could be purchased to go or, in locations with seating, eaten there.

AUTOPILOTS

Though the majority of the world drives on the right-hand side of the road, there are countries where medieval habits die hard. Centuries ago, before the days of motorized transportation, men fought with swords and traveled on horseback. Since most people are right-handed, men would keep their scabbards to their left, drawing—and, if need be, fighting—with the sword in their right hand. Riding on the left side of a road kept their right side, and hand, free for fighting. Today, residents of 166 countries drive on the right side of the road; those in 74 nations (many of which were once colonies of European states) drive on the left.

LINCOLN ASSASSINATION THEORIES

1. Vice President Andrew Johnson—Lincoln's nemesis—was involved with Booth's assassination plan. Allegedly, Johnson received a note written by Booth on the day Lincoln was assassinated.
2. A simple conspiracy, organized by John Wilkes Booth, was responsible for Lincoln's assassination. Booth, a southern patriot and racist, led a small group by himself.
3. Lincoln's assassination was the result of a Confederate plot—the Confederacy's position weakened as the Civil War progressed, and assassination seemed the only resolution. This was a popular theory that arose almost immediately after the president's death.
4. Lincoln's assassination was the result of a conspiracy of powerful international bankers. Not only did the president turn down money from the Rothschilds to finance the war, but they and other European bankers opposed many of his policies, so they hired Booth to kill him.
5. The Roman Catholic Church was behind Lincoln's assassination. The majority of American Catholics were in favor of slavery and opposed to a Lincoln presidency.
6. The secretary of war, Edwin Stanton, was the mastermind behind Lincoln's assassination, as he desired much more stringent Reconstruction policies.

HOW HAPPY?

Why would anyone want to be happy as a clam? The full adage is "Happy as a clam at high tide," and since clams are caught only at low tide—by hand, foot, or rake—it's no wonder these tasty mollusks are indeed happiest at high tide.

WHEN PHIL SPEAKS . . .

Groundhog Day is a distinctly American holiday that arose from the influx to Pennsylvania of German settlers, who brought a Candlemas Day tradition with them to their new country. As far back as the Roman conquest, Germans believed that any animal that cast its shadow on this day signaled six more weeks of winter. With the plethora of groundhogs in the Keystone State, they—and Punxsutawney Phil in particular—got the job. Back in Europe, there was even an old English song:

> If Candlemas be fair and bright,
> Come, winter, have another flight;
> If Candlemas brings clouds and rain,
> Go winter, and come not again.

THE NOT-SO-WORLDLY SERIES

Legend has it that the World Series got its name from the *New York World*, a newspaper that was said to have sponsored early baseball championship games. But it's not true; the *World* never played such a role. By 1886, the postseason contest was called the World's Championship (and so cited in *Spalding's Base Ball Guide* for 1887), since both American and National League winners wished to call themselves "America's Champions"; it was assumed that teams from other countries would one day enter the contest. By the time of the Red Sox–Pirates series in 1903, the playoffs were referred to as the World Championship Series, eventually shortened to World Series. To this day, only U.S. and Canadian teams have competed in the World Series.

LIGHT SHOW

The aurora borealis, or northern lights, and the aurora australis, or southern lights, are the heavenly result of the inter-
action between the solar wind and earth's magnetic field.
The sun emits highly charged particles, or ions, that speed
through space, forming a cloud of ions called plasma. The
stream of plasma coming from the sun is called solar wind.
When plasma hits the earth's magnetic field, some of the
ions become trapped by the earth's magnetic forces and follow magnetic lines into the ionosphere (more than 30 miles
above the earth's surface), where they collide with various
atmospheric gases, mostly oxygen and nitrogen, generating
up to 1 million megawatts of electricity and the characteristic
sky glow. Generally red, green, blue, and violet in color, the
aurora appears in a variety of forms, from simple patches of
light to streamers, arcs, banks, rays, and curtains.

COME 'N' GET IT

Why do mosquitoes seem to zoom in on some people while
completely ignoring others? Mosquitoes have a complex set
of sensors that lead them to human prey from as far as 100
feet away. These sensors can detect chemicals that both
mammals and birds emit, including those in sweat. Mosquitoes can also detect movement, and they assume anything
moving is alive and therefore full of blood. They can also
detect heat and can find warm-blooded mammals at close
range. All in all, avoiding mosquitoes might just be a losing
battle.

◆

Our present-day usage of the word ALIBI has never changed
from the Latin: it is an adverb meaning "elsewhere."

VERY SLIPPERY

Scientists used to think that ice was slippery because the pressure exerted on it from a skate, puck, or even a pair of galoshes created friction, and the resultant heat melted a thin top layer of ice. But by examining ice crystals up close, they've discovered that the molecules on the surface of the ice vibrate more than usual for a solid—though they vibrate only up and down, not in all directions, as would be the case in a liquid. The result is a quasi-fluid layer on the top of the ice, making slipping and sliding practically inevitable.

THE GREAT WAR

In 1918, the Committee for Public Information, an office of the United States government whose purpose was to elicit support for World War I, published a set of official reasons why America opted to enter the war. They were:

1. Germany's continued submarine warfare
2. Imperial Germany becoming an international outlaw
3. Prussian militancy and autocracy disturbing the balance of world power and international equilibrium
4. Autocratic nations threatening world democracy
5. Isolationism no longer being a viable option in an age of growing global interdependence
6. The threat to America's independence

◆

It is not likely that you will sink in QUICKSAND unless you dive in headfirst. Your body is less dense than the quicksand; if you relax, you will eventually float to the top, as you would in water.

OW! HA HA

Not so funny, the funny bone. Frankly, it hurts when you hit it. It's not a bone, of course—it's the ulnar nerve, which runs down the length of the arm. It lies close to the skin's surface, and since most of us have very little fat for cushioning at the back of the elbow, when that spot is struck just right, the ulnar nerve presses into the humerus, which is the long bone that runs from your elbow to shoulder. The result is a tingling sensation that runs down the ulnar nerve through your forearm and into your ring and little fingers.

RAINING CATS

Cats are said to have nine lives because they are rarely injured when they fall. Some veterinarians believe that the longer a cat's fall, the better chance it has for survival. Cats have a finely tuned sense of balance in their inner ears, their whiskers are highly sensitive to surrounding vibrations, they use all four feet evenly to cushion a fall (they bend their knees on impact, too), and they instinctively spread their limbs like a feline umbrella, which slows their fall considerably. All of these advantages add up to at least nine happy lives!

FOR WHOM DOES THE BELL TOLL?

It tolls for Sir Benjamin Hall. Big Ben is not the clock atop London's House of Parliament, but the thirteen-and-a-half-ton bell inside the clock tower. Cast in 1858, its installation was directed by Sir Benjamin, who was the commissioner of works at the time. The moniker was probably coined by the *Times* (not by Sir Benjamin as an act of self-promotion).

MOUNTIES' MISSION

In 1873, the Canadian government established the North-West Mounted Police—the forerunner of the Royal Canadian Royal Mounted Police—to form law enforcement detachments throughout the prairies and establish friendly relations with the native population (now known as the First Nations), contain the whiskey trade and enforce prohibition, supervise treaties between the First Nations and the federal government, assist the settlement process by ensuring the welfare of immigrants, and fighting prairie fires, disease, and destitution. The first detachment left Dufferin, Manitoba, on July 8, 1874, and arrived in southern Alberta in October. The detachment included about 275 officers and men, 142 draft oxen, 93 head of cattle, 310 horses, 114 Red River carts, 73 wagons, a pair of nine-pounder field guns, a couple of mortars, mowing machines, portable forges, and field kitchens.

"HERE, HORSEY . . ."

The reason firehouses have circular stairways dates back to the days when fire engines were pulled by horses. Horses were stabled on the ground floor but occasionally got out of their stalls. The curved stairs prevented them from getting onto the upper floor.

◆

Only three of the 263 previous POPES have been called "the Great"—Pope Leo I, Pope Nicholas I, and Pope Gregory I. The "Great" title is merely bestowed as a popular acclamation by the people and is not any sort of official title.

VIGILANTE JUSTICE

The term *lynching*—to put to death without legal sanction—comes from Captain William Lynch (1742–1820), a man who, along with his neighbors, decided to rid Pittsylvania County, Virginia, of bands of thieves. Edgar Allan Poe reported that Captain Lynch and his "lynch men" had drawn up an agreement, dated September 22, 1780, that read, "If they will not desist from their evil practices, we will inflict such corporal punishment on him or them, as to us shall seem adequate to the crime committed or the damage sustained."

Lynch and many others felt that large Virginia cities and their courts were too far away (nearly 150 miles from Richmond) for swift and reasonable justice, especially when crimes of violence had been committed. They considered lynching, along with other forms of frontier punishment, appropriate and necessary, declaring that they were "aiding the civil authority."

JUST A MIRAGE

Seeing things? When light passes through two layers of air with different temperatures, you may see a mirage. It's especially common in the desert—sun heats the sand, which in turn heats the air just above it. The hot air bends light rays, and so when you think you're seeing a lake, what you're really looking at is a reflection of the sky above.

GOOD DOG

Fido may be a favorite puppy name dating from Roman times: it comes from the Latin *fidus*, meaning "faithful."

SPLITSVILLE

Over half of all marriages don't last. Here are the most common reasons, according to several surveys, married couples split:

- Lack of commitment to the marriage
- Dramatic change in priorities
- Couple's marital satisfaction decreases
- Desertion
- Bigamy
- Personal safety and protection of children
- Imprisonment
- Institutionalization
- Poor communication
- Financial problems
- Irretrievable breakdown of some kind
- Chronic abuse—sexual or physical
- Chronic substance abuse
- Sexual infidelity
- Betrayed trust
- Falling in love with another person

HOW DOES IT KNOW?

DuPont's nonstick Teflon seems to be a conundrum: If it's a nonadhesive surface, how do they get it to stick to the pan? Teflon won't chemically bond to anything except itself, but it can be forced into nooks and crannies. The metal surface of the pan is roughened, and then a primer is applied; the Teflon is embedded in the primer, and then additional layers of Teflon are applied on top of that.

SLEEP ON IT

The phrase "You made your bed—now lie in it" is more literal than one could imagine. Centuries ago, as soon as spring
came, people took their mattresses outside, slit them open,
and aired out the straw, horsehair, and whatever else they
had used to stuff the mattress. But after the long winter (and
given what passed for cleanliness at the time), it was not
unusual to find mites, bedbugs, mice, and all manner of surprises inside. The job was to clean out the stuffing and
restuff the mattress—and however well or poorly you did the
job, you had to sleep on it, hence the saying.

THE PURPLE HEART

The Purple Heart is the oldest military decoration for the
common soldier still in use in the world, and the first
American award made available to common soldiers. When
the Continental Congress told General George Washington
there was no money for new commissions, he designed a
new badge of honor: "Whenever any singularly meritorious
action is performed, the author of it shall be permitted to
wear on his facings, over his left breast, the figure of a heart
in purple cloth or silk edged with narrow lace or binding.
Not only instances of unusual gallantry but also of extraordinary fidelity and essential service in any way shall meet with
due reward."

Today the Purple Heart is awarded to members of the
U.S. armed forces who are wounded by an instrument of war
in the hands of the enemy, and posthumously to the next of
kin for those killed in action or who die of wounds received
in action. It is specifically a combat decoration.

FIFTY WAYS TO NAME YOUR COUNTRY
The Origins of Each of the United States

Alabama: Believed to come from two Choctaw words, *alba*, meaning "vegetation" or "plants," and *amo*, "gatherer."

Alaska: Derived from the Aleut word *alyeska*, meaning "great land" or "that which the sea breaks against."

Arizona: A combination of Indian words *aleh* and *zon*, meaning "little spring."

Arkansas: Ohio Valley Indians referred to the local Quapaw Indians as the Arkansas, or "south wind."

California: A mythical Spanish island, ruled by a queen named Califia, which appeared in a Spanish romance (c. 1500) called *Las Sergas de Esplandián*.

Colorado: From the Spanish word for "colored."

Connecticut: From the Indian name Quinnehtukqut, which means "beside the long tidal river."

Delaware: Named after Delaware River and Delaware Bay, which were named for Sir Thomas West, Baron de la Warr.

District of Columbia: Built on land known as the Territory of Columbia.

Florida: From the Spanish festival day Pascua de Florida, or "feast of flowers," referring to Easter.

Georgia: Named in honor of George II of England.

Hawaii: Origin uncertain, but one theory has it that the name comes from Hawaii Loa, who in traditional lore discov-

ered the islands, or it may be named after the legendary ancestral home of the Polynesian people.

Idaho: An invented word from an unknown source.

Illinois: Algonquin for "tribe of superior men."

Indiana: Meaning "land of Indians," the name was given to the Indiana Territory by the U.S. Congress when Indiana was created from the Northwest Territory.

Iowa: The tribal name of the Iowa Indians, Ayuxwa, was spelled *Ioway* by the English and means "this is the place" or "beautiful land."

Kansas: From the Sioux *kanze,* meaning "south wind."

Kentucky: From the Iroquois word *ken-tah-ten,* meaning "land of tomorrow."

Louisiana: The area was named La Louisiane after Louis XIV of France.

Maine: So named to distinguish the mainland from the off-shore islands; also thought to be a compliment to Henrietta Maria, wife of Charles I and queen of England, who owned the province of Mayne in France.

Maryland: For King Charles's wife, Queen Henrietta Maria.

Massachusetts: Opinions differ, but the most popular theory is that it's a combination of the Indian words *massa,* "great," and *wachusett,* "mountain-place."

Michigan: Derived from the Chippewa word *majigan,* referring to a clearing on the lower peninsula.

Minnesota: From the Dakota word *mnishota,* meaning "cloudy water."

Mississippi: From the Chippewa word meaning "father of waters."

Missouri: Named after the local Sioux tribe, meaning "he of the large canoes."

Montana: Derived from the Latin word *montaanus*, "mountainous."

Nebraska: From an Oto word meaning "flat water."

Nevada: Spanish sailors originally called the California mountains the Sierra Nevada, meaning "snowcapped range"; the name of this new territory was a shorter version, meaning simply "snowcapped."

New Hampshire: Captain John Mason named the land he had been granted after the English county he had lived in as a child.

New Jersey: After the Channel isle of Jersey.

New Mexico: Named after Mexitli, an Aztec god.

New York: Named by the British to honor the Duke of York.

North Carolina: Named in honor of Charles I of England.

North Dakota: From the Sioux word for "friend."

Ohio: From the Iroquois word meaning "great river."

Oklahoma: A combination of two Choctaw words, *ukla*, "person," and *humá*, "red."

Oregon: The origin is in question, although the Columbia River, along the state's northern border, was called the Ouragan, which is French for "hurricane"; others believe the name arose from a mapmaker's error in the 1700s.

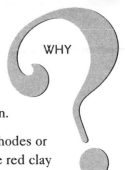

Pennsylvania: "Penn's woods," after William Penn.

Rhode Island: Either from the Greek island of Rhodes or from the Dutch *roodt eylandt*, "red island," for the red clay along the shore.

South Carolina: Like North Carolina, named in honor of Charles I of England.

South Dakota: Like North Dakota, from the Sioux word for "friend" (the two states were one territory until 1899).

Tennessee: From the Tennessee River, which took its name from Tanasi, two Cherokee villages on its banks.

Texas: From the Caddo word *teysha*, meaning "hello, friend."

Utah: *Yuttahih*, an Apache name for the Ute tribe, means "people of the mountains."

Vermont: Anglicized version of French explorer Samuel de Champlain's choice *Vert Mont*, meaning "green mountain."

Virginia: For Elizabeth I of England, the "Virgin Queen."

Washington: The Washington Territory, established in 1853, was named for President George Washington.

West Virginia: Like Virginia (West Virginia was not a separate state until 1861), named in honor of Queen Elizabeth I.

Wisconsin: From the French version of the Chippewa word for "grassy place" or "gathering of the waters."

Wyoming: From the Delaware Indian word, meaning "mountains and valleys alternating" (the Delawares lived much farther east, but the name is taken from the Wyoming Valley in Pennsylvania).

PLACE NAMES FROM AROUND THE WORLD

Argentina: From the Latin *argentum*, "silver."

Barbados: The term *os barbados* means "the bearded ones" in Portuguese, a reference to the island's fig trees, whose long roots resemble beards.

Brazil: From the native brazilwood tree, named because its wood was the color of red-hot embers (*brasil* in Portuguese).

Britain: From Pritani, a Celtic tribe mentioned as early as the first century B.C.E. by Diodorus Siculus as the island's original inhabitants.

Canada: *K'anata* meant "little settlement" to the Algonquins, and referred to Stadacona, a village near what is now Quebec City.

Christmas Island: Discovered by Captain William Mynors on Christmas Day in 1643.

Costa Rica: Spanish for "rich coast," so named because Christopher Columbus thought there was gold there.

Cyprus: Named for the copper (Greek *kypros*) that was found on the island.

Ethiopia: From the Latin *Aethiopia*, meaning "land of burned faces."

Gambia: Probably from the Portuguese *câmbio*, meaning "trade"; the Portuguese monopolized trade there in the sixteenth century.

Hong Kong: In Cantonese, *heung gong* means "fragrant harbor" or "spice harbor."

Hungary: From the Turkic *on-ogur*, for "people of the ten spears," after the seven Magyar tribes and three Khazar tribes who settled there.

Israel: From the Genesis story; an alternative Hebrew name for Jacob, meaning "he struggles with God."

Japan: English pronunciation for the Chinese for "land of the rising sun," a reminder that the country is east of China.

Kenya: After the Kikuyu people's *kirinyaga*, the "mountain of whiteness," referring to Mount Kenya; the British mispronounced it as "Kenya."

Kyrgyzstan: Derives from three Persian words meaning "land of forty tribes."

Luxembourg: From *lucilemburrugh*, a combination of Celtic and German words meaning "little castle."

Malta: Most likely derived from the Latin *melitta*, "honey," which was the island's major export during classical times.

Mongolia: First used by the Chinese, meaning "brave" or "fearless."

Namibia: From the Nama language, referring to the Namib Desert (*namib* means "enormous").

Nepal: Means "wool market" in Tibetan.

Pakistan: An acronym created by Muslim nationalist Choudhary Rahmat Ali in 1933:

P	Punjab
A	Afghania
K	Kashmir
S	Sindh
TAN	Balochistan

The *I* was added for ease of pronunciation. However, in his 1947 book *Pakistan: the Fatherland of the Pak Nation*, Ali modified his own acronym:

P	Punjab
A	Afghania
K	Kashmir
I	Iran
S	Sindh
T	Turkharistan
A	Afghanistan
N	Balochistan

Papua New Guinea: The neighboring Malays, who have straight hair, called the natives *papua*, "frizzy hair."

Sudan: From the Arabic for "land of the blacks."

Ukraine: From *krajina*, a Slavic term for "border territory."

Uruguay: From a Guarani word meaning "river of shellfish."

Vatican City: From *Mons Vaticanus*, the Roman hill on which the Papal palace stands.

Viet Nam: From a Chinese term meaning "beyond the southern border."

◆

SO ROMANTIC

Don Juan came up with the cocktail-party phrase "breaking the ice." At least that's the derivation based on Lord Byron's description of the British in his famous 1821 poem "Don Juan": "And your cold people are beyond all price, / When once you've broken through their confounded ice."

AVAST!

What ho? Could it be that Moby-Dick did indeed live and breathe? There had long been a story about an actual white whale told by whalers who sailed the Pacific Ocean, and an article written by Jeremiah Reynolds and published in 1839 in *The Knickerbocker* told the tale. Captain Nathaniel Palmer, while aboard the whaler *Penguin*, told of his victory battling a leviathan known as Mocha Dick, which was often spotted in the waters near the Mocha Islands off Chili. Herman Melville's novel did not appear until 1851, but Reynolds's description has a strangely familiar sound: "From the effect of age, or more probably from a freak of nature, as exhibited in the case of the Ethiopian Albino, a singular consequence had resulted—*he was white as wool!*"

COCKROACH VS. HUMAN

For millions of years, humankind has lost the fight against cockroaches; there are plenty of reasons. A cockroach can:

- Be frozen for two days and still survive
- Go three months without any food at all
- Live a week without its head
- Hold its breath up to forty minutes
- Be as much as six inches long with a one-foot wingspan
- Live through a thermonuclear explosion
- Navigate perfectly if both deaf and blind

◆

Our word INCH comes form the Latin *uncia*, meaning "a twelfth part."

SHIVER ME TIMBERS!

Goose bumps (so named because they make a person look like a plucked goose) are a signal from the hypothalamus, the body's thermostat, that we need to warm ourselves. It's part of the shivering reflex, in which the body's muscles and glands begin working to heat up the body. This reflex is involuntary, contracting and relaxing the skeletal muscles; the hair on your body pulls up and the ducts to the sweat glands contract, conserving heat. The entire body can go to work in an extreme situation: every muscle in the body, except those in the eyeballs, can shiver—even the tongue.

SOME LIKE IT HOT

Crickets make a variety of chirping sounds, called stridulation (males are the "singers"), for a variety of reasons:

- A loud, monotonous sound to attract a female
- A quick, soft chirp to court and impress a female
- An aggressive sound to warn male intruders away from his territory

This language, spoken by scraping one wing against another, is simply a variation of courtship and survival that is often observed in the animal kingdom. But the cricket offers a singular service to humans that no one else in nature seems to have mastered: They tell the temperature. To get a rough idea of what to wear and how to prepare for a picnic or outdoor concert, check your watch and count the number of chirps you hear in fifteen seconds. Add 37 to that number, and you'll have the approximate temperature in degrees Fahrenheit.

THE GRIM REAPER

The American Medical Association's List of the Major Causes of Death in the United States (as of 2000)

Tobacco (smoking)	435,000
Poor diet and physical inactivity	365,000
Alcohol (includes alcohol-related motor vehicle deaths)	85,000
Microbial agents	75,000
Toxic agents	55,000
Adverse reactions to prescription drugs	32,000
Suicide	30,622
Incidents involving firearms	29,000
Motor vehicle crashes	26,347
Homicide	20,308
Illicit drug use, direct and indirect	17,000
Anti-inflammatory drugs such as aspirin	7,600

HAIL, SPARKY!

Dalmatians enjoyed a long and illustrious career before catching the imagination of Walt Disney. Centuries ago they were known as "coach dogs" and ran alongside stagecoaches, guarding against marauders and highwaymen. When horse-drawn fire engines came into use, dalmatians were used because they bonded with horses and were easily trained to run ahead of them and clear streets quickly in emergencies.

◆

For centuries people believed that the VEIN in the fourth finger of one's left hand went directly to the heart, which is why wedding rings are traditionally worn there.

SHALL WE DANCE?

The Whirling Dervishes are Sufis who trace their origin to the thirteenth-century Ottoman Empire. The dervish's dance is a mystical exercise, part of a sacred ceremony. The dervish spins in a precise rhythm, emptying himself of all thought in order to enter a trancelike state.

During the ritual dance, or *sema*, there are four *selams*, or musical movements, each with a distinct rhythm. The first *selam* represents the human being's birth to truth through feeling and mind. The second *selam* expresses the rapture of the human being witnessing the splendor of creation in the face of God's greatness and omnipotence. The third *selam* is the rapture of dissolving into love and the sacrifice of the mind to love. In the fourth *selam* the dervish, after the ascent of his spiritual journey, returns to his task, servanthood to God.

ROADSIDE AMERICA

Miniature golf was first introduced in 1916 with a course designed by James Barber in Pinehurst, North Carolina (legend has it that when Barber saw the finished course, he declared, "This'll do!"—providing the course with its name, Thistle Dhu). It became particularly popular during the Depression, as a round of miniature golf cost less than seeing a movie; also, in a decade seemingly gone haywire, it offered a place where the world was brought down to a manageable size. It became one of America's first roadside franchises in the 1930s and 1940s, and the industry grew even as other businesses failed. By midcentury, miniature golf was enjoying a pint-sized form of the suburban sprawl taking place in much of the United States.

CRAZY CAT

Catnip (*Nepeta cataria*) is a common herb in the mint family that grows easily in any garden. Nepetalactone is the secret ingredient that makes cats crazy, and it's recently been found to repel cockroaches and the mosquitoes that carry yellow fever. Herbalists recommend catnip for human use as a treatment for colic, headache, fever, toothache, colds, and spasms. It is also an excellent sleep inducer (try a cup of catnip tea).

But back to the cats. About 30 percent of the feline population—including most tiny kittens and old cats—do not respond to catnip at all. Reaction from interested cats lasts only five to fifteen minutes; once the cat acclimates to the catnip, it loses interest for an hour or more, at which point the cycle starts over again.

CATNIP BEHAVIOR

1. Sniffing
2. Licking and chewing the toy or plant, head shaking
3. Chin and cheek rubbing
4. Rolling and body rubbing
5. Grasping and kicking

SHAZAM!

The term *hanky-panky* was not originally used to connote sexual hijinks, as one might think, but is instead a magician's term from the 1800s. Prestidigitators used to wave handkerchiefs to distract the audience from whatever trick they were performing with their other hand. Like the rhyming *hocus-pocus*, which was already in use, *hanky-panky* became a catchphrase for anything suspicious or sneaky, like a little romance on the side.

THE PSYCHOLOGY OF COLOR

Color is never just about the way it looks, whether it's on your back or on your walls; it's about how it makes you feel, and the message it sends about you to others. Much research has been done on meaning of color—how it affects people's lives, their temperaments, and even their buying habits.

Red: This color represents fire, passion, warmth, heat, and love; power, excitement, and aggression. It's no wonder it can elevate blood pressure, quicken breathing, and cause people to make snap decisions. Red is known to be an appetite stimulant, though an entire room of scarlet will make one anxious. Bars, casinos, and restaurants often use scarlet accents in the hope that it will, as experts say, help people lose track of time.

Orange: The hue most associated with appetite, orange is almost universally appealing, and is wholesome and warm. Orange is often used in packaging to make an expensive product appear more affordable.

Yellow: The most visible of all the colors, yellow is the top attention getter; since it enhances concentration, it has become the color of choice for legal pads and Post-Its. Yellow speeds up the metabolism and is the most fatiguing color to the eye.

Green: This shade is the most popular for decorating. It's soothing to the mind and eye and is familiar and calming, because it's seen so much in nature. Not only is it easy on the senses, but experts say it can actually improve vision. Hospitals and other institutions rely on its peaceful and relaxing qualities.

Blue: Blue causes the body to produce chemicals that relax the nervous system. Research has proven that people are more productive in blue rooms—students test better, and weight lifters lift more. Both men and women most favor blue, and retain more information when the text is blue.

Purple: Magisterial, luxurious, and sophisticated, this color can evoke passion and romance. However, because it is so rarely found in nature, it can easily appear artificial.

Brown: Brown is solid, earthy, and reliable, and men are apt to cite it as one of their favorite colors. Its solidity and strength promote comfort and openness.

Pink: Less in-your-face than its scarlet counterpart, people find it romantic and tender. It can be calming (some go so far as to say tranquilizing) when in a room, causing visitors to be soft-hearted.

Though black and white are technically not colors, as they don't appear in the spectrum, their place in color psychology is as important as all the others:

Black: Priests wear black to signify their submission to God, and other people wear it to connote formality. Color psychologists consider it the most controversial of colors: it's associated with both witches and demons, sturdiness and reliability. Black is not a true color—in pigmentation, it's the presence of all color; in light, it's the absence.

White: This color symbolizes innocence and purity. Doctors and nurses wear it to imply a sterile environment. White pigmentation is the absence of any color; white light indicates the presence of all colors.

TAPHOPHOBIA

Psychologists tell us that taphophobia—the fear of being buried alive—is very common. Some famous examples:

"All I desire for my own burial is not to be buried alive."
—LORD CHESTERFIELD

"Have me decently buried, but do not let my body be put into a vault in less than two days after I am dead."
—GEORGE WASHINGTON

Prior to the advent of embalming, being buried alive was a common fear—though a rare occurrence. The eighteenth century brought about the invention of the signaling, or escape hatch, coffin. There were several types of these coffins, but they all had in common a mechanism that allowed communication from the buried person to the world above. Some of the accoutrements of these rigged-up coffins included firecrackers, bells, flags, and breathing tubes—one version even provided a shovel, food, and water. The fad didn't last long, however, and the signaling coffin soon disappeared. But not the fear of being buried alive: a patent for a "coffin alarm" was applied for as recently as 1983.

◆

MEXICAN JUMPING BEANS are real, all right—they even have a Latin name: *Laspeyresia saltitans.* However, they're not beans at all, but moth larvae, which grow inside the seed capsules of a Mexican desert shrub. The larvae roll around inside the seed capsule when they detect warmth and light, causing the seed capsule to "jump." After three to five months, these larvae spin a cocoon, and a small number of them hatch as moths, living only a few days.

COLOR ME ASLEEP

Dreaming in color is one thing, but what about dreaming in particular colors? What do colors in dreams mean?

Colors	Representation
Beige	The basics, neutrality
Black	The unknown, danger, death, hate
Black and white	Need for more objectivity in making decisions
Blue	Truth, justice, heaven, tranquility
Brown	Practicality, domestic comfort, the earth
Burgundy	Wealth, success, the potential for power
Fuchsia	Spirituality, meditation, emotional stability
Gold	Spiritual rewards, richness, refinement
Gray	Fear, depression, ill health
Green	Growth, hope, healing, peace, wealth; jealousy
Hot pink	Sex, lust
Ivory	Slightly tainted purity
Maroon	Courage, strength
Orange	Friendliness, warmth, courtesy
Peach	Innocent love
Pink	Love, joy, sweetness
Purple	Devotion, compassion
Red	Intense passion, power, anger, courage; also shame, sexual impulses
Silver	Justice and purity
Teal	Trustworthiness, devotion
Turquoise	Healing power, natural energy
Violet	Religious aspiration, purification
White	Purity, peace, innocence, new beginnings
Yellow	In a positive dream, energy, harmony, optimism; in a negative dream, cowardice and sickness

SCHOOL UNIFORMS

The wearing of caps and gowns for graduation is the last vestige of a long tradition of both keeping vows and keeping warm. When European universities developed in the twelfth century, teachers and students alike began to wear long gowns. Gowns were standard clerical garb, and scholars of the day took a type of minor vow with the Church. As university connections to the Church began to dissipate, the gowns stayed, providing warmth to students and faculty who lived and taught in the cold, drafty buildings. Gowns are still de rigueur in many universities throughout the world, but they are worn for ceremonial use only in the United States, though their design is regulated. The shape of the sleeve and hood show the degree a student has pursued: a bachelor's gown has no hood and pointed sleeves, the master's has closed sleeves with arm slits and a narrow hood; the doctor's has bell sleeves and a draped, wide hood. The hood's lining denotes the college. And as for caps, velvet is worn by doctors only, please.

HEAVY STUFF

The materials that go into making an airplane's flight information data recorder—the "black box"—include stainless steel and high-temperature insulation, which surround a locator beacon and memory unit. If you've ever wondered why an entire plane isn't made out of the black box material, since they always seem to make it through a crash without substantial damage, it's simply that it would be too heavy: the plane would never get off the ground. And by the way, the black box is painted orange.

SO FUNNY I FORGOT TO LAUGH

"Why did the chicken cross the road?" is perhaps the best-known example of what is called anti-humor, a strangely twisted brand of comedy that relies on irony for a humorous response. The listener expects a punch line to be obvious, and when the answer is nonsensical, this seems funny.

Oh, the answer? "To see his friend Gregory Peck."

THE TWELVE LINKS OF DEPENDENT ORIGINATION

Buddhism teaches the ultimate elaboration of the principles of cause and effect, or conditions, which explain the concept of the interdependency of existence.

1. Ignorance is the condition for mental formation.
2. Mental formation is the condition for consciousness.
3. Consciousness is the condition for name and form.
4. Name and form are the condition for the six senses.
5. The six senses are the condition for contact.
6. Contact is the condition for feeling.
7. Feeling is the condition for craving.
8. Craving is the condition for clinging.
9. Clinging is the condition for becoming.
10. Becoming is the condition for birth.
11. Birth is the condition for aging and death.
12. Aging and death are the condition for ignorance.

◆

Israeli POSTAGE STAMPS are special: the glue on the back is certified kosher.

MOVING RIGHT ALONG

History repeats itself in myriad ways, and people's reasons for emigrating have not changed much over time, according to experts at the Ellis Island Immigration Museum:

Religious or ethnic persecution
Natural disaster
Famine
Homeland economic problems
War (or fear of war)
Feudalism and its overthrow
Political strife
No son to provide economic protection for the
   parents in later life
Oppression
Following family and friends
Adoption
Slavery
Criminal incarceration
Being deported

DRINK UP

Alcohol does not kill brain cells but rather damages dendrites—the branched ends of nerve cells that serve as electrical connections to the cells. Losing function of these ends means cutting off incoming messages, which disrupts brain function. Thankfully, most of this damage is not permanent. But that's nothing—back in the day, promoters of temperance also claimed that excessive amounts of alcohol in the blood could cause one to easily catch fire and burn alive.

MONEY FOR NOTHING?

Here are the ten most common reasons grant applications for funding from philanthropic organizations and agencies are declined:

1. "The organization does not meet our priorities."
2. "The organization is not located in our geographic area of funding."
3. "The proposal does not follow our prescribed format."
4. "The proposal is poorly written and difficult to understand."
5. "The proposed budget and grant request are not within our funding range."
6. "We don't know these people—are they credible?"
7. "The proposal doesn't seem urgent—and I'm not sure it will have an impact."
8. "The objectives and plan of action of the project greatly exceed the budget and timelines for implementation."
9. "We've allocated all the money for this grant cycle."
10. "There is insufficient evidence that the program will become self-sufficient and sustain itself after the grant is completed."

(Source: Grant Guides Plus, Inc.)

A LITTLE SOMETHING ON THE SIDE

Before it was food, it was a building. The literal meaning of the French phrase *hors d'oeuvre* was an outbuilding that was not part of the main architectural design. The culinary community borrowed it to describe an appetizer served apart from the main course.

ROOM AT THE INN

America was booming by the 1820s, and the number of travelers—transients, businessmen, even vacationers—was increasing dramatically. To serve them, a new type of hostelry was born. The hotels that sprang up in the center of towns offered meeting rooms, fine restaurants, and a variety of other creature comforts. The most American touch of all? The best lodgings were no longer reserved for guests with impressive titles, as they had been in Europe. Only money got you top-of-the-line service.

WASH ME CLEAN

You washed your hands. Then you washed your dog's dirty paws. So why isn't that bar of soap dirty?

Soap is made from a compound with two components, one hydrophobic (water-insoluble), the other hydrophilic (water-soluble). The former attaches itself to dirt and dissolves it, while the latter keeps the dirty, greasy stuff that was just on your clothes or hands suspended in water, ready to wash away.

As for when hands are really clean: an old wives' tale proposes that to make sure children wash their hands extremely well, they should sing their ABCs. It takes approximately fifteen seconds, the amount of time suggested for a good, germ-ridding scrub.

◆

The OPOSSUM has changed so little since the Cretaceous period, when dinosaurs still roamed the earth, that it's often referred to as a living fossil.

THE DANGERS OF MARRIAGE

The nuances of a wedding are mired in custom and fraught
with superstition, and even the days of the week and months
in when one marries were thought to carry their own special
connection to the couple's ultimate success.

Monday for wealth
Tuesday for health
Wednesday the best day of all
Thursday for losses
Friday for crosses
Saturday for no luck at all.

Advice on the month is even more specific:

Married when the year is new, he'll be loving, kind, and true.
When February birds do mate, you wed nor dread your fate.
If you wed when March winds blow, joy and
sorrow both you'll know.
Marry in April when you can, joy for maiden and for man.
Marry in the month of May, and you'll surely rue the day.
Marry when June roses grow, over land and sea you'll go.
Those who in July do wed, must labor for their daily bread.
Whoever wed in August be, many a change is sure to see.
Marry in September's shrine, your living will
be rich and fine.
If in October you do marry, love will come but riches tarry.
If you wed in bleak November, only joys
will come, remember.
When December snows fall fast,
marry and true love will last.

POINT IN QUESTION

The question mark probably first appeared in the ninth century, though a point or dot at the end of a sentence had long been used to show a full stop. For a query it was followed by a curved line tilted upward to the right. This indicated the cadence and intonation of the voice of the speaker.

WELCOME CHAOS

Who says chaos theory has nothing to do with real life? For over a decade, washing machine manufacturers have been selling a consumer product that exploits randomness. The washing machine maker added a second tiny pulsator to stir the water; it relies on predictable movements while working in a nonlinear way, the basis of chaos theory. Results? The clothes come out cleaner and less tangled.

THE SMELL OF VICTORY, AND THEN SOME

Perfume has a long history as more than a come-on. The Greeks used scents for medicinal purposes—for example, rose petals were worn around the neck to ward off hangovers. Both the Romans and the Crusaders put perfume on before battle, believing that it brought good luck. And Nero had an obsession with beautiful odors—his first-century palace had pipes hidden throughout to spray his guests with rich scents.

◆

Scientists believe that OCTOPI, like humans, turn red when angry and blanch white when afraid.

WHY DIE?

Suicide prevention organizations list these as the leading reasons people attempt and/or commit suicide:

Depression
Schizophrenia, personality disorder, etc.
Alcoholism and substance abuse
Illness and physical infirmity
Revenge, anger, punishment
Sacrifice for others or the community
Politics
Suicide bombers
Loss of a loved one
Loss of job, economic distress
Sexual orientation, gender conflicts

WHAT FLOATS YOUR BOAT?

It's about buoyancy, the upward force a fluid exerts on an object less dense than itself—that's what allows even gigantic things to float in liquid. An object's density determines whether or not the liquid it's placed in can offset the pull of gravity on the object and push it up, allowing the object to float instead of sink. Density depends on weight and size, so if two objects are different sizes but weigh the same, the smaller object is the denser one. Ocean liners, freighters, and sloops may be large, but they're all hollow inside, which makes their overall density less than that of water—and that's why they float rather than sink.

◆

SPAM is an acronym for shoulder pork and ham.

541

TURN TO THE CHASE

We use the phrase "cut to the chase" to cue someone to hurry a story along. And although it sounds like a movie director's request for a quick move to an action scene, it was not first heard on the screen: its first known usage was as a script direction in a 1927 novel, *Hollywood Girl*.

HOLE-Y COW

Bacteria? How can something so bad taste so good? Yet bacteria are essential for making cheese, and different kinds of bacteria give each cheese a specific flavor. *Propionibacter shermani* is just one of three species of bacteria that go into the making of Swiss cheese, but it's the one that makes it holey. As the cheese is being made, the bacteria produce bubbles of carbon dioxide, which leave the distinctive holes—"eyes" is the technical term—that make Swiss so different from all other cheeses.

STOP IT, I LOVE IT!

How is it that being tickled can drive you crazy—and yet when you try to tickle yourself in the very same place, it doesn't work? From birth, stimuli begin to bombard you; one of the first things an infant learns to do is filter them. Consequently, the first signals you ignore are the ones that your own body produces. It's why you don't notice your vocal cords, blinking, the feel of your feet on the sidewalk . . . or self-tickling. The laughter that erupts when someone else is after you is sheer panic.

DID I DO THAT?

When you have a few drinks, your body reacts the same way every time. Once alcohol enters the bloodstream, different parts of the brain are affected, one by one:

Part of Brain Affected	Effect on Behavior
Cerebral cortex	Inhibition of language and information processing
Limbic system	Mood and attitude changes, leading to strong emotion, depression, pursuit of sexual activity
Cerebellum	Changes in coordination and cognition
Hypothalamus and pituitary gland	Increases blood pressure and decreases body temperature
Medulla	Effects on respiration, heart rate, and other vital functions

GLIMPSES OF THE SOUL

The onus of bad luck in breaking a mirror is a comparatively modern version of an ancient belief. Before mirrors, when people checked their appearance in a pool of water, many believed that they were actually seeing a glimpse of their soul. If their reflections were disrupted in any way—a breeze, a stone, a sudden wave—their soul was disturbed as well, and bad luck would befall the viewer.

A DIFFERENT STRIPE

For centuries, stripes have been worn by social outcasts—serfs, prostitutes, jugglers, clowns, hangmen, Jews, lepers, cripples, and heretics, to name just a few. Eventually, stripes adorned the uniforms in most prison systems around the world.

In the United States, the striped outfits were meant to symbolize just what they look like: prison bars. During the Great Depression, many Americans ended up in jail for crimes that were poverty-related, such as petty theft, vagrancy, and debt, and prison uniforms changed to jeans and denim shirts, partly as a way to lessen the humiliation these first-and-only-time offenders experienced or felt. Today, many states are returning to the old-fashioned stripes to make prisoners easy to spot. And for the record, they sell for about $12 a set and are available in red, green, orange, and blue stripes on a white ground—although the black-and-white version is by far the best seller.

THIN STRIPES AND PINSTRIPES

The New York Yankees are famous for their pinstriped home uniforms, but both stories of how their uniforms came to feature the stripes are false. Some say they were used to disguise the gigantic girth of the Bambino, Babe Ruth. But the truth is, the Yankees were already playing in stripes both before Ruth joined the team and while he was still in shape. Others say the Yankees thought the moving stripes would distract the competition during play. But the Bronx Bombers were just jumping on the fashion bandwagon: the fad for stripes had started in other clubs years before.

WHO THE HECK IS OLLIE?

However you used to say it as a kid, "Ollie, Ollie, oxen free," "Ollie, Ollie enfry," or whatever, all agree it was the universal call for every game player still out in the field to come on in. Most likely, kids originally called, "All the outs in free."

NO STRINGS ATTACHED?

Why don't spiders get caught in their own webs? Seems they've got a terrific sense of both design and direction. It helps that the tips of their legs secrete an oily substance to help them slip over the sticky threads they've woven. But the real trick is that not all of the threads in a spiderweb are sticky. The silk for the hub and the spokes radiating out from it are not, but the thread spiders use to make the spiral portion of the web is sticky, to ensnare insects. The spiders know which is which, of course, and manage to sidestep the danger.

FALL INTO . . .

In 1969 a man named Donald Fisher opened a store that sold only records, cassette tapes, and every size of Levi's imaginable—important stuff that parents wouldn't understand because of the generation gap. He named his store . . . The Gap.

◆

Though COLORBLINDNESS is mostly a genetic dysfunction, it can also be caused by nerve or brain damage or by drug use. It occurs in 5–8 percent of men and only 0.5 percent of women.

JUST-WAR THEORY

Why war? Most historians will agree that St. Augustine originated just-war theory, perhaps the most influential perspec-
tive on the ethics of war and peace. According to the Hague
and Geneva Conventions, just-war theory can be divided
into three parts:

1. *Jus ad bellum*, which concerns the justice of resorting
to war in the first place:

Just cause
Right intention
Proper authority and public declaration
Last resort
Probability of success
Macro-proportionality—weighing the universal goods ex-
pected to result from the war against the universal evils

Just-war theory insists all six criteria must each be fulfilled
for a particular declaration of war to be justified.

2. *Jus in bello*, which concerns the justice of conduct within
war, after it has begun:

Discrimination—soldiers are only entitled to target those
who are "engaged in harm."
Micro-proportionality—soldiers may only use force proportional to the end they seek
No means *mala in se*—soldiers may not use weapons or
methods that are "evil in themselves," e.g., mass rape,
genocide, ethnic cleansing, or torture

3. *Jus post bellum,* which concerns the justice of peace agreements and the termination phase of war:

Just cause for termination
Right intention
Public declaration and legitimate authority
Discrimination—between, e.g., police, government officials, general population
Proportionality—the terms of peace must be proportional to vindication

(Stanford Encyclopedia of Philosophy)

LIAR, LIAR

A recent study shows that most people lie in everyday conversation, mainly to appear to be more likable and competent. Nearly 60 percent of the people tested in the study lied at least twice during a ten-minute telephone call. Women tend to lie to make the person they're speaking to feel good, while men lie to make themselves look better.

BECAUSE I'M THE AUTHOR

Many science fiction writers use what's called the "tooth fairy rule," which states that a mysterious outside force may be invoked once—but only once—per story to explain away the inexplicable.

The modern NECKTIE is a descendant of the cloths worn by Roman orators around their necks to keep their vocal cords warm. Subsequently they became clothing that proclaimed status, occupation, or identity.

547

UBER-BRRR?

Though people talk about whether it's "too cold to snow," it's more accurate to ponder whether it's too *dry* to snow. Heavy snowfalls occur when the temperature is right around the freezing point—warmer air holds more moisture than cold air. The conditions for snow include saturated air and an air temperature profile that allows snow to reach the surface. In a city such as Buffalo, New York, its close proximity to Lake Erie results in the perfect moisture-rich conditions to guarantee a large annual snowfall—cold arctic air moving over the warmer surface of the lake picks up moisture and is cooled as it rises, creating clouds and eventually snow.

A STARRY, STARRY POISONED NIGHT

Much has been made of Vincent Van Gogh's mental illness and early death, but it seems his addictions could very well have hastened his demise. Not only was he an alcoholic, but his drinks of choice were paint thinner and the "green fairy," absinthe. It's also possible that Van Gogh was poisoned by digitalis, a common treatment at the time for epilepsy, with which he was afflicted. Many experts believe his digitalis use accounts for his depiction of haloed light sources, as the drug often causes ultrasensitivity to light.

GLASS OR PLASTIC?

Why is it when you go to unload the top rack of the dishwasher, the glass is nice and dry while the plastic containers are still dripping with water? Because glass is a better heat conductor than plastic and therefore dries faster.

WHICH COLOR IS BETTER FOR CHOCOLATE?

If you thought you were getting cheated out of your favorite color of M&M's in your last bag, you're probably not alone. The numbers of each color are controlled and are a result of heavy consumer testing. Here's the color mix, in percentages:

Flavor	Brown	Yellow	Red	Green	Orange	Blue
Plain	3	14	13	16	20	24
Peanut	12	15	12	15	23	23
Peanut butter	10	20	10	20	20	20
Almond	10	20	10	20	20	20

BUGGY

Life imitates art imitates science? The word *bug* used as a term for a problem in technology (now most often computers) was yet another Edison innovation. He coined the word in 1889 while working on the phonograph; it was an expression he evidently used when he ran into difficulty, implying that there was an imaginary bug inside, wreaking havoc. Over half a century later in 1947, the bug joke was picked up by computer geeks when a moth flew into the Mark II computer at Harvard University and actually stopped up the works. The bug was captured, taped down, and logged in. The entry? "First actual case of bug being found."

◆

A PRINCIPALITY is a sovereign territory that is ruled by a prince or princess.

EDWARD BARLEYCORN

It was no mathematician but King Edward I of England who standardized measurements back in 1305. He dictated that an inch would be defined as the length of "three barleycorns, round and dry." His purpose was to set a standard of accuracy in certain trades; British cobblers were among the first to adopt the idea.

TRADE AGREEMENT

Back in the day, a betrothal was much more of a family affair. The bride's dowry, set by her parents, was something substantial, equal to the bride's perceived worth and meant to bring value to the marriage. The groom did his part, too, by paying a brideprice to her family, which helped pay for the wedding costs, and by promising to support her faithfully.

FINE FRIGID FRIENDS?

Why is it we humans need cashmere and snowsuits to keep warm, while birds fly about year-round only in feather suits? Frankly, our heating systems aren't as good.

In human bodies, the further hot blood is pumped from the heart, the more it cools. Birds' circulatory systems, on the other hand, have a different kind of network, called a *rete mirabile*, or "wondrous network." A bird's arteries lie extremely close to the veins, so close that their proximity causes heat to be evenly transferred from the warmer artery to the cooler vein. That's why, for birds, feathers are enough, and they're virtually always warm all over.

THE BAD-TEMPERED LILY

The onion is a member of the lily family. Such a nice family . . . and yet the onion has a reputation as a tearjerker. When you slice an onion, you release sulfur compounds that evaporate and become a volatile gas, and that gas irritates eyes. Slicing the onion under running water helps—many of the sulfur compounds will dissolve in water. Cutting out the root first works, too, because that's where the compounds originate.

ANIMAL LOGIC

"Hair of the dog" is only part of the longer, original expression, "the hair of the dog that bit you." People used to believe that the antidote for a dog bite should include some of the guilty dog's hair. Same for a hangover: a little more of the same should set everything straight.

NUMBER, PLEASE

Why does every movie character live in the same neighborhood?

Surely you've noticed: Every single solitary time a phone number is given on TV or in the movies, it's strangely familiar. First, the appropriate area code—but after that? The exchange always seems to be "555," or, in older cases, "Klondike 5." It's because 555 is reserved for information nationwide in the United States. So any, er, fan who tries to call the number the pretty girl just gave the handsome detective is guaranteed to be out of luck.

FABULISTS

Aesop's fables, Mother Goose, nursery rhymes—speculations on their origins are numerous. Historians are split as to whether Aesop was born a slave or even existed at all. Mother Goose may be the pseudonym of Queen Bertha of France. But by the seventeenth century, nursery rhymes were imbedded in culture, with roots in tales centuries old. Based in oral tradition, they disappear and resurface, sometimes slightly changed. Many historians believe the versions of nursery rhymes we know today concern themselves with British history and personalities. Some theories:

> A FROG HE WOULD A-WOOING GO . . .
> *So there's an end of one, two, and three, the Rat,*
> *the Mouse, and little Froggy.*

Concerns a French suitor of Queen Elizabeth I, the Duke of Anjou, who was not successful in his pursuit.

> BAA, BAA, BLACK SHEEP . . .
> *One for the master,*
> *One for the dame,*
> *And one for the little boy*
> *Who lives down the lane.*

Having to divide up the bags is said to be about the export tax on wool in 1275.

> GEORGIE, GEORGIE, PUDDING AND PIE . . .
> *Kissed the girls and made them cry.*
> *When the boys came out to play,*
> *Georgie Porgie ran away.*

King George IV apparently enjoyed women and wealth but

was fearful of political reform. Other guesses as to the secret identity of "Georgie" have been King George I, the Duke of Buckingham (George Villiers), and King Charles II.

HICKORY, DICKORY, DOCK . . .
The mouse ran up the clock
The clock struck one
The mouse ran down.

Said to be about Richard Cromwell, who could neither preserve the republic put in place by his father, Oliver Cromwell, nor prevent the restoration of the monarchy.

HUMPTY DUMPTY SAT ON A WALL . . .
Humpty Dumpty had a great fall.
All the king's horses and all the king's men
Couldn't put Humpty together again.

Though some believe the original Humpty to be King Richard III, it most likely refers to King John's loss of power to the barons.

JACK AND JILL WENT UP THE HILL . . .
To fetch a pail of water.
Jack fell down and broke his crown,
And Jill came tumbling after.

A ditty about the failure of a plan to marry Queen Mary I to the King of France.

JACK SPRATT COULD EAT NO FAT . . .
His wife could eat no lean.
And so between the two of them,
They licked the platter clean.

This is allegedly about King Charles I and his wife, Queen Henrietta, who were quite opposite in their personalities.

LITTLE BOY BLUE, COME BLOW YOUR HORN . . .
The sheep's in the meadow,
The cow's in the corn.
But where is the boy who looks after the sheep?
He's under the haystack,
Fast asleep.
Little Boy Blue is Cardinal Wolsey, who was "found asleep"
by King Henry VIII and lost his power when he could not
win the King a divorce. (Wolsey was a butcher's son, who
undoubtedly looked after his father's livestock.)

LITTLE JACK HORNER SAT IN A CORNER . . .
Eating a Christmas pie:
He put in his thumb and pulled out a plum,
And said, "What a good boy am I!"
A story about the English Reformation, when Henry VIII
became Protestant and seized all Roman Catholic Church
properties, especially the monasteries.

LITTLE MISS MUFFET SAT ON A TUFFET . . .
Eating her curds and whey.
Along came a spider,
Who sat down beside her,
And frightened Miss Muffet away.
Mary, Queen of Scots, is Miss Muffet, and a Catholic who
displeased the Presbyterian preacher John Knox, who stars as
the frightening arachnid.

OLD MOTHER HUBBARD WENT TO THE CUPBOARD . . .
To give her poor dog a bone.
But when she got there, her cupboard was bare,
And so the poor dog had none.

This describes Cardinal Wolsey's efforts to compensate himself for loss of the king's favor by securing various offices and titles.

THREE BLIND MICE, SEE HOW THEY RUN . . .
They all ran after the farmer's wife,
Who cut off their tails with a carving knife.
Did you ever see such a sight in your life,
As three blind mice?

The mice most likely represented Lattimer, Ridley, and Cranmer, Protestant clergymen who died at the stake. The farmer's wife was Queen Mary I.

◆

LIGHTNING GLASS

Lightning strikes somewhere on earth approximately one hundred times per second. The strikes occasionally result in fulgurites, or "lightning glass"—hollow, carrot-shaped tubes formed when a lightning bolt courses through sand at 2,950 degrees Fahrenheit, instantly superheating the sand and melting and fusing its grains. Sand, of course, is commonly used in the manufacture of commercial glass, along with soda ash, limestone, and borax. The largest fulgurite on record was found in Florida and was nearly seventeen feet long.

CHEERS, INDEED!

Ancient Greeks would toast to good health to let guests know that their drinks had not been spiked with poison. A toast requires the host to take the first sip.

THE TWELVE DAYS OF CATECHISM

As Christmas approaches, "The Twelve Days of Christmas" becomes the Yuletide season's "99 Bottles of Beer on the Wall." Its monotony and repetition originally had a purpose, though: it was written as a catechism song. Between the years 1558 and 1829, English Catholics were not permitted to practice their faith, and the song was composed to mask lessons. "My true love" was God himself, and the partridge stood for Jesus Christ. Herewith the rest of the code:

Two turtledoves	The Old and New Testaments
Three French hens	Faith, hope, and charity
Four calling birds	The four Gospels
Five golden rings	The first five books of the Old Testament, which give the history of humankind's fall from grace
Six geese a-laying	The six days of creation
Seven swans a-swimming	The seven gifts of the Holy Spirit
Eight maids a-milking	The eight Beatitudes
Nine ladies dancing	Nine choirs of angels
Ten lords a-leaping	The Ten Commandments
Eleven pipers piping	The eleven faithful Apostles
Twelve drummers drumming	The twelve points of belief in the Apostles' Creed

◆

HERRING PARTS are used in ceramic glazes, nail polish, lipsticks, and even some automobile paint to give them shine. The fish scales are transformed into "pearl essence" to brighten commercial products.

DEAD GRANDMOTHER REDUX

A major job search Web site reports that the three top reasons for calling in sick when you're not sick are:

Personal business and errands
Catching up on sleep
Relaxing

Here are some other reasons—clearly not entirely true—in case you want to be more creative:

Sprayed by a skunk
Tripped over dog and knocked unconscious
Bus broke down and was held up by robbers
Arrested as a result of mistaken identity
Forgot to come back to work after lunch
Couldn't find shoes
Hurt during bowling
Spit on by a venomous snake
Being pursued by a hit man
Scalp burned by curlers
Brain went to sleep
Cat unplugged alarm clock
Had to attend husband's grand jury trial
Forgot what day of the week it was
Got slipped drugs in a drink
Tree fell on car
Pet monkey died

◆

Legend has it that ST. FABIAN was elected pope in 236 because a dove landed on his head, and the clergy took it as an anointment from above.

PREMATURELY, OF COURSE

Whether we embrace it, color it, or blame it on our children, the majority of us can expect our hair to go gray with age. Recent studies have indicated that as we grow older, melanocytes—pigment-producing cells—play a part in not only skin color but hair color as well. The pigment is located in the hair follicle, and when with time these melanocytes become depleted, there goes the golden pate of your youth. (Take heart: scientists in Japan are working with a type of pepper that may reinvigorate the melanocytes.)

FLIGHT SCHOOL

Scientists have long theorized that birds fly in a V formation to gain lift from the bird in front of them—vortices form as a result of the first bird's flight, and the following bird, if in the right position, flies in an area of greatly reduced air resistance. Recent discoveries show other benefits of decreased drag: the heart rates of some birds were lower while in formation, allowing then to glide more often and conserve energy. It is believed that a flock of geese can fly 70 percent further while in formation, with birds taking turns as lead flier. The V formation also offers each bird an unobstructed view, so flock members can avoid collisions and communicate while in flight.

◆

BENJAMIN FRANKLIN never patented a single one of his inventions. He insisted that he was wealthy enough and that his ideas were for the benefit of the American people, not for his own profit.

FORTY WINKS

Experts say that while a full night's sleep is necessary to restore and perform many vital body functions, a short sleep may boost learning and memory. A 60-to-90-minute nap can be as beneficial to some as a full night's sleep, as long as the napper experiences both slow-wave sleep and rapid eye movement (REM), which are stages of deep sleep. Bosses are also finding that sleep deprivation is all too common among employees and is costing them plenty. Some sleep deprivation consequences in the workplace are:

- Increased errors and accidents
- Increased absenteeism
- Increased drug use
- Increased turnover
- Higher group insurance premiums
- Decreased productivity

A LONG WINTER'S NAP

Animals hibernate for the simplest of reasons: It is their only alternative to starvation. Once cold sets in and food and water become unavailable, these animals find a safe place to sleep, and slow their heartbeat dramatically and lower their body temperature, sometimes to nearly freezing, both of which diminish their need for food.

BLISTERS appear on a patch of skin where damage has occurred—whether from a burn, a pinch, or simply friction. It protects the flesh from further irritation, allowing it a chance to heal.

SINCERE BUT FLOWERY

Since Victorian times, giving different types of flowers as a gift signified different feelings or purposes.

Amaryllis: splendid beauty, pride
Ambrosia: mutual love
Baby's breath: fruitful marriage
Bluebell: constancy
Calla lily: magnificent beauty
Camellia: gratitude
Carnation: strong love, beauty
Chrysanthemum (red): love
Chrysanthemum (white): truth
Cornflower: delicacy
Cyclamen: modesty and shyness
Daffodil: high regard
Daisy: innocence
Dogwood: love's durability
Fern: fascination and beauty
Flowering almond: hope
Forget-me-not: remembrance
Forsythia: anticipation
Geranium: comfort
Heliotrope: devotion, faithfulness
Hibiscus: delicate beauty
Honeysuckle: generosity
Hyacinth (white): loveliness
Hydrangea: boastfulness
Iris: faith, wisdom
Ivy: eternal fidelity
Japonica: loveliness
Jasmine: joy and amiability
Lilac: first love

Lily (white): purity, happiness
Magnolia: love of nature, nobility, dignity
Maidenhair: discretion
Mimosa: sensitivity
Orange blossom: purity, fertility
Orchid: love, beauty
Pansy: think of me
Peach blossom: captivity
Periwinkle: pleasing memories
Rose (red): love
Rose (yellow): friendship
Rose (coral): desire
Rose (peach): modesty
Rose (dark pink): thankfulness
Rose (pale pink): grace
Rose (orange): fascination
Rose (white): innocence
Rosemary: remembrance, loyalty
Sage: wisdom
Snowdrop: hope
Stephanotis: happiness in marriage
Stock: lasting beauty
Sunflower: adoration
Sweet pea: lasting pleasure
Sweet William: sensitivity
Tulip: true love
Verbena (pink): family unity
Veronica: fidelity
Violet: purity, modesty, fidelity
Wheat: prosperity, friendliness

◆

The SWASTIKA was chosen for use by the Nazis because it is an ancient symbol of prosperity and good fortune.

THE ORIGINAL HOME SHOPPING NETWORK

Much of Sears Roebuck and Company's success came from its early dependency on mail order. Shortly after Richard Sears began to sell watches to railroad station agents like himself in 1886, he wrote and printed a mailer to sell watches and jewelry by mail under the name R. W. Sears Watch Co. This was 1888, and both the westward railroad expansion and the postal system were working in Sears's favor. Not only were the catalogs permitted to be mailed as aids in the dissemination of knowledge (at one cent per pound), but the advent of rural free delivery in 1896 made distribution of the catalog economical. Farmers and others who lived outside of towns and cities began to rely on the Sears catalog, "the Cheapest Supply House on Earth." The catalog expanded from watches and jewelry, adding sewing machines, sporting goods, musical instruments, saddles, firearms, buggies, bicycles, baby carriages, clothing, and eyeglasses. Nearly every word was written by Sears himself, using familiar stories and personal experiences to sell his wares, much the same way many of today's most successful mail order catalogs and Internet companies do.

FORE . . . AND A QUARTER

The universal diameter for a golf cup is 4¼ inches. It started when a particular hole at St. Andrews in Scotland continually filled with sand after a period of rain. Two golfers found a drainpipe—it happened to be 4¼ inches—and absconded with a piece to temporarily stem the tide of wet sand. It was the first "cup" installed on the course, and became the standard at St. Andrews and subsequently the world.

PUT A HOLE IN ONE

There are two schools of thought on why the doughnut has a hole—and both have the ring of truth. The first is based in logic: The fried cakes bakers made would often be too doughy in the middle if cooked until the outer part was done, but too crisp around the edges if left to fry a little longer. A hole was the perfect solution for even cooking.

Captain Hanson Gregory is at the center of the second theory. While at the helm of his ship one stormy night, he found it impossible to get a good grip on the helm while eating his fried cake. He impaled the pastry on one of the wheel's spokes, forming a temporary rest area for the cake and a long-term culinary delight for posterity.

NOW AND LATER

It sounds like something from outer space: microencapsulation. But actually it's the secret behind scratch 'n' sniff. The essence of a fragrance is distilled into a perfume so that millions of tiny bubbles are suspended in a liquid; this is then incorporated into a plastic that can be used and printed like ink. After the plastic dries, the trapped fragrance is released from a few bubbles each time the area is activated. That's why a scratch 'n' sniff item can last for years—this microencapsulation process holds each drop of fragrance better than if it were in a stoppered bottle.

◆

MAYDAY, the international radio distress call, has nothing to do with traditional spring celebrations—the French term *m'aider*, or "help me," has merely become anglicized.

NEW YEAR—IT'S WHAT YOU EAT

It's universal to wish others happiness and good luck at the new year. Some countries believe eating special food will help that good fortune along:

Belarus: Each piece of meat eaten during New Year's Eve dinner brings your happiness.

Germany: Eating carp is thought to be such good luck that people place some of the fish's scales in their wallets for financial good fortune.

Holland: For good luck in the new year the Dutch eat *olie bollen*, puffy doughnuts filled with diced apples, raisins, and currants.

Hungary: Eat something sweet for the first bite in the New Year so that the whole year is sweet. No chicken or fish for New Year's Day lunch and dinner: Fish swim away with your luck, chickens scratch it away. Lentils and pork will bring wealth, health, and luck.

Ireland: This one's not for consumption: Bang on the door and walls with Christmas bread to chase the bad luck out and bring good spirits to the household, along with the promise of enough food for the new year.

Italy: Drinking beer after midnight brings good luck. For New Year's Day supper, have thirteen courses for good fortune. Caviar will bring you riches all the year. Lentils and *zampone* (a stuffed pig's trotter) bring luck. Chickpeas bring health and fortune. And *chiacchiere*, honey-drenched balls of

dough, ensure a sweet year. (Slip some of those lentils in your purse for luck, too.)

Korea: *Ttokguk,* or rice cake soup, is eaten as part of sunrise celebrations. Koreans believe that each bowl eaten adds a year to your life.

Mexico, Spain, and Cuba: These countries enjoy a custom of eating twelve grapes at the stroke of midnight while making twelve wishes, each grape signifying one month of the up-coming year. If the grape for the respective month is sweet, expect a good month; if it's sour, the month will be a bad one.

Philippines: Food on the table at midnight encourages an abundance of food throughout the year.

Poland: Folklore suggests that eating herring at the stroke of midnight will bring luck for the next year.

Scotland: The first one who draws and drinks water from a well will be lucky, usually in love: "The flower o' the well to our howse gaes / And the bonniest lad'll be mine."

Slovakia: Cut an apple, and if the seeds are healthy, you will be, too. Mothers cross their children with honey on their foreheads for a sweet life.

Southern United States: Black-eyed peas are eaten for luck, with corn bread, cabbage, collard greens, or kale for wealth.

Worldwide: In many places, eating ring-shaped food (dough-nuts especially) symbolizes coming full circle, and good luck will follow. Cabbage is also considered a sign of prosperity.

FLAG WAVING

When you see flag decals on a bus, plane, or taxi, the flag's field of stars should be on the left side when placed on the left side of the vehicle. But on the right side of the vehicle, the decal should be placed with the stars facing right so that the flag will appear as if the vehicle's forward motion is causing the flag to blow in the wind.

WHAT A DUMB HAT

John Duns Scotus, an influential thirteenth-century philosopher, founded a school of scholasticism known as Scotism. Over time, Scotism fell out of fashion, and his followers, thought of as tedious hairsplitters, became known as "Dunses." Scotus believed that conical hats were an aid to brainpower (look at wizards, for example), and insisted that they funnel knowledge to the wearer. Eventually Scotus's "Duns caps"—later called dunce caps—were objects of ridicule and by the nineteenth century students were forced to wear them as a symbol of shame.

MURDER MOST FRIENDLY

What's a little homicide between pals—at least in the United States, Canada, or Greece? In these countries, friends or acquaintances account for almost half of all killings. In the majority of cases, there's a single victim and a single offender; most often both are male. The scene of the crime is frequently a residence, with both victim and offender having been drinking.

AM I BORING YOU?

You may not be tired, and it's been proven that it has nothing to do with lack of oxygen. Yawning is contagious, and just thinking about it right now may cause you to open wide.

Sometimes yawning is a response to a visual stimulus. Scientists point to mirror neurons, which cause people to react with the same behavior they sense in someone else. Up to 60 percent of people who watch a video or hear others talk about yawning are apt to follow suit. And others believe that it's an evolutionary remnant that communicates a need for rest or a desire to be alone (which explains our feeling that we're boring someone when they yawn).

Other interesting things about yawning:

- After the age of five, children begin to yawn contagiously.
- Schizophrenics rarely yawn.
- Yawning often precedes a major activity change—thus an athlete may yawn while in the starting blocks, a soprano before the curtain goes up.

SMALL STUFF

What of the word *trivia* itself? In medieval times, education was divided into seven sections. The sciences were arithmetic, geometry, astronomy, and music; the liberal studies were grammar, rhetoric, and logic. The former list of studies—the quadrivium, which is from the Latin for "four ways"—was thought to consist of the more important subjects. The other, more general group of three was known as the trivium, and thus anything learned on these subjects was, well, trivial.

SOME WHO HAVE ASKED WHY

"There is occasions and causes why and
wherefore in all things."
—WILLIAM SHAKESPEARE, HENRY V

"Why don't you speak for yourself, John?"
—HENRY WADSWORTH LONGFELLOW,
"THE COURTSHIP OF MILES STANDISH"

"Every why hath a wherefore."
—WILLIAM SHAKESPEARE, THE COMEDY OF ERRORS

"You see things; and you say, 'Why?' But I dream things
that never were; and I say 'Why not?'"
—GEORGE BERNARD SHAW, BACK TO METHUSELAH
(quoted by and often misattributed to
Robert F. Kennedy)

"Love's stricken 'why'
Is all that love can speak—
Built of but just a syllable
The hugest hearts that break."
—EMILY DICKINSON, "NO. 1368"

"My advice to you is not to inquire why or
whither, but just enjoy your ice cream while it's on
your plate—that's my philosophy."
—THORNTON WILDER, THE SKIN OF OUR TEETH

"Saul. Saul, why persecutest thou me?"
—ACTS OF THE APOSTLES 9:4

WHY

YOU WORM!

First of all, it's not tequila, it's mescal. That's where you'll find the worm at the bottom of the bottle. There's even some logic for it being there: It's the agave worm (actually a butterfly larva), found on the plant mescal is made from. Many believe that the worm (which was very nearly nixed recently by Mexican officials as too low-class) is an essential component to the alcohol's *je ne sais quoi*. Not only does it add to mescal's flavor and color, they insist, but the worm brings good luck. And some even go so far as to say it's an aphrodisiac.

HIGHWAYS OR SKYWAYS?

General—and subsequently President—Dwight D. Eisenhower was extremely impressed during his World War II stay in Germany with the Germans' well-designed autobahn system. It led him to a crack world leader–cum–military genius idea of his own. All the interstate highways that were planned in the United States during the Eisenhower administration required that one mile in every five be straight. These straight sections would be usable as airstrips in times of war or other emergencies.

◆

The term JAILBIRD was coined in England centuries ago, when criminals were placed in cages, which were then hung three feet off the ground.

The main reason people want to remove their TATTOOS is that they have fallen out of love with the person they've memorialized on their body in ink.

569

FIELDS OF GLORY

The miles of breathtaking tulip fields in Holland are a beautiful sight to see. But why the Netherlands . . . and why tulips?

The popular perennial is actually indigenous to central Asia; in fact, the Turks of the Ottoman Empire were the botanists who really took to the tulip and began to cultivate it with ardor as early as 1000 C.E. The tulips that Europeans eventually imported now grow in parts of Russia, around the Black Sea, and the Crimea.

In the 1500s, with world exploration on the rise, Europeans became obsessed with the importation of beautiful flowers. Botanical drawings became popular to hang in one's parlor, tulip drawings chief among them. This fueled what was becoming "Tulip Mania," though this frenzy was largely driven by a botanist named Carolus Clusius, who in 1593 was appointed the head botanist, or *Hortulanus*, at the University of Leiden's Hortus, the first botanical garden in Western Europe. Clusius had befriended a man named de Busbecq, an ambassador to Constantinople, who had given him some tulip bulbs—long thought to be a sign of wealth and power in the Ottoman Empire—which he brought back to Holland. Though Clusius's interest in the tulips was scientific, the combination of the drawings, the plants' rarity, and their foreign popularity proved too much for the Dutch, and some of Clusius's bulbs were stolen. Now Tulip Mania was in full swing.

Prices skyrocketed, and tulip buying and trading became heavy. Hybrids became coveted, with prices as high as $1,500 per bulb for a flower we can purchase today for about fifty cents; the highest recorded trade for a single bloom was

$2,250 plus a horse and carriage. Prices eventually settled down, and the Dutch have made tulip exporting one of the most successful businesses in the world. About 7 million of the 9 million tulips grown there are sold in other countries, at a value of $750 million. And that still leaves enough for locals and tourists to enjoy.

A romantic tulip aside: While the rose is universally thought of as the most romantic of flowers, there is a Turkish fable about Prince Farhad and his lady love, Shirin. Inconsolable upon hearing that she had been killed, the prince rode his horse off a cliff to his own death. It is said that for every drop of blood he shed, a red tulip sprang up in her memory, making the tulip the Turkish symbol of perfect love, and Turkey's national flower.

DIAL-A-RIDDLE

Why—and when—did zero become the number after nine? Look around: cell phones and remote controls are just a couple of places numbers are set up like this, though calculators still have the zero preceding the number one.

It's a throwback to the old rotary phones, when the telephone signal was a series of pulses, and zero, needing to have ten pulses, logically appeared on the dial after the nine. When touch-tone phones came on the market and the numbers started to appear in a grid, the zero followed the nine, because that's what people expected.

◆

The human STOMACH needs to produce a new layer of mucus every two weeks, or digestive acids will cause it to digest itself.

FEET ON THE GROUND

Men atop their mounts have long been a paean to famous or fallen leaders, and over the centuries the belief has grown that the number of horse's hooves touching the ground on a statue has to do with the fate of the rider. This is the supposed relationship of the rider's posture and the way he died:

> If the horse has both front legs in the air, the rider died in battle.

> If the horse has only one front leg in the air, the rider died as the result of wounds suffered while in battle.

> If the horse has all four feet on the ground, the rider died of natural causes.

Recent research by buffs suggests the legend may be untrue. Most of the statues at Gettysburg do comply with the rules, save one, however, so some say this is where the notion began. The exception: The horse of General John F. Reynolds, who was killed at Gettysburg, has one foreleg and one hind leg raised, instead of both forelegs.

COPYCAT

When the Haloid Company set out to brand its electrophotography machine, they hired a scholar of classical languages to come up with a name. He suggested the process be called xerography, from the Greek words for "dry" and "writing." The copier itself he named the Xerox machine.

SEEING EYES

One of the many dark surprises of growing older is that our vision begins to fail. By your forties, you may find the menu in a candlelit restaurant hard to read, instructions on a pill bottle impossible to read. You've got presbyopia, and you can't put it off anymore: You need reading glasses or bifocals. If glasses on a beaded chain around your neck don't appeal, what do you do? Now there are bifocal contact lenses.

Like bifocal glasses, there are two prescriptions per lens—one to see things up close, and one for distance. But since contact lenses float in your eye and don't stay perched on your nose where you can control exactly where to look, how do they know? How *do* they work?

Here are the three types currently available, and how they're made:

Aspheric: Prescriptions for both near and distance vision are close to the middle of the lens, though the near prescription is at the center.

Concentric: The near prescription is in the middle of the lens, while the prescription for distance is around the outside.

Translating: The near prescription is on the bottom, and the distance prescription is on the top. The bottom part of the contact is flat, as if the bottom of a circle were cut off, so that it doesn't rotate when you blink.

Some doctors may instead prescribe two completely different lenses—one eye for distance, the other for close work: a dizzying effect for a bit, but once their eyes adjust, many people swear by this method.

LAUGH, LAUGH, LAUGH

The human being is the only species capable of laughter as we know—and hear—it. On average, we experience it seventeen times a day. And it not only feels good—it really *is* good for you, healthwise:

- It reduces our stress levels by reducing the level of stress hormones
- It helps us cope with serious illnesses
- It promotes healing by lowering the blood pressure
- It increases vascular blood flow
- It increases oxygenation of the blood

And though we do talk of "breaking" or "bursting" into laughter, it is a quite orderly communicative response. It may feel spontaneous, but in fact it occurs during pauses in conversation or at the end of stories, after the punch line. This is why scientists call it the "punctuation effect."

Laughter is triggered not only by humor, but by sociological or psychological situations: when people are comfortable with each other, shared relief, the passing of danger, social situations that need easing. The brain responds simultaneously with both sound and movement: not only are our facial muscles involved, but there are involuntary movements in the muscles of the arms, legs, and trunk as well.

◆

The RABBIT'S FOOT is considered good luck because the rabbit, with its ability to reproduce at astonishing speed, was seen as a symbol of fertility.

MONEY FROM THE SEA

The Narragansett Indians of New England were the first to use wampum, cylindrical beads to measure value. It preceded the use of currency in the United States by several hundred years but was used most often not as money, but as trade; when woven into intricate belts and other jewelry, it was a means of solemnizing agreements.

Wampum is actually a mispronunciation of the Narragansett word for the inner part of the whelk shell, *wompam*. The purple beads were valued at five times more than the white ones. The beads were often strung and measured on a six-foot string, which they dubbed a "fathom," echoing the sea term. Eventually, wampum use became more widespread, and it was used for a wider variety of transactions. Historians note that wampum was used for ransom for captives, compensation for crimes, presents between friends, prizes for victory in games or sport, paying fines, incentives to maintain peace or to wage war, payments for services of shamanism, marriage proposals, and, possibly, bribes and rewards for murder. Perhaps the most unusual payment? One could pay for an education at Harvard with wampum beads.

ON THE CLOCK

Clocks run clockwise most likely because they were made to run the same way a sundial did. Both the sundial and the clock were invented in the Northern Hemisphere, and the east-to-west direction of the sun during the day causes the shade on a sundial to run clockwise—or sundialwise. All would be different if the sundial had been invented in the southern hemisphere.

THE WHY OF WHO

An eponym is the name of a person for whom something is supposedly named. But why do they come into use? A few reasons and examples:

- By association with a person (derrick)
- In honor of (einsteinium)
- Infamy (bowdlerize)
- Interjections (Geronimo!)
- Invention (shrapnel)
- Metonymy ("Dad burned the steaks on the Weber")
- Possessives and Compound Nouns (Planck's constant, Doppler effect)
- "Pulled a _____." (Winona)
- Self-promotion (daguerreotype)
- Simple metaphor (quisling)
- With Suffixes
  - -esque (Kafkaesque)
  - -ia (dahlia)
  - -ian/-ean (Orwellian)
  - -ism (spoonerism)
  - -ite (rammelsburgite)
  - -ium (curium)
  - -ize (grangerize)
  - -mander (gerrymander)
  - -phone (sousaphone)
  - -type (daguerreotype)
- Trademark (Frisbee)
- "Verbing" (boycott, lynch)

WHAT PRICE, BEAUTY?
From the "Don't Try This at Home" Files

In what was thought of as a great improvement, the Romans changed the basic toothpaste formula concocted by the Egyptians in the fourth century. Various mixtures were used early on: One was salt, pepper, mint leaves, and irises; a later concoction was crushed pumice stone and wine vinegar. The Romans replaced the vinegar with human urine, which contains ammonia, a whitening agent. In the eighteenth century, straight ammonia took its place.

SMELLY LOGIC

Perhaps it's not the very best food for your social life*, but there are plenty of healthy reasons to keep garlic in one's diet. In fact, for more than five thousand years, the good clove has been said to heal everything from snakebites to the plague. Some of today's more popular uses:

- It lowers the risk of stomach cancer
- Studies show it may impede other cancers
- It helps hypertension
- It may help prevent heart disease
- It can lower blood cholesterol
- It can even be used as an antiseptic, killing fungus and some types of bacteria
- It clears acne in its raw form
- It's a natural mosquito repellent
- It prevents cold and flu

*You can always try the less-pungent pill form.

THE MARCH (AND MAY AND JULY) OF TIME

The months of the year—and for that matter, the entire year itself—went through several permutations before the advent of the Gregorian calendar, which is the one in use by most of the world today. In the Roman calendar, which is thought to have been constructed by Romulus, Rome's founder, there were only ten months (which is why, for example, September, the ninth month, is named with the Latin root for the word seven). The year was then only 304 days long; harsh winter times without any agricultural activity remained unnamed; and the new moon in March started another year, in line with the lunar cycle. With the reign of Rome's second king, Numa Pompilius (c. 700 C.E.), what are now the first two months of the year were added.

Julius Caesar abolished the lunar year and implemented a calendar ruled by the sun. The new length of the Julian calendar year was 365 days, with an extra day every four years. Now we had twelve months and a leap year.

The Gregorian calendar was devised by Neapolitan Aloysius Lilius, and adopted in 1582 by Pope Gregory XIII, basically to correct the errors of the Julian calendar; now the tropical year would be 365 97/400 days.

So the months of the year are, not surprisingly, an array of words composed of Latin roots, Roman gods, and unanswered questions:

January: After Janus, the Roman god of beginnings, doors, sunrise, and sunset. He had one face that looked forward and one that looked back.

February: Romans celebrated *februa* the festival of forgiveness (from the Latin "to purify").

March: The first month of the old Roman year, it is named after Mars, the god of war.

April: Possibly from *aperire*, "to open," signaling the signs of spring; or perhaps from Aphrodite, original Greek name of Venus.

May: Probably from a Roman goddess: either from Maiesta, the Roman goddess of honor, or Maia, mother of Mercury.

June: Named to honor Juno, the chief Roman goddess.

July: This was the month Julius Caesar was born, and named for him in 44 B.C.E., the year of his assassination.

August: Formerly called Sextilis (the sixth month in the Roman calendar), it was renamed in 8 B.C.E. to honor Augustus Caesar.

September: *Septem*, Latin for seven in the Roman calendar.

October: The eighth month (*octo* in Latin) in the Roman calendar.

November: The ninth Roman month, from *novem*.

December: *Decem*, for the Roman tenth month.

◆

The word BALLOT comes from *balotta*, the Italian word for "ball" or "small pebble," the latter of which was used in ancient times to cast a vote.

SEE THROUGH

The reason we can see through glass is the same reason we can see through water: they're both liquids. As opposed to most liquids, which basically remain the same color, opaqueness, and viscosity, glass becomes stiffer as it cools. At room temperature, its rate of flow is so slow that it would virtually never lose its shape. Formally the scientific term used for glass was "supercooled liquid;" this implies that in the process of being made, the glass has been rapidly chilled past its normal freezing point, and though for all intents and purposes looks and acts like a solid, its loosely spaced molecular structure allows for light to pass through, and thus ensures its clarity. More recently, the term "amorphous solid" is more often applied; this refers to an apparently solid substance that lacks crystalline structure, and instead has the random organization of liquids.

Need it be said? In the case of glass, seeing is *not* believing.

SEASON FOR SNEEZIN'

Sneezing, of course, expels whatever is bothering you and your nose, whether it's dust, pepper, or even cold air. But it's not just the nose that gets the message. Lots of different muscles have to react all at once in order for the process to take place. Abdominal muscles, the diaphragm, vocal chords, and even eyelid muscles work all at once. And then there are photic sneezers, who *ahchoo* when they are exposed to bright light; one in three people do it, and there's no way to cure yourself of it. It's inherited.

CHOOSING POLITICAL SIDES

Have you ever noticed how people tend to take the same seat, if it's available, in a recurring situation? At the dinner table, in a classroom, at a meeting, everyone tends to gravitate to the same chair, time after time. It's thought that this is how the terms Left and Right began for political liberals and conservatives.

When the French legislature met for the first time after the French Revolution, in October 1791, all 745 members arrived and looked to sit with their like-minded friends. It so happened that the radicals sat on the left side of the room, with the more traditional-minded people choosing seats to the right of the aisle. A custom—and a new way of defining politics—had begun.

LIFE BLOOD

Top 10 reasons people give the Red Cross for not giving blood:

1. I don't like needles / I am afraid to give blood.
2. I'm too busy.
3. No one ever asked me—I didn't realize my blood was needed.
4. I already gave this year.
5. I'm afraid I'll get AIDS.
6. My blood isn't the right type.
7. I don't have any blood to spare.
8. I don't want to feel weak afterward.
9. They won't want my blood (I am too old / I've had an illness).
10. I have a rare blood type, so I'll wait until there is a special need.

WHY CAN'T I GO?

Why is a movie unsuitable for kids (or for your very own precious ears and eyes)? Is it raunchy, trash-talking, or pornographic? Actually, the movie rating system—a voluntary system sponsored by the Motion Picture Association of America and the National Association of Theatre Owners—was designed to guide people with just a little bit of generalized advance warning on what types of things might take place when the lights go down.

General Audience—All ages are admitted. This film contains nothing most parents will consider offensive for even their youngest children to see or hear. Nudity, sex scenes, and scenes of drug use are absent; violence is minimal; snippets of dialogue may go beyond polite conversation but do not go beyond common everyday expressions.

Parental Guidance Suggested—Some material may not be suitable for children. Explicit sex scenes and scenes of drug use are absent; nudity, if present, is seen only briefly, horror and violence do not exceed moderate levels.

Parents Strongly Cautioned—Some material may be inappropriate for children under 13. Rough or persistent violence is absent; sexually-oriented nudity is generally absent; some scenes of drug use may be seen; one use of the harsher sexually derived words may be heard.

Restricted: Under 17—Requires an accompanying parent or adult guardian. An R may be assigned due to, among other things, a film's use of language, theme, violence, sex, or its portrayal of drug use.

No One 17 and Under Admitted—The rating board believes that most American parents would feel that the film is patently adult. May contain explicit sex scenes, an accumulation of sexually oriented language, or scenes of excessive violence. Does not, however, signify that the rated film is obscene or pornographic.

THE DIRT

Pica is an eating disorder quite unlike the types one reads about in magazines. It is an addictive craving for non-food substances such as dirt, clay, chalk, even ice chips. It is seen mostly in pregnant women, children, or third world countries where there may be a mineral-deficient diet. The name *pica* comes from the Latin word for magpie, a kind of bird known for its reputation to eat almost everything. Geophagy—eating dirt or clay—is a common form of pica; particular types of chalky dirt are sold in stores in parts of the southern United States. Native Americans concoct a form of acorn bread today in which clay is an important ingredient.

EYES WIDE SHUT

It sounds like something we only read about, on top of just sounding plain suspicious, but hysterical blindness is real. It's called conversion disorder, and is a psychiatric condition in which emotional distress expresses itself through physical symptoms. Inability to speak and paralysis are other forms of the disease. The symptom, though not usually life-threatening in itself, usually—and often spontaneously—disappears in the space of a few days or weeks.

COMATOSE

A coma is an extended period of unconsciousness from which a person may or may not eventually recover; while in a deep coma, one cannot be aroused with even the most painful stimuli. One can fall into a coma for several different reasons. It can be a symptom of a disease, or the result of an event such as a severe head injury, a metabolic problem, or a seizure, head injury being the most common. Other causes are diabetes, hemorrhage, shock, or the result of large amounts of morphine or alcohol, which is called a toxic coma.

Most comas last from two to four weeks; the chances of recovery—without brain damage—after more than three months is less than 10 percent. Comas do not all resemble a deep sleep; there are different stages of a coma, and the progress of recovery is measured by the patient's increasing awareness of surrounding stimuli. Patients may begin to make movements or sounds, and become agitated; they may even make reflexive motions that mimic waking activities.

Some coma victims fall into a persistent vegetative state: Normal bodily functions continue, but without the patient's awareness. Breathing, blood pressure, food intake, and elimination are normal, and this vegetative state can last for years, or even decades; most who do wake have suffered severe brain damage and do not ever recover completely.

If and when a person begins to emerge from a coma, he or she begins by reacting to different stimuli. Gaining consciousness is not instant, like in the movies: It may take several days or weeks. First awakening may last only a couple of minutes, to the frustration of family and friends. But in the following days, the patient may awaken for gradually increasing intervals.

Sometimes a coma is chemically induced by a doctor—usually after a head injury—to aid in medical treatment and recovery.

The Glasgow Coma Scale is used to assess the severity of a coma by measuring three components: eye opening response, verbal response, and motor response:

The Glasgow Coma Scale

EYE OPENING RESPONSE

    E1 = None;
    E2 = To pain
    E3 = To speech
    E4 = Spontaneous

VERBAL RESPONSE

    V1 = None
    V2 = Incomprehensible
    V3 = Inappropriate
    V4 = Confused
    V5 = Oriented

MOTOR RESPONSE

    M1 = None to pain
    M2 = Extension to pain (decerebrate posturing)
    M3 = Flexion to pain (decorticate posturing)
    M4 = Withdrawal to pain
    M5 = Purposeful movement/localized response to pain
    M6 = Obeys commands

A score of E4V5M6 indicates the normal state; a score of E1V1M1 indicates complete unresponsiveness.

TOP 10 REASONS TO STOP SMOKING

The National Heart, Lung, and Blood Institute suggests that anyone trying to give up cigarettes use these reminders of the benefits when the going gets difficult:

1. I will reduce my chances of having a heart attack or stroke.
2. I will reduce my chances of getting lung cancer, emphysema, and other lung diseases.
3. I will have better smelling clothes, hair, breath, home, and car.
4. I will climb stairs and walk without getting out of breath.
5. I will have fewer wrinkles.
6. I will be free of my morning cough.
7. I will reduce the number of coughs, colds, and earaches my child will have.
8. I will have more energy to pursue physical activities I enjoy.
9. I will treat myself to new books or music with the money I save from not buying cigarettes.
10. I will have more control over my life.

FRIEND OR FOE?

The handshake's origin was not so much a sign of greeting, but one of wary goodwill. Generally travelers who came upon each other on the road would draw their daggers with their right hand. When—and if—it became apparent that physical danger was not imminent, the daggers were sheathed and and the strangers would clasp hands as a sign of goodwill.

YES, THEY ARE WATCHING YOU

Part of the scariness of scary stories, camping, the woods, or just nature in general is the feeling you get at night that animals are skulking about, watching you. They can see you; you can't see them. In fact, every once in a while you get a glimpse—a pair of bright, yellow-green orbs, like mirrors, following you in the dark.

You're not imagining it. Wolves, raccoons, crocodiles—they all give off a sort of "eyeshine" from a mirror-like layer of cells in or behind the retina called the tapetum lucidum. Many nocturnal animals have it; the retina captures some of the light that enters the eye, but the rest of it passes through. The tapetum lucidum bounces it back to the retina, virtually giving the animal another chance to see, and making the animal's eyes essentially light up.

On a more domestic level, house cats are equipped with this kind of vision as well, allowing them 130 times better night vision than the human eye. The consolation? Humans have some of the best daytime vision in the animal kingdom.

'NIGHTY-'NIGHT!

Warm milk contains melatonin, a known sleep aid, and tryptophan, the ingredient in turkey that makes you doze off after Thanksgiving dinner—so it makes perfect sense that a glass may help you nod off at bedtime.

◆

The telephone AREA CODE in a portion of northeastern Florida that includes Cape Canaveral is 321. As in "3-2-1, LIFT-OFF!"

587

DREAM ON

It seems there are as many types of dreams as there are interpretations for them. Here are just a few of life's more common sleep stories, with the reasons why you dream them:

Animals: Of course it depends on the type of animal; dreaming about your pets or other domesticated animals may mean
good fortune; wild animals denote fear and bad luck. Insects
in general mean something in your waking life is nagging
you.

Bed: An extremely common element in dreams (see HOUSE),
and though Freud may call it the womb, it can denote a sexual encounter, sickness, or death.

Car: Also a very common object, symbolizing power, status,
and sexuality. Generally it's about new life, but of course it
depends on who's driving and what type of journey and car
it is. Is it dangerous? Do you trust the person behind the
wheel? Is it a long trip? Who's really in control?

Celebrities: Meeting a famous person in a dream may indicate a profitable offer is coming your way.

Chase: Running away is one of dreamdom's most frightening
motifs, a response to threats in out waking lives. This is why
so often we feel unable to move. But dreaming about being
pursued may be a good way of coping with fears and stress.
If, in your dream, you are caught by whoever is chasing you,
you have a lot of work do to about the real-life problem; if
you escape, you are nearly free.

Child: Especially if the child is an infant, this could be anxiety for men as much as it means wish-fulfillment for women;

either way, it's about great responsibilities.

Death: If the experience is a near-death event, it is often the result of a lucid dream, which occurs as the body is going to sleep. This dream is about a sense of vulnerability and of being out of control of the circumstances surrounding you.

If you do actually die in your dream, it can signify a release from current anxieties in your life, and point toward a rebirth that is about to occur.

Dreaming of the death of a loved one means you're feeling worried about their well-being.

Devils, Demons: If a demon helps you in your dream, it may signify the moral dilemma you feel about the task you've completed—a deal with the devil. If the demon is working against you, it could be you feel some evil—perhaps in the form of a person—is working against you in your waking life. If the demon threatens others, you may be worried about how to protect those important to you.

Exam: How many times have you had others tell you about having this dream? "I got to the class, and I realized I hadn't once opened the book/had never attended the class all semester, and here I was at the final!" Sometimes the test is in another language, time is running out, or you're late.

It's a self-esteem/self-confidence dream, and is indicative of feeling that you're not good enough or ill-prepared for what's coming your way. Though life is a constant test, this dream may stand for a particular approaching challenge you fear you can't meet.

Falling: It's an old wives' tale that you will die in your sleep if you hit the ground; there are many who have lived to tell the tale. Falling is the most common dream of all. You may *feel* like you want to check out; this dream indicates a sense of inferiority or fear of failure in school, work, finances, or love. These dreams often occur in the first stages of sleep, accompanied by muscle spasms in the arms, legs, or whole body; these sudden contractions are known as myoclonic jerks. Sigmund Freud said falling may indicate a desire to give in to an urge—perhaps an indiscreet one—sexual or of some other kind.

Fire: This is a common dream regardless of the dreamer's culture. It very often signifies purification, and passing through the flames in the dream is very positive. If you are burned, however, you perceive life as painful.

Flying: Flying dreams are lucid dreams, a category of dreams in which you become aware that you are dreaming. We think of flying as the ultimate freedom: If, in your dreams, it is exhilarating, joyful, and liberating, and you are enjoying the scenery below, you are feeling in control and on top of life. But if you are having difficulties staying in the air, and are fearful, you may be afraid of meeting challenges, out of control and afraid of success.

Food: Preparing or eating food means happiness and domestic contentment. Being hungry or thirsty often indicates spiritual dissatisfaction.

Garden: A lush garden in bloom means healthy growth of the soul; dead or weed-infested gardens mean you are aware of the need for spiritual growth.

House: It's generally a symbol of many things, and is second most common after falling as a dream motif. The house represents you, each room an aspect of your waking life. Doors may come as a complete surprise ("I've lived here forever

and I never saw that!") and represent opportunities—sometimes scary ones—and should be opened.

Lost: Driving, shopping, and amusement parks often play a part; your opportunities are questionable and you feel you lack the ability to make the right choice. As in your waking life, you feel isolated, and that life is not progressing as you had hoped.

Naked: You're hiding something in your waking life, or feeling shameful. You're sure, in the dream, that everyone can see what a fraud you are, now that you're undressed before them. Many people see this with the exam dream.

Sexual: Sexual dreams are not unusual and can be extremely healthy if the emotions in the dream are not abnormal; it is not unusual to awake sexually aroused.

Teeth: In dreams they express your thoughts about your physical appearance and how others see you. Teeth can be power: They bite, tear, chew; conversely, losing them in your dream may indicate a feeling of powerlessness. Some cultures think dreaming of teeth signifies the death of someone close to you (the Chinese believe that your teeth fall out if you tell lies). There is also a theory that losing teeth symbolizes money, like our old friend the Tooth Fairy taught us.

Time: Dates and numbers may represent a time or event that is serving as the trigger for the dream.

Water: Again, as in life, so it is in dreams. Traditionally, calm water means good times ahead, clear sailing. Rough waters signify caution, and a warning to reconsider your course of action.

DOG GONE

The top reasons dogs are given up by their owners and brought to an animal shelter are behavioral. Unfortunately, pets often don't live up to their owners' unrealistic expectations: Chewing, hyperactivity, and soiling the house are often cited. Other reasons often given are:

- Moving from one's home
- Landlord prohibits pets
- Too many animals in the household
- Cost of veterinary care
- Owner's personal problems
- Inadequate facilities
- Aggression toward other pets
- Hostility toward other people

LUCK OF THE DRAW

In the Middle Ages, children and teenagers didn't send valentines to the other kids they had a crush on. They drew names from a bowl, and the name you picked was your special valentine for the entire week. They wore these slips of paper on their sleeves for all seven days; now we say you "wear your heart on your sleeve" when you make it obvious to everyone how you feel.

◆

Some theorize that the tradition of throwing SALT over the left shoulder to ward off bad luck originates from Judas's having spilled salt at the Last Supper.

WHY, ROBOT

Author Isaac Asimov (1920–1992) devised the Three Rules of Robotics, which the robots in his books and short stories were obligated to follow. Many authors have adopted these rules for their fictional robots as well.

First Law: A robot may not harm a human being, or, through inaction, allow a human being to come to harm.

Second Law: A robot must obey the orders given to it by human beings, except where such orders would conflict with the First Law.

Third Law: A robot must protect its own existence, as long as such protection does not conflict with the First or Second Laws.

BIRD FEED

Why do chickens have white breast meat and dark thigh meat? Dare we ask if it has to do with chicken exercise? The muscles in constant use have high myoglobin content, which is caused by higher levels of oxygen and produces red muscle fiber, or dark meat. This is true of all fowl, including chicken, turkey, duck, and goose.

This also explains why fowl have white muscle tissue. White meat comes from the parts of a bird where muscles are less used and require less oxygen. Since neither chickens nor turkeys fly regularly, their chest muscles are used for bursts of speed on an as-needed basis, using glycogen as fuel instead of myoglobin. The less exercised meat looks white when cooked, and the more constantly used legs and wings appear dark.

BYE-BYE, LOVE?

Why and how people bury their dead like they do

Funerary customs are as old as death itself, and have grown out of fear, religion, gender, ignorance, and of course, love and respect. Most cultures have ceremonies, which often include a wake or other viewing of the deceased, a sacred place for the dead, and memorialization of the dead.

Some early burial rituals addressed the fear of the dead coming back to haunt the living and perhaps settle old scores; some believed they needed to protect themselves from whatever evil spirits had taken their beloved.

A few of the ways—some traditional or historic—people have said good-bye to their loved ones throughout time around the world:

- Some African tribes grind the bones of their dead and sprinkle them into their food.
- The Calatians ate their dead— it was not only the duty of the family, but an honor.
- Zulus burn the dead's belongings to drive spirits from the area.
- Cypriots visited a mummified relative as a family, changed the clothing of the dead, and had family chats with them.
- Hara kiri is an old Japanese death sacrifice, but upon the death of a nobleman, twenty or thirty slaves would commit suicide.
- A Hindu tradition, outlawed by the British, required *suttee*, or the immolation of a spouse, upon the death of a married man. The widow would dress her best, climb upon the funeral pyre, lie down next to her husband, and allow their eldest son to light the pyre. She would be cremated alive.

594

- On Bali, widow sacrifice was also common, with the women drugged and hypnotized before their cremation.
- At an Amish funeral, the number of mourners in attendance varies according to the deceased's age.
- Fear most likely underlies the custom of cremation; people burned the dead to destroy the evil spirits. Even today, some primitive tribes simply leave their dead to rot or be eaten by predators, while they flee the spirits left behind.
- Zororastrians also leave their dearly departed to the forces of nature. They believe fire is too sacred and that mother earth should not be defiled.
- The ringing of bells at a funeral service is a medieval carry-over; it was believed that evil spirits would never near a bell that had been blessed.
- Covering the face of the deceased originated not from concerns of privacy or discomfort about viewing the dead, but from pagan tribes who believed that the spirit of the dead escaped from the mouth. Mourners wore special clothing, believing them to be a disguise—they would trick any returning spirits from recognizing them.
- The Hindi may honor the dead by walking around the funeral pyre, but do not look at the flames; however, they are supposed to see to it that the skull bursts in the pyre, as the soul lives there and must be released.
- Hungarians put unchristened children, suicides, and murderers in boxes that are buried—without any services—in a churchyard trench.
- Often, men and women are treated differently in death: The Cochieans buried women and hung men from trees; Ghonds buried women and cremated men; and the Bongas buried men facing north, and women facing south.
- Feasts, wakes, parties, and memorials are remnants of offering food and drink to the deities.

THE UNWELL

The American Psychiatric Association defines a personality disorder as an enduring pattern of inner experience and behavior that:

- deviates markedly from the expectation of the individual's culture
- is pervasive and inflexible
- has an onset in adolescence or early adulthood
- is stable over time
- leads to distress or impairment

Types of Disorders

ANXIETY DISORDERS

Acute Stress Disorder: anxiety symptoms following recent exposure to trauma

Panic Disorder: short-term attacks of anxiety, often without warning

Agoraphobia without History of Panic Disorder: anxiety about leaving home and/or being in public places

Social Phobia: extreme anxiety in social situations

Specific Phobia (formerly Simple Phobia): an irrational fear of a situation or object

Obsessive-Compulsive Disorder: recurring unwanted thoughts or repeated actions

Post-Traumatic Stress Disorder: long-term anxiety resulting from a particularly traumatic event

Generalized Anxiety Disorder: excessive, frequent worry with no specific cause

CHILDHOOD DISORDERS

Attention-Deficit Hyperactivity Disorder: inability to concentrate or control impulses, most often in young people

WHY

Asperger's Syndrome: milder variant of autism

Autistic Disorder: lifelong developmental disability characterized by impaired communicative and interactive skills

Conduct Disorder: inappropriate, disruptive childhood behavior

Oppositional Defiant Disorder: long-term pattern of hostility, disobedience, et al toward authority figures

Separation Anxiety Disorder: excessive and inappropriate distress about separation from home or an individual

Tourette's Disorder: neurological disorder characterized by body or verbal tics

EATING DISORDERS

Anorexia Nervosa: characterized by mistaken belief one is overweight

Bulimia Nervosa: characterized by bingeing and vomiting

MOOD DISORDERS

Major Depressive Disorder: pattern of hopelessness, helplessness, worthlessness, thoughts of suicide

Bipolar Disorder (Manic Depression): characterized by alternating episodes of mania and depression

Cyclothymic Disorder: mild form of bipolar disorder

Dysthymic Disorder: long-term depressive disorder characterized by more days of feeling down than positive

COGNITIVE DISORDERS

Delirium: state of mental disturbance and agitation

Multi-Infarct Dementia: partial loss of brain function due to series of strokes

Dementia: the loss of intellectual function; causes may include alcoholism or Alzheimer's disease

PERSONALITY DISORDERS

Paranoid Personality Disorder: characterized by extreme distrust

Schizoid Personality Disorder: pattern of social isolation and indifference to others

Schizotypal Personality Disorder: mild form of bipolar disorder

Antisocial Personality Disorder: extreme disregard for feelings of others, obsession with personal gain

Borderline Personality Disorder: continual instability in personal relationships

Histrionic Personality Disorder: overdramatic reactions in unwarranted situations

Narcissistic Personality Disorder: inflated, unrealistic feelings of self-worth

Avoidant Personality Disorder: persons stay away from any chance of conflict

Dependent Personality Disorder: overreliance on others

PSYCHOTIC DISORDERS

Schizophrenia: general term for wide range of disassociative disorders

Delusional Disorder: consistent persecutory, jealous, grandiose feelings

Brief Psychotic Disorder: short-term episode brought on by stressful events

Schizophreniform Disorder: short-term schizophrenic episode characterized by hallucinations and delusions

Schizoaffective Disorder: marked by both schizophrenic and manic-depressive symptoms

Shared Psychotic Disorder: a system that develops in two or more extremely close persons, one of whom is delusional

DEPRESSIVE DISORDERS

Depression: characterized by feelings of inadequacy and inertia

Major Depressive Episode: loss of interest in almost all activities for at least two weeks

Dysthymia: chronic and mild depression

Seasonal Affective Disorder: depression during fall and winter

Postnatal Depression: sadness in the days and weeks after giving birth, often leading to inability to care for child

SUBSTANCE-RELATED DISORDERS

These include dependence on alcohol, drugs (cocaine, amphetamines, marijuana, opiates, sedatives, hallucinogens, or inhalants), or nicotine.

◆

COLOR MY WORLD

Chromotherapists use color combined with light to balance a person's energy in their physical, spiritual, emotional and mental capacities:

RED—awakens both physical and mental energies
ORANGE—beneficial for the solar plexus and the lungs
YELLOW—stimulates the nerves
BLUE—heals organic disorders like colds, allergies and liver problems
GREEN—alleviates stress
INDIGO—acts on fever and skin problems

◆

Metal atoms in the red pigment of HEMOGLOBIN can carry the large quantities of oxygen humans and other large vertebrates require.

THE STATE OF YOUR ESTATE

Lawyers say that these are some of the most common reasons people should do their estate planning in advance:

1. To designate an executor and someone who will manage your affairs should you become disabled or pass away.
2. To assure that your estate remains sound should you need to go to a nursing home or assisted living facility.
3. To avoid probate, during your life and after.
4. To protect children from a prior marriage should you pass away first.
5. To protect your heirs from lawsuits and similar claims, such as those arising from divorce.
6. To help children and grandchildren who have no experience managing money, or who may have special needs.
7. To insure that specific monies or gifts from your estate go to the people, institutions, and charities you wish.
8. To protect your estate for the rest of your family in case you predecease a spouse who remarries.
9. To care for the different needs of different children.
10. To prevent challenges to your estate.
11. To reward or encourage heirs who make wise life decisions, and prevent the depletion of the estate by those who may not.
12. To set aside money for childrens' and/or grandchildrens' education, regardless of the wishes of their parents.
13. To assure a new stepparent doesn't spend your children's inheritance.
14. To be sure that the portion of your estate meant for your spouse does not go to his/her new spouse and that spouse's family.

THANKS, WALT

After audiences' delighted response to Walt Disney's first full-length animated film, *Snow White and the Seven Dwarves*, the studio knew it had a good thing going. It started a long history of animated successes, including:

Fantasia (1940)
Pinocchio (1940)
Dumbo (1941)
Bambi (1942)
The Adventures of Ichabod and Mr. Toad (1949)
Cinderella (1950)
Peter Pan (1953)
Lady and the Tramp (1955)
Sleeping Beauty (1959)
101 Dalmations (1961)
The Aristocats (1970)
Robin Hood (1973)
The Many Adventures of Winnie the Pooh (1977)
The Fox and the Hound (1981)
The Great Mouse Detective (1986)
The Little Mermaid (1989)
Beauty and the Beast (1991)
Aladdin (1992)
The Lion King (1994)
Pocahontas (1995)
The Hunchback of Notre Dame (1996)
Mulan (1998)
Tarzan (1999)
The Emperor's New Groove (2000)
Lilo & Stitch (2002)

ALWAYS GREENER
Why is there such lawn envy?

Until the Industrial Revolution, only the wealthy were lucky enough to have manicured lawns. English gardens and lawns had long been the envy of homeowners around the world, but either one had a staff of men with scythes or, as both George Washington and Thomas Jefferson had, a flock of sheep on the front lawn, keeping things trim.

Early in the nineteenth century, an Englishman named Edwin Budding developed a lawn mower, which he designed after a machine that sheared the nap on velvet. In 1870, Elwood McGuire improved on it, and fifteen years later, Americans were buying 50,000 lawnmowers a year. Still, the lawns didn't look like those across the pond.

The American Garden Club sponsored contests and worked to persuade homeowners that a beautiful lawn and was a public duty. Meanwhile, the U.S. Department of Agriculture and U.S. Golf Association joined forces in 1915 to concoct the right combination of grasses for both a beautiful fairway and a gorgeous backyard. Pesticides and herbicides were now in the increasingly expensive picture.

Though few countries in the world have the dewy, temperate climate that makes the English garden possible, they continue to try. In the United States alone, homeowners spend $17 billion on outdoor improvements, and more than 26 million households hire professionals to help with their yard work, landscaping, and gardening.

Recently, however, environmentalists have criticized the plethora of manicured lawns for many reasons:
- Single species plants reduce biodiversity, and local biodiversity suffers when plants are imported simply for reasons of beautification.

602

- Pesticides (over 136 million pounds in 1997) and other chemicals often do environmental damage; 99 percent of urban stream samples tested positive for pesticides in 1999.
- Use of water for lawns in climates that don't normally support grass puts strain on local water supplies; 30 to 60 percent of it is urban fresh water.
- A gas lawn mower pollutes as much in one hour as a car does in 350 miles.
- An acre of wetland or prairie costs $150 a year to maintain; an acre of lawn, approximately $1,000; there are more than 20 million acres of lawn in the United States—more than any other single crop in the country.

◆

SPACE HEROES

A Short Calculation of Those Who Have Given
Their Lives for Science

3	*Apollo 1* (US)
1	*Soyuz 1* (USSR)
3	*Soyuz 11* (USSR)
7	*Challenger* space shuttle (US)
7	*Columbia* space shuttle (US)
50	Plesetsk launchpad employees (USSR)
71	Total

◆

One's NAME DAY is the feast of a (usually lesser known) saint bearing your first name. Sometimes there is more than one saint with the same name and hence multiple name days: for example, the name day for Rebecca is either March 23 or July 19, and the name day for Philippa is either February 27 or May 7.

TO YOU!
Why and how we lift a glass around the globe

Toasts began as thanks and a prayer to the gods before a feast. Perhaps this is why we still refer to liquor as "nectar of the gods." Here are some toasts from around the world:

Albania	*Gezuar*
Armenia	*Genatzt*
Austria	*Prosit*
Azerbijan	*Noosh Olsum*
Bali	*Selamat*
Belgium	*Op Uw Gezonheid*
Brazil	*Saude*
Burma	*Auug Bar See*
China	*Wen Lei*
China	*Yam Sing (Cantonese)*
China	*Ganbei (Mandarin)*
Croatia	*Na Zdravlje*
Denmark	*Skaal*
Egypt	*Fee Sihetak*
England	*Cheers*
Estonia	*Tervist*
Ethiopia	*Letenatchie*
Finland	*Kippis*
France	*A Votre Sante*
Germany	*Prosit*
Georgia (Republic)	*Gaumardjos*
Greece	*Iss Ighian*
Greenland	*Kasugta*
Hawaii	*Okele Maluna*
Hawaii	*Hauoli Maoli Oe*
Holland	*Proost*

Hungary	*Kedves Egeszsegere*
Iceland	*Samtaka Nu*
India	*Aancllld*
Indonesia	*Selamat*
Ireland	*Slainte*
Israel	*Le Chaim*
Italy	*Alla Tua Salute*
Italy	*Per cent'anni!*
Japan	*Kampai*
Japan	*Banzai*
Korea	*Kong Gang Ul Wi-Ha Yo*
Kyrgyzstan	*Den Sooluck Yuchun*
Latvia	*Lai ta Buda Ruc*
Latvia	*Prieka*
Latvia	*Uz Veselibu*
Lebanon	*Vesar*
Lithuania	*I Sveikata*
Malaysia	*Yam Seng*
Malaya	*Slamat Minum*
Mexico	*Salud*
Morocco	*Saha Wa Afiab*
New Zealand	*Kia-Ora*
Norway	*Skaal*
Old English	*Wes Thu Hale*
Pakistan	*Zanda Bashi*
Persia (Iran)	*Salaamati*
Phillipines	*Mabuhay*
Poland	*Na Zdrowie*
Portugal	*A Sua Saude*
Romania	*Noroc*
Romania	*Sanatatee*
Romania	*Dumneavoastrua*
Russia	*Za Vashe Zdorovia*

Scotland	*Shlante*
Slovak	*Nazdravie*
South Africa	*Gesondheid*
Spain	*Salud*
Sudan	*Sabatuk Fy*
Swahili	*Afya*
Sweden	*Skål*
Syria	*Kull Sana Wo*
Syria	*Enta Salem*
Tagalog	*Mubuhcly*
Tanzania	*Kwa Afya Yako*
Thailand	*Sawasdi*
Thailand	*Chai-o*
Tibet	*Tashidelek*
Tibet	*Phun Tsun Tsok*
Turkey	*Sherefe*
Ukraine	*Budjmo*
Ukraine	*Na Zdorovya*
Wales	*Lechyd da*
Yugoslavia	*Na Zdraviye*
Zulu	*Oogy Wawa*
Zulu	*Poo-zim-pee-La*

As a last word, the Swedish *skål* means "drinking vessel," and is derived from the word for skull—which is exactly what the Swedes used to drink from.

◆

The PANAMA CANAL has two parallel sets of locks so that vessels may pass through the canal in both directions simultaneously. The lock chambers are 1,000 feet long, 110 feet wide, and 40 feet deep.

AND THE AWARD GOES TO . . .
Academy Award–winning movies that go by their own name

REAL FOLKS

The Great Ziegfeld (1936)
The Life of Emile Zola (1937)
Lawrence of Arabia (1962)
Patton (1970)
Gandhi (1982)
Amadeus (1984)
Schindler's List (1993)
Braveheart (1995)

AND FICTIONAL ONES

Rebecca (1940)
Mrs. Miniver (1942)
Hamlet (1948)
All About Eve (1950)
Marty (1955)
Gigi (1958)
Ben-Hur (1959)
Tom Jones (1963)
Oliver! (1968)
The Godfather (1972)
The Godfather, Part II (1974)
Rocky (1976)
Annie Hall (1977)
Kramer vs. Kramer (1979)
Driving Miss Daisy (1989)
Forrest Gump (1994)

HE LOOKS AWFULLY SUSPICIOUS

The FBI often look at suspects based on their sociopsychological profile when searching for serial killers:

Disorganized, Nonsocial Offenders	Organized, Asocial Offenders
IQ below average, 80–95	IQ above average, 105–120
Socially inadequate	Socially adequate
Lives alone, usually does not date	Lives with partner or dates frequently
Absent or unstable father	Stable father figure
Family emotional abuse, inconsistent	Family physical abuse, harsh
Lives and/or works near crime scene	Geographically and occupationally mobile
Minimal interest in news	Follows the news
Usually a high school dropout	May be college educated
Poor hygiene/housekeeping	Good hygiene/housekeeping
Keeps a secret hiding place in the home	Does not usually keep a hiding place
Nocturnal (nighttime) habits	Diurnal (daytime) habits
Drives a clunky car or pickup	Drives a flashy car
Returns to crime scene to relive memories	Returns to crime scene to see what police have done
Usually leaves body intact	May dismember body

Disorganized, Nonsocial Offenders	Organized, Asocial Offenders
May contact victim's family to play games	Usually contacts police to play games
No interest in police work	Police groupie or wannabe
Experiments with self-help programs	Doesn't experiment with self-help
Kills at one site, considers mission over	Kills at one site, disposes at another
Attacks in a "blitz" pattern	Attacks using seduction into restraints
Depersonalizes victim	Personalizes, holds a conversation
Leaves a chaotic crime scene	Leaves a controlled crime scene
Leaves physical evidence	Leaves little physical evidence
Responds best to counseling interview	Responds best to direct interview

◆

THE SCOTTISH PLAY

Traditionally, actors don't mention the name of Shakespeare's *Macbeth*. There are various theories about the source of the superstition: the witches' incantation in the play is said to be real; during an early performance, the actor playing Lady Macbeth, Hal Berridge, is thought to have died backstage; it's often performed when a theater company is in trouble because it's a box office winner.

"WHY DIDN'T I ORDER THE HOMARINE SALAD?"

Probably because you didn't know "homarine" was the adjective for lobster. Some other animal adjectives:

MAMMALS

Anteater	myrmecophagine
Antelope	bubaline
Ape	simian
Armadillo	tolypeutine
Ass	asinine
Auk	alcidine
Badger	musteline
Bear	ursine
Calf	vituline
Cat	feline
Cow	bovine
Deer	cervine
Dog	canine
Fox	vulpine
Goat	caprine
Hamster	cricetine
Leopard	pardine
Leo	lionine
Mouse	murine
Otter	lutrine
Pig	porcine
Porcupine	hystricine
Rabbit	leporine
Rhinoceros	ceratorhine
Ram	arietine

Sable	zabeline
Sheep	ovine
Shrew	soricine
Skunk	mephitine
Squirrel	sciurine
Tiger	tigrine
Whale	cetacean
Wolf	lupine
Zebra	zebrine

BIRDS

Blackbird	icterine
Bluebird	turdine
Buzzard	beuteonine
Cormorant	phalacrocoracine
Crow	corvine
Cuckoo	cuculine
Dod	didine
Dove	columbine
Duck	anatine
Eagle	aqualine
Falcon	accipitrine
Goose	anserine
Gull	larine
Jay	garruline
Ostrich	struthionine
Owl	strigine
Peacock	pavonine
Quail	coturnine
Sparrow	passerine
Stork	ciconine
Swan	cygnine

Turkey	meleagrine
Wren	troglodytine

FISH

Barracuda	percesocine
Dolphin	delphine
Fish	piscine

INSECTS

Ant	formicine
Bee	apian
Flea	pulicine
Mosquito	aedine
Moth	arctian
Wasp	vespine

MARSUPIAL

Kangaroo	macropodine

REPTILES

Alligator	eusuchian
Rattlesnake	crotoline

◆

New Orleans JAZZ owes some of its roots to military marching bands. When a band was (pardon the expression) disbanded as impractical to modern warfare at a military base in Louisiana, many of the instruments were repurposed by local musicians, who adapted them to their own musical style.

HOGGING THE TRUFFLES

Often one hears of a truffle-hunting pig, specially trained to ferret out the world's best, most prized and hard-to-find mushrooms. In the United States, most truffles are found in in Oregon and Washington, states whose weather and topography are similar to the truffle-rich parts France and Italy. In Europe, truffle hunters use pigs and mixed-breed dogs for hunting—the dogs are preferred because the pigs enjoy a truffle as much as a human, and are as likely to eat them as find them. A truffle hunter will often carry a staff to force the pig away from the prize.

Dogs are the better bet, because they prefer other foods besides mushrooms. The hunter brings treats for the dog, who is not fed the night before; he is not eager to eat a truffle, but he knows finding one will earn him a reward.

PLANE MAGIC

The first American air shows began around 1910. Realizing that this new, exciting form of transportation had grabbed people's imaginations, small groups of pilots banded together and put on shows to promote aviation, entertain, or simply to make a living. Where daredevils and large egos meet, competition is not far behind, and contests for highest, fastest, and best stunt performances became a popular new type of entertainment. Families came to the airfields on the outskirts of town, picnics and all, and made a day of it. By the beginning of World War I, air shows had become a worldwide phenomenon. The United States was a bit behind: The first international air show took place in Reims, France in August 1909—with nearly 500,000 spectators.

WHAT ARE YOU TRYING TO SAY?

When you see symbols like this on your computer screen, you can be sure someone is saying *exactly* what they mean. Whether you find them annoying or adorable, these symbols are certainly universal. They're called emoticons, and they're the "flower-dotted i" of the computer age. Herewith enough for a short novel:

:-) or :)	Smile
:-D or :d	Open-mouthed
:-O or :o	Surprised
:-P or :p	Tongue out
;-) or ;)	Wink
:-(or :(	Sad
:-S or :s	Confused
:-| or :|	Disappointed
:'(	Crying
:-$ or :$	Embarrassed
(H) or (h)	Hot
:-@ or :@	Angry
(A) or (a)	Angel
(6)	Devil
:-#	Don't tell anyone
8o|	Baring teeth
8-|	Nerd
^o)	Sarcastic
:-*	Secret telling
+o(	Sick
:^)	I don't know
*-)	Thinking
<:o)	Party

8-)	Eye rolling
|-)	Sleepy
!-)	Proud of black eye
#-)	Wiped out; partied all night
#:-o	Shocked
$-)	Won the lottery; money on the brain
%-(	Confused
%-)	Dazed or silly
%-\	Hung over
%-|	Worked all night
%-}	Humorous or ironic
>-	Female
>-)	Devilish wink
>:)	Little devil
>:-<	Angry
>:-(	Annoyed
>:-)	Mischievous devil
<:->	Devilish expression
<:-(	Dunce
<:-)	Innocently asking dumb question
(8(|	Homer
(<> .. <>)	Alienated
()	Hugging
(-:	Left-handed smile; smiley from southern hemisphere
(:-&	Angry
(:-(	Unsmiley
(:-*	Kiss
(:-\	Very sad
(::()::)	Bandaid, meaning comfort
(:|	Egghead
*	Kiss
*<:-)	Santa Claus

+<:-|	Monk or nun
+<||-)	Knight
+:-)	Priest
+O:-)	The Pope
-)	Tongue in cheek
-=	Snuffed candle to end a flame message
/\/\/\	Laughter
0:-)	Angel
2B|^2B	To be or not to be
5:-)	Elvis
8	Infinity
8 :-)	Wizard
8-#	Death
8-o	Shocked
8-O	Astonished
8-P	Yuck!
8-[	Frayed nerves; overwrought
8-]	Wow!
8-|	Wide-eyed surprise
: (	Sad
:)	Smile
: [	Bored, sad
:( )	Loudmouth; talks all the time;
:*	Kiss
:*)	Clowning
:**:	Returning kiss
:+(	Got punched in the nose
:,(	Crying
:-	Male
:-#	My lips are sealed; wearing braces
:-&	Tongue-tied
:->	Smile of happiness or sarcasm
:-><	Puckered up to kiss

:-<	Very sad
:-,	Smirk
:-/	Wry face
:-6	Exhausted
:-9	Licking lips
:-?	Licking lips; tongue in cheek
:-@	Screaming
:-C	Astonished
:-c	Very unhappy
:-D	Laughing
:-d~	Heavy smoker
:-e	Disappointed
:-f	Sticking out tongue
:-I	Pondering; impartial
:-i	Wry smile or half-smile
:-J	Tongue in cheek
:-l	One-sided smile
:-M	Speak no evil
:-o	Surprised look; yawn
]:->	Devil
]:-)	Happy devil
][	Back to back

◆

RISING TO THE OCCASION

Yeast does double duty: It makes bread rise and it makes alcoholic beverages ferment. Yeasts are single-celled fungi that produce energy by converting sugars to carbon dioxide and ethanol. In bread, the carbon dioxide makes the dough rise (the ethanol evaporates); in beer, the ethanol is captured in the bottle. Saccharomyces cerevisiae is the most commonly used type of yeast.

617

WAS IT AN INCREDIBLY BUMPY SILK ROAD?
And why some silks are not so smooth

Silk was supposedly discovered by accident: Yuen Fei, a Chinese emperor's concubine, accidently dropped a cocoon into her tea, whereupon it unraveled, and the thread attracted sufficient attention to become a luxury fabric.

The gathering and waving of silk remained secret processes—some say for nearly thirty centuries, until Japan discovered it around 300 B.C.E. By that time, silk had become such a valuable commodity that it was often traded for luxuries from Europe. It is said that Julius Caesar allowed no one else in the Roman empire to wear silk but himself. Until the sixth century, silk came entirely from Asia, until Emperor Justinian I sent monks undercover to steal mulberry seeds and silkworm eggs and hide them in their staffs and bring silk to Europe.

Only a few moths (after their lives as caterpillars) are used to produce silk, the mulberry silk moth, *Bombyx mori*, being the most common. Herewith a few fascinating facts, from worm to weave:

- One ounce of eggs produces about 20,000 worms; they will consume about one ton of mulberry leaves before they die.
- Tusah silk is produced by silkworms that feed on oak, not mulberry, leaves.
- 5,500 silkworms will produce only 2¼ pounds of raw silk.
- The very popular dupioni, or shantung, silk is produced from two silkworms spinning a cocoon together. In weaving, the double strand is not separated, and the uneven, irregular feel has become its hallmark.

TOWER OF FAITH

The flying buttress made an amazing difference in the architectural beauty of cathedrals when the Gothic era, with its increased knowledge of engineering, arrived in the eleventh century. Along with other features such as ribbed vaults, steeply pointed spires and arches, the design allowed much more space for the advent of huge and numerous stained glass windows, and therefore increased natural light. The flying buttress was the key to this more open and gracious structure; it allowed for higher ceilings, and most importantly, the buttress carried the weight of roofs that were heavier than the roofs common in the churches that came before.

HURRY SUNDOWN?

Though most of the world uses daylight saving time, there is some opposition to the idea.

Farmers, for whom an extra hour of sunlight would seem to be a boon, often say that it's all right with them, but not so much with the animals. Chickens and cows take several weeks to get used to the new time, making the farmers' routines difficult. And Orthodox Sephardic Jews have issues around the dark mornings during the month of Elul, when penitential prayers are recited.

There is a benefit to the time change that can't be denied: the number of traffic accidents and fatalities decrease in the United States and the United Kingdom by nearly one percent by virtue of having more light later at night, when drivers tend to have more accidents.

WORDS TO WRITE BY

The Turkey City Lexicon is a set of terms that writers use as shorthand to describe certain types of flaws in each other's prose. It was compiled by authors Lewis Shiner and Bruce Sterling. Some examples:

Brenda Starr Dialogue: Long sections of talk with no physical background or description of the characters. Such dialogue, detached from the story's setting, tends to echo hollowly, as if suspended in mid-air. Named for the American comic-strip in which dialogue balloons were often seen emerging from the Manhattan skyline.

"Burly Detective" Syndrome: The hack writers of the Mike Shayne series showed an odd reluctance to use Shayne's proper name, preferring such euphemisms as "the burly detective" or "the red-headed sleuth." This syndrome arises from a wrong-headed conviction that the same word should not be used twice in close succession.

Brand Name Fever: Use of brand name alone, without accompanying visual detail, to create false verisimilitude.

Gingerbread: Useless ornament in prose, such as fancy sesquipedalian Latinate words where short clear English ones will do.

Not Simultaneous: The misuse of the present participle is a common structural sentence-fault for beginning writers. "Putting his key in the door, he leapt up the stairs and got his revolver out of the bureau." Alas, our hero couldn't do this even if his arms were forty feet long.

Pushbutton Words: Words used to evoke a cheap emotional response without engaging the intellect or the critical faculties. Commonly found in story titles, they include such bits of bogus lyricism as "star," "dance," "dream," "song," "tears," and "poet," calculated to render the audience misty-eyed and tender-hearted.

Roget's Disease: The ludicrous overuse of far-fetched adjectives, piled into a festering, fungal, tenebrous, troglodytic, ichorous, leprous, synonymic heap.

"Said" Bookism: An artificial verb used to avoid the word "said." The term "said-book" comes from certain pamphlets, containing hundreds of purple-prose synonyms for the word "said," which were sold to aspiring authors from tiny ads in American magazines of the era before World War II.

Tom Swifty: A compulsion to follow the word "said" with a colorful adverb, as in "'We'd better hurry,' Tom said swiftly." This was a standard mannerism of the old Tom Swift adventure dime-novels.

Countersinking: A form of expositional redundancy in which the action clearly implied in dialogue is made explicit. "'Let's get out of here,' he said, urging her to leave."

Dischism: The unwitting intrusion of the author's physical surroundings, or the author's own mental state, into the text of the story. Authors who smoke or drink while writing often drown or choke their characters with an endless supply of booze and cigs. "Dischism" is named after Thomas M. Disch, who first diagnosed this syndrome.

False Interiorization: A cheap labor-saving technique in which the author, too lazy to describe the surroundings, afflicts the viewpoint-character with a blindfold, an attack of space-sickness, the urge to play marathon whist-games in the smoking-room, etc.

Fuzz: An element of motivation the author was too lazy to supply. The word "somehow" is a useful tip-off to fuzzy areas of a story. "Somehow she had forgotten to bring her gun."

WHY CAN'T I GET THE BLUE PLATE SPECIAL?

Because it's been "86ed"—and other tidbits of diner slang

Like so much slang, its etymology is lost in time; though with diner slang, there appears to be some proof that as far back as the 1870s, black waiters were using at least some of the phrases listed here. One thing's for sure: it's all based in good fun, made up to lighten the mood in stressful environments. Listen closely next time you sit down at a lunch counter, and see if you can spot your order.

Numbers Slang:

41 = lemonade
51 = hot chocolate
55 = root beer
86 = the kitchen is out of it, or, cancel the order
95 = customer jumping the check
99 = report to the manager

Eggs:

Adam and Eve on a raft = poached eggs on toast
deadeye = poached egg
wreck 'em = scrambled eggs
Fry two, let the sun shine = 2 fried eggs with unbroken yolk

Meat:

first lady = spare ribs (another Adam and Eve reference)
Pittsburgh = rare meat, cold in the middle, charred on the outside
on the hoof = meat cooked rare

Noah's boy = ham (Ham was Noah's second son)
groundhog, bow wow, Coney Island = hot dog
burn one, clean up the kitchen = hamburger
two cows, make 'em cry = two burgers with onions
hockey puck = hamburger, well done
take a chance = hash
bowl of red = chili
Irish turkey = corn beef and cabbage
radio = tuna (like saying "tuna" or "turn it down")
Bossy in a bowl = beef stew
zeppelin = sausage

Drinks:

city, city juice, 81, dog soup = water
moo juice, cow, 5 = milk
java, joe, draw one = coffee
pair of drawers = two coffees
an M.D. = a Dr. Pepper
blonde and sweet = coffee with milk and sugar
sinkers and suds, life preservers = doughnuts and coffee
squeeze one = orange juice
creep = draft beer

Desserts:

fish eyes = tapioca pudding
bucket of mud = bowl of chocolate ice cream
houseboat = banana split
nervous pudding = Jello
Eve with the lid on = apple pie

Staff and surroundings:

bubble dancer = dishwasher

gallery = booth
lumber = toothpick
soup jockey = waitress

Other:

sand, yum-yum = sugar
twins, Mike and Ike = salt and pepper
burn the British = English muffin, toasted
birdseed = bowl of cereal
hail = ice
shingle with a shimmy = toast with jelly
blowout patches = pancakes
machine oil = syrup
rabbit food = lettuce
keep off the grass = no lettuce
pin a rose on it = with onions
Frog sticks = French fries
A Murphy = a potato
cut the grass = no relish (on a hot dog or hamburger)
paint it red = with ketchup
sea dust = salt
warts = olives
put a hat on it = add ice cream
boiled leaves = tea
a spot with a twist= a cup of tea with lemon
in the alley = served on the side
high and dry = served plain
a million on a platter = a plate of baked beans
crowd = three of anything (as in "Two's company . . .")
on wheels, take it for a walk = order to go
whiskey = rye bread (as in rye whiskey)
dog biscuit = cracker

MAGIC METAL
The amazing new world of "memory metal"

A certain alloy made of nickel and titanium has changed the, well, shape of metallurgy. It's called memory metal, and its special shape memory effect, or SME, makes it possible for objects to be deformed, and then subsequently retain, their original shape.

The metal can be twisted and reshaped in any way, then reheated and brought back to "square one" at a certain temperature. This memory metal's crystal structure is transformed, but not destroyed; heating causes the atoms to reassume their original order. There are two types of "memory": a one-way SME can be changed, then recover its original shape when heated. A two-way alloy holds its first-position shape at one temperature, and can take on a completely new shape when heated at another temperature.

NASA began to explore this technology in the 1960s, and finally employed it in building the space station in the 1980s. At that point, commercial adaptations were beginning to appear, and home and industrial products hit the market. One of the most astounding innovations is a tube made of this special alloy which is crushed and inserted into clogged blood vessels. The metal has a memory transfer temperature that is very close to the body temperature of a human, so that the tube will expand once inside, and open the clogged arteries.

Some other devices that have benefited from this technological advance:

- Antennas for mobile phones
- Spectacle frames
- Medical guide wires and tools

- Stents for vascular and nonvascular surgery
- Staples and plates for the repair of fractured bones
- Orthodontic archwires
- Fire security and protection devices
- Motor protectors
- Security door locks
- Heating and ventilation controls
- Food cooking safety indicators
- Steam vent controls

◆

FAMILY OF CAT

Unspayed adult female cats remain in heat for about five days, and may mate with more than one male during that time. The litter (born about two months later) may include the offspring of more than one father, so the kittens may not look at all alike.

But you might not be able to tell how different at the outset. The kittens are not always born with their markings. Those develop over weeks: blue Persians, for example, are born with tabby-like markings. Eye colors change, too, from blue to the more common green or gold.

◆

LAST WORDS

"I have six honest serving men
(They taught me all I knew);
Their names are What and Why and When
And How and Where and Who."

—Rudyard Kipling, *The Elephant's Child*

INDEX